The Art of John Lennon
Drawings, Performances, Films

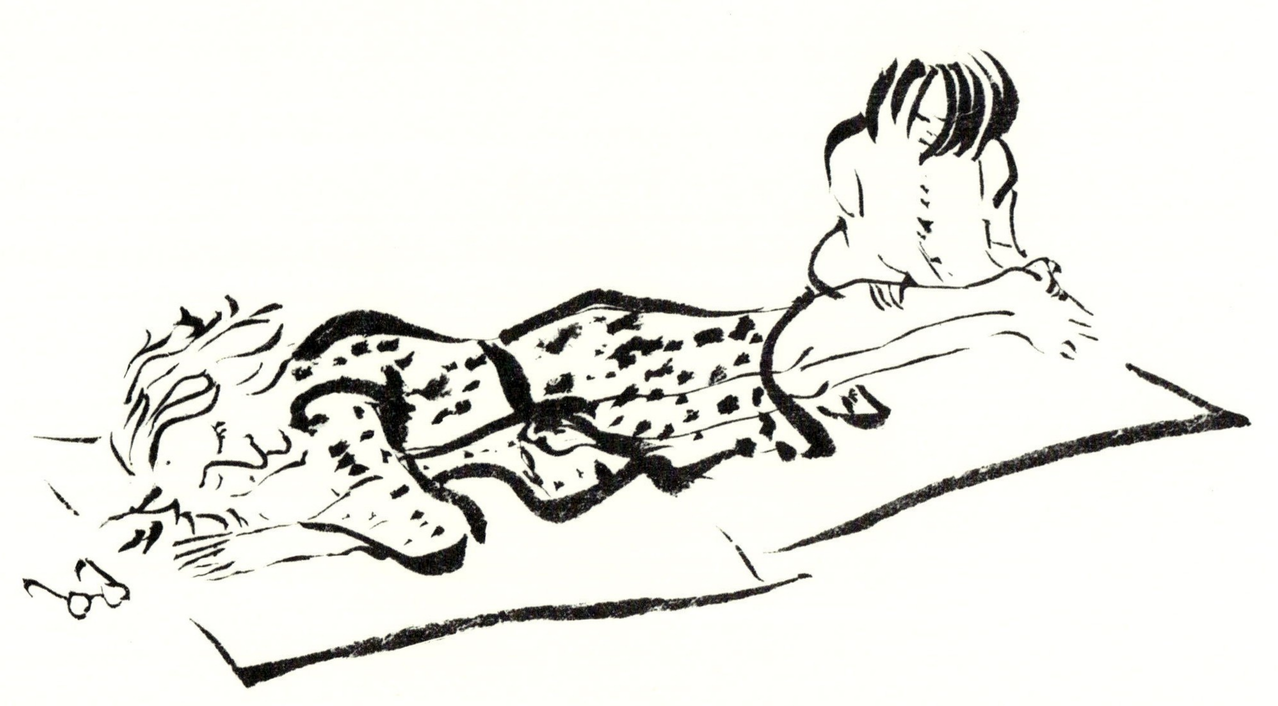

John Lennon

Drawings
Performances
Films

Edited by Wulf Herzogenrath
and Dorothee Hansen

Cantz

The editors express their grateful thanks to:

Yoko Ono, New York, who supported us generously from the very beginning, contributed a text, made all of the drawings available on loan and arranged for us to have access to the Lenono Photo Archive as well as
Sam Havadtoy for many useful suggestions
Lynne Clifford (Bag One Arts)
Karla Merrifield (Studio One, archivist)

for loans and advice:
Matthias Höllings

the authors:
Thomas Grötz, Trier
Jörg Helbig, Berlin
Astrid Kirchherr, Hamburg
Jann Wenner, New York

the photographers:
Robert Freeman
Ruud Hoff
Nico Koster
Iain Macmillan
Keith McMillan
David Nutter
Ben Ross
Annette Yorke

the board of directors of Radio Bremen, in particular intendant Karl-H. Klostermeier and programme directors Dr. Rüdiger Hoffmann and Hermann Vinke, as well as the many television and radio staff members, particularly coordinator Marion Gerhard

Peter Pickert, exhibition designer

Hartmut Brückner, typography

Cantz Verlag, Stuttgart:
Bernd Barde
Markus Hartmann
Cornelia Plaas

Senator for Commerce, Trade and Technology, Bremen:
Senator Claus Jäger

the HVG Hanseatische Veranstaltungs-Gesellschaft mbH, Bremen

the Concerto Culturmarketing GmbH:
Helmut Hadré
Hermann J. Pölking-Eiken
Frank Wendler
Barbara Janzhoff

the sponsor:
Sony Deutschland GmbH, Cologne

Contents

7 On the Exhibition in the Kunsthalle Bremen
Yoko Ono

8 John Lennon, Artist
Or: Why was it impossible for so long to
acknowledge him as an artist – and why
do we still find it difficult today?
Wulf Herzogenrath

14 Seeing John Lennon Again
Astrid Kirchherr

18 Remembering John Lennon
Jann Wenner

The Drawings and Lithographs

24 Early Watercolours, 1952

29 Early Caricatures, around 1955

36 Drawings from the years 1968 to 1979

71 The Japanese Dictionary, 1977

138 Bag One, a series of
15 original lithographs, 1970
Dorothee Hansen

The Performances
Dorothee Hansen

158 "John" by Yoko Ono and
"Yoko" by John Lennon

162 You Are Here

168 Bed-In for Peace

172 War is over!

176 Bagism

Films, Record Sleeves, Writings

182 The Films
Dorothee Hansen

188 John Lennon's Solo Albums –
Cover Concept and Design
Thomas Grötz

202 John Lennon as a Writer:
Shun the Punman!
Jörg Helbig

210 Biographical Notes
John Lennon: The Visual Artist
Matthias Höllings

225 Selected Bibliography

227 The Authors

John Lennon and Yoko Ono
drawing at their Greenwich
Village apartment,
New York 1972.
Photo: Ben Ross

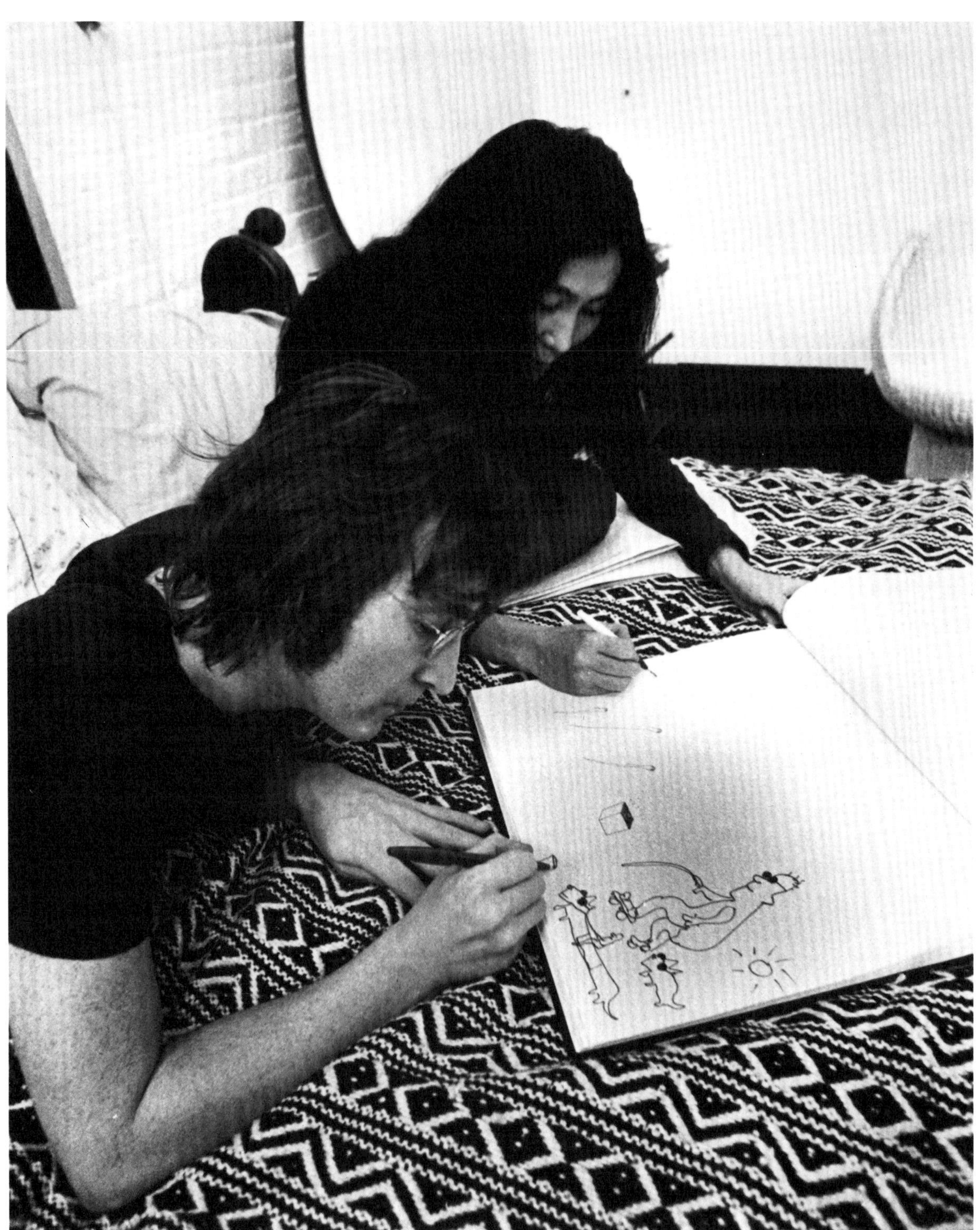

In his lifetime, John Lennon, the artist, remained an "outsider" to the art world, largely because of his fame as a Beatle and how he was viewed by the world as a result of it. In hindsight, that was fortunate, in the sense that it allowed his works to maintain their purity, free from comments and "suggestions" by the critics and dealers. He maintained his unique style, untouched by the trends.

John did his drawings with inspiration and speed, very much like how he created his songs. It was obvious that there was a strong innate need for John to keep creating these works. Most of the time, the drawings reflected his mood. Though once when John was in a dark mood, I looked over his shoulder and found him drawing a very funny picture. Another time, John was in a happy mood, drawing a picture with black humour. Only John would do that, I thought. It was as though John was using the act of drawing to balance and unite his two minds – one the dark and pessimistic, and the other the joyful and optimistic. Along with his guitar, pen und paper seemed to have served as ideal tools to express John's complexe emotions.

Now, over a decade after his death, there is no difficulty in getting galleries to exhibit John's artworks. In fact, some of his works have become part of the collections of major museums. I wonder what John would have thought of all that. He would have accepted it with his usual wry humour, maybe.

I am not unaware of the significance of showing John's original drawings for the first time in Bremen, Germany. This country, as you know, played a significant role in his life as he started as a musician thirty odd years ago. John often spoke of his Hamburg experience with nostalgia and love.

I hope you enjoy the show.

Yoko Ono

John Lennon, Artist

Or: Why was it impossible for so long to acknowledge him as an artist –
and why do we still find it difficult today?
Wulf Herzogenrath

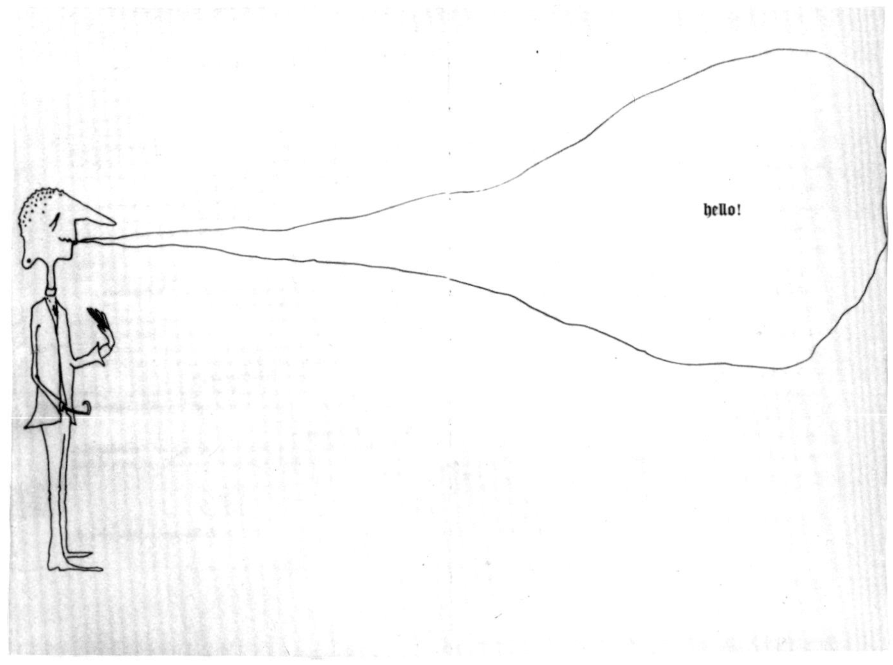

John Lennon, *Hello,* from:
In His Own Write, 1964

An introduction to the first book about John Lennon as a visual artist must answer two questions: first of all, why should the brilliant musician, songwriter and megastar John Lennon be called a visual artist at all, and secondly, why was he not recognised as a visual artist until the nineties? Although he published his drawings in his two books, his lithograph portfolio *Bag One* was exhibited several times in the early seventies and the international media covered his performances – it is nevertheless remarkable and indeed odd that our publication (issued in conjunction with the exhibition at the *Kunsthalle Bremen*) should be the first to address this important field in the oeuvre of John Lennon.

If we are to ascertain why the art world took so little notice of his drawings, events and performances, films, nonsense literature and his extremely innovative design of the record sleeves, we must first of all examine the mechanisms of the art scene in the seventies and the changes it underwent between that period and the nineties – for it is the transformation that has taken place since the mid-eighties which has made it possible for such works as those of megastar John Lennon to gain broader acceptance. I would like to address this point first before moving on to the actual works Lennon created.

In the 20th century, the provocation occasionally caused by a controversial work of art has tended to be due not so much to the nature of the work itself, but to the fact that it has rolled back accepted frontiers or evaded a form of categorisation previously taken for granted. As early as 1914, Marcel Duchamp transposed his "readymades" – everyday objects purchased cheaply in department stores – to the aura of the art exhibition and art museum, giving them titles, signing them with his name, and so creating a work of art. To achieve this, he altered the object's coordinates of reference, changed our ways of perceiving it and broke the mould of what had hitherto been regarded as an unassailable law: the tenet of the hand-crafting, uniquely individual artistic genius. He showed that we regard the same object with different eyes depending on whether we see it in a department store or a museum; the functional, commercial and aesthetic coordinates of reference change with the change of location.

In the last few decades, we have been confounded by artists who wrench works of art from their familiar contexts, rearranging them or completely ignoring considerations of saleability and art market structures, using reproducible media and even connecting into the Internet because in this way they can achieve direct effects and responses that they could not otherwise find in the traditional, static art media.

In presenting the artistic oeuvre of John Lennon, we wish to leave aside his role as an internationally acclaimed musician whose work in that field has been frequently analysed. Our aim is to free the visual and literary aspect of his oeuvre, and his holistic approach to it, from the shadow of his media fame as a Beatle and in this way to open it up for discussion for the first time. In the sixties and the beginning of the seventies,

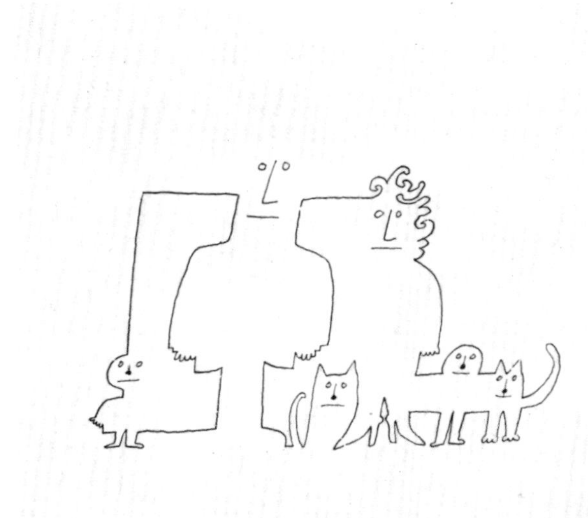

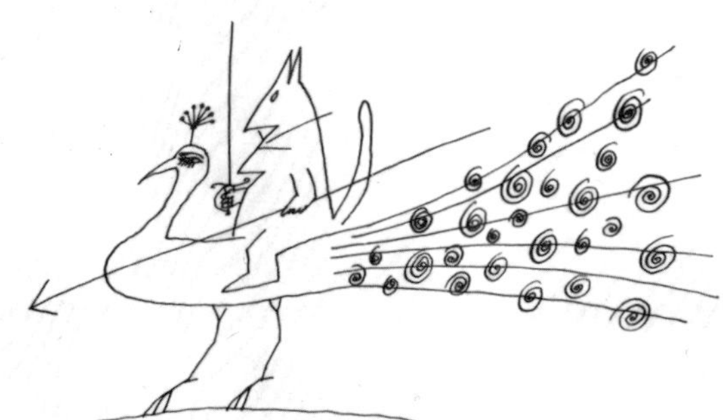

when Lennon was creating his drawings, writing nonsense literature and performing events – in short, when he was actively engaged as a visual artist –, the public dismissed this work as the rumblings of the rainbow press, the latest gossip about a pop star or the usual media ballyhoo. Even when Lennon worked with the artist Yoko Ono, he was still unable to escape the cult of stardom and could not return to the "normal" world of visual art. There he came up against limits as clear as the laws of the art market.

When two people do similar things, they tend to be categorised according to their individual backgrounds rather than on the basis of their action or individual work. Art naturally evolves more from the activity of artists and takes its identification from the fact that we can accept an extension of the concept of art if it is posited by an artist. But we in the art world seem to find it very difficult to accept gatecrashers or to accept the work of outsiders as something artistic or creative, especially if we already regard them rather suspiciously because they are successful stars. The art of caricature, for example, even in its highest artistic form as practised by Saul Steinberg, Roland Topor or Tomi Ungerer, took decades to be taken seriously in the official art world (and where are the major retrospectives in the art museums even for these heroes?). The same can be said of photographers, copywriters and advertising people who are extremely successful in the glamorous world of magazines, albeit usually at the price of being disdained by the art world; the late success of Helmut Newton or Michael Schirmer bears witness to this. It was not until 1987, at the documenta 8 in Kassel, that designers or architects received any widespread recognition in the art scene – once again, it was often the commercial success of certain designers that tended to hinder their breakthrough and acceptance by the art world. Even more blatant is the disregard for or even rejection of the creative forces in the field of pop music, even though this field has had an enormous influence on the visual arts through the work of such artists as David Byrne or Laurie Anderson, who are both visually and musically innovative.

It is as though we were now paying for the attitude adopted by many intellectuals from the early fifties onwards in reaction to the functionalisation of culture in Nazi Germany, or in Stalin's Russia or Mao's China for that matter. All forms of popular art became suspect, and the critical world held that high art should transcend the taste of the masses. In the theories of these philosophers, whose works were widely read in

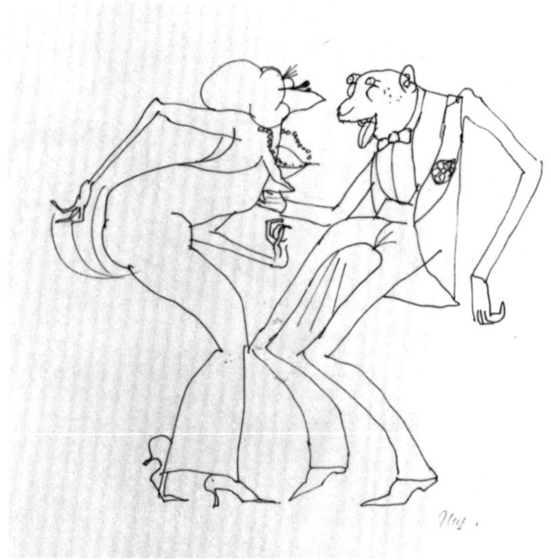

the fifties and sixties, from Ortega y Gasset to
Adorno, the taste of the masses is scorned. In
general, prevailing opinion tended to agree with
Oscar Wilde's quip that a work of art could not
be authentic if it was liked by more than two
people. Only art which was inaccessible, difficult
and complex was regarded as avant-garde, and in
an inversion of this principle, critics saw a clear
distinction between highbrow and lowbrow art,
allowing them to differentiate between good art
and bad, while in their eyes the taste of the public
at large always trailed two generations behind.

The new media, however, radically altered
such prejudices in two particular ways. First of
all, artists began to use the media in a new,
creative way as part of their work: Andy Warhol
did so by founding his magazine *Interview,*
Joseph Beuys by founding a party and a
university, and Nam June Paik by creating his
video works – and in this context we also have
to include John Lennon and Yoko Ono, who
accepted their popularity as media stars and not
only used it creatively in their performances, but
even addressed it as a specific issue. And
secondly, the general public rapidly began to
change its way of perceiving things as a result
of developments in the areas of film, video,
computer, MTV etc., while at the same time the

intellectual criticism of the traditional art world
remained entrenched in its attitudes from the
seventies, cosseting its ideal of an avant-garde
couched in intellectual obscurity.

John Lennon's drawings are creative master-
pieces situated between free drawing, caricature
and illustration. Even today, they still bear
witness to the keen sense of observation, wit and
profound irony with which Lennon saw the
world around him. In his works he is always
interested in people, and even if they sometimes
get on his nerves, certain characters, scenes or
chance occurrences touch him. His works are
precise observations, often based on personal
experience, always reflecting his own sentiments.
Just as his lyrics invariably express not only his
mood of the moment, but also his general
attitude, so too can we assume that behind almost
every drawing there is some situation that has put
him on the defensive, often reacting with sarcasm.

He draws with simple stroke and clear line,
often concluding with a single confident flourish.
Without haste or hatching, but with a fine sense
of composition on the white paper. He likes to
complement his writing with a drawing, often
combining the two forms in his books without a
direct or even illustrative connection. The figures
and forms that stretch and sprawl across a double
page are nevertheless chosen with care, while
some larger drawings are then printed in a relatively small format. We sense in this approach
a deliberate creative intention that places
importance not only on the drawing itself, but
also on its afterlife and mass circulation in the
reproduced form of the book, and it therefore
deserves consideration of its artistic intent.

On the other hand, the more than 100 drawings Lennon made in connection with his studies
of the Japanese language are more or less precise
illustrations – though invariably highly original –
of the English and Japanese sentences written
beside them. It is here, especially, in the small
format of this seemingly incidental work that we

can discern a confident hand and a sure line. Some of his other drawings are more illustrative or fleeting, as though they had been sketched carelessly and quickly; these, too, are reproduced here, along with four surviving drawings Lennon made as a child and which he himself published on a record sleeve.

For John Lennon, the exterior visual design of the phonograph record was not a matter to be left to the advertising staff of the record companies. He was the first to take the visual appearance of this primarily acoustic medium consistently seriously, undertaking an extremely wide range of design approaches and liberating this popular medium from its otherwise purely commercial orientation. For this reason, we have published here for the first time all the works connected with the visual design of the records, and have moreover drawn attention to the nonsense texts published in his two books during his lifetime as well as in a third volume compiled from his estate and published after his death. In these works, Lennon stands in the singularly British tradition of nonsense literature that revels in iconoclastic neologisms, puns and poking fun at lofty maxims. Many authors have pointed out the kinship to Lewis Carroll's *Alice in Wonderland* and even to James Joyce, though Joyce certainly moved in a different direction.

For me, however, the real revelation – apart from the drawings – is Lennon's frequent participation in events or performances, as we called them in the late seventies, but which in the sixties were referred to in the popular press by the rather derogatory catchword "happenings" – after all, in this context the event was soon reduced to a household term for any action that did not quite fit in with the norm.

There is, however, one more reason why the performances by John Lennon and Yoko Ono tended to be dismissed as nothing more than entertaining media happenings instead of being acknowledged as artistic events. As I already

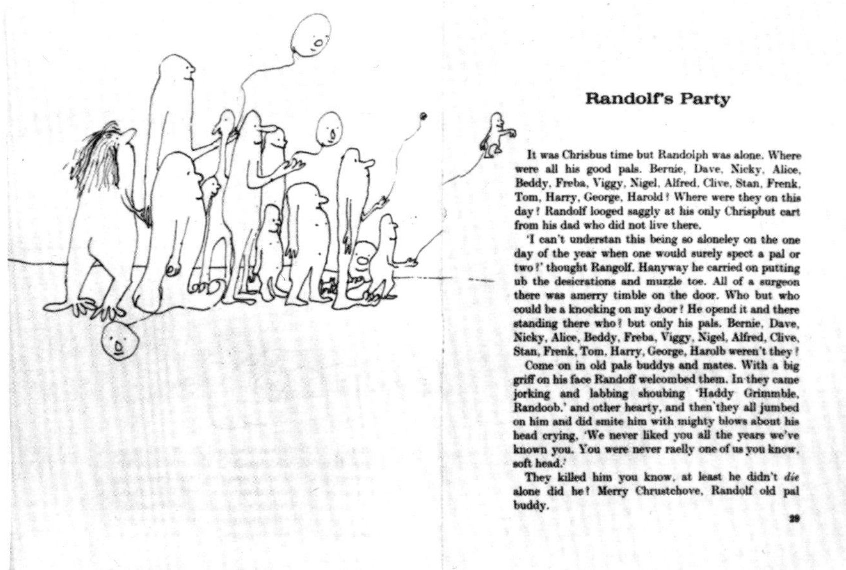

It was Chrisbus time but Randolph was alone. Where were all his good pals. Bernie, Dave, Nicky, Alice, Beddy, Freba, Viggy, Nigel, Alfred, Clive, Stan, Frenk, Tom, Harry, George, Harold ! Where were they on this day ? Randolf looged saggly at his only Chrispbut cart from his dad who did not live there.

'I can't understan this being so aloneley on the one day of the year when one would surely spect a pal or two !' thought Rangolf. Hanyway he carried on putting ub the desicrations and muzzle toe. All of a surgeon there was amerry timble on the door. Who but who could be a knocking on my door ? He opend it and there standing there who ! but only his pals. Bernie, Dave, Nicky, Alice, Beddy, Freba, Viggy, Nigel, Alfred, Clive, Stan, Frenk, Tom, Harry, George, Harolb weren't they !

Come on in old pals buddys and mates. With a big griff on his face Randoff welcombed them. In they came jorking and labbing shoubing 'Haddy Grimmble, Randoob.' and other hearty, and then they all jumbed on him and did smite him with mighty blows about his head crying, 'We never liked you all the years we've known you. You were never raelly one of us you know, soft head.'

They killed him you know, at least he didn't *die* alone did he ! Merry Chrustchove, Randolf old pal buddy.

29

John Lennon, *Randolph's Party*, from: *In His Own Write*, 1964

mentioned in my remarks on the borderline between the megastar and the artist, the art world quite simply did not want to pay attention to them, on grounds of principle. One the other hand, however, it should be stressed that these early performances addressed subjects and adopted forms which were only to become accepted and commonplace in the art world much later. In other words, John Lennon and Yoko Ono were simply too far ahead of their time.

For example:

1. The *Acorn Event* in front of Coventry Cathedral in summer 1968 (see p. 158) and the mailing action in December 1969 in which leading international politicians were sent acorns to plant for peace. A dozen years later, Joseph Beuys initiated his "city forestation instead of city administration" event for the *documenta 7* (1982) in which he proposed to plant *7000 Oaks* (or similar trees) in or near Kassel, which was then finally completed by the following *documenta 8* in 1987.

2. When John Lennon and Yoko Ono were finally able to move to New York, they planned to display a huge photo of themselves without

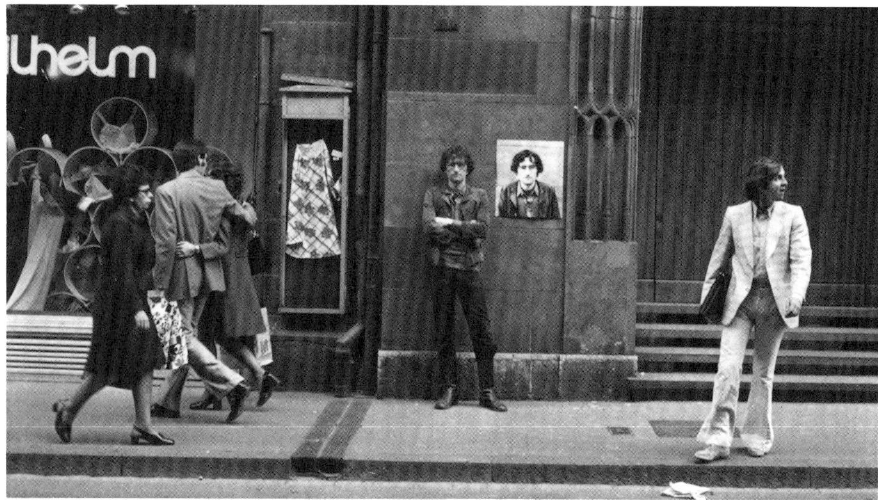

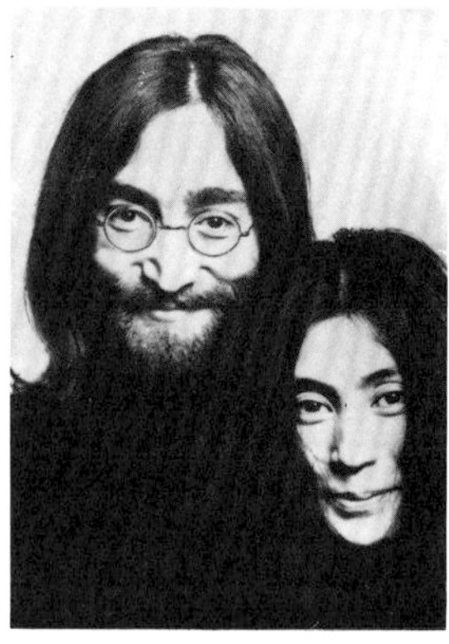

John Lennon and Yoko Ono planned to have this photo displayed on the largest advertising space at New York's Times Square in 1971.
Photo: Iain Macmillan

Jochen Gerz, *Exhibition of Jochen Gerz beside his photographic reproduction,* Basel 1972.
Photo: Galerie Stampa, Basel

any comment and without any specific commercial connection, such as a new record, on Times Square. This is pure Concept Art, playing with the context of art and a certain knowledge as a starting point. In a similar event that was actually carried out by Jochen Gerz (*Exhibition of Jochen Gerz beside his photographic reproduction,* 1972) in Basel, the artist stood on the street beside a photo of himself. In this case, of course, nobody took any note of the presentation because the passers-by were unaware of the situation and the person portrayed; the artist was demonstrating the tautology and, at the same time, the conceptual realisation of Magritte's assertion in his painting of a pipe that this is not a pipe, but merely a picture of one.

3. The *Bed-In* in Amsterdam combined new elements in 1969: real time and time extension, with John Lennon and Yoko Ono spending not hours, but several days in bed. Their event gives visual expression to the unity of space and time, of unrepeatable and unforeseeable action, and the subject of "peace" is demonstrated, written of, sung of, elucidated in leaflets — yet all this is misconstrued as a media spectacle, for the reporters are not there to visit a performance, they want facts and stories — and John Lennon and Yoko Ono provide them only to a limited degree. When artists like Marina Abramović and

Ulay carried out lengthy events ten years later, they could be sure of an attentive audience. In 1969, the media transformed the Lennon/Ono performance into a "peace demonstration" which was registered unwillingly by the public — an audience of reporters was unable to understand it as an artistic event. Some years later, the American artist Colette organised performances in which she lay in bed on decorative fabrics more or less like Goya's Maja in a further variation on the same theme.

4. Lennon's London exhibition *You Are Here* at the Robert Fraser Gallery in 1968 (see p. 162) in which the charity boxes of various non-profit charitable organisations were displayed is one of his most profound and complex actions. These banal objects are generally kitschy, shaped to represent the cause for which the donations are collected: animals and ships, in plastic and ceramics — the trivial objects of Jeff Koons in the eighties are certainly not far away. But for Lennon, who received many begging letters himself every day, this may well have been a desperate attempt to break out of the dilemma of the rich man confronted by the multiplicity of poverty and its demands, as well as being a sarcastic comment on the role of the artist in a commercial situation, as the western art market certainly is. Lennon refused to seek the position in the art world he may well have desired because he realised that it would be impossible for him to be free as an artist — free, that is of his Beatles fame — and nevertheless he presented his artistic work with a highly conceptual gesture by addressing the role of the star as artist, and the impossibility of crossing that border.

5. The *War is over!* posters (1969) use minimal aesthetic means: black lettering on a white ground, simple, clearly legible typeface. In the midst of mass advertising with Pop Art elements and cinema painting, with Op Art effects and flashing coloured lights, this simple surface with its clear text "*War is over!*" leaps out

– and everyone who sees it automatically wonders which war is meant and how come it is over, for there is, of course, always a crisis somewhere. Because Lennon/Ono rented the billboards themselves without a sponsor or government backing, without a museum or a collector covering the costs, this was seen as a PR gag for themselves – and not as art. It is not mentioned in any history of art – what an omission! After all, at the end of the seventies, this kind of minimalistic textual simplicity took hold in advertising and, at the same time, Jenny Holzer created an entire system of socio-critical aphorisms directed against consumer society – again at Times Square on the huge commercial advertising spaces. This was immediately accepted by the art world – as were Barbara Kruger's simple sentences such as "we don't need another hero" combined with photos of everyday life.

By way of conclusion it may be said that John Lennon's artistic oeuvre falls into two categories. The first is the work of the traditional artist who draws, writes, illustrates and then even designs his publications. Until now, the art world has failed to give this the attention it deserves, because a megastar simply cannot be an artist, even if he went to art school and has always practised his craft – in this case drawing. The second category is the work that addresses the issue of the media reception of fame itself – only the photographers and reporters took any note of these actions; the art world completely missed the inherently artistic aspects of events and performances that dealt directly with the permanent reality of the media and of a life spent facing the media. Lennon/Ono gave several press conferences hidden in a bag in order to be both present and invisible at the same time, so that they could respond without appearing as Lennon/Ono – and at the same time becoming even more of a media event than ever.

How can the artist address the question of

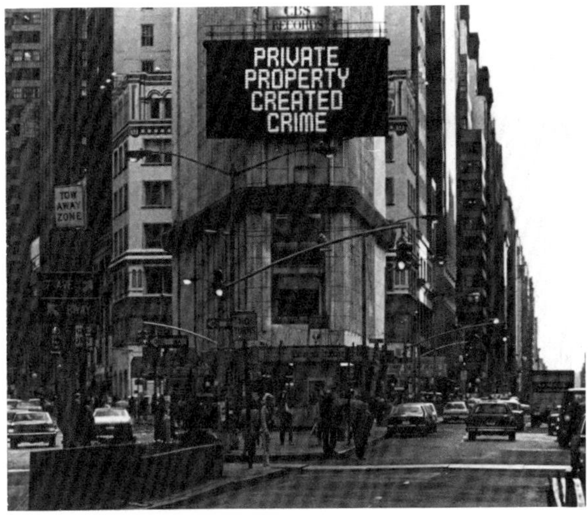

John Lennon/Yoko Ono, The *War is over!* poster event, December 1969

Jenny Holzer, *Private Property Created Crime*, luminous advertisement on Times Square, New York 1982

dropping out of art in the midst of the art world? It is an impossible Catch 22 of the kind that Duchamp, the Futurists, Dadaists and Constructivists all experienced. The reception of art has always continued to develop, as have the museums, galleries and collectors – and whatever has tried to escape it has invariably (fortunately for the spectators and the museums!) been caught up with in the end.

Now it's John Lennon's turn.
Would he have liked that?
"I am the Walrus!"

Seeing John Lennon Again
Astrid Kirchherr

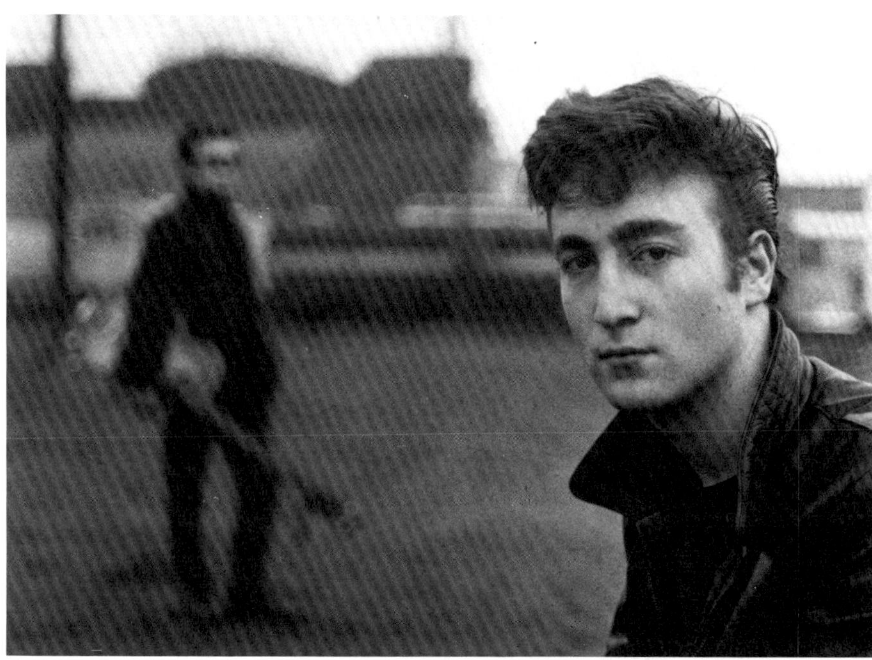

Astrid Kirchherr, *John Lennon,* Heiligengeistfeld, Hamburg 1960

I first met John Lennon in October 1960. In those days, he and the other Beatles were doing gruelling nine-hour gigs night after night in the *Kaiserkeller* on the Reeperbahn. To this day I still remember so well how enthusiastic my boyfriend at the time, Klaus Voormann, was about the Beatles and their music, and how he insisted on taking me along to one of their concerts. Being the "daughter of a respectable family", I used to spend most of my time in chic, "existentialist" bars, and the idea of going to the run-down *Kaiserkeller* on Hamburg's notorious Reeperbahn gave me the creeps. But the moment I saw the Beatles on stage, any misgivings I might have had evaporated. From the first glimpse, John's charisma fascinated me. Standing like a beacon in a storm: legs bent, head forward, hair tousled – with his incredible voice he seemed to be wringing his soul right out of his body! He radiated an electrifying mixture of recklessness, youthful aggression and cool which I had never seen before. To me, John was the perfect embodiment of rock'n'roll. He had that magical aura about him even then. On the same night I also met the great love of my life, Stuart Sutcliffe,

who played bass for the Beatles at the time.

John and Stuart had been great friends ever since their days together at the Liverpool College of Art. Whereas painting and drawing were always Stuart's primary interest, John – himself a gifted draughtsman – lived entirely for his music. Through their friendship my relationship with the Beatles quickly began to develop. I had my first long conversation with John in November 1960, when I was photographing the Beatles at *Heiligengeistfeld,* the fairground in Hamburg. I still remember perfectly well picking them up around noon on the corner of Reeperbahn and Grosse Freiheit in my "Beetle" convertible. They were all polished up for the occasion and very excited. I wanted to photograph them exactly as they appeared: natural, full of energy and outrageously good-looking, just like real "hoods". But how different they were from the other young toughs with their motorcycles and black leather jackets: These boys had brains!

John in particular behaved like a true professional at these photo sessions. He followed my instructions enthusiastically, in part because he was apparently quite impressed by me. To him I represented an independent young woman working as an artist who made no secret of her intellectual background and knew exactly what she wanted. He quickly realised that the macho behaviour he sometimes indulged in failed to impress me in the slightest.

I believe I made him feel insecure yet curious at the same time. As it is, this positive curiosity about the world was one of John's most pronounced characteristics. When he visited me, for instance, it was impossible to tear him away from my bookshelves. He was constantly asking about this or that author, and Stuart was once amused to relate how stunned John was at finding a book by the Marquis de Sade on my shelves. Sometimes he and Paul McCartney would spend hours rummaging through my record collection which consisted, for the most part, of French chansons, jazz and classical recordings. Since all of this was new to them, it was very inspiring. John was like a sponge, eagerly soaking up whatever came his way and getting to the bottom of things. I am certain that he instinctively knew he would one day find a use for this "artistic raw material".

Hamburg: City of Sin

The time John Lennon spent in Hamburg had a formative influence on him, not only in terms of his music but also regarding his own individual cultural development. You have to recall the situation at the time. The Hamburg of 1960 was still very much scarred by the war, and we were still considered the recent enemy by many of the English. Having just flown in from Liverpool, the Beatles must have imagined that Germany consisted mainly of little Hitlers and round, stubby-legged "Fräuleins" devouring huge amounts of sauerkraut. And then of course there was the Reeperbahn myth. For them, Hamburg was the "City of Sin": prostitutes everywhere you looked, nightclubs, pimps, sailors with tattoos the size of hubcaps – the whole gamut of clichés. So when they met Klaus and me, and later on our circle of artist friends, they were completely bowled over. Suddenly, they realised that this country also had sensitive, attractive people in it. On the other hand, we "Krauts" considered England a different planet. We had access to very little information about the country and its people, let alone any personal contacts, a fact which greatly enhanced our capacity for pigeonholing. John had his prejudices, just like the rest of us, but was quickly prepared to revise them or even discard them altogether. He consciously freed himself more and more from the preconceived notions he had formerly held. I would venture to maintain that the time they spent in Hamburg contributed initial, significant impulses to the development of the marked political consciousness he later displayed.

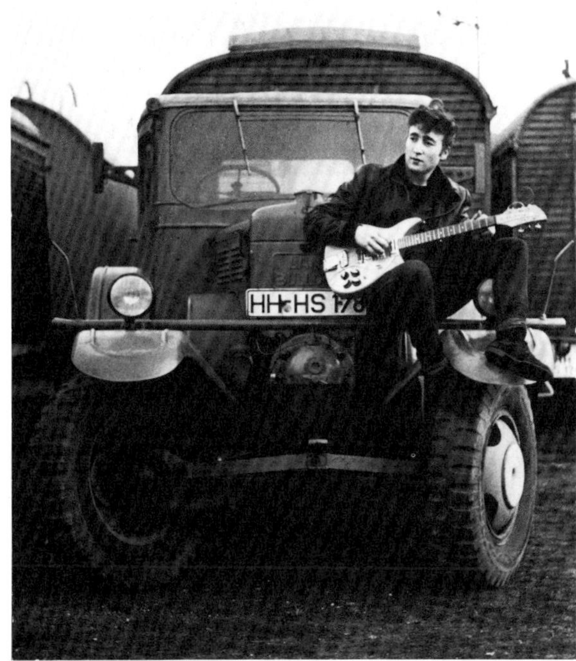

Astrid Kirchherr, *John Lennon,* Heiligengeistfeld, Hamburg 1960

The Beatles' "lifestyle" was naturally also shaped by their time in Hamburg. Musically speaking, they acquired their final, professional polish by appearing in clubs on the Reeperbahn. The famous "look", however, only developed little by little. Stuart and George Harrison were, by the way, the only two whom I gave a moptop haircut. John and Paul only later acquired the taste. At the time, I was in awe of Jean Cocteau. His favourite actor, Jean Marais, had such a haircut in one of his films, which I am certain was inspired by the ancient Greeks. It must be remembered that changes were always made by the band as a whole: no one wanted to be different. This homogeneity was an important prerequisite for their phenomenal success.

The influence was naturally reciprocal: I learned, for example, a lot about discipline and stamina from the Beatles.

The time in Hamburg was a continuous, highly energetic maturing process. It was particularly fascinating for me to watch how John and

Stuart inspired each other. At the time, Stuart was clearly the person to whom John felt the closest. Stuart gave him the support he so desperately needed. Yet this intimacy was mostly confined to their private, emotional lives. John naturally preferred solving musical problems with Paul. As a visual artist, he was conspicuously independent, if not to say self-sufficient. Although he very much admired Stuart's paintings, I never saw him paint himself, either in watercolour or oil. His great talent lay in drawing, something he always did on the side to pass the time, without giving it much thought. He simply accepted his talent as a given and never paid much attention to it. His greatest challenge was always music.

A great many of these drawings accompanied me for a long time. His letters were full of pencil sketches and curious vignettes. Once he even took my big black book, a kind of artist's diary, and scribbled in it from cover to cover. It was one huge swarm of octopus-like figures with large heads, and of course a few of samples of those "Jesus cartoons" with Jesus hanging on the cross and a pair of slippers on the ground in front of him. The drawings were very similar to those which later served as illustrations in the two marvellously quirky nonsense books, *In His Own Write* and *A Spaniard in the Works*. It was particularly amazing to watch how unbelievably fast he could draw, all in one movement without lifting his pencil once, just like Picasso and Cocteau, his role models at the time. I was especially happy to receive a birthday card from the Beatles once, which showed cut-off photographs of their heads below which John had drawn octopus bodies.

Mind Games
Apart from having diverse artistic talents, John Lennon possessed a high degree of sensitivity, something his biographers tend to overlook. Not only was he a provocateur, a cynic, and a genius – he was above all a kind, sensitive person. I will never forget the touching way he looked after me after Stuart's death. He often came to me and said: "Let's take some beans and talk!" (By "beans" he meant the appetite-stemming drug "Preludin"). We would then talk about everything that troubled us for hours on end. One time, after much hesitation, he asked whether I would give him something that had belonged to Stuart. When I asked him if there was anything in particular, he eventually admitted he would like Stuart's college scarf. That moved me a great deal.

I had the impression that John needed those "beans" in order to overcome his inhibitions and to give free rein to his emotions. I believe that we must view his later consumption of drugs in this light. For him it was in fact an attempt to broaden his consciousness. I am absolutely certain that John was a born surrealist, and that he inherited the facets of the eccentric and the incomprehensible, and, in my opinion, he took drugs precisely to enable others to experience the incomprehensible.

As with all real artists, John's creative appetite was difficult to sate. This is not insignificant, I think, in understanding why Yoko Ono held such great fascination for him. When John met her at an exhibition in 1966, she was already an established artist – labelled "progressive" at the time – easily able to arouse his enthusiasm for everything new and unusual. He was only too willing to break through boundaries, investigate new paths and live out his desire for experimentation. The two of them later combined many of their artistic activities – from recordings to films and those spectacular "happenings" and *Bag-Ins,* and Yoko was most certainly his source of inspiration for the erotic lithographs in his portfolio *Bag One.*

The last time I saw John Lennon was in 1966 at the shooting of Richard Lester's *How I Won the War.* I naturally kept close track of his life and work up until his incredibly tragic death, and

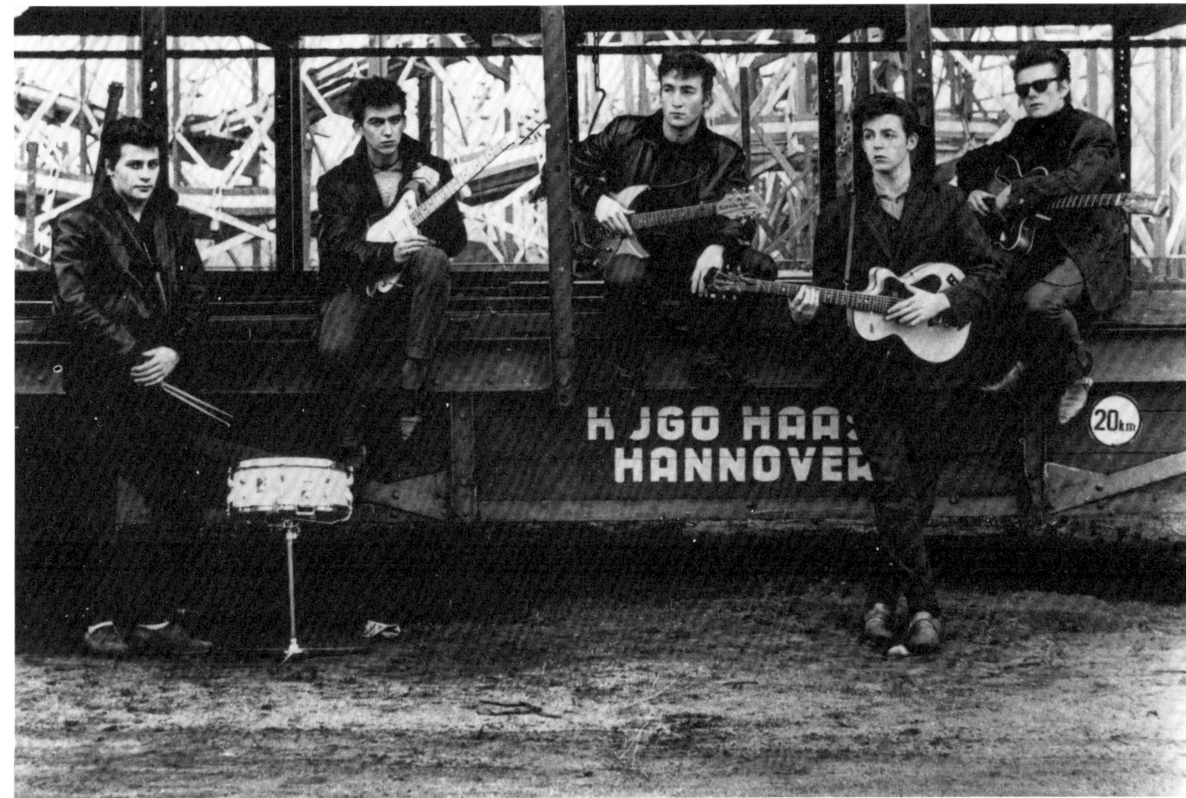

Astrid Kirchherr,
The Beatles (Hugo Haase),
Hamburg 1960

continued to feel very close to him all those years.
I was very pleased to see how the rough diamond
I first met in Hamburg became an accomplished
man of the world who in the end gave us *Imagine*.

What remains is not only a memory – still very
much alive – of an extraordinary human being,
but also a quiet feeling of happiness that John was
able to develop his artistic and human potential in
such a wonderful way.

It is a great pleasure for me to be able to see
John again in this exhibition.

Remembering John Lennon
Jann Wenner

John Lennon was a great musical artist, but his life was about far more than music. He was a visionary in every respect who sought to challenge and inspire his audience, not simply to please them. His ambitions transcended all boundaries. He sought nothing less than to have people transform their consciousness, to free their minds. He saw his life and his work, his marriage and his music, his visual art and his political activism, all as part of an ongoing, integrated effort to put his gift to great purpose. John was a dreamer, as he himself said, but he never doubted that, through hard work and subversive play, his dreams could be made a reality and the world could change for the better.

The visual arts in all their various forms were an extremely important part of how John expressed himself and brought his ideas to the rest of us. They certainly were an important avenue through which he entered and forever changed my life. I first fell in love with the Beatles when, as a college student in California, I saw them in Richard Lester's 1964 film, *A Hard Day's Night*. No one could have foreseen at that time what a monumental figure John would become, of course; it was enough that in that movie he defined his identity as the "smart Beatle" – witty, acerbic, intolerant of fools.

Over the course of the next few years the Beatles would help to reinvent and ultimately redefine popular music and its place and potential in society. Suddenly what had once been an amusement for teenagers became perhaps the most significant means of communication for a generation that found itself engaged in crucial social, cultural and political battles.

Despite the role he had already taken on as a cultural provocateur – this was the man who declared that the Beatles were more popular than Jesus, remember – John was beginning to feel trapped by his identity as a Beatle and was looking for other ways to create, another way to be. Tellingly, he turned again to film, acting in Richard Lester's 1967 anti-war protest, *How I Won the War*.

By the time of that movie I had started publishing *Rolling Stone*, and John Lennon appeared on our first cover in his cinematic role as Private Gripweed. "I feel I want to be them all – painter, writer, actor, singer, player, musician," John said in that issue. "I want to see which one turns me on and what I'll be like when I've done it." In that spirit of adventure, that willingness to explore his own identity and try anything, to test and shatter limits, John embodied much that I wanted *Rolling Stone* to aspire to. Choosing him to be on that first cover was, in retrospect, not really a choice at all.

One year later, towards the end of 1968, John and I had the opportunity to crash through the boundaries of good taste together. He had fallen in love with Yoko Ono by then and he wanted to release *Two Virgins*, the tape of experimental music he and Yoko had made in his home on their first night together. The problem was the cover art: their record company did not want to put the album out with the frontal and rear nude portraits John and Yoko had chosen for the front and back covers.

Because of our sympathetic coverage of them, John and Yoko understood that *Rolling Stone* would be willing to work with them to get their message out. So when they offered to let us run the portraits in the magazine I jumped at the opportunity to help them and to associate *Rolling Stone* with their work and their daring. One of the nude photographs (rear) that John took of himself and Yoko with an automatic camera appeared on the cover of the first anniversary issue of *Rolling Stone*. (The frontal portrait was the centerspread!)

Does it surprise you to learn that that was the first issue of *Rolling Stone* to completely sell out on the newsstand? The response was overwhelming – and hilariously funny. Even before the issue went on sale, our hometown newspaper,

The San Francisco Chronicle, ran a story with a four-column headline that announced: "Nude Beatle Perils S.F." Distributors protested and post offices in some cities refused to deliver subscription copies. As I wrote in our next issue: "The phones were ringing and all manner of readers and readers-to-be were traipsing down to our office … to get copies of the issue. And not just one copy, but three or four apiece. The point is this: 'Print a famous foreskin and the world will beat a path to your door.'"

Beyond all the surreal fun, however, it seemed to me then – and I am even more certain now – that John and Yoko were making important points with those photos. In their relationship and in their love for each other they had been reborn, made innocent again. They wanted people to accept them for who they were, stripped of John's Beatle past. They also wanted people to accept themselves and their sexuality, to realize that sex was not bad, but beautiful.

John and Yoko's bodies were ordinary, and they were saying that it's okay not to be physically perfect, that you shouldn't worry about the size of your penis or your breasts. It's enough to be who and what you are, human beings. "Even the president of the United States sometimes must have to stand naked," Bob Dylan wrote in 1965 – but, with typical disdain for restraint of any kind – John and Yoko acted on it.

Two Virgins was soon followed by other conceptual provocations by John and Yoko, as they began to turn their lives into works of art and social comment: Bed-Ins for peace, performance art events, political protests, erotic drawings. While all this was going on, a lot of people on the music scene – artists, executives and journalists alike – began to wonder about John. What was the matter with him? Had he lost his mind? How could he break up the Beatles? How could he make such a spectacle of himself? And what they said about Yoko was even worse.

What those people didn't understand was that Yoko had liberated John, had freed him to become the person he had always wanted to be. In her fearlessness, Yoko gave John the means to become himself. He would always be grateful to her for that. He had the greatest respect for Yoko's artistic achievements and viewed her avantgarde background as a new way to seeing things, of defamiliarizing the familiar, and an invitation to be both fun and serious.

Though they would never admit it – nor would they ever say it in public, so intimidated were they by John's genius – many people on the music scene envied John's willingness to defy convention; for all their hipness, they were too uptight to take the risks John and Yoko took.

No doubt about it – in taking those risks John sometimes made a fool of himself. But he was willing to do so if that was the price of being more than a fool – and maybe even shockingly wise – the rest of the time. And, in John's case, a certain kind of gifted foolishness could be its own reward. John's drawings, for example, seem much more relaxed and whimsical, almost Thurberesque, than his music, which always tended to look at the big picture, ever was.

As in his books, *In His Own Write* and *A Spaniard in the Works,* John felt free and unfettered in his drawings, able to experiment without feeling compelled to make major statements. The result was a charming, candid day-to-day portrait of a man and what mattered to him when he wasn't in the public eye: his wife, his son Sean, his sexual desires, his friends, his travels, his morning coffee.

All this was a counterpoint to the reach of John's solo musical work. If John's songs with the Beatles forever altered the landscape of popular music, his solo work gave voice to the John Lennon the world remembers: the evolutionary utopian who dug for the truth within himself as fiercely as he demanded it of the world.

Still, the private world of family and daily pleasures became increasingly important to John

after all the tumult of the sixties and early
seventies. It was a deserved respite from the fray.
Then, just as he was re-entering the public world,
he was lost to us.

How it broke our hearts when he died. How
encouraging it would be to have John Lennon
with us now, helping us to sort out the brutal
complexities of our time, helping us to find a way
into the future. John always seemed able to give
us hope.

I feel privileged to have known John Lennon
and blessed by my continuing friendship with
Yoko. John's death meant that we lost a great and
loving man, and that we would never enjoy all the
terrific work he would have gone on to do. But he
left us a great deal to sustain us. Painter, writer,
actor, singer, player, musician, composer: That's
what he was and those are the sources of his gifts
to us and all who come after.

Drawings
Lithographs

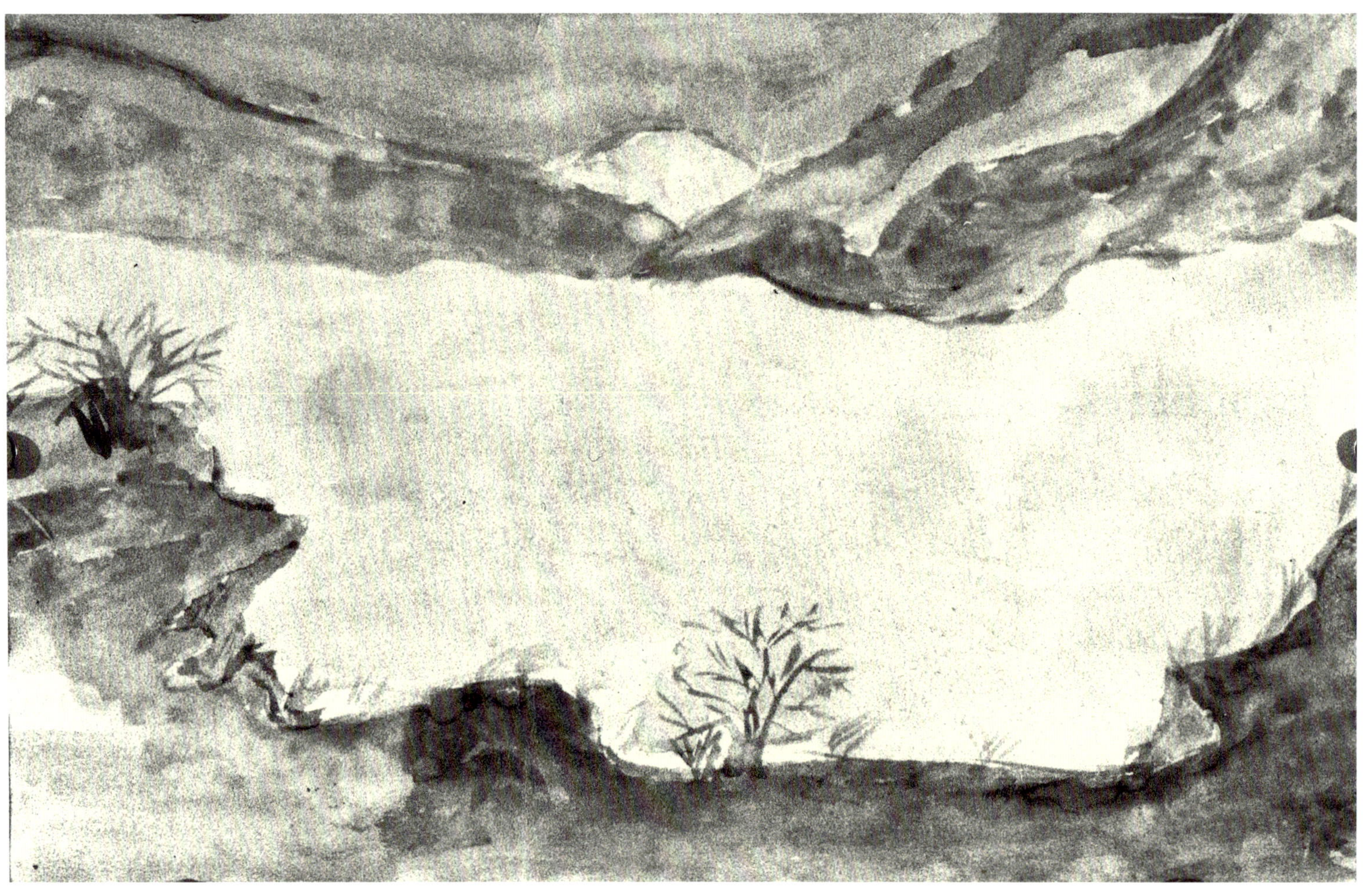

Untitled
1952
10½″ x 6¾″
Watercolour
signed: J. Lennon 1952

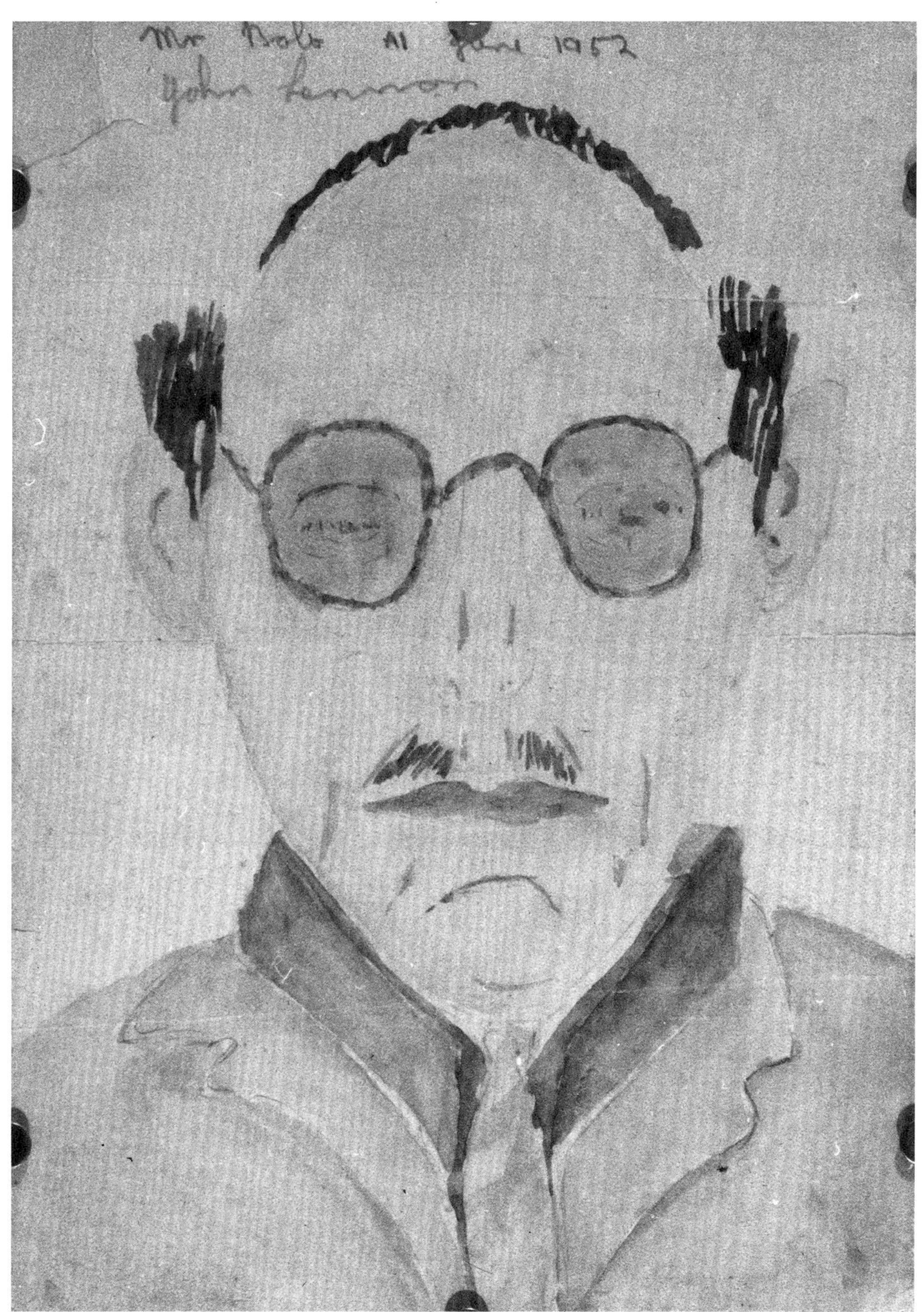

Mr. Bob
1952
7½″ x 10½″
Watercolour
signed: John Lennon,
June 1952

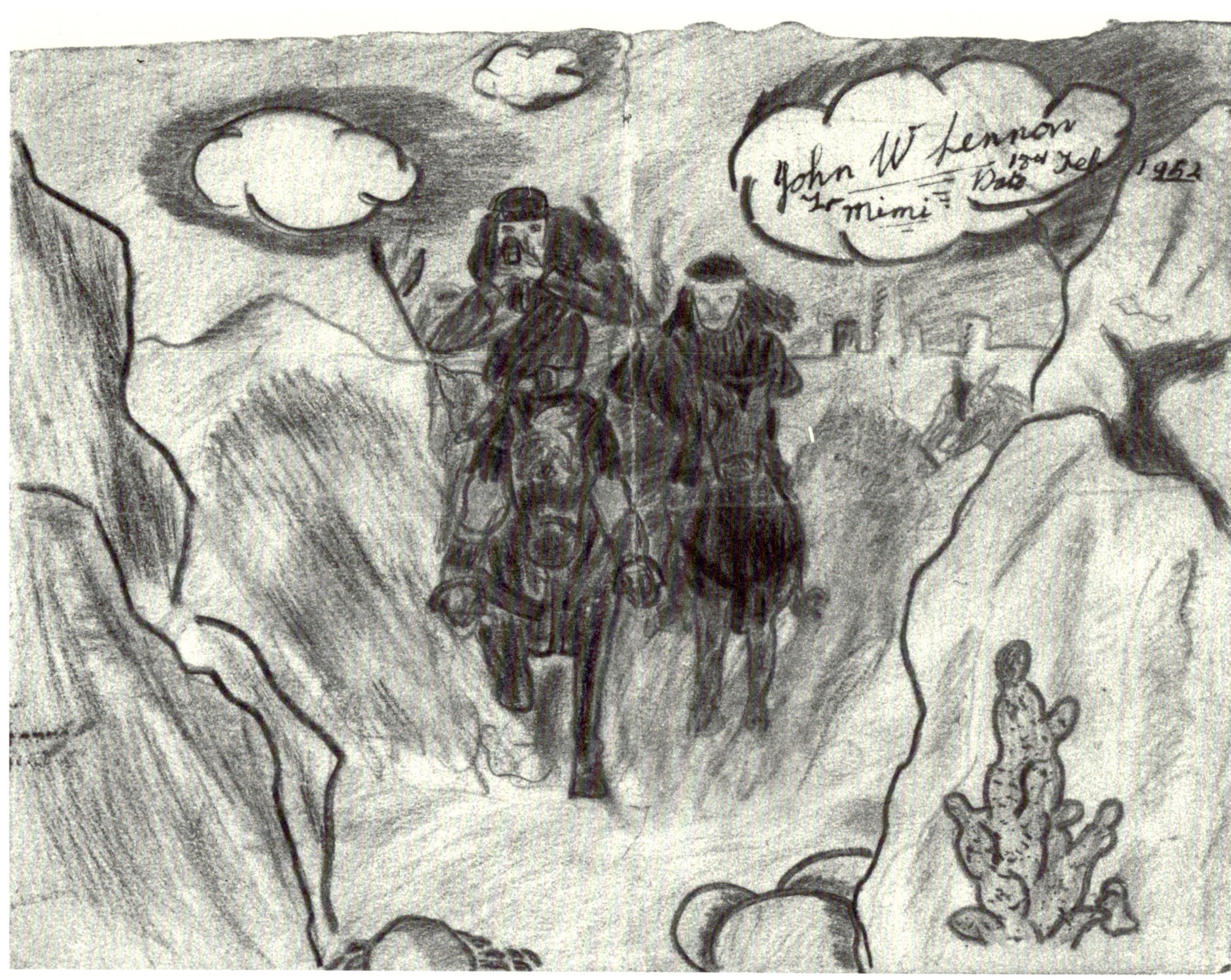

Untitled
1952
8″ x 6¾″
Colourpen
signed:
John W Lennon 1952

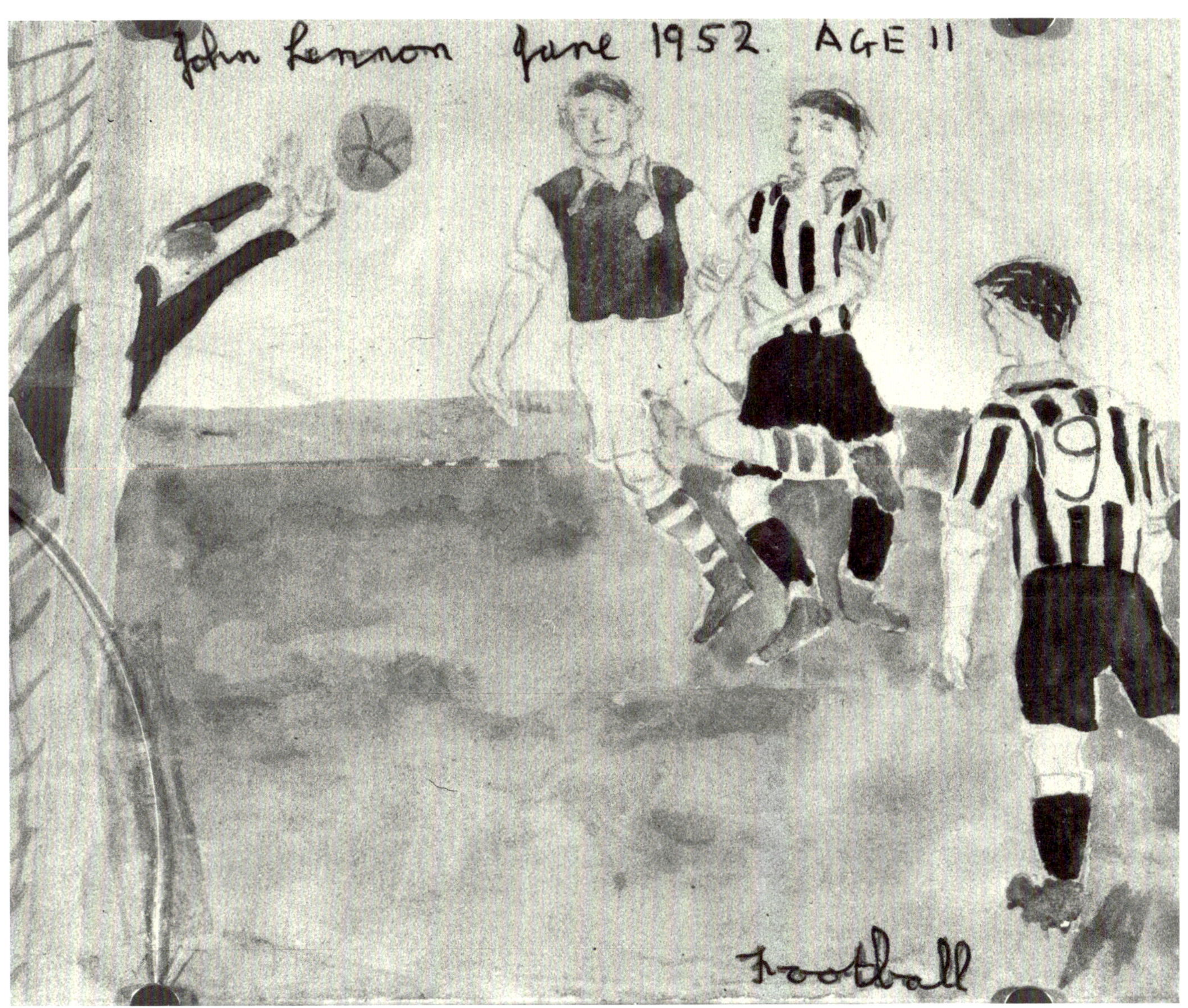

Untitled
1952
9″ x 7½″
Watercolour
signed: John Lennon,
June 1952, age 11

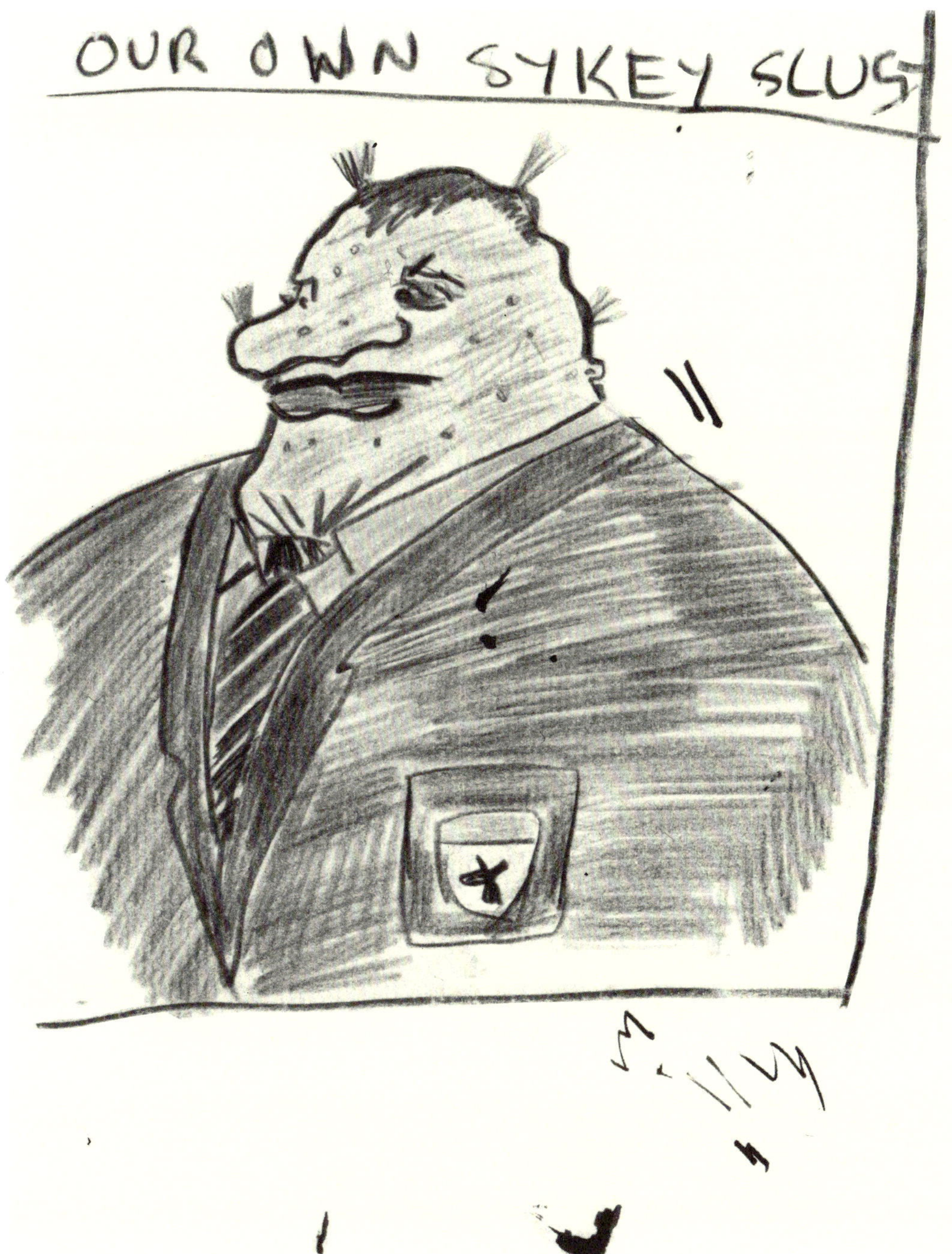

Our Own Sykey Slug
(from the sketchbook)
around 1955
5¾" x 7¾"
Colourpen

A Primitive Mrs. Vaughn
(p. 1 from the sketchbook)
around 1955
5¾″ × 7¾″
Pen

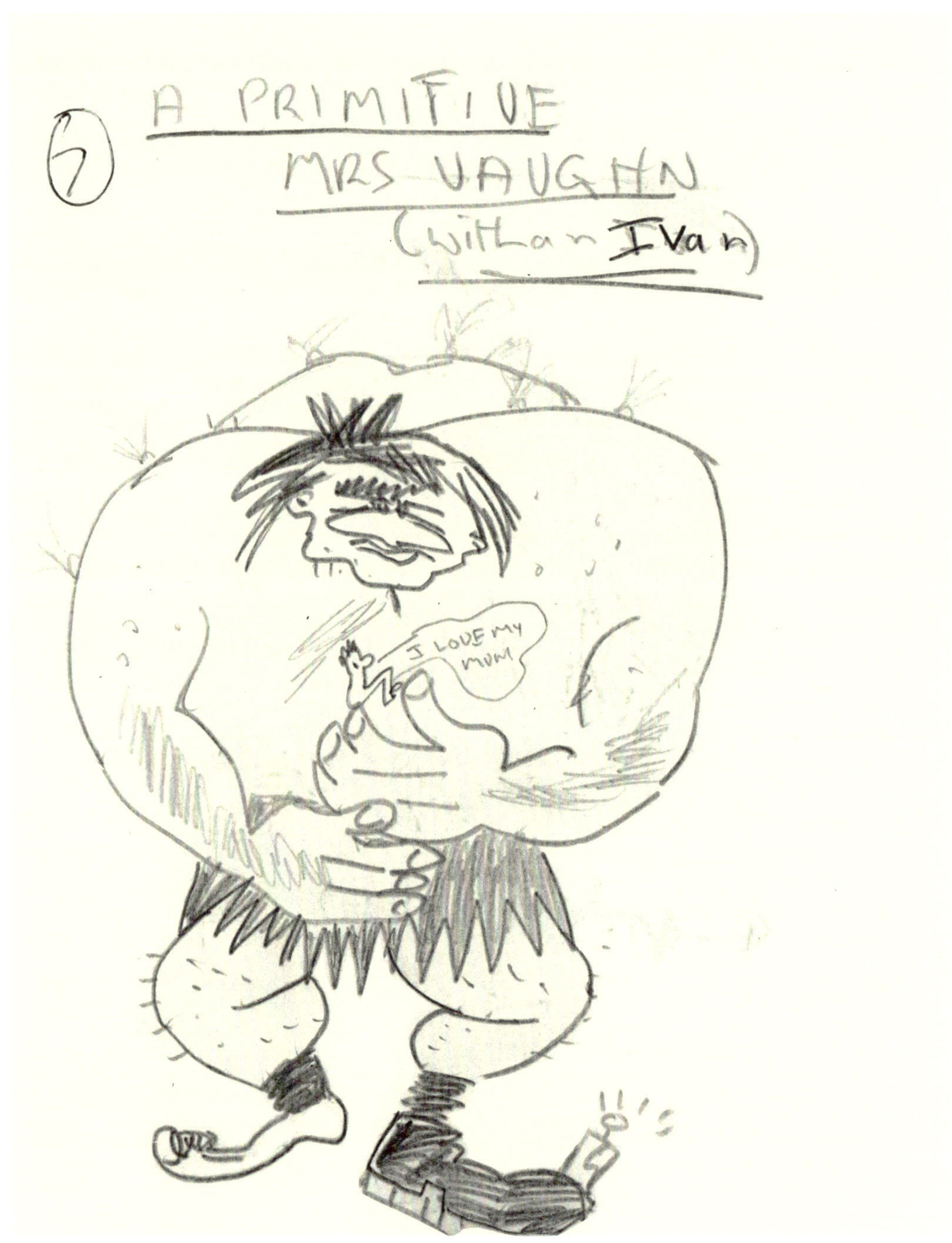

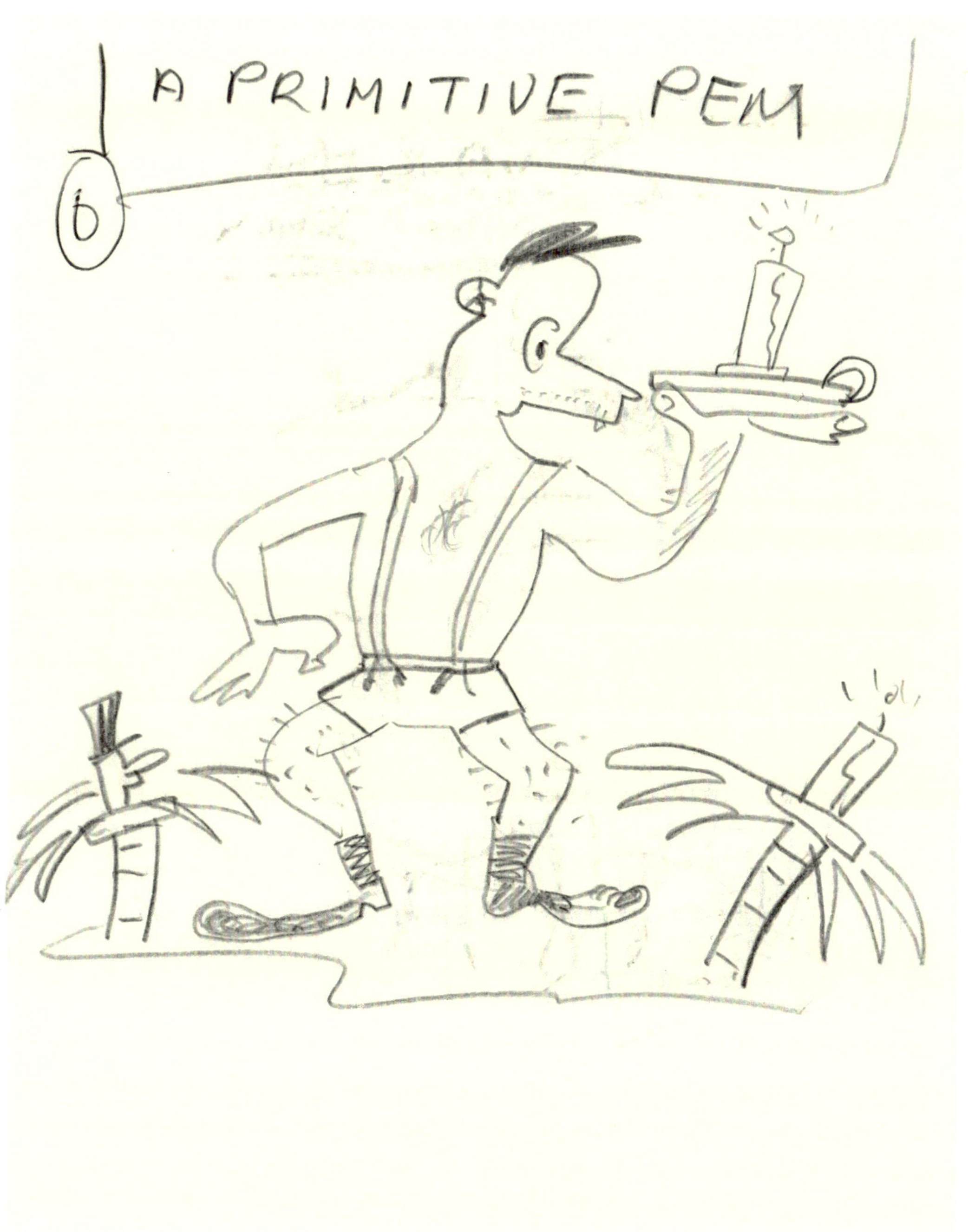

A Primitive Pem
(p. 6 from the sketchbook)
around 1955
5¾″ x 7¾″
Pen

A Warty Walley
around 1955
(p. 9 from the sketchbook)
5¾″ x 7¾″
Pen

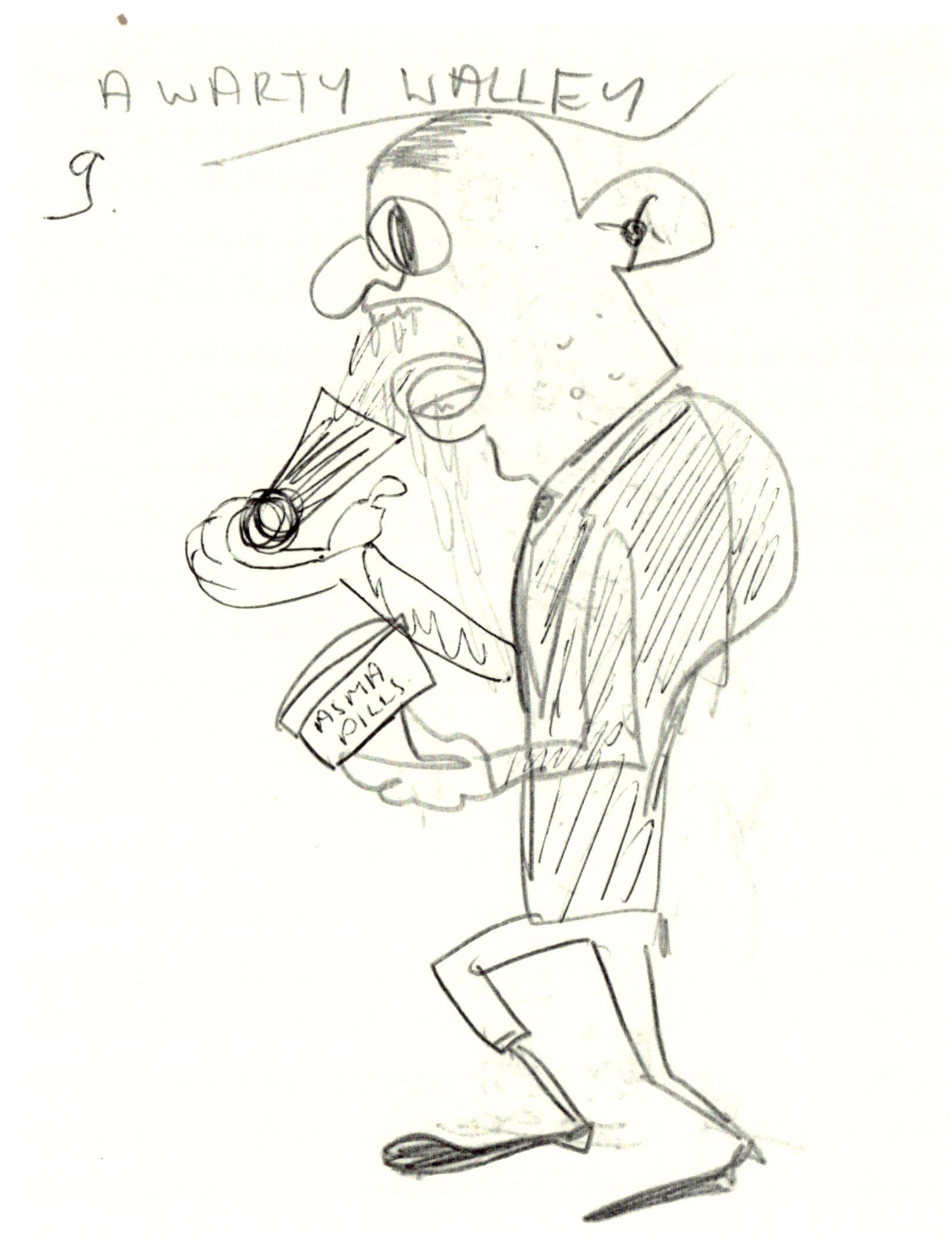

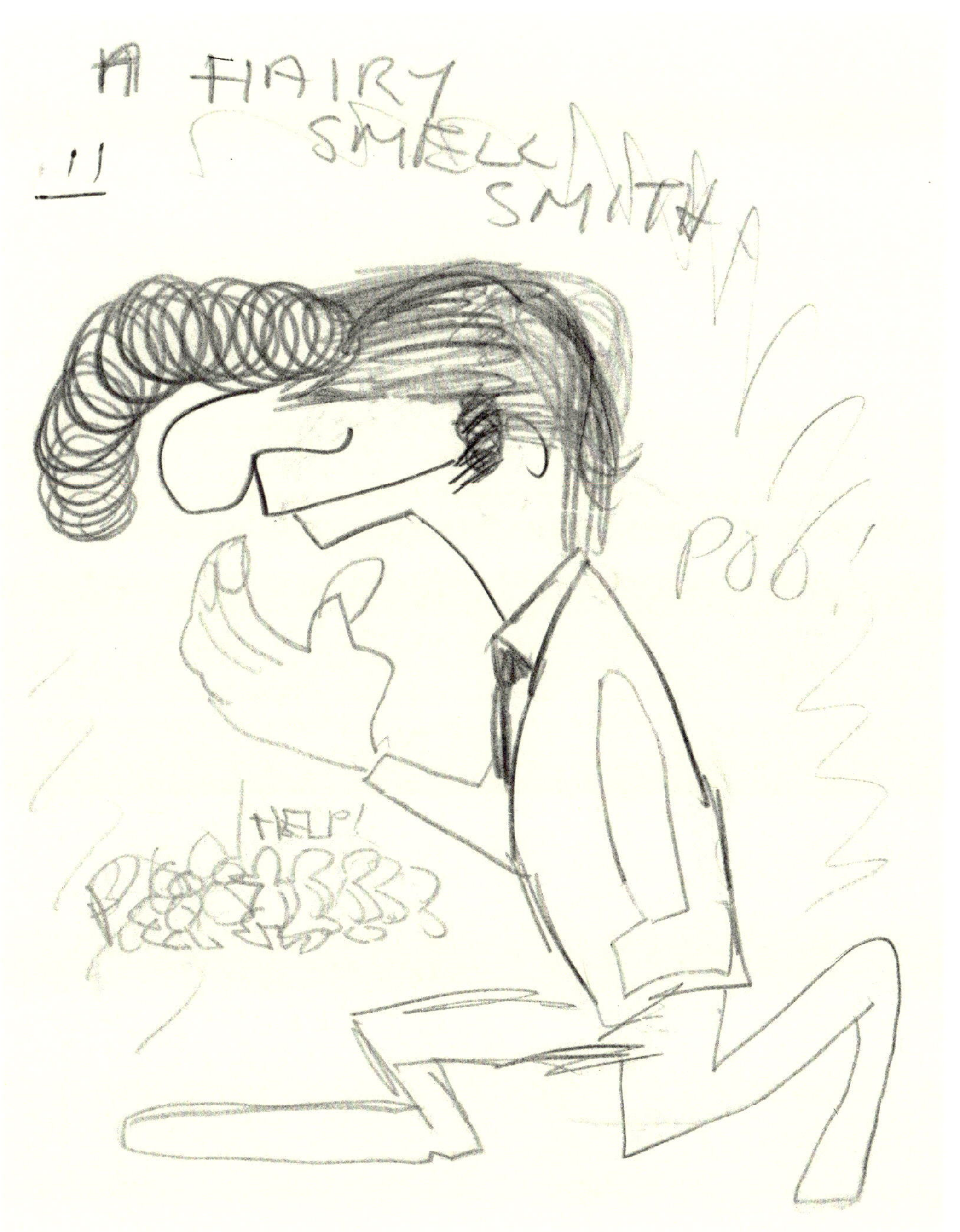

A Hairy Smell Smith
(p. 11 from the sketchbook)
around 1955
5¾″ x 7¾″
Pen

Moi Dad
(p. 12 from the sketchbook)
around 1955
5¾" x 7¾"
Pen

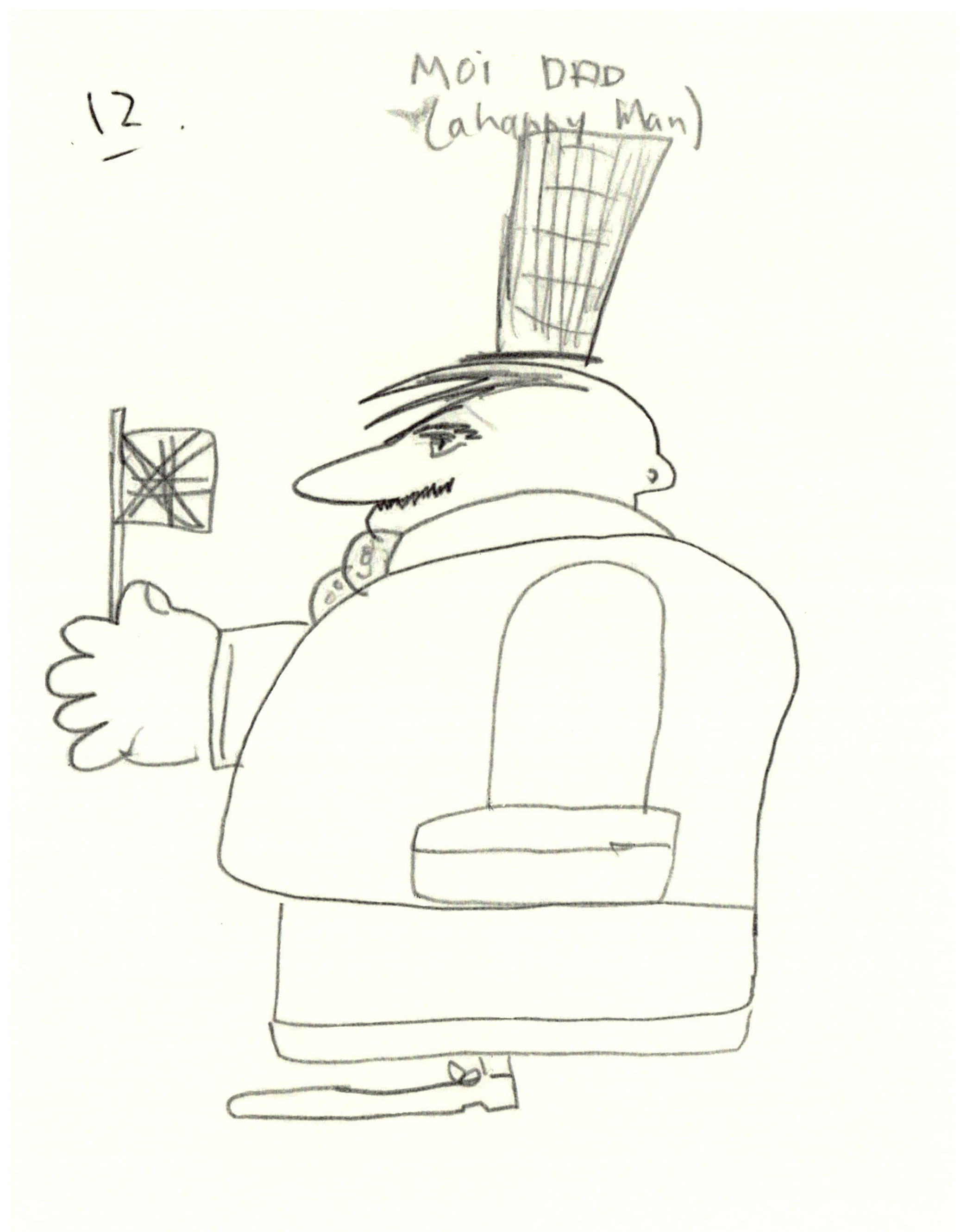

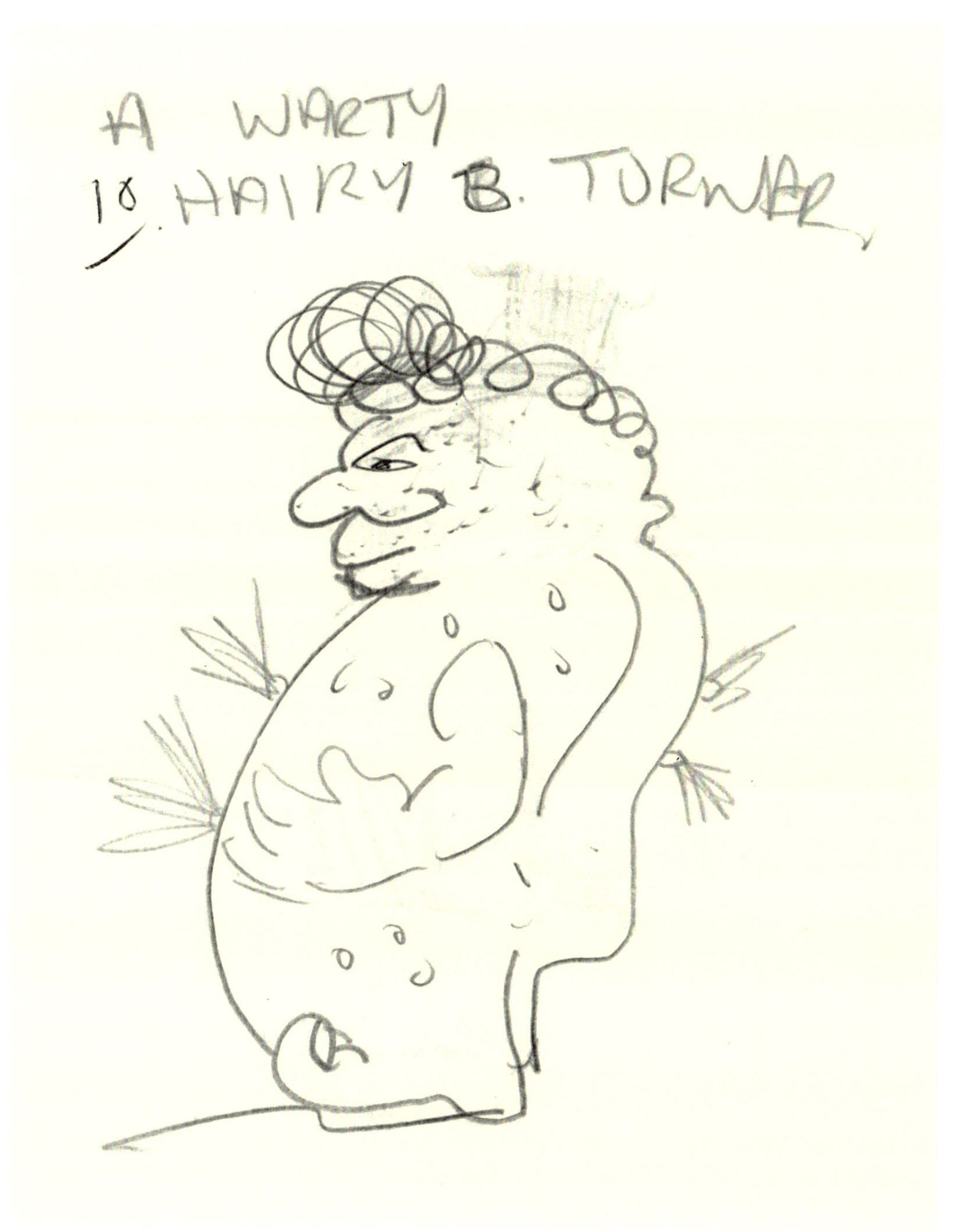

A Warty Hairy B. Turwal
(p. 10 from the sketchbook)
around 1955
5¾″ x 7¾″
Pen

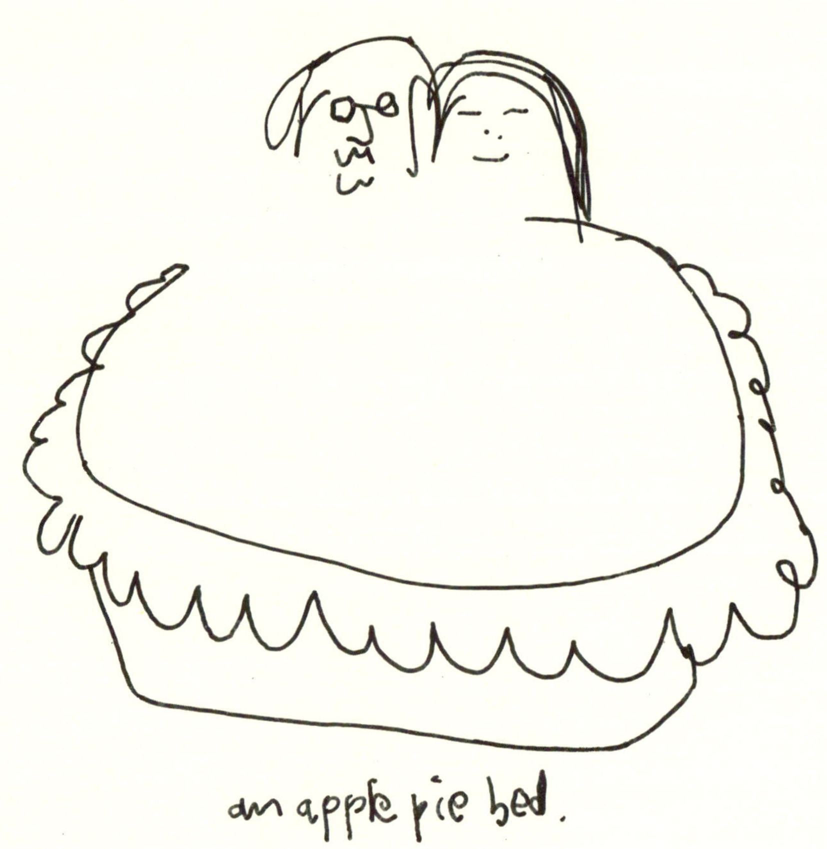

Apple Pie Bed
1969
8¾" x 7¼"
Ink

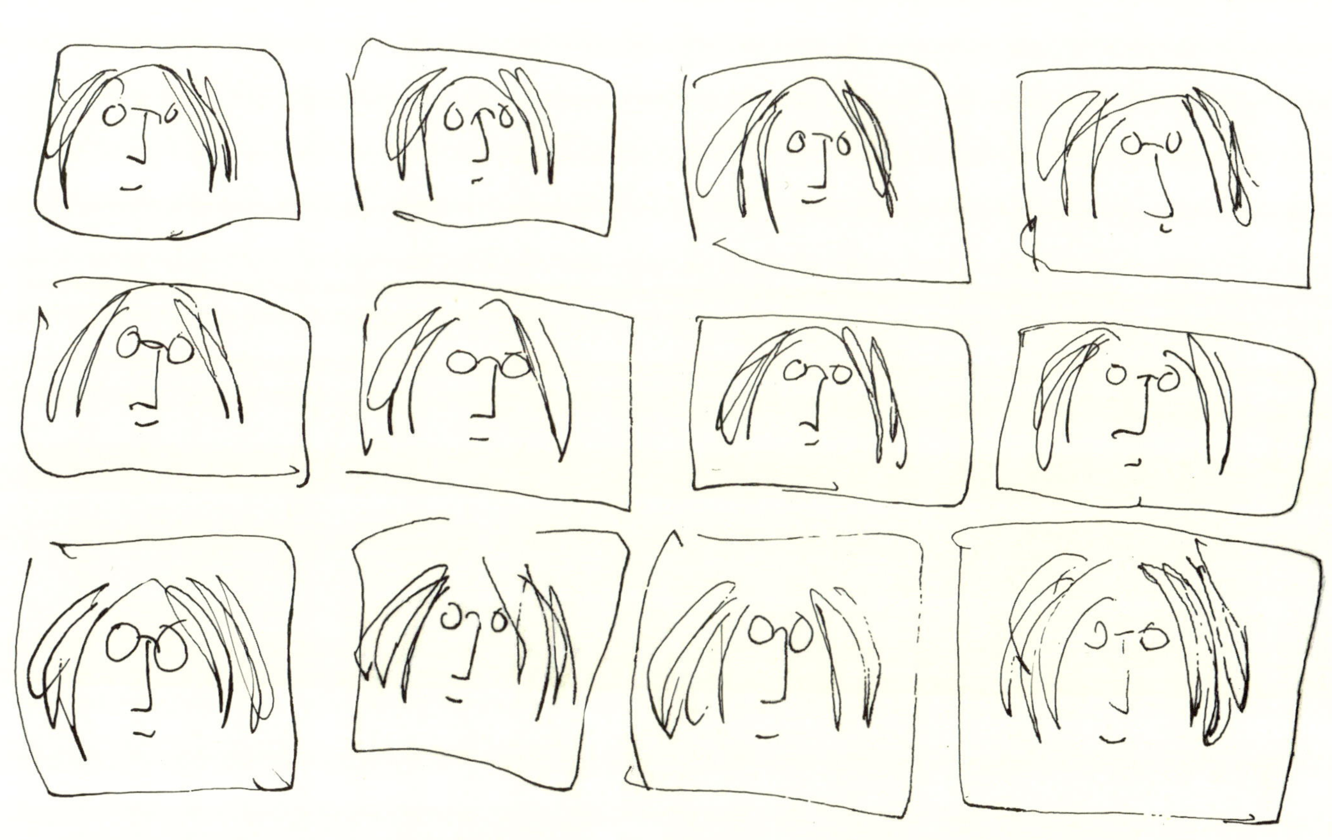

Multiple Self-Portrait
1968
9¾″ x 7¾″
Ink
signed: J.L. 68

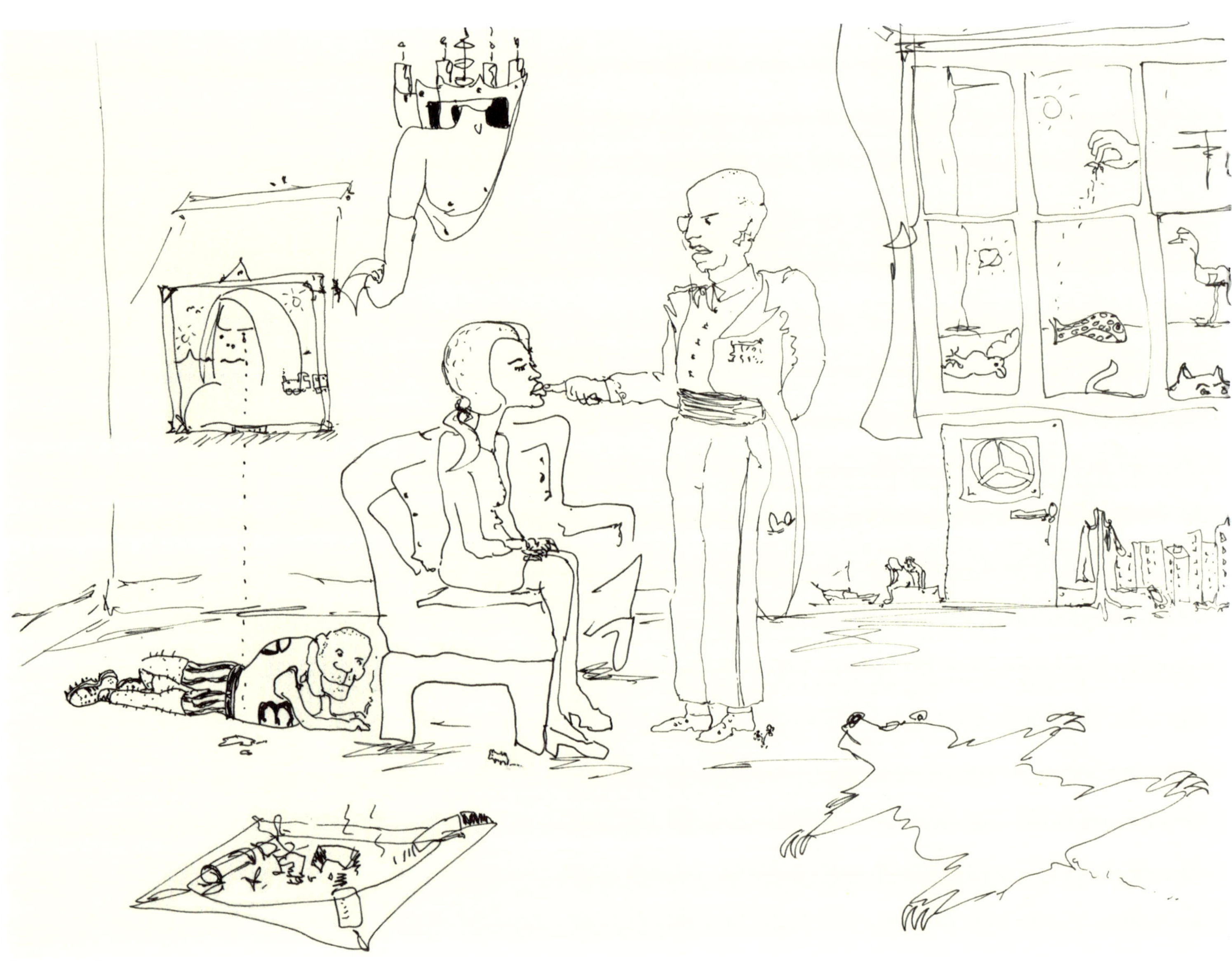

Untitled
1970
13¾" x 10½"
Ink

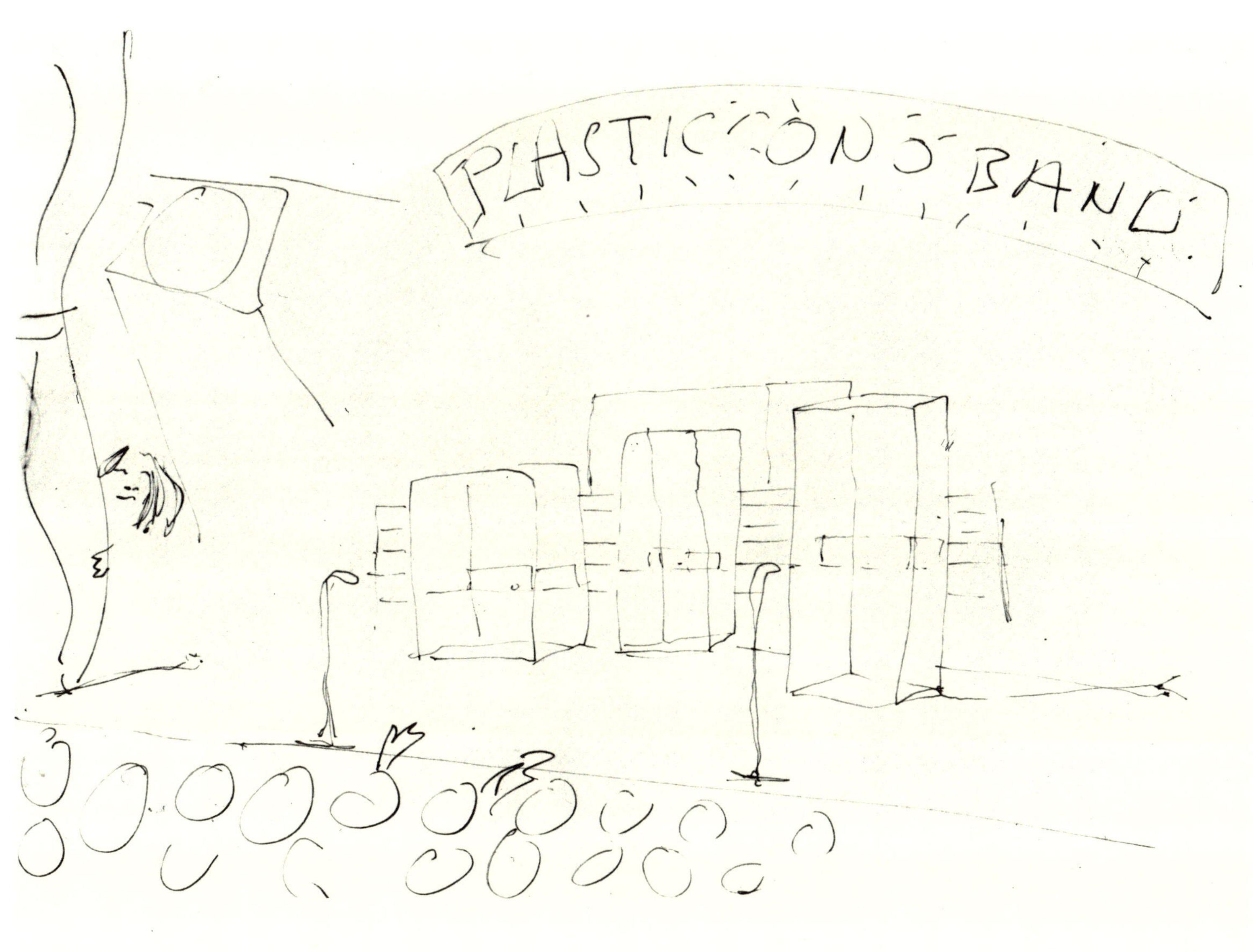

Plastic Ono Band
1970
11 ½″ x 8″
Ink

Back off Boogaloo
1976
10½″ x 12″
Ink

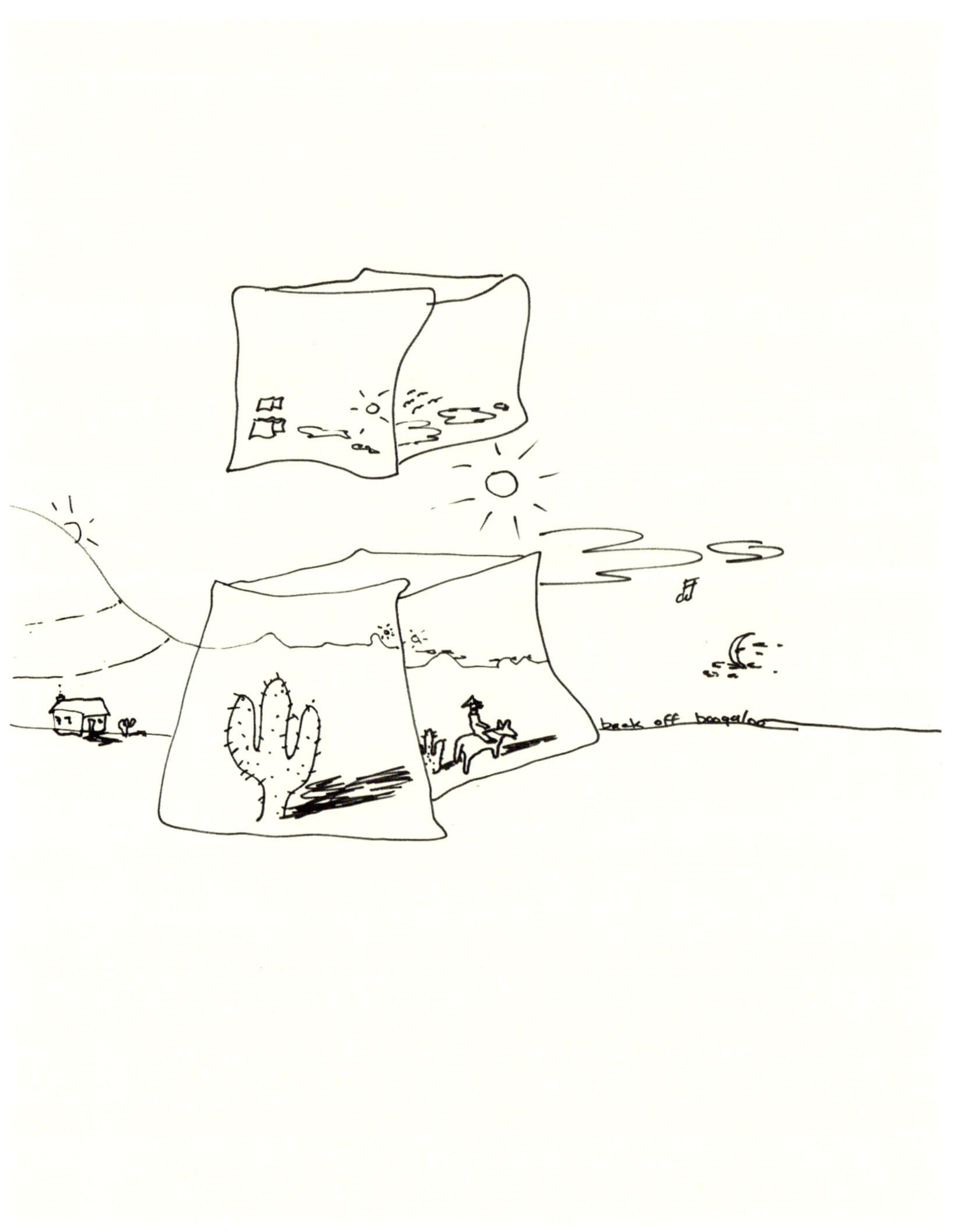

New York Woman
1972
8″ x 9½″
Ink
Signed J.L. 72.

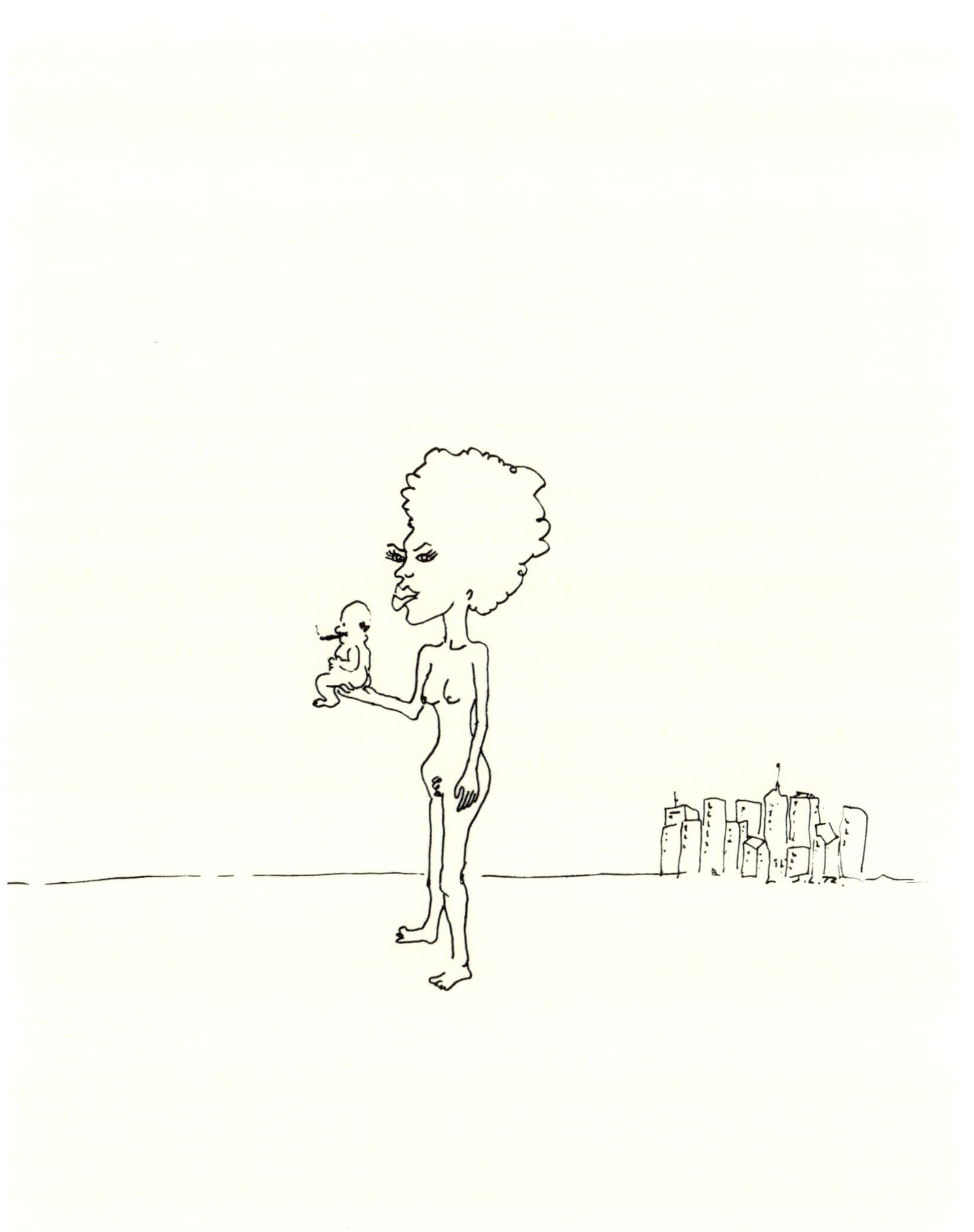

Yoko with Cat
1977
9″ x 10½″
Ink

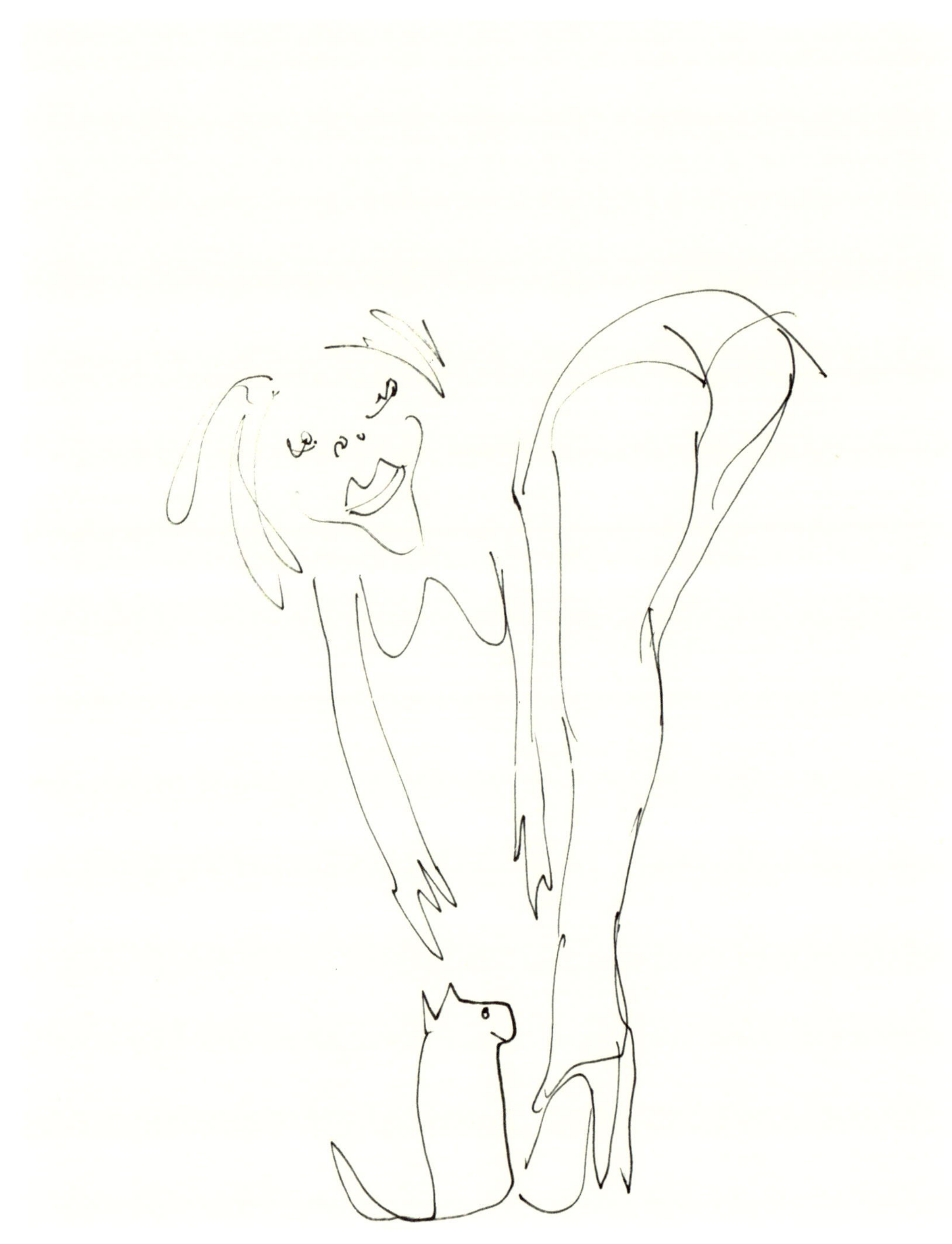

Looking Back
1977
9″ x 11″
Ink

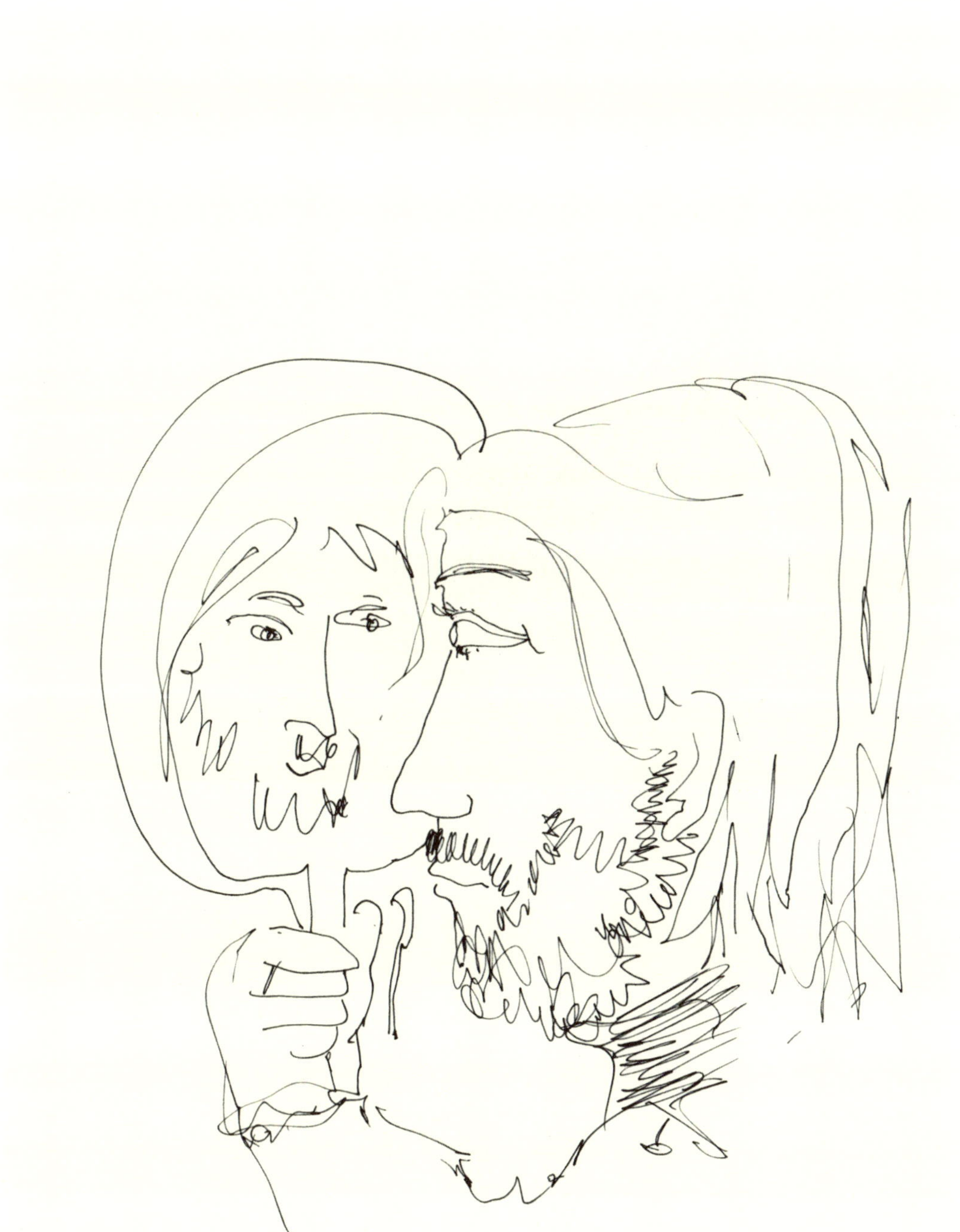

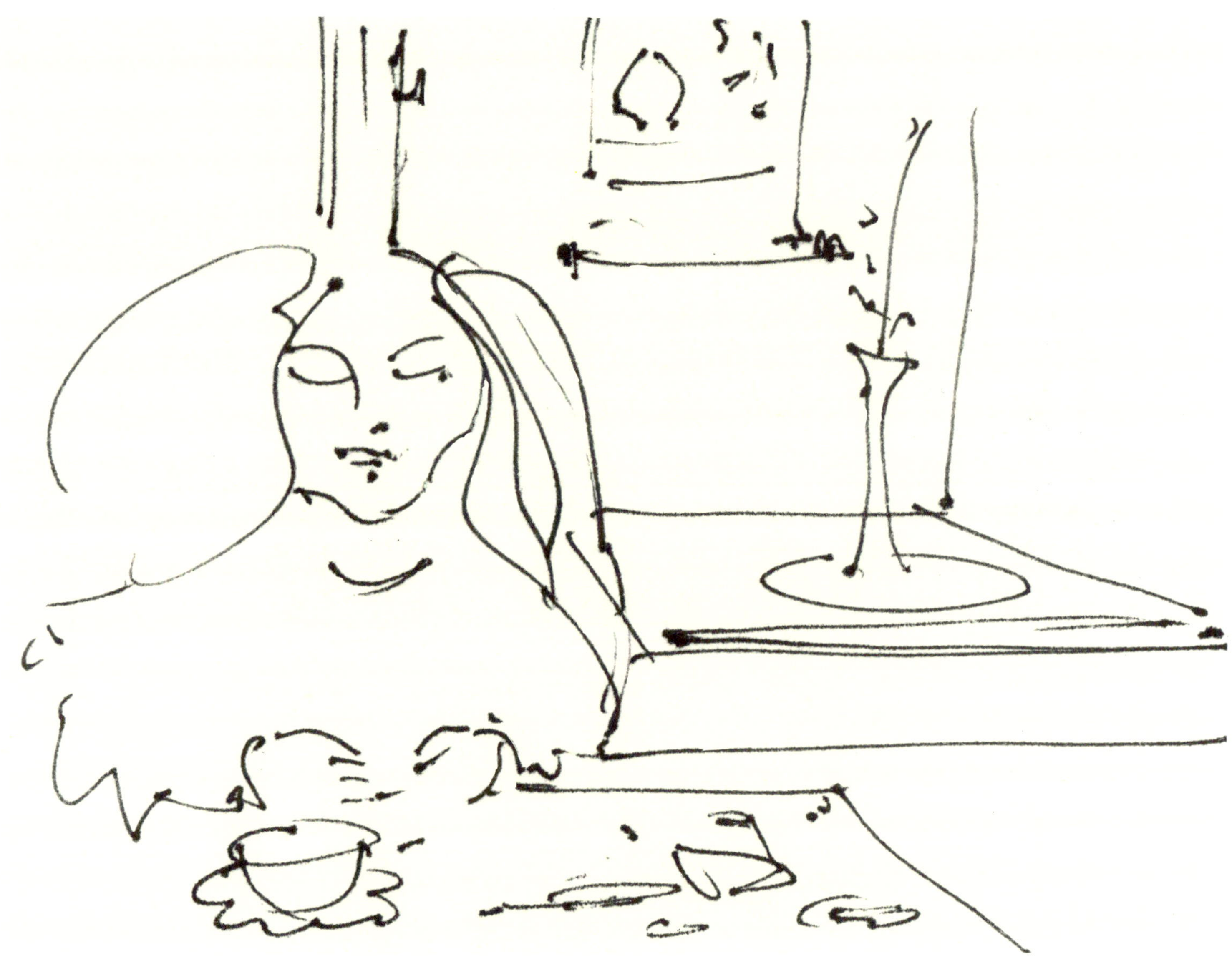

Morning Coffee
1977
4½″ x 3½″
Sumi Ink

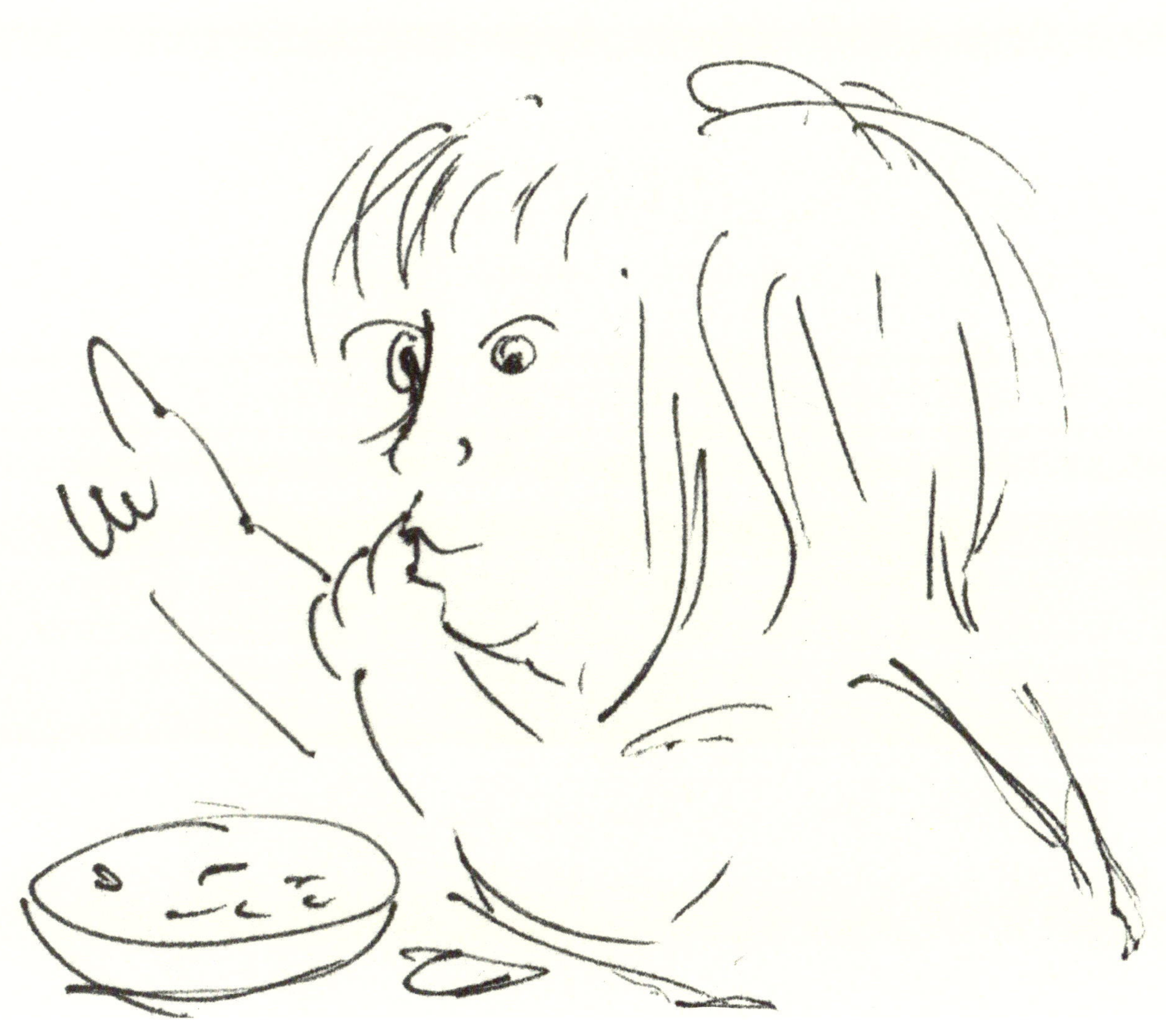

Sean
1977
4 ½" x 3 ½"
Sumi Ink

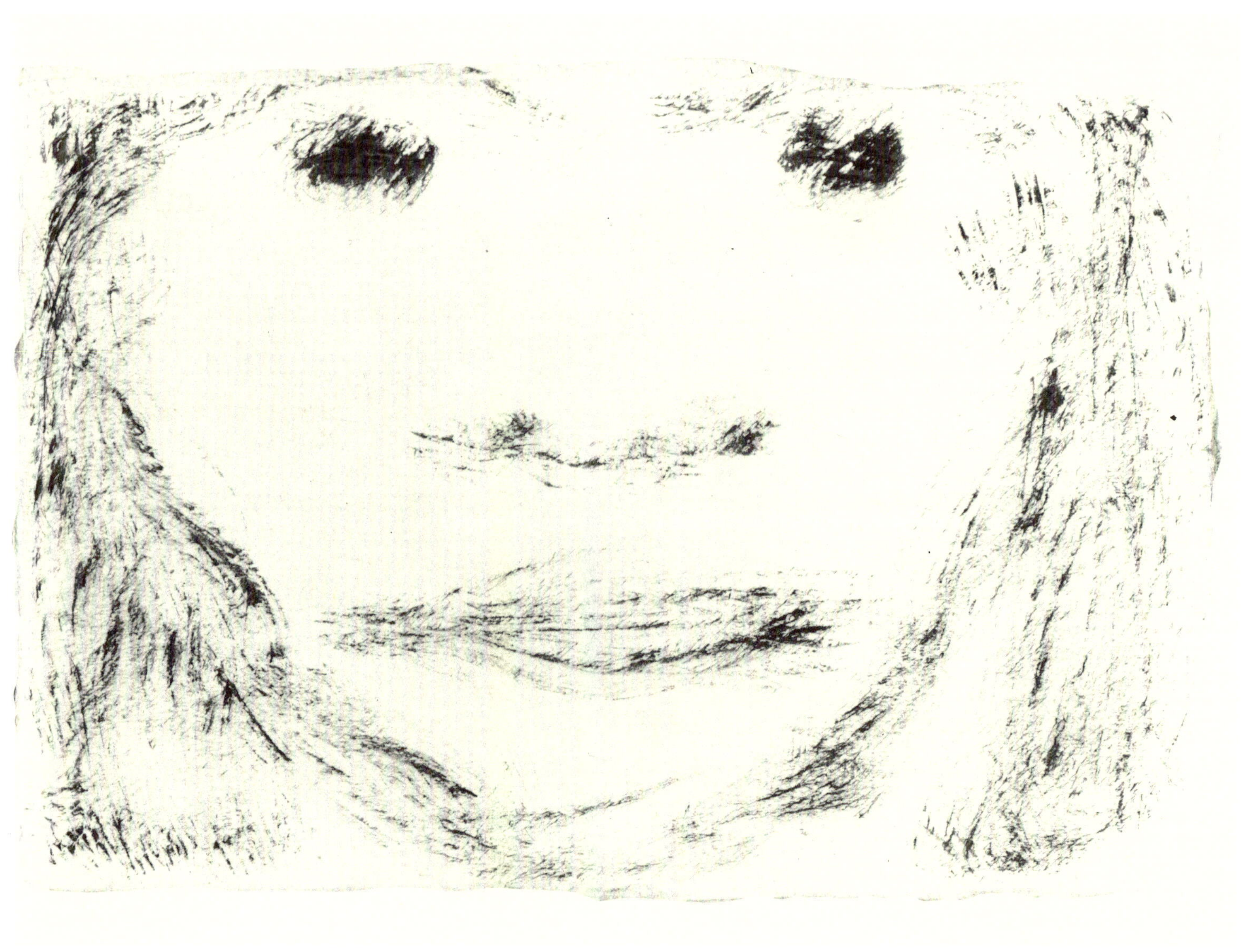

Yoko (Subject)
1977
5 ½″ x 3 ¾″
Sumi Ink

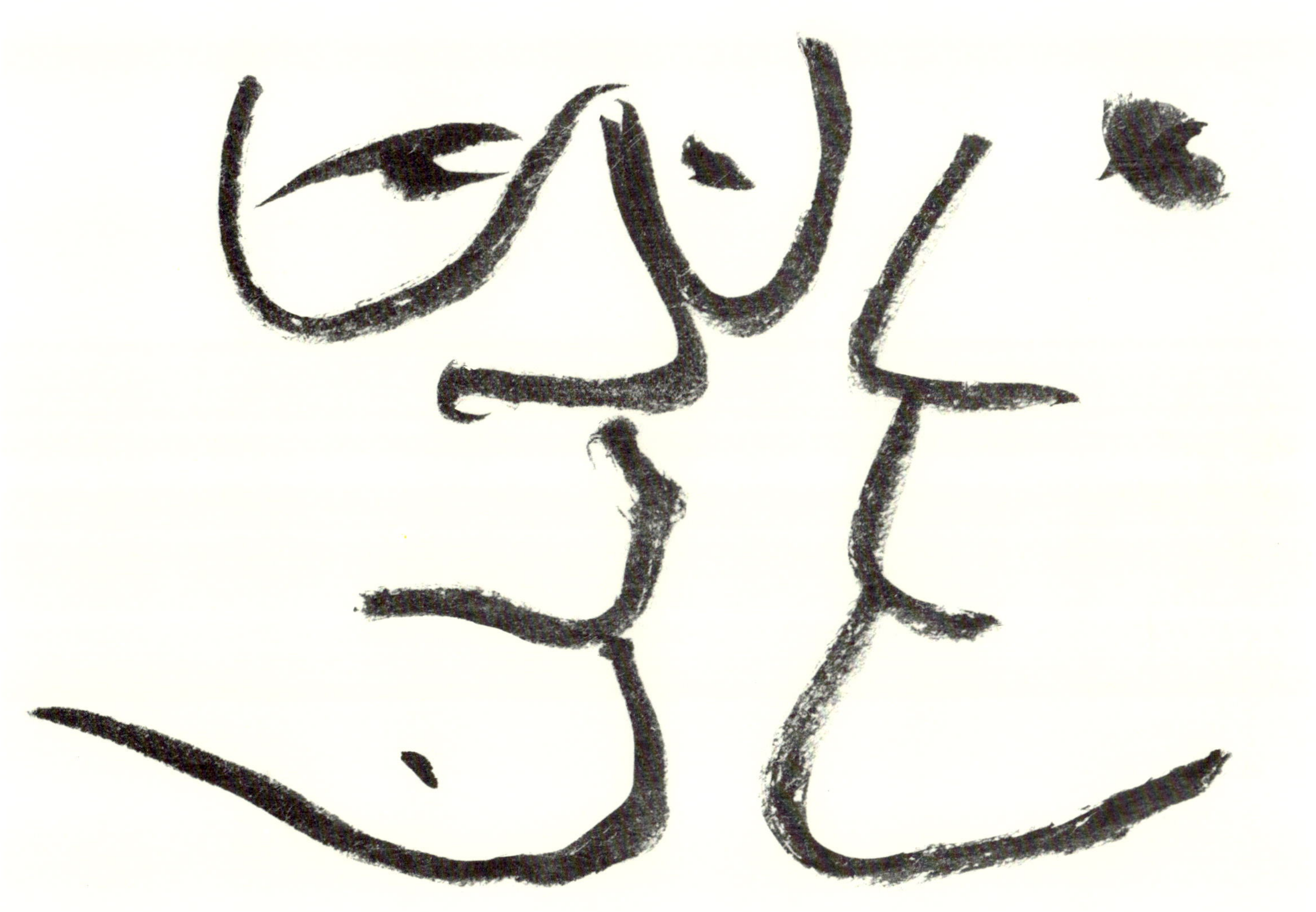

Untitled
1977
5¾″ x 3¾″
Sumi Ink

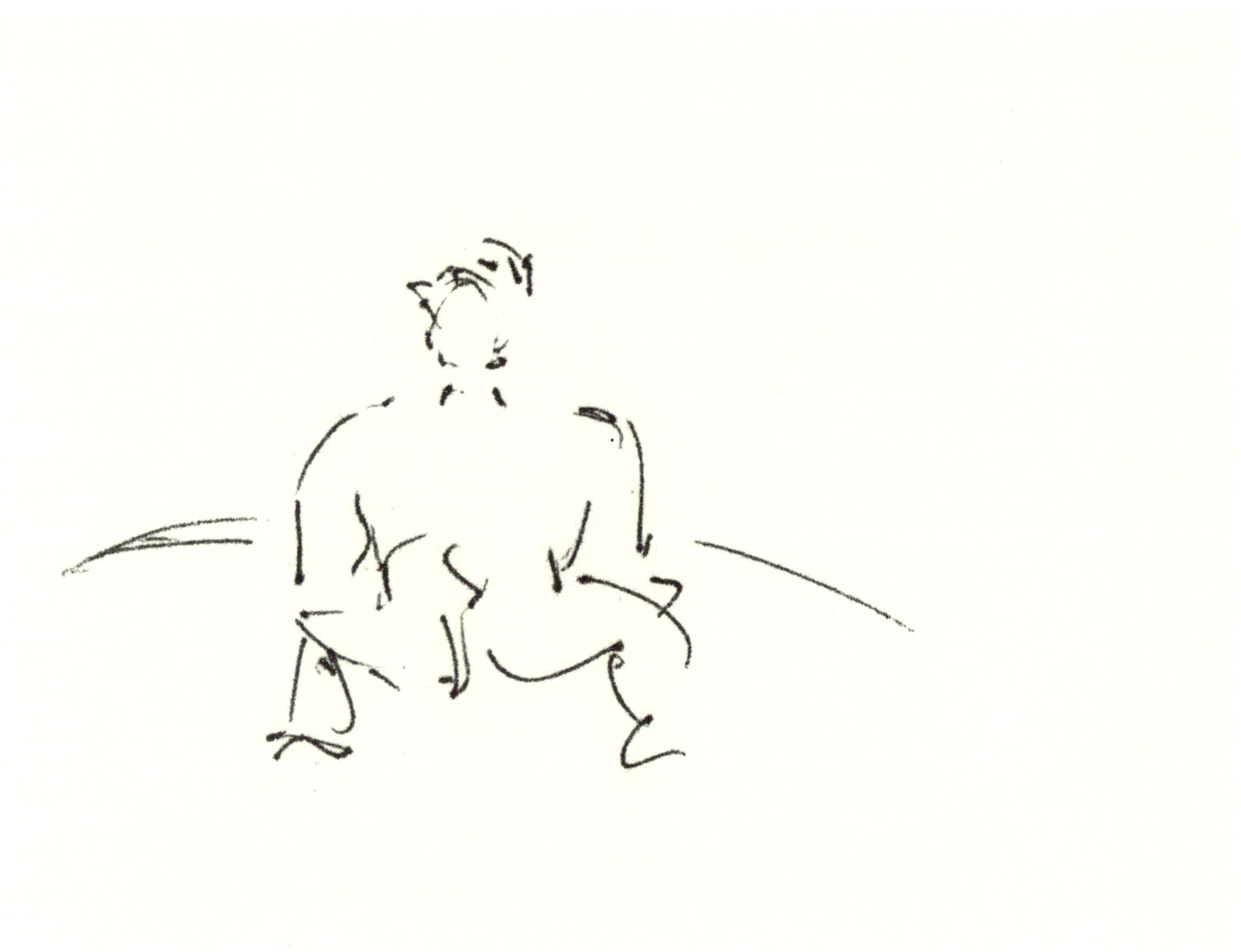

Sumō
1977
3 ½″ x 3 ½″
Sumi Ink

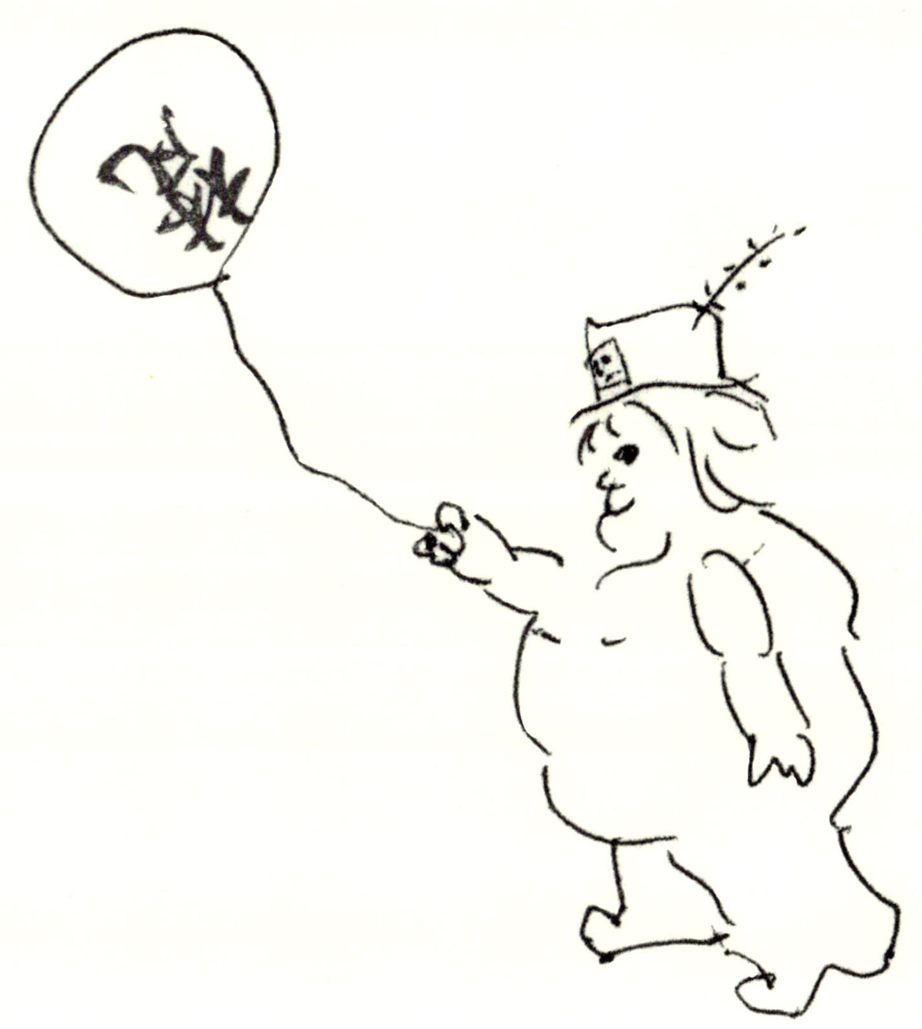

Obon
1977
3 ½″ x 3 ½″
Sumi Ink

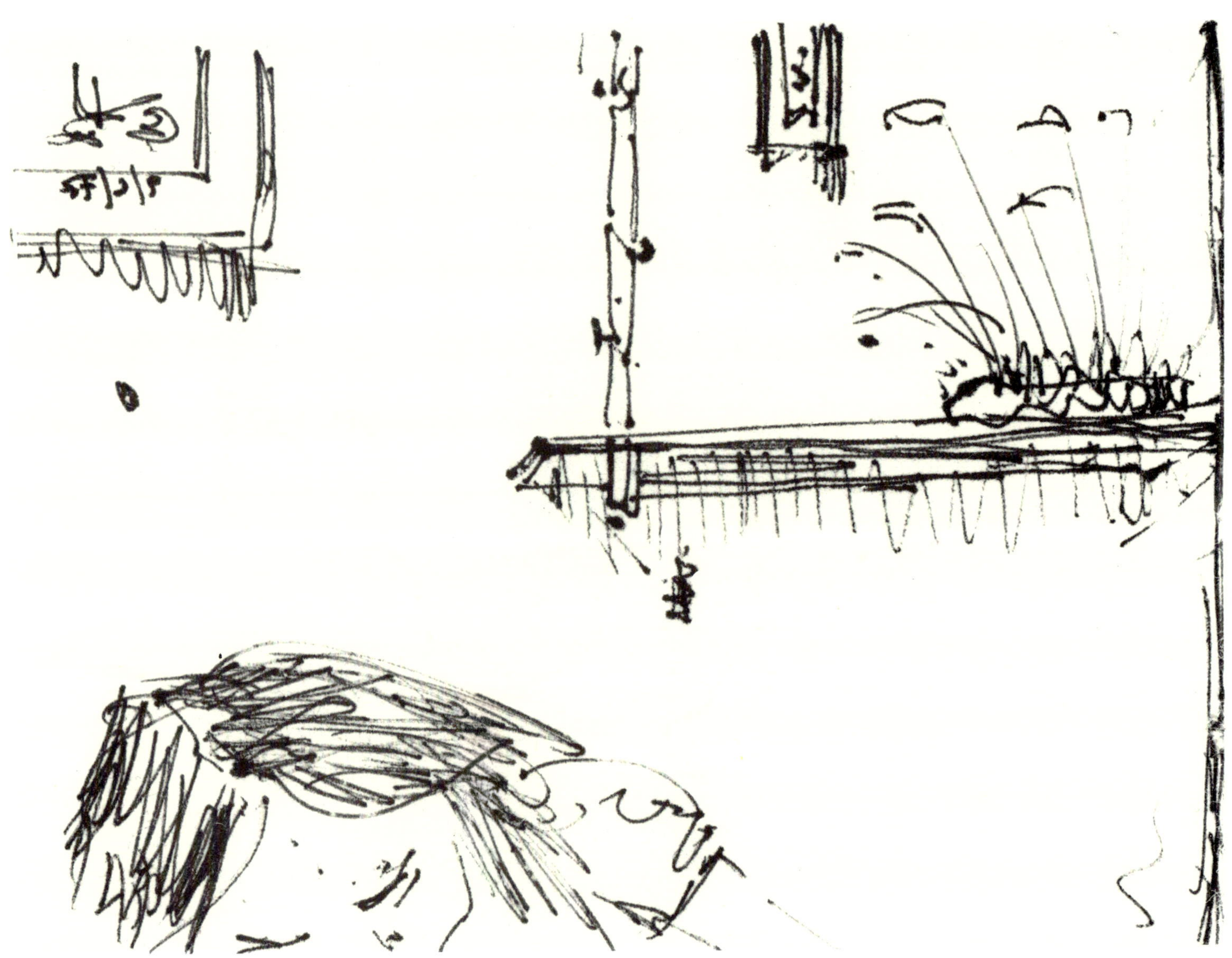

Summer in Japan
1977
4½″ x 3½″
Sumi Ink

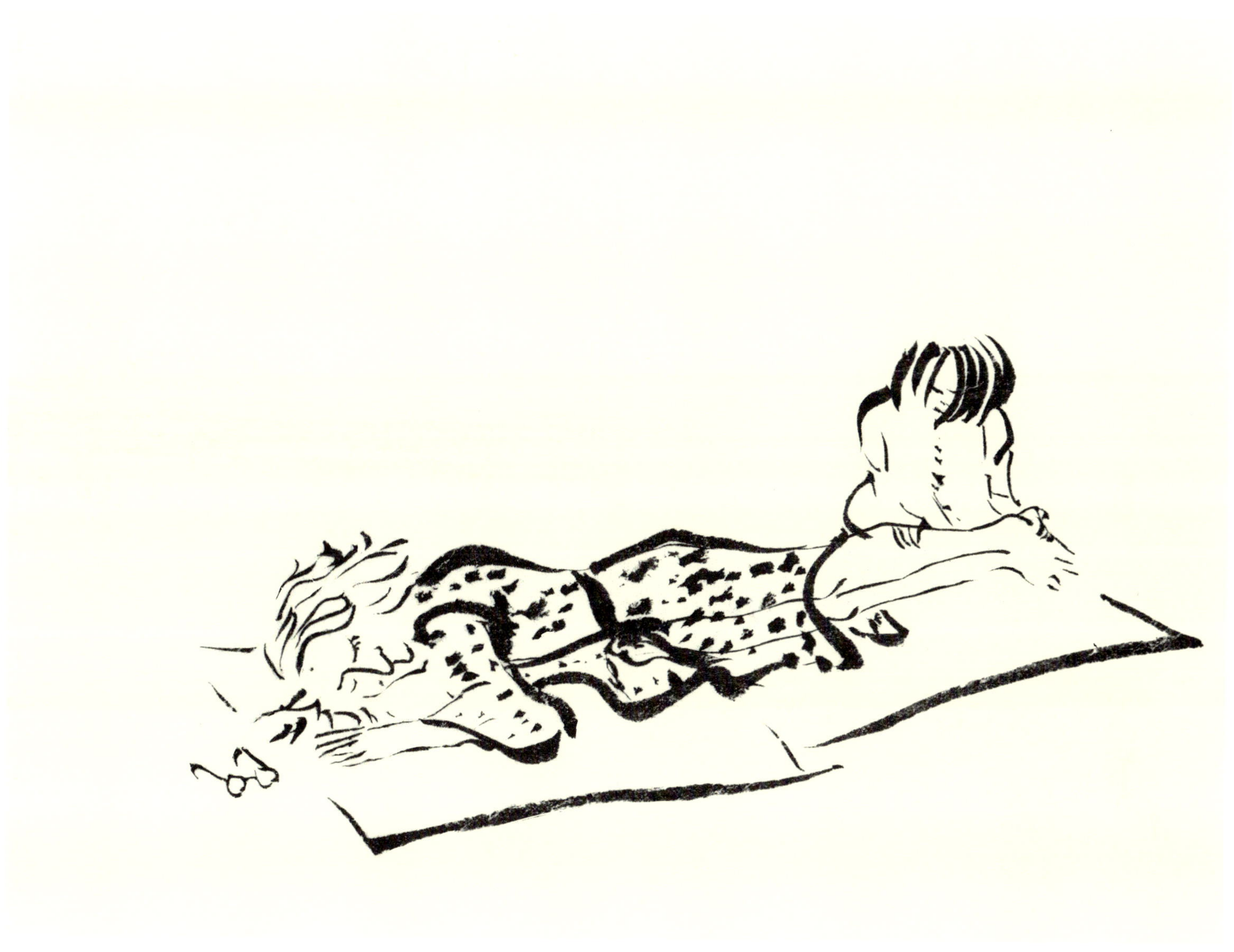

Karuizawa '77
1977
5 ½″ x 3 ¾″
Sumi Ink

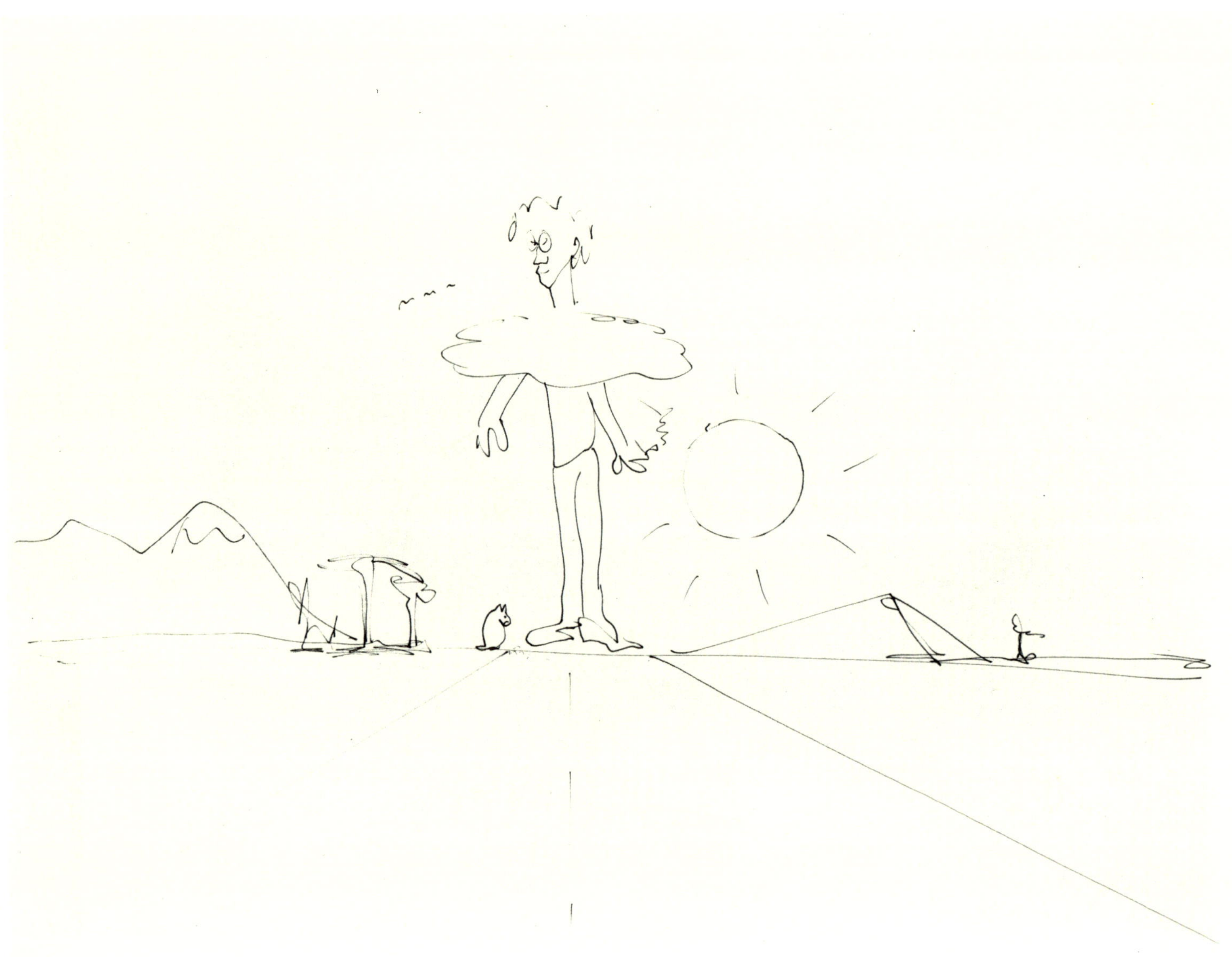

Untitled
1978
13½″ x 10½″
Ink

John Liberty
1978
10½″ x 14″
Ink

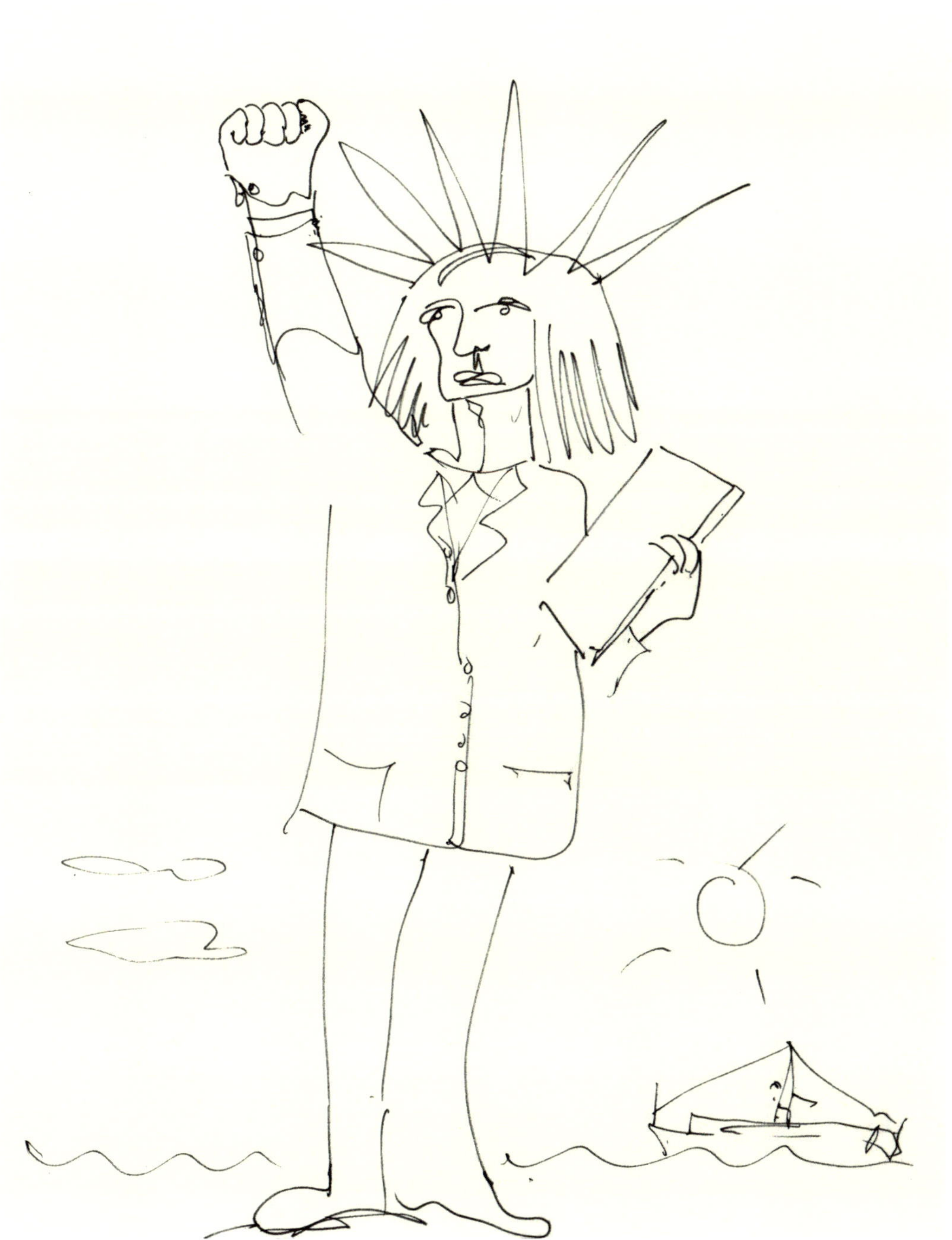

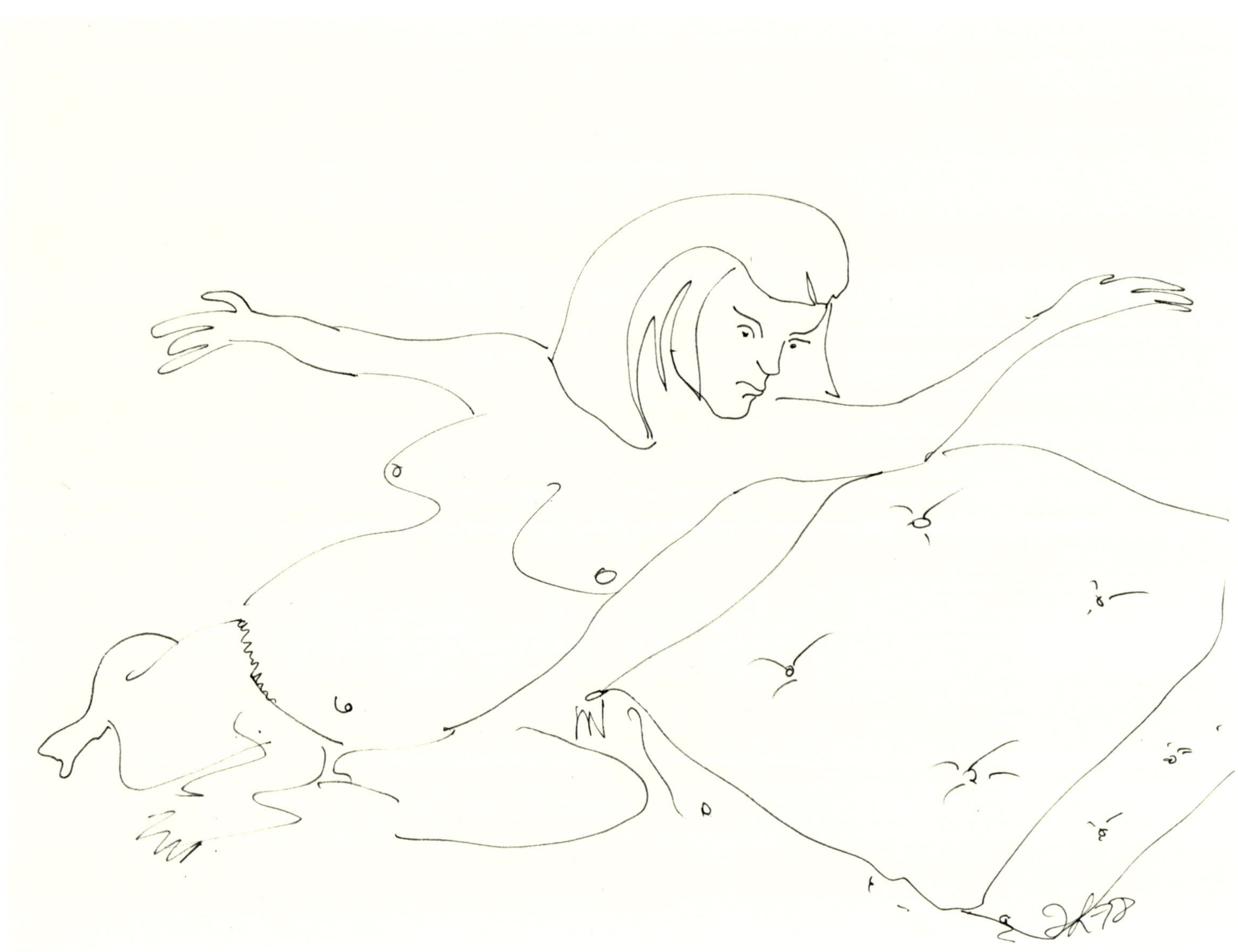

Untitled
1978
13 ½″ x 10 ½″
Ink
Signed JL 78

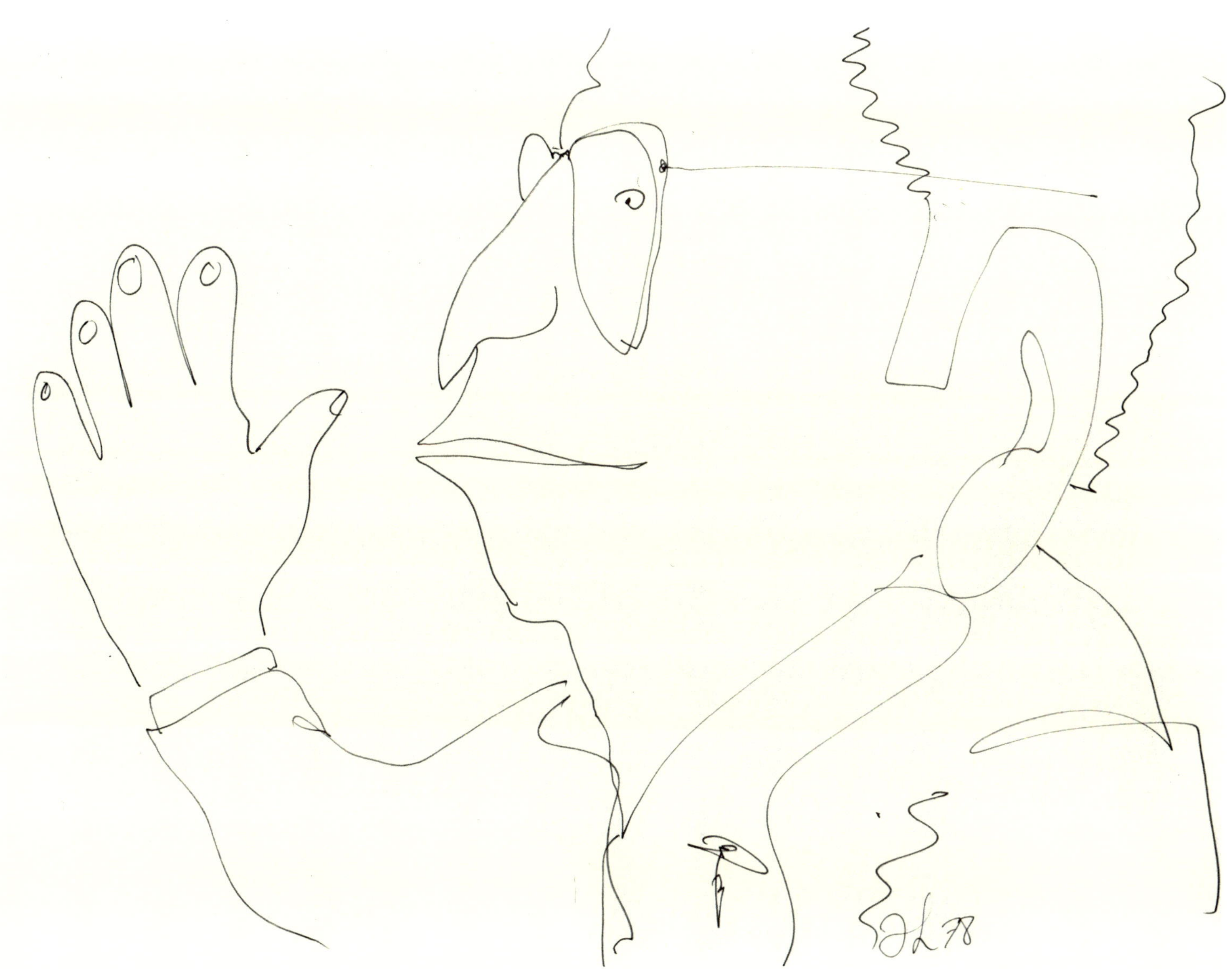

Untitled
1978
13½" x 10¾"
Ink
Signed JL 78

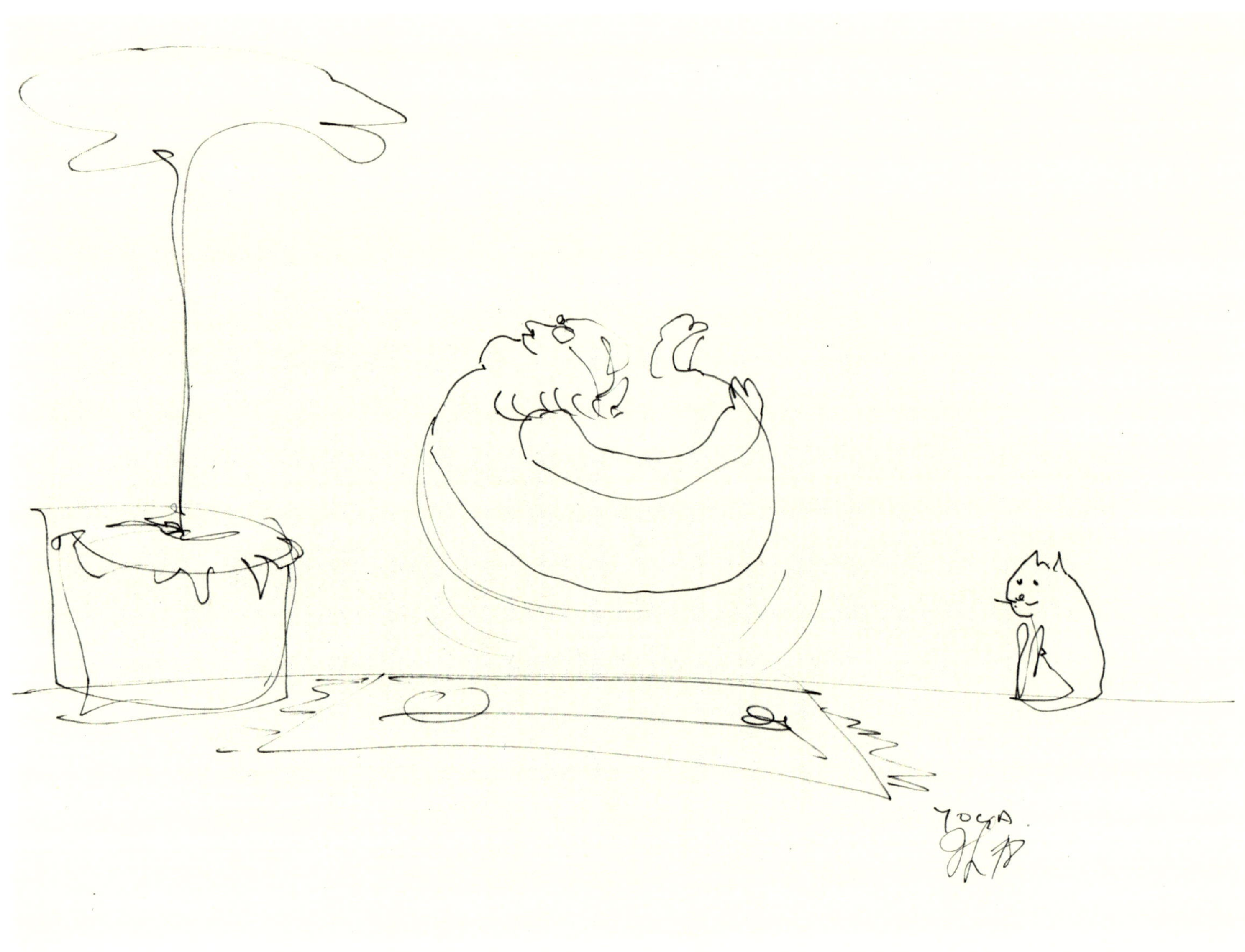

Yoga
1978
12½" x 10⅓"
Ink
Signed JL 78

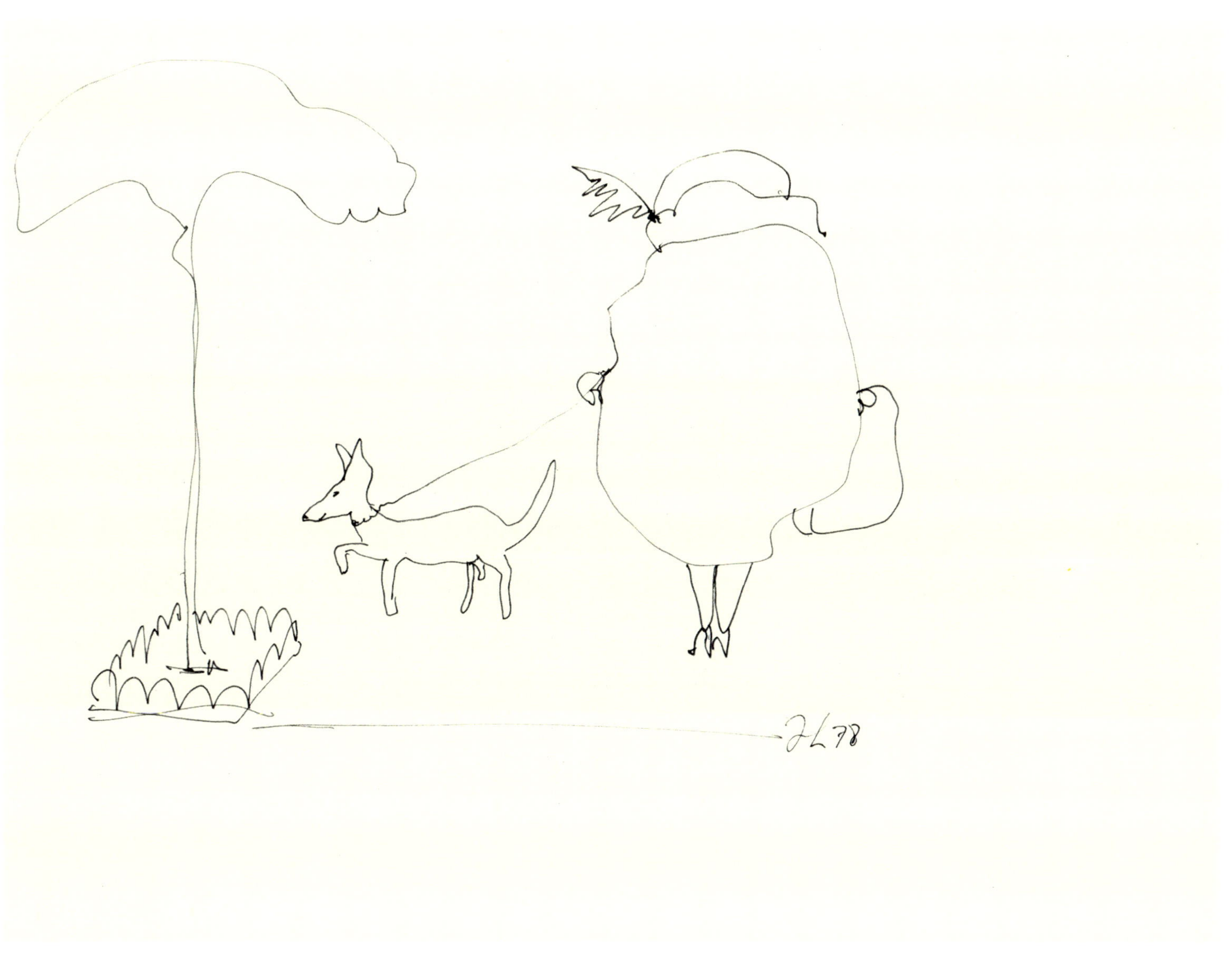

Morning Walk
1978
11½" x 9"
Ink
Signed JL 78

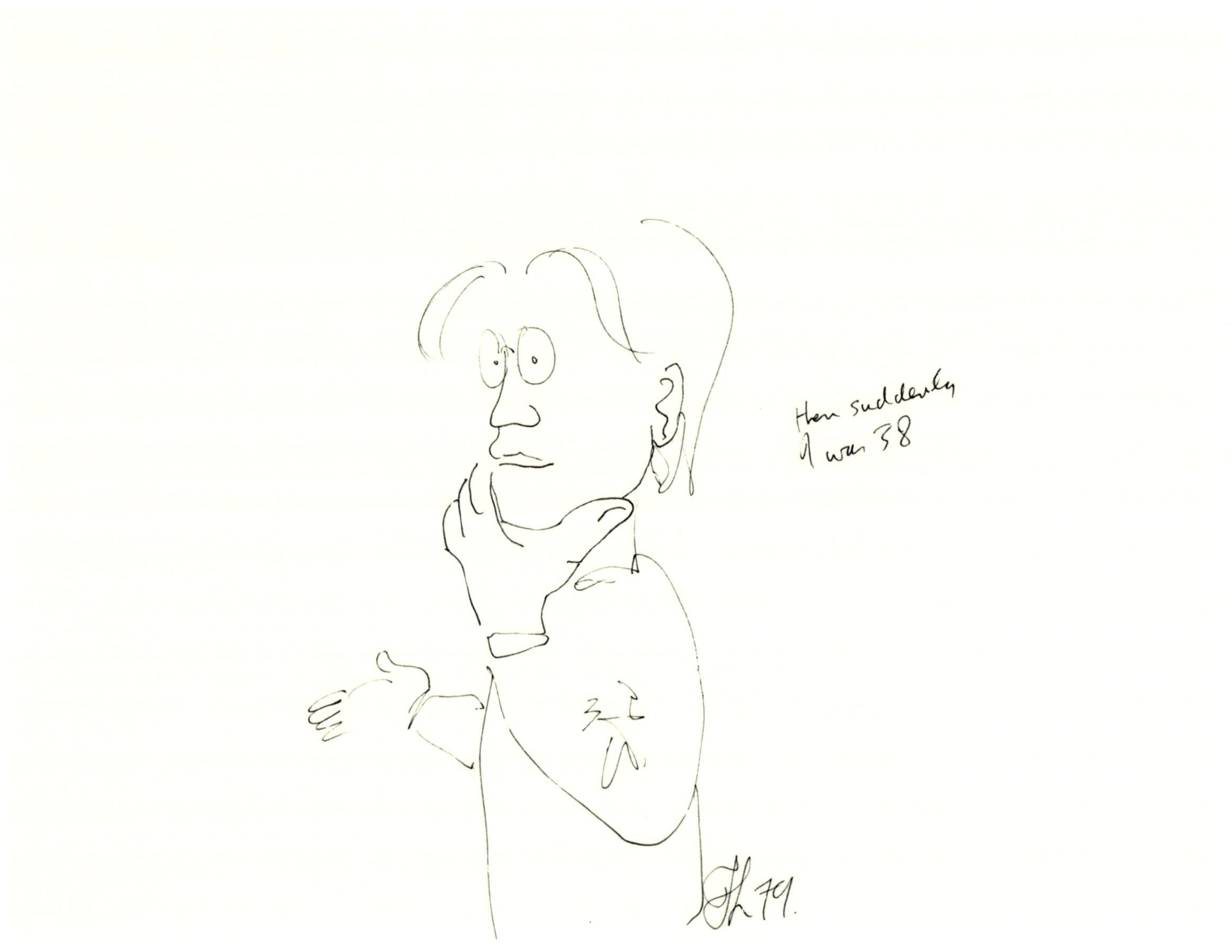

Then suddenly I was 38
1979
9½"x9"
Ink
Signed JL 79.

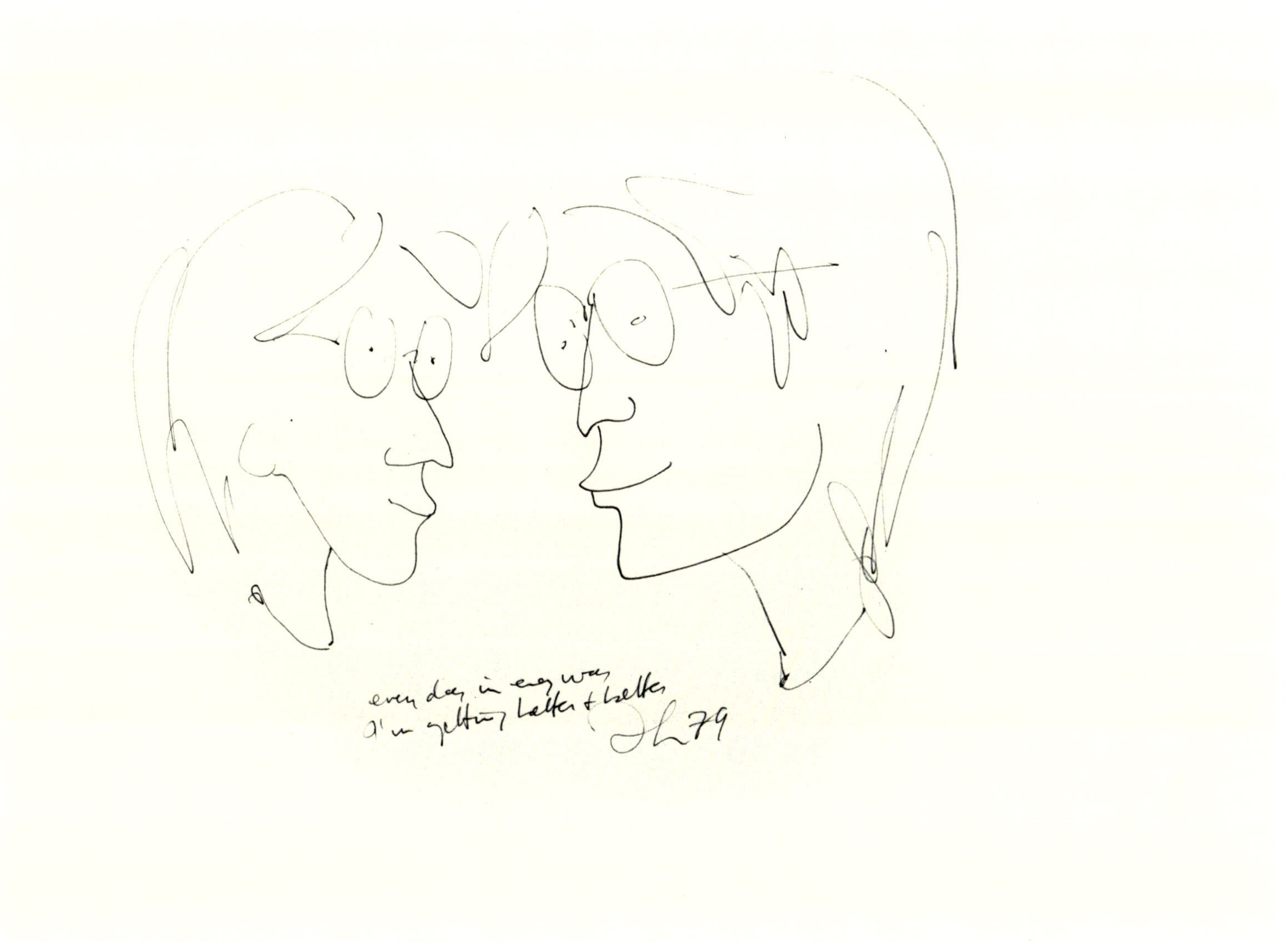

Every day, in every way
1979
11½" x 9¼"
Ink
Signed JL 79

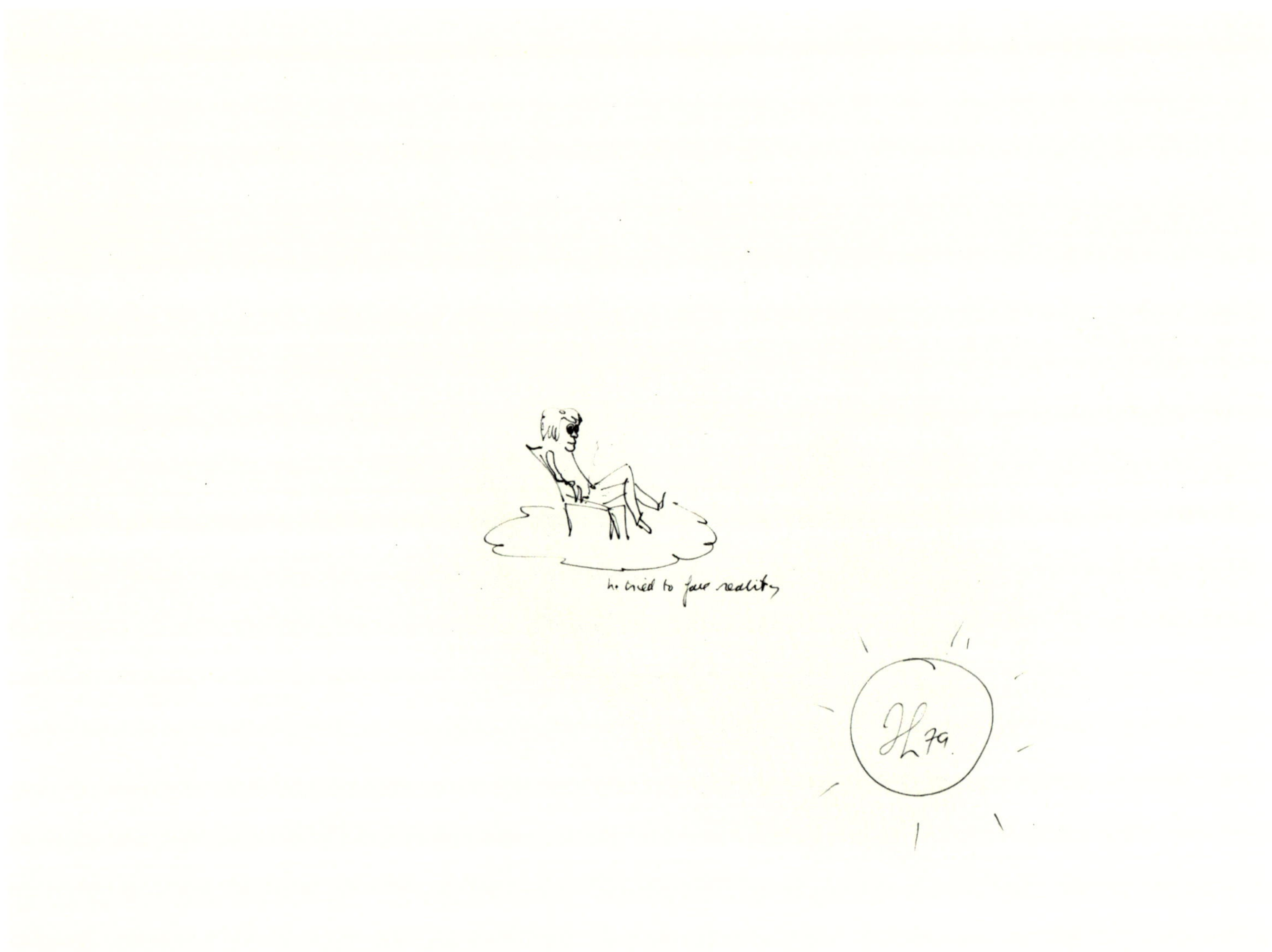

He tried to face reality
1979
9½″ x 7½″
Ink
Signed JL 79.

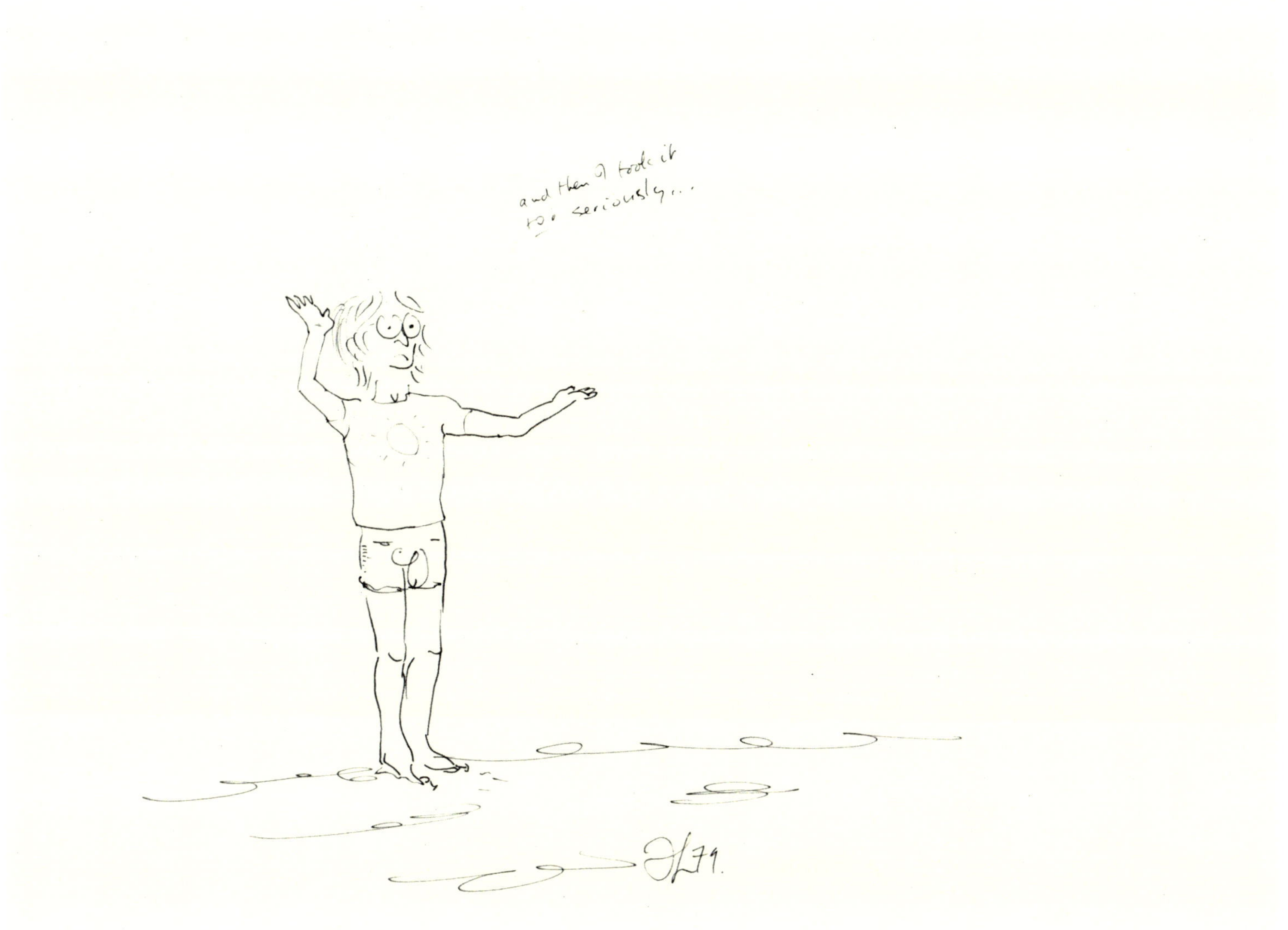

And then I took it too
seriously…
1979
11½″ x 9½″
Ink
Signed JL 79.

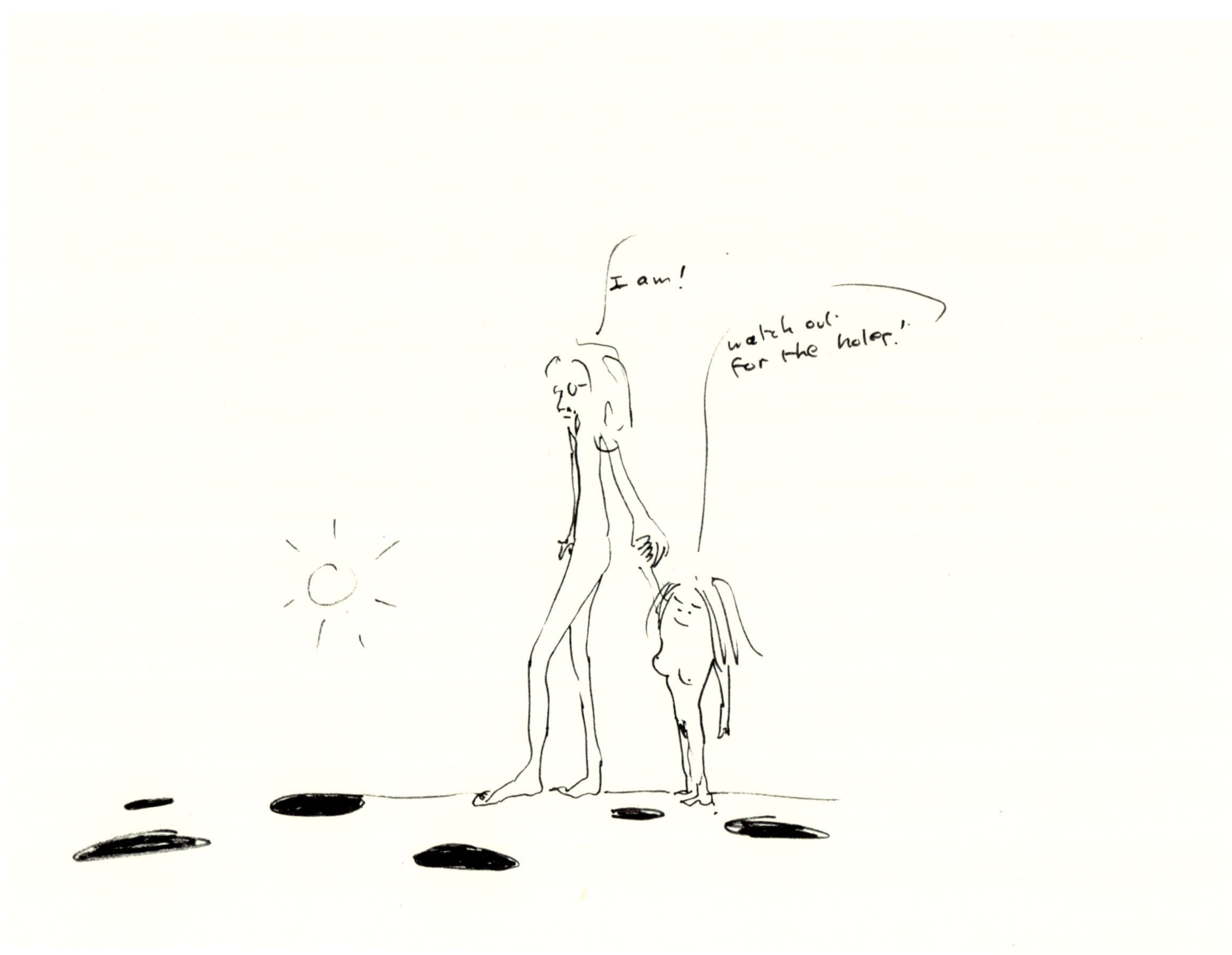

Watch out for the holes!
1979
9″ x 7″
Ink

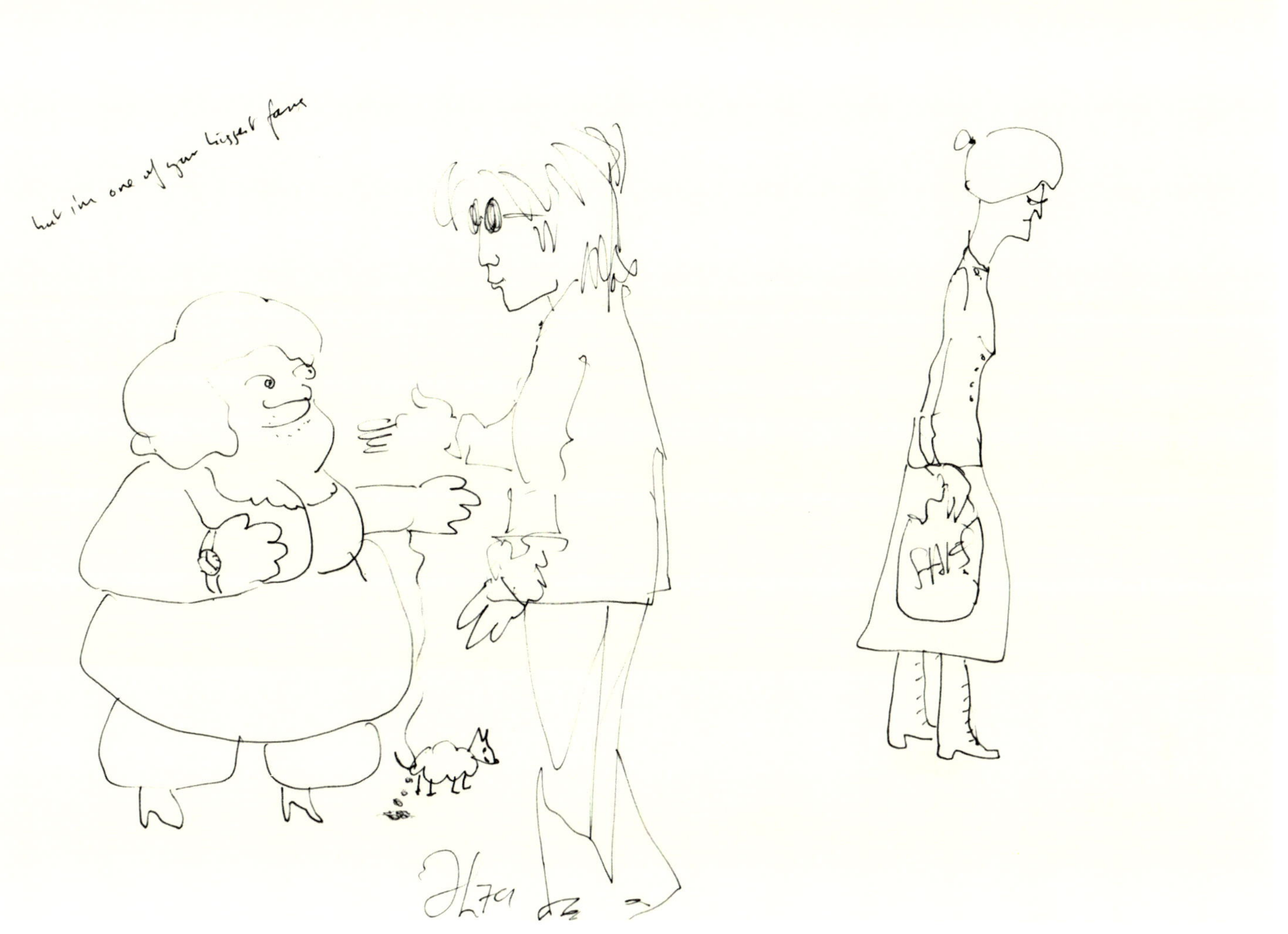

But I'm one of your
biggest fans
1979
11½" x 9"
Ink
signed: JL 79

Best of Both Worlds
1979
10½″ x 13½″
Ink
Signed JL 79

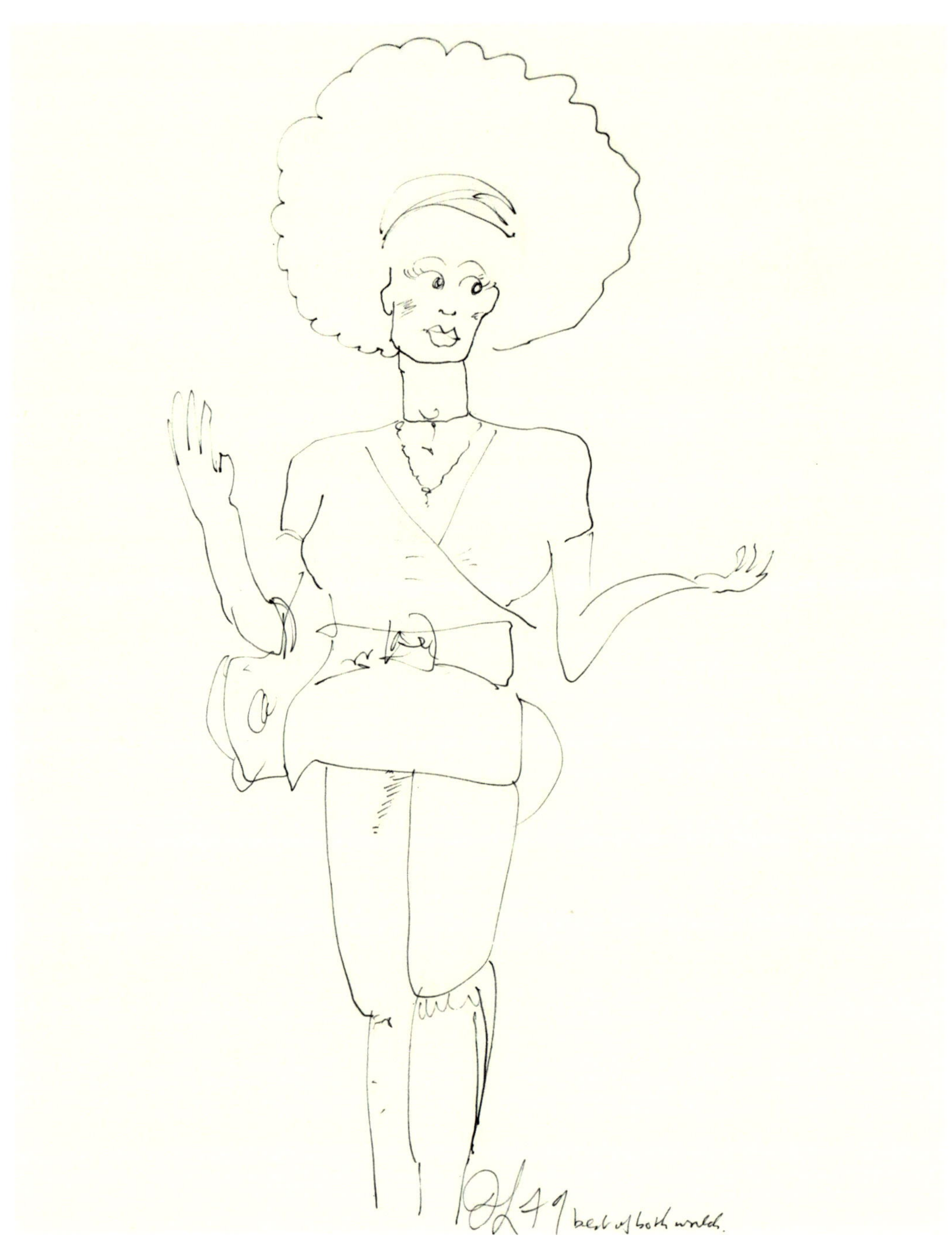

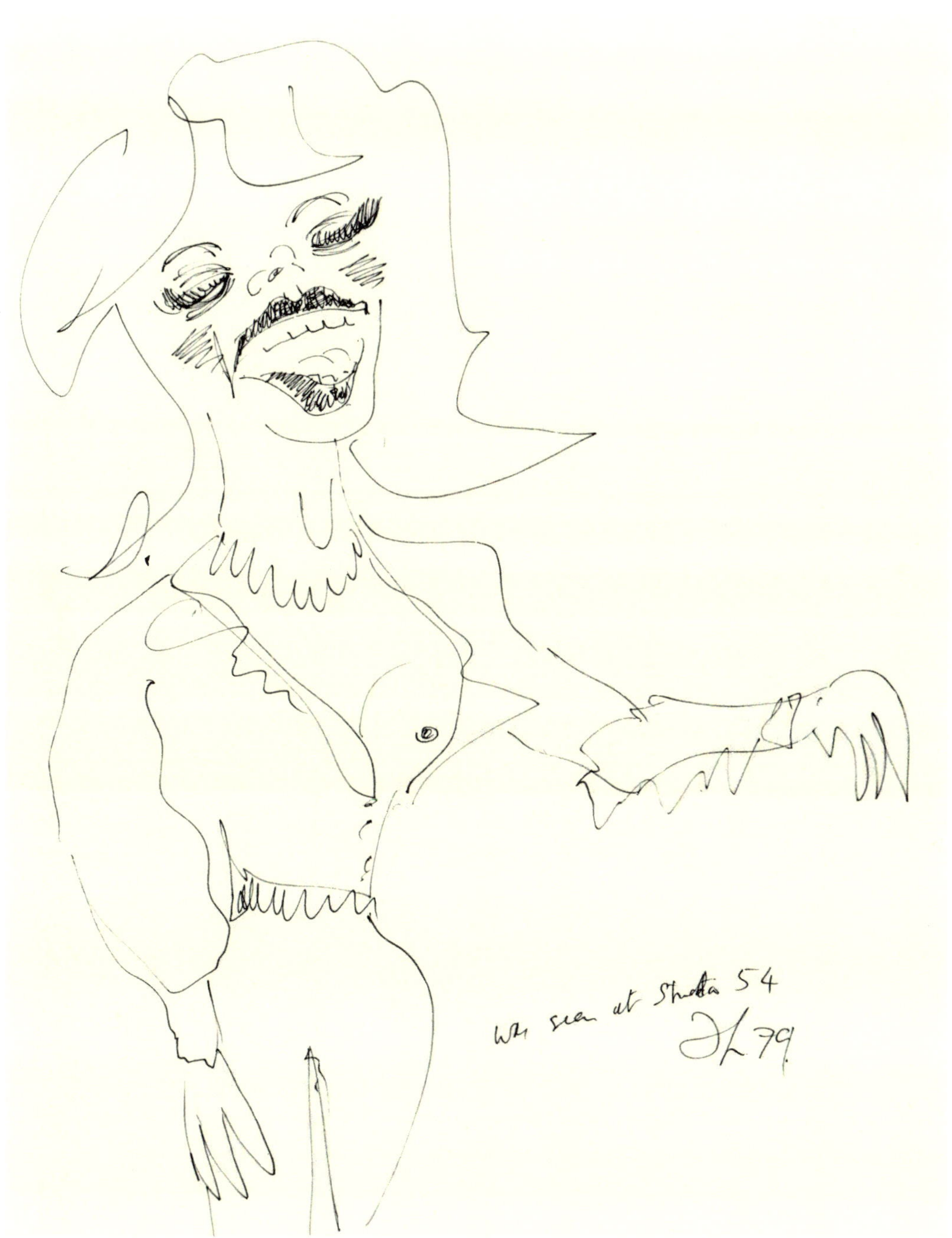

Studio 54
1979
10½" x 13½"
Ink
Signed JL 79.

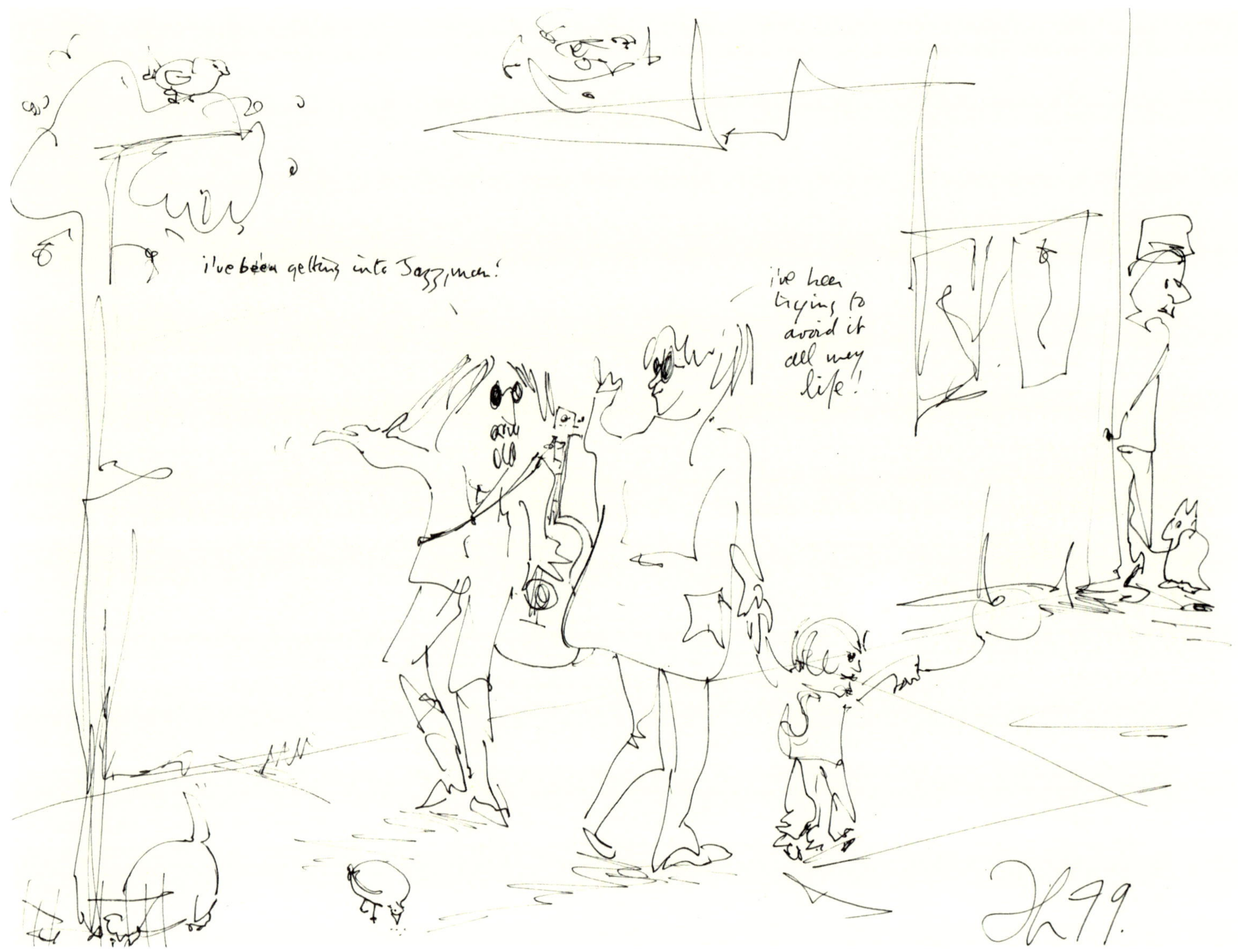

The Jazz Man
1979
13½″ x 10¾″
Ink
Signed JL 79.

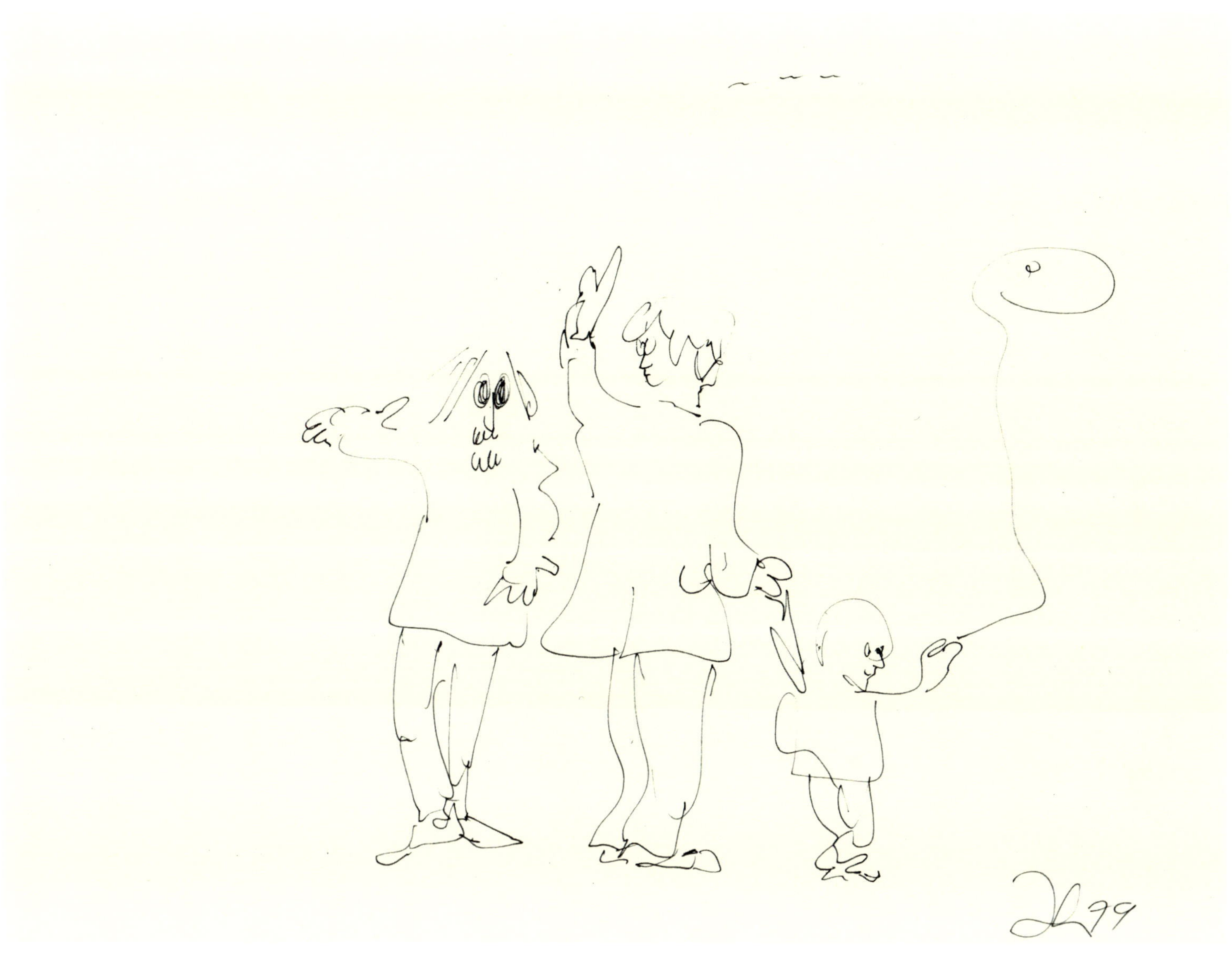

Peace, Brother
1979
12¾″ x 9¾″
Ink
Signed JL 79

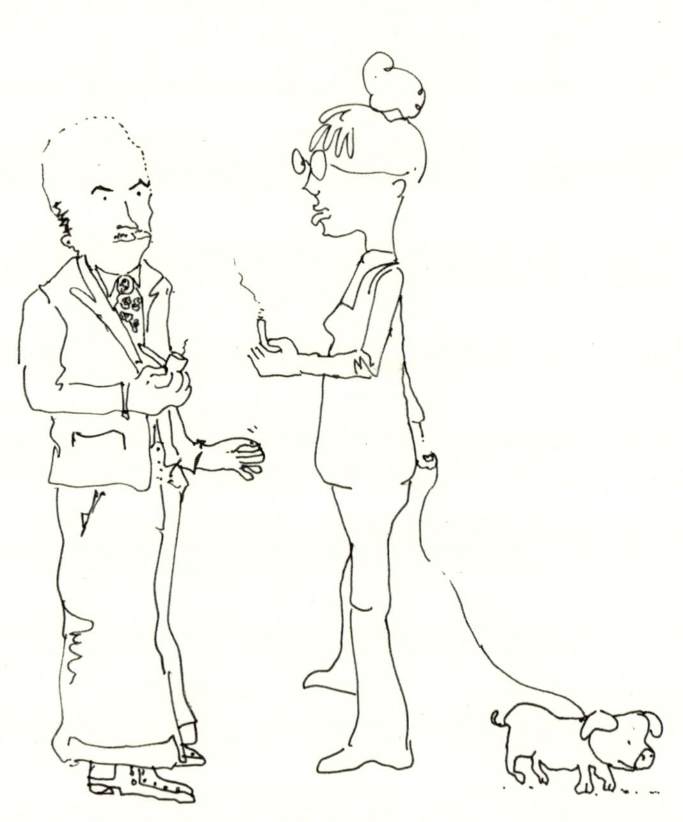

Woman with Pig
1979
9½" x 8¼"
Ink

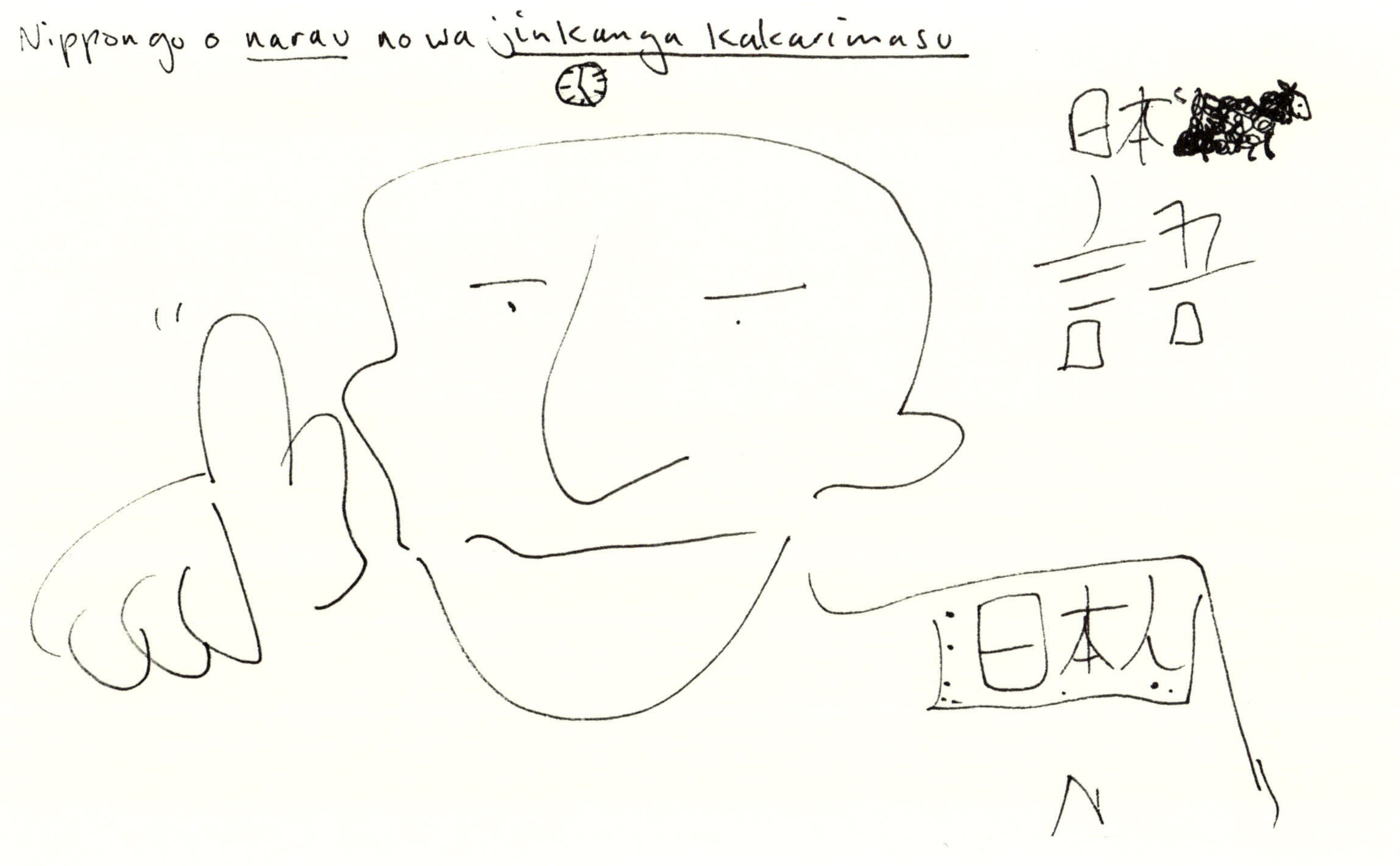

Nippon go o narau
It takes time to learn
Japanese
1977
8″ x 4¾″
Ink

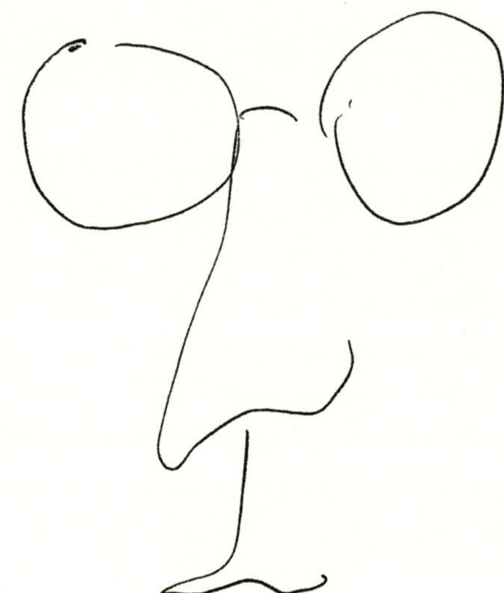

Jibun
Myself
1977
8" x 5"
Ink

TSUKURIMASU
uta o tsukuru toki piano o tsukaimasu. TSUKAIMASU

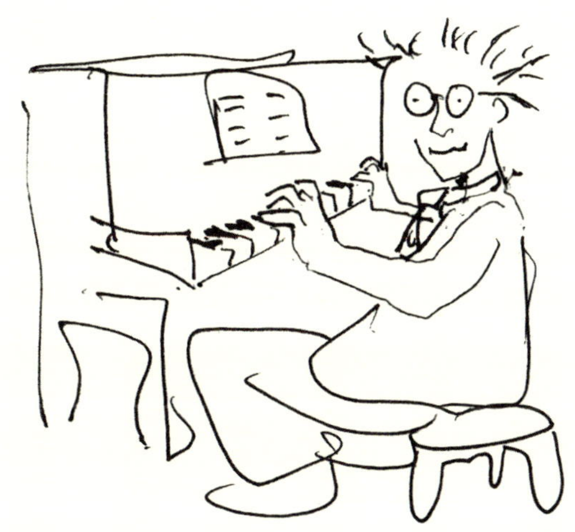

Uta o tsukuru toki, piano
o tsukaimasu
When I create a song, I use
a piano
1977
8" x 5"
Ink

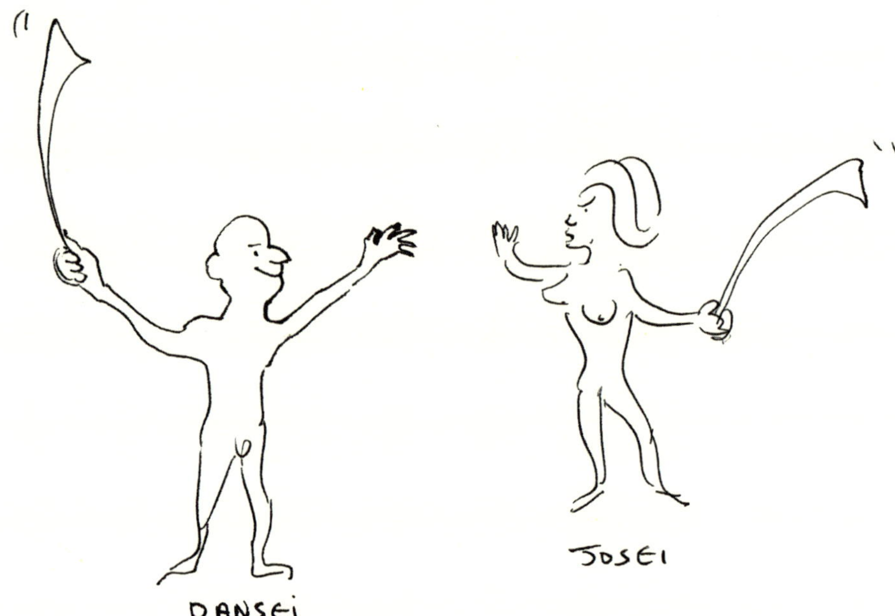

Dansei – Josei
Man – Woman
1977
8″ x 5″
Ink

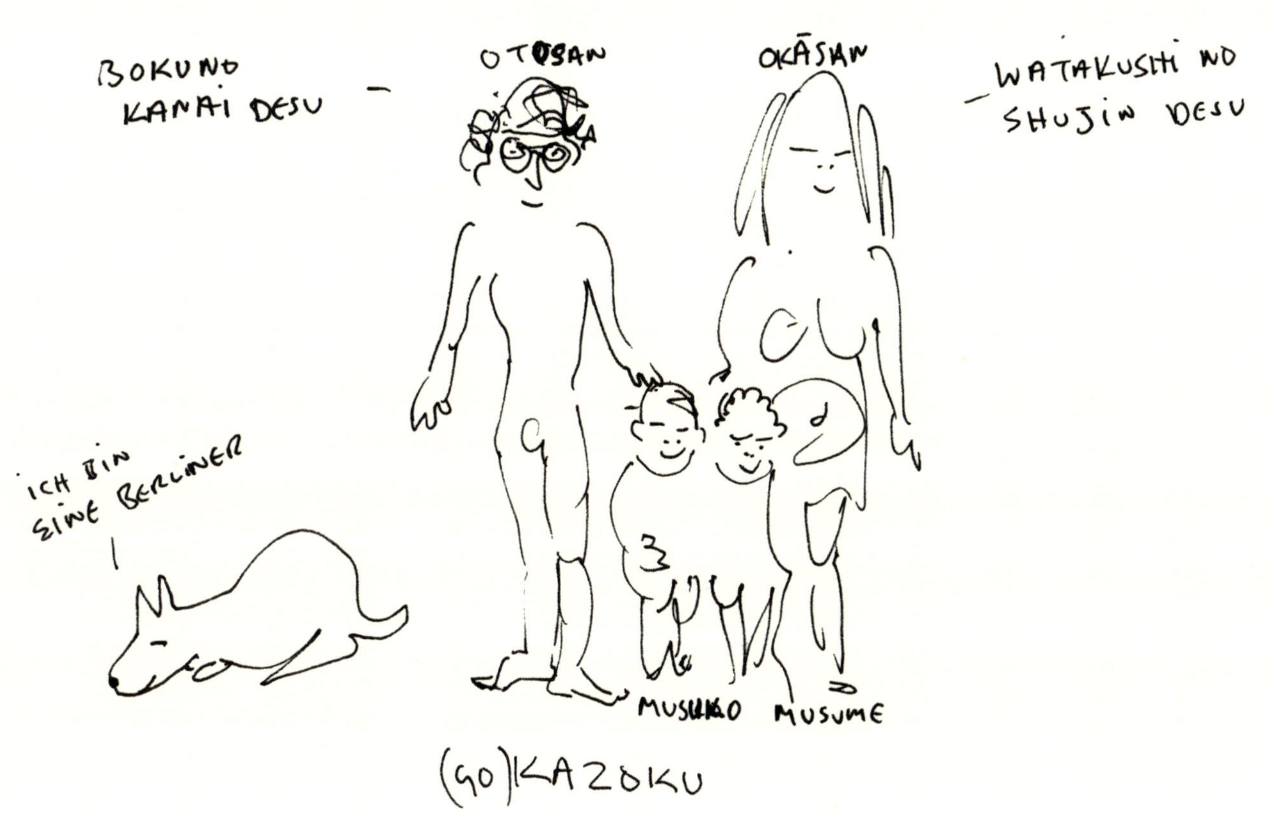

(Go)kazoku – Boku no kanai
desu – Watakushi no shujin
desu
Family – This is my wife –
This is my husband
1977
8″ x 5″
Ink

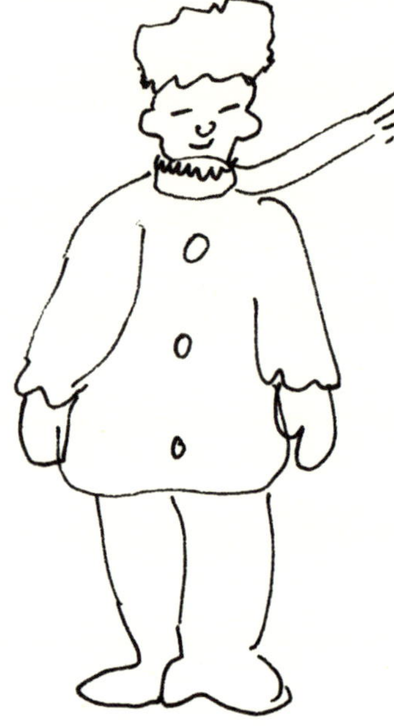

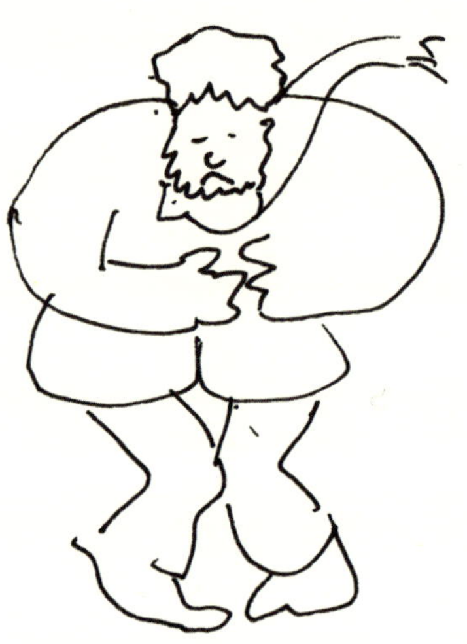

Sōtoni samui desu –
Hijōni samui desu!
It's cold outside –
it's very cold outside!
1977
8" x 5"
Ink

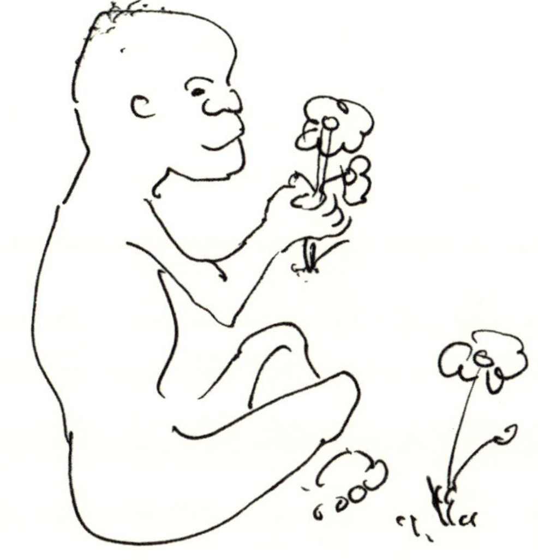

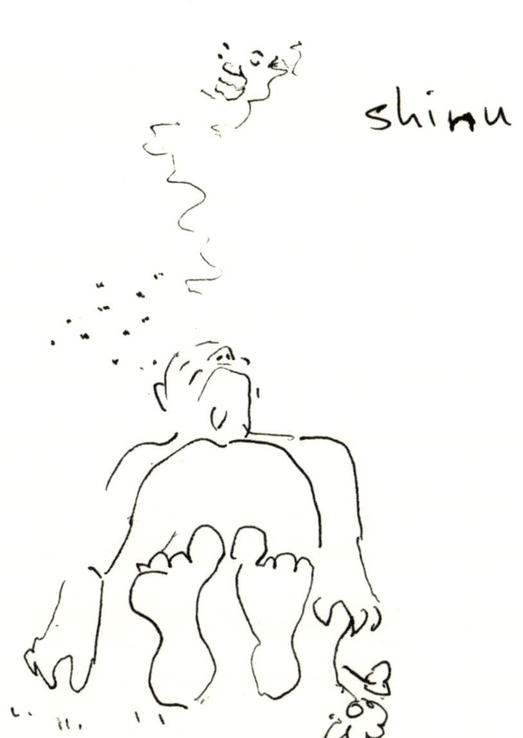

Ikiru – shinu
Live – die
1977
8″ x 5″
Ink

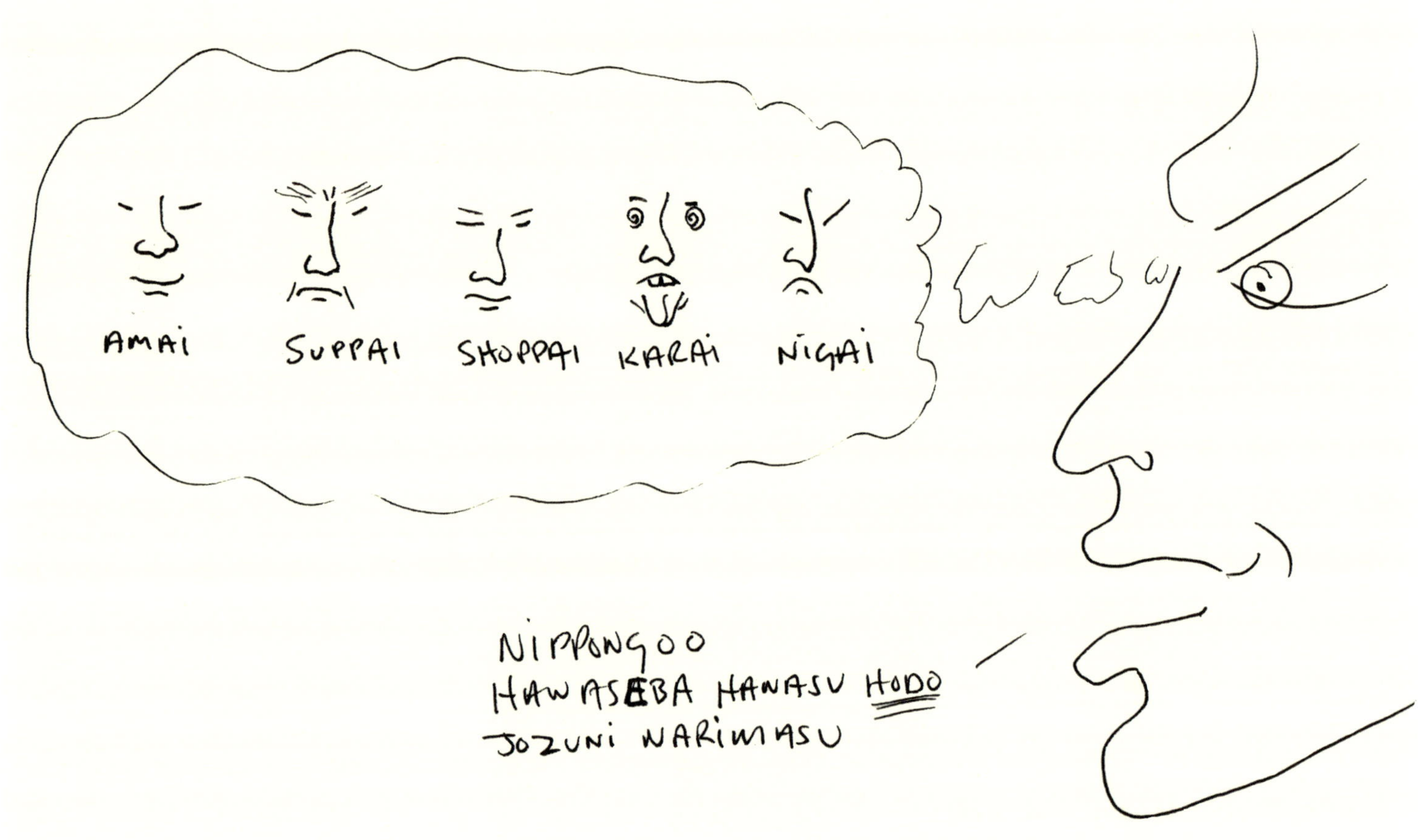

Amai – suppai – shoppai –
karai – nigai
Sweet – sour – salty –
hot – bitter
1977
8″ x 5″
Ink

KURABETE

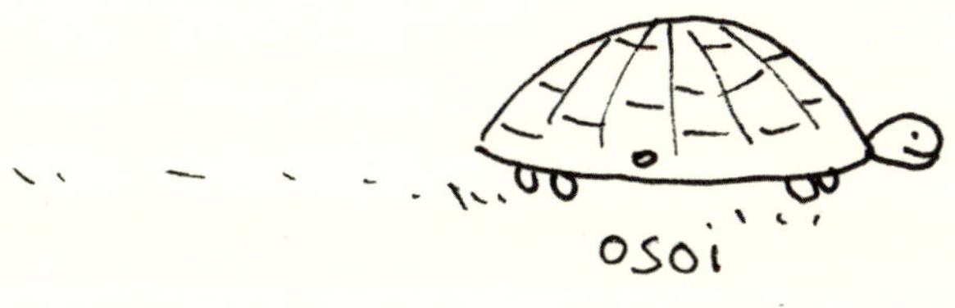

Kurabete – osoi – hyai
Compare – slow – fast
1977
8″ x 5″
Ink

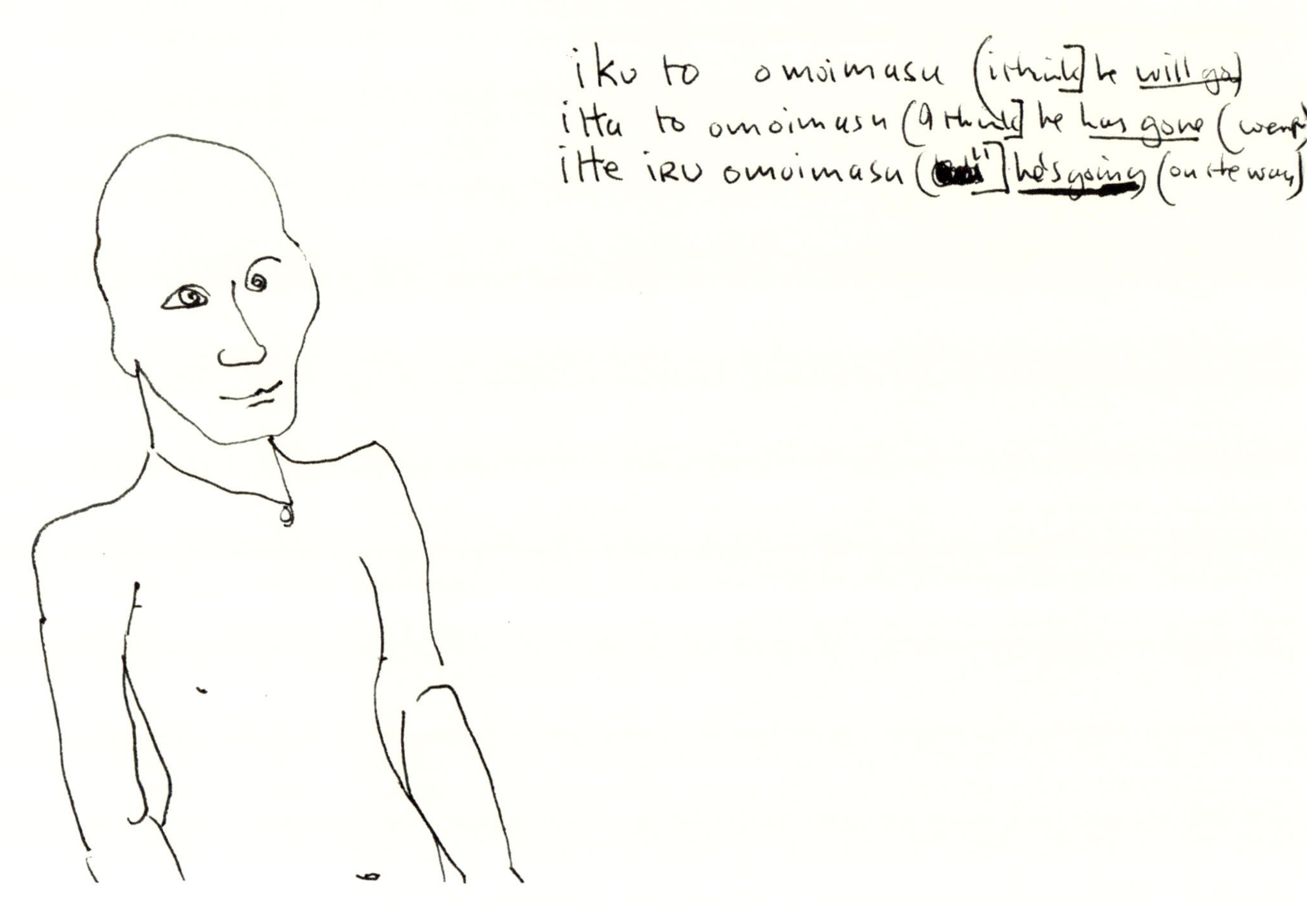

Iku to omoimasu
On the Way
1977
8″ x 4¼″
Ink

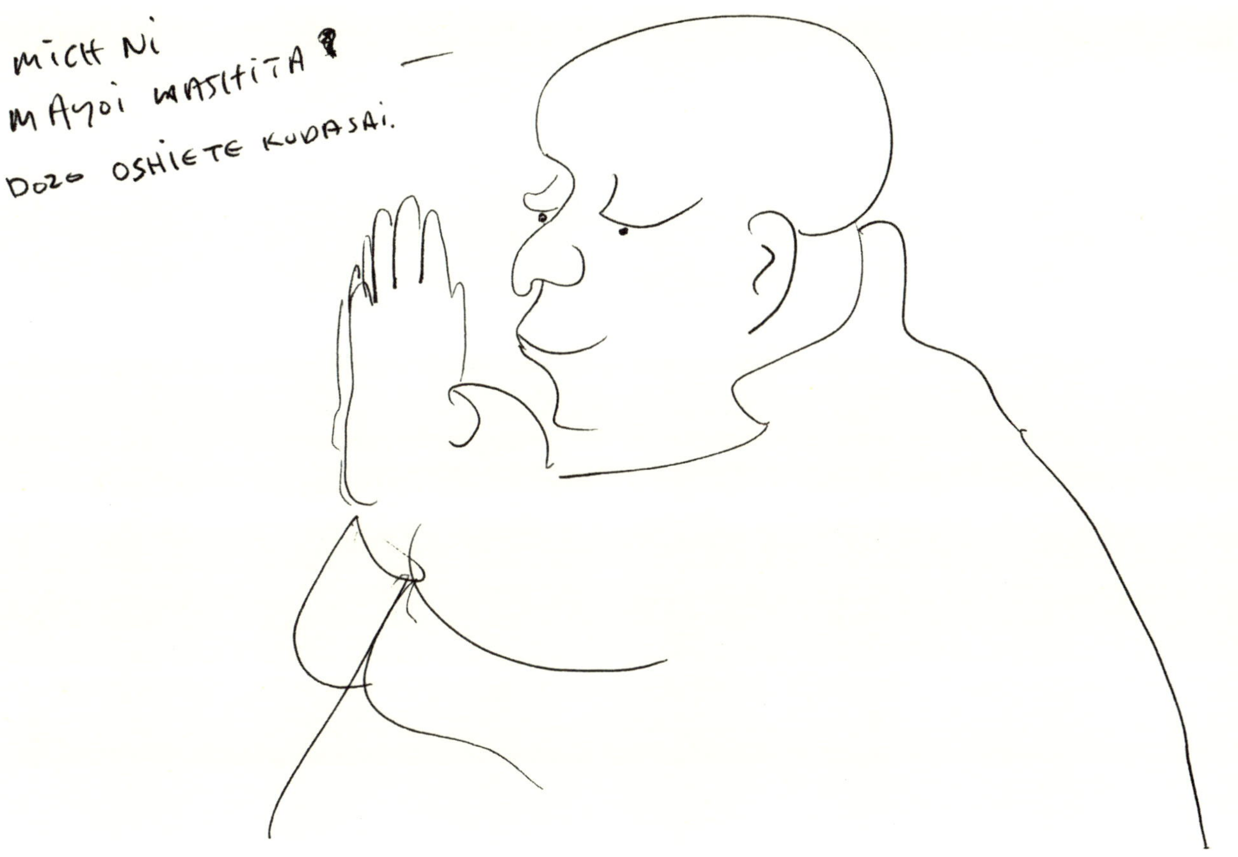

Michi ni mayoi mashita.
Dōzo oshiete kudasai.
I am lost. Please show
me the way.
1977
8″ x 5″
Ink

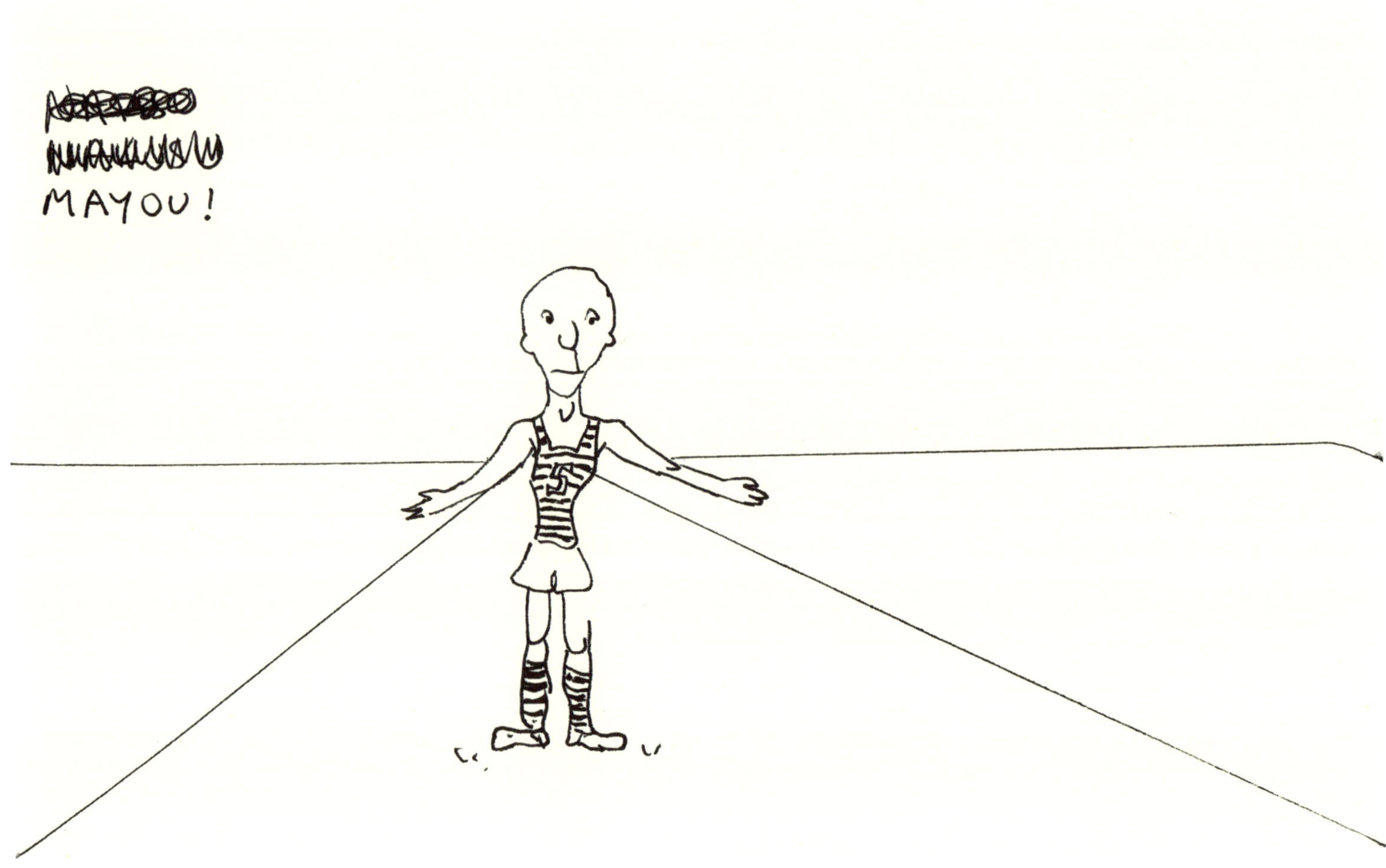

Mayou!
To loose your way!
1977
8″ x 5″
Ink

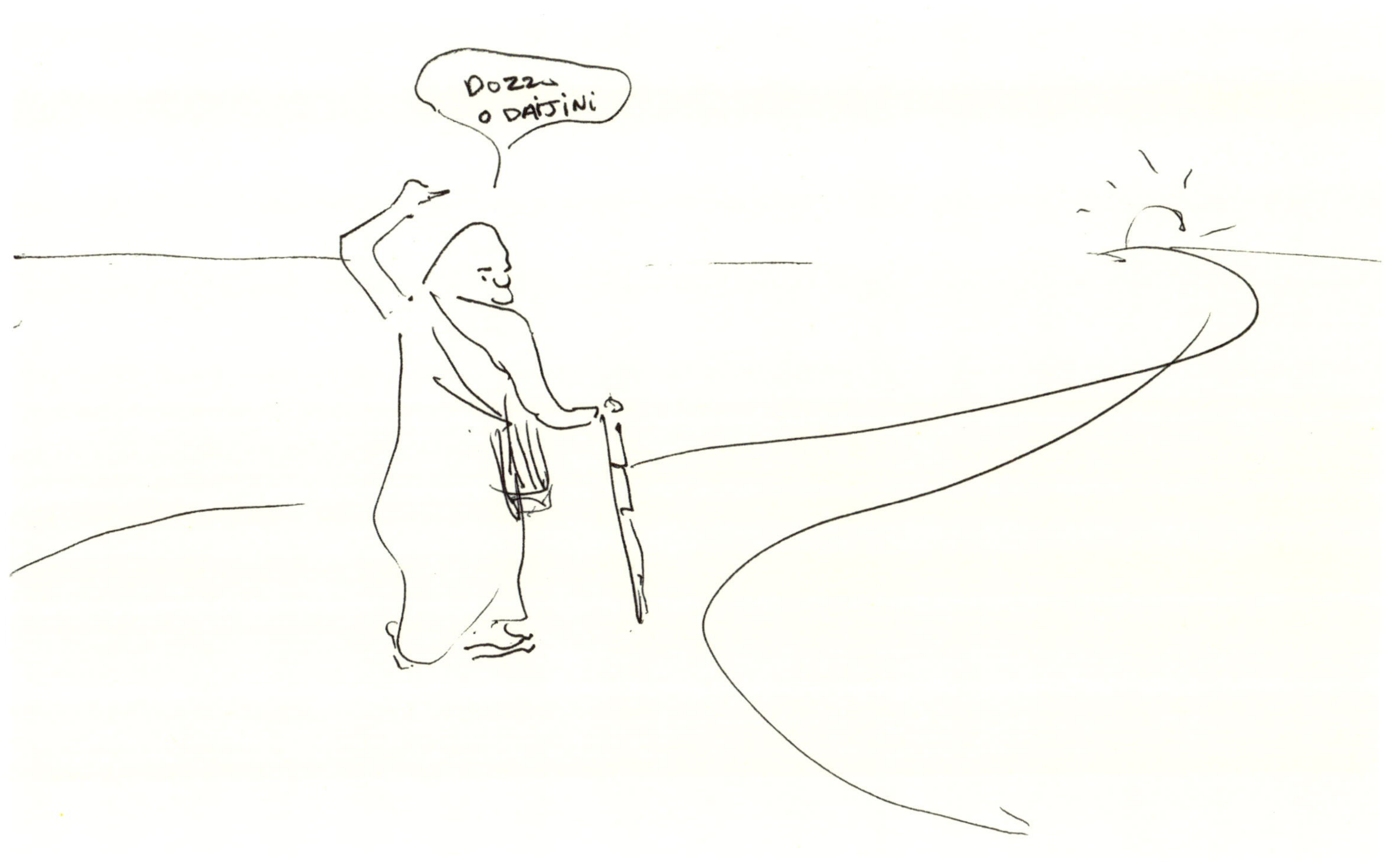

O-daiji ni
Take care
1977
8" x 5"
Ink

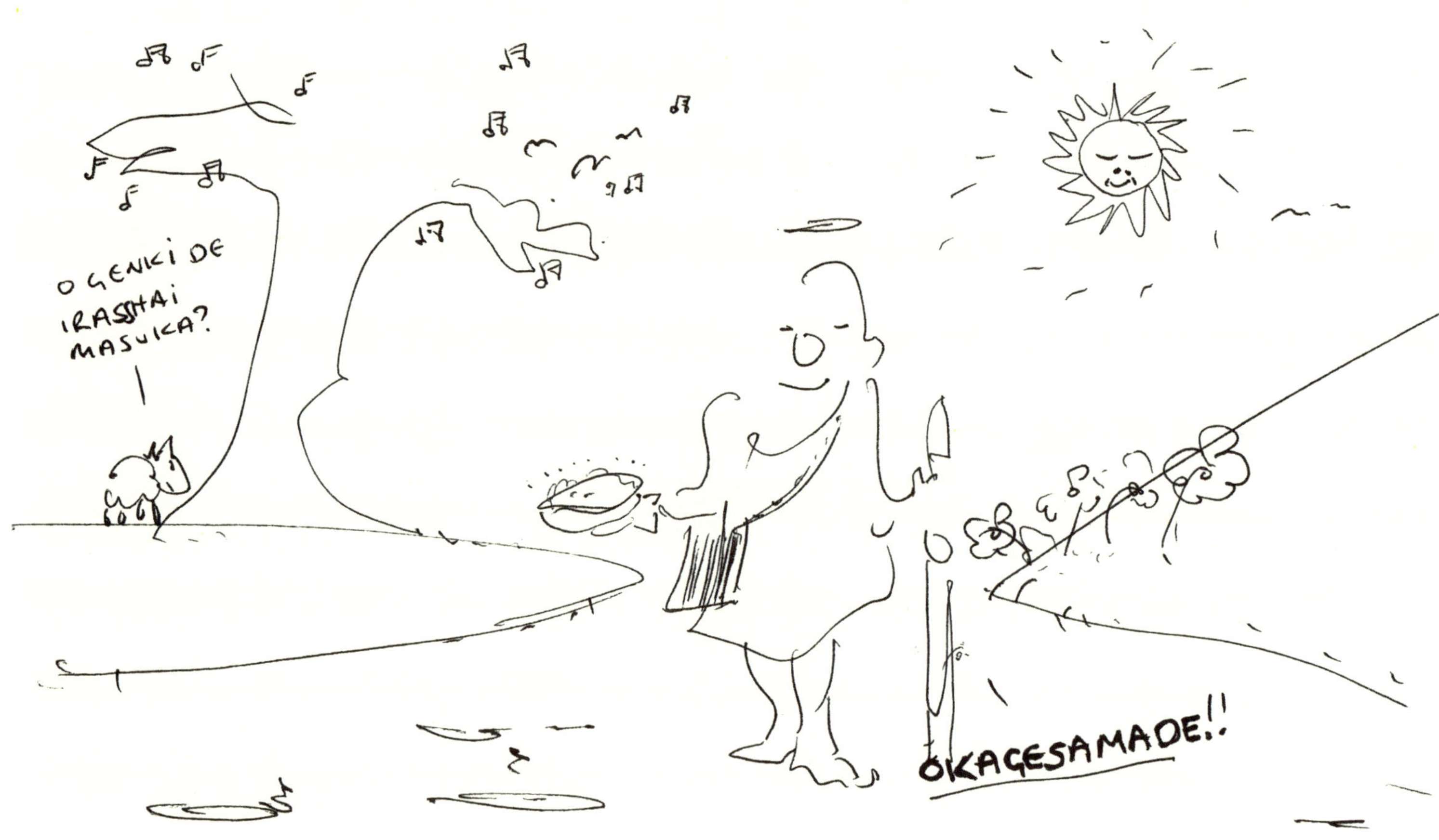

Ogenki de irasshaimasu ka?
Okagesamade!!
Are you doing well? – Yes,
thank you (and all the
others)!!
1977
8″ x 5″
Ink

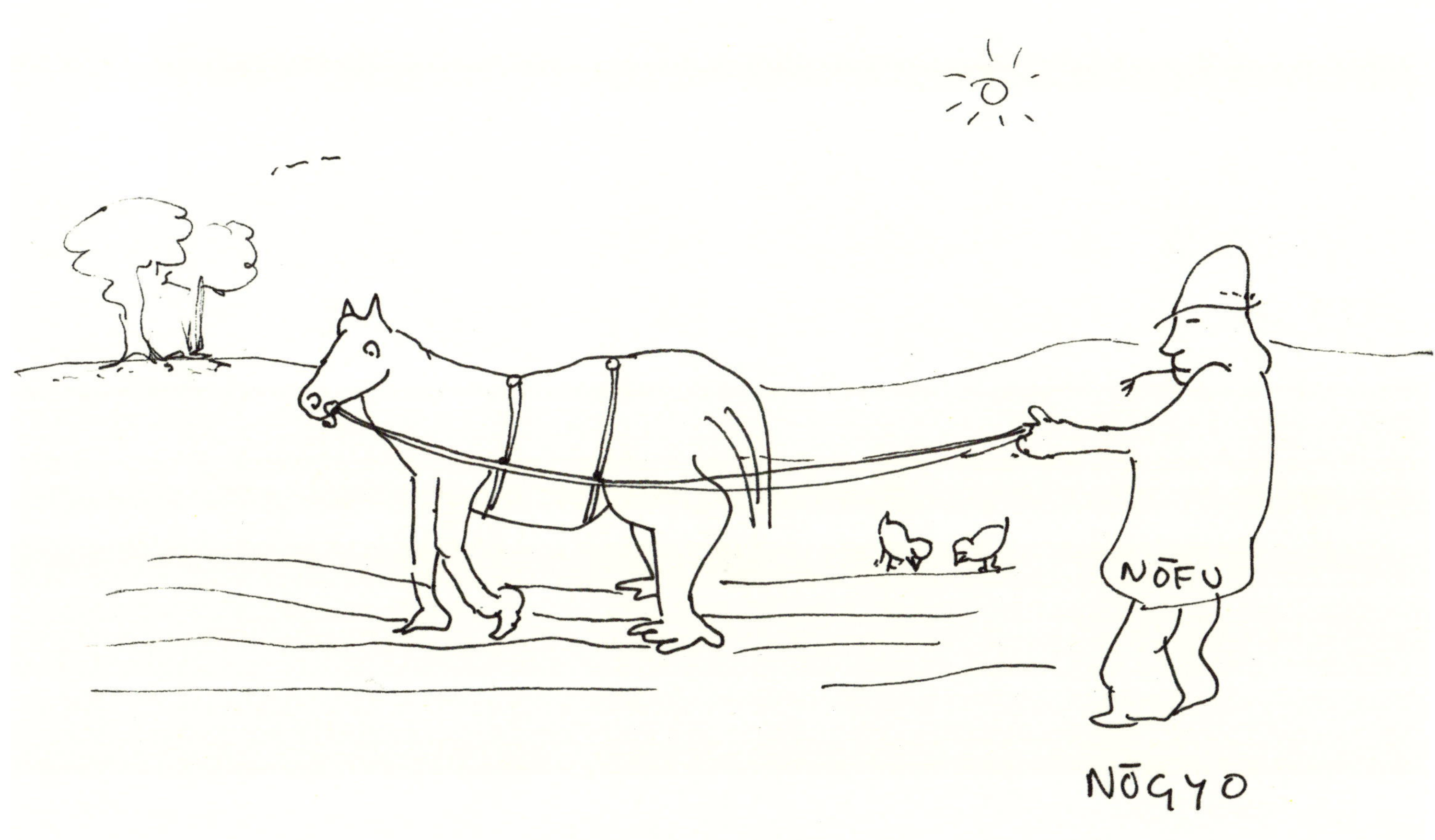

Nōfu – nōgyo
Farmer – agriculture
1977
8″ x 5″
Ink

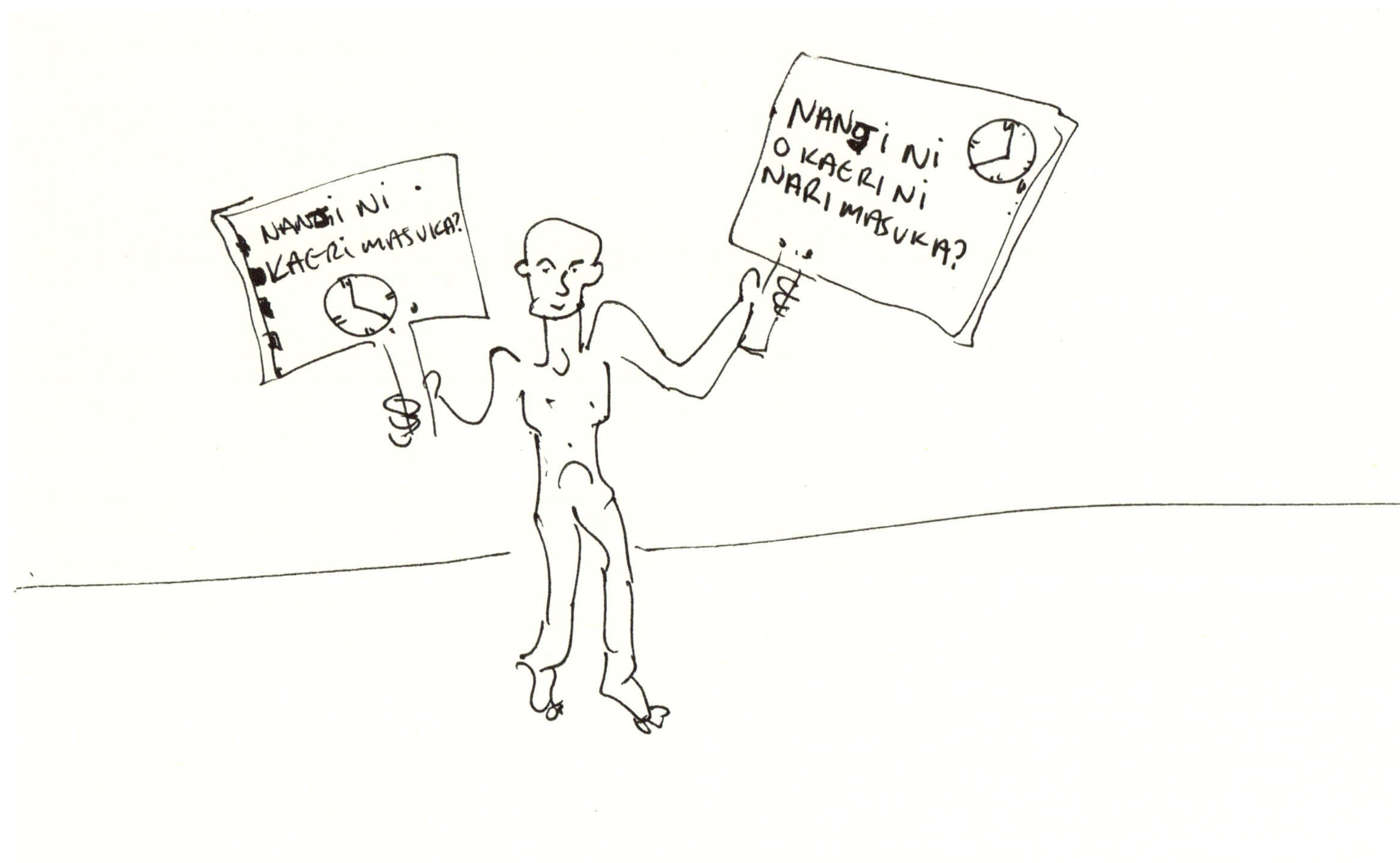

Nanji ni kaeri masuka?
What time are you
coming back?
1977
8″ x 5″
Ink

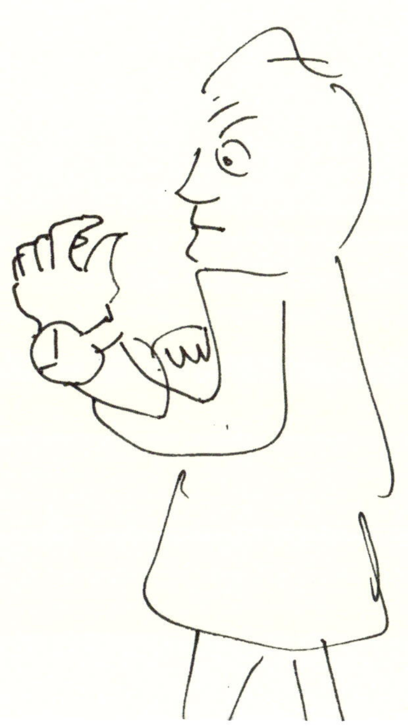

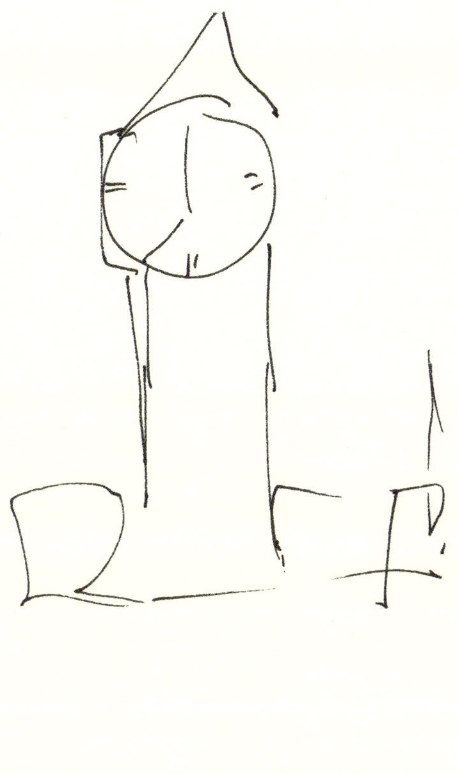

Jikanga nai desu
Didn't have time
1977
8″ x 5″
Ink

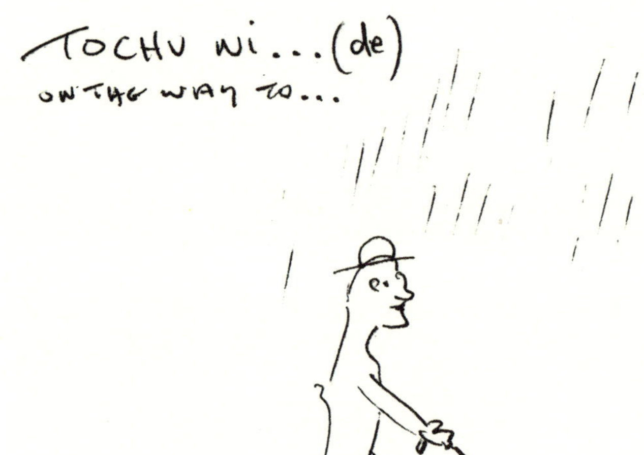

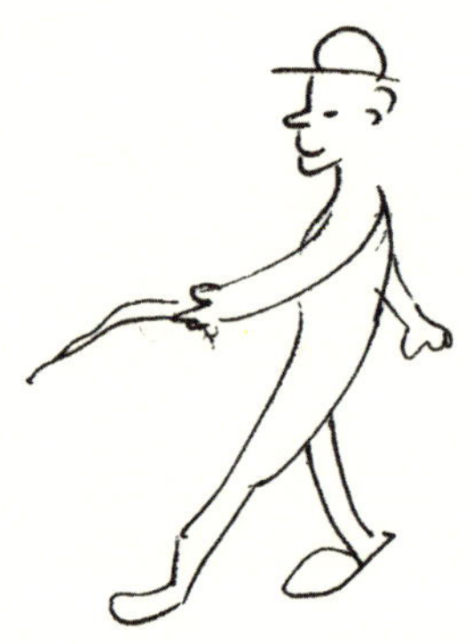

Tochu ni… (de)
On the way to…
1977
8″ x 5″
Ink

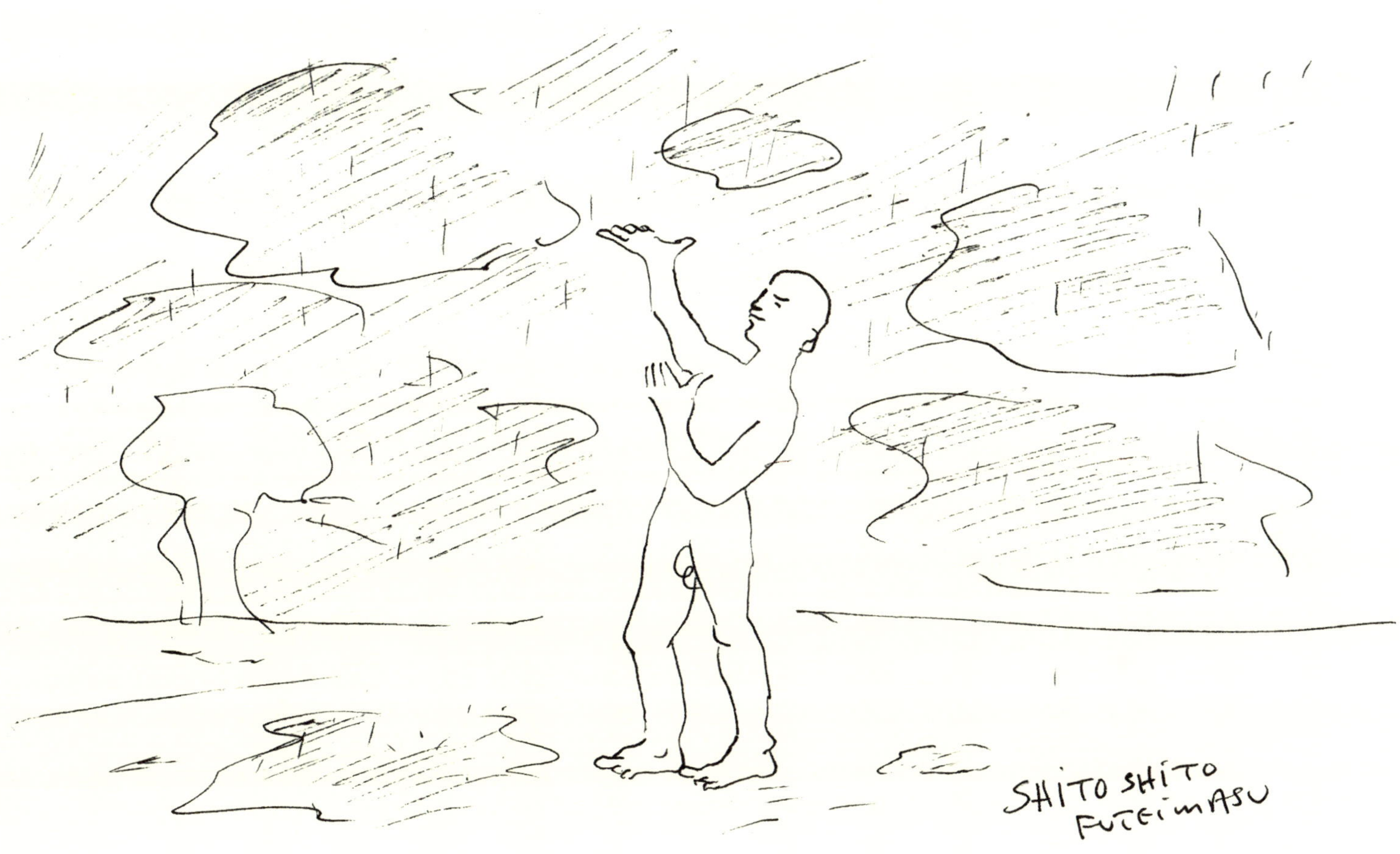

Shito shito futteimasu
It's raining
1977
8″ x 5″
Ink

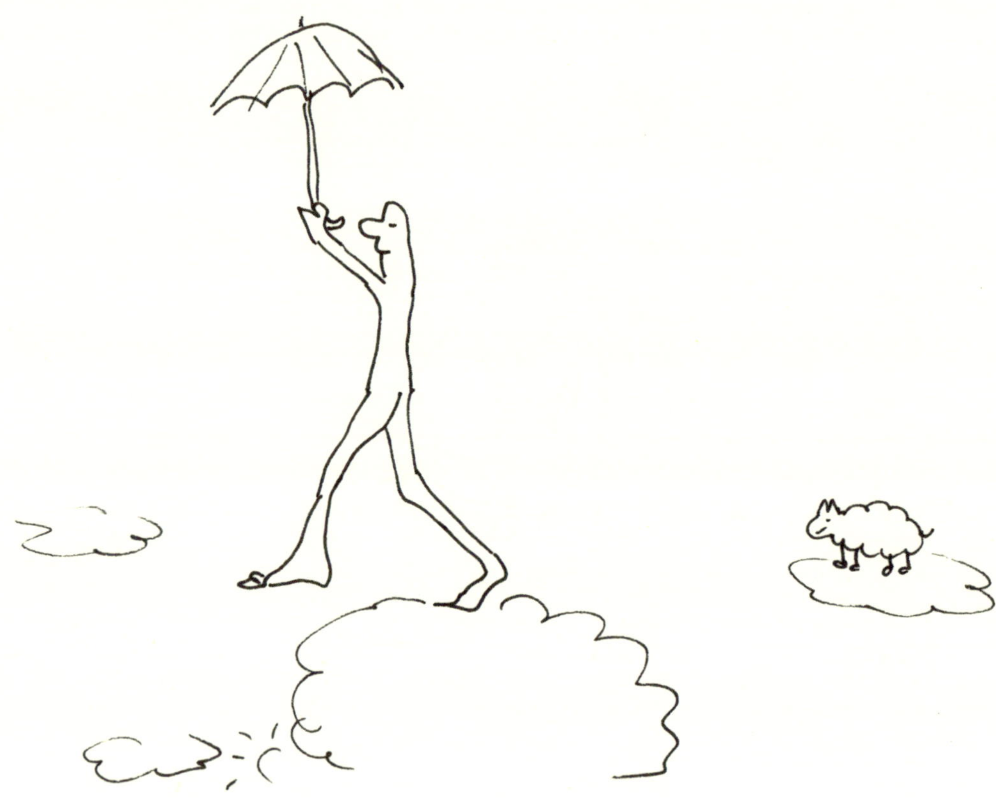

Dandan takaku narimasu
Gradually getting higher
1977
8″ x 5″
Ink

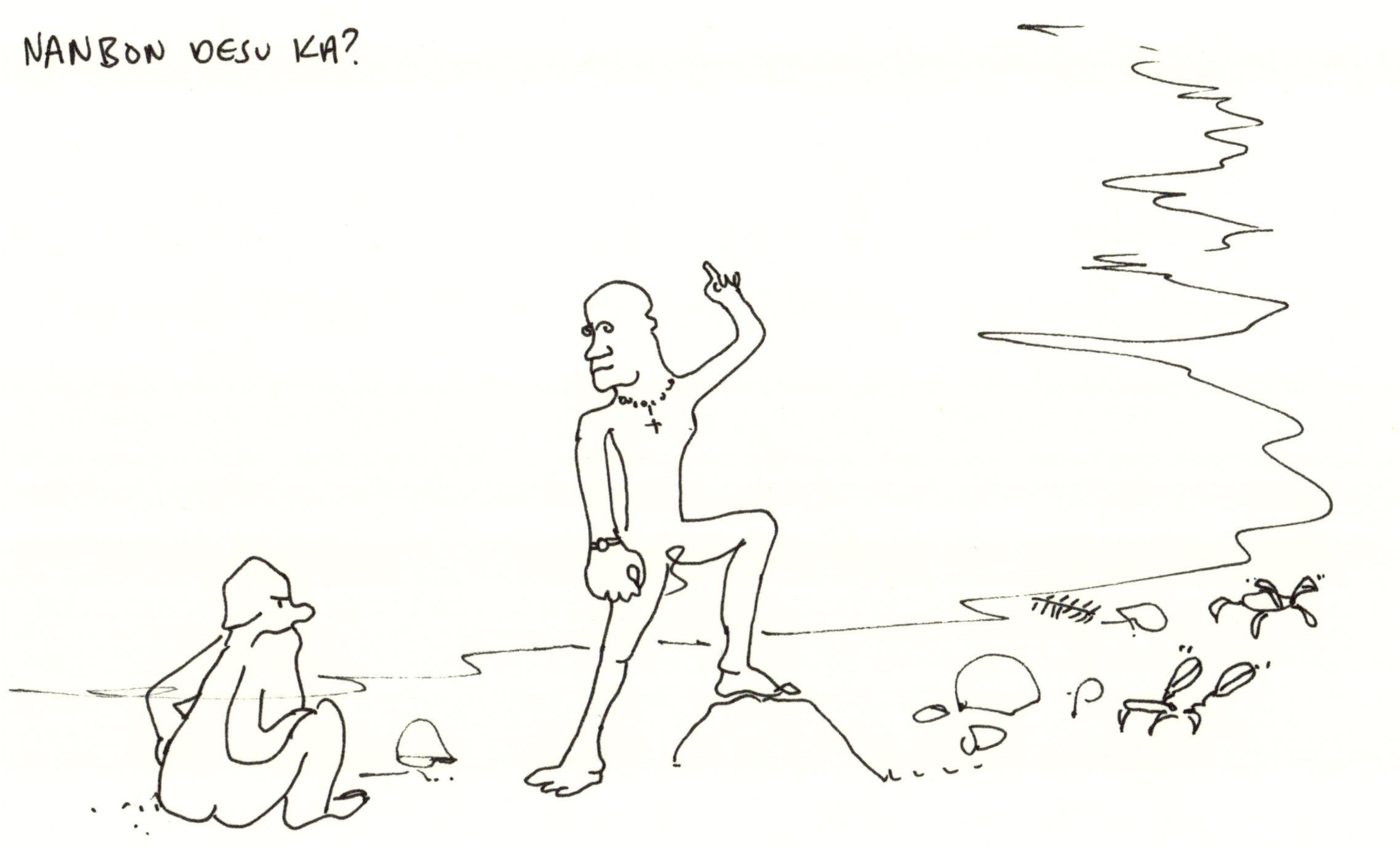

Nanbon desu ka?
How much would you like?
1977
8" x 5"
Ink

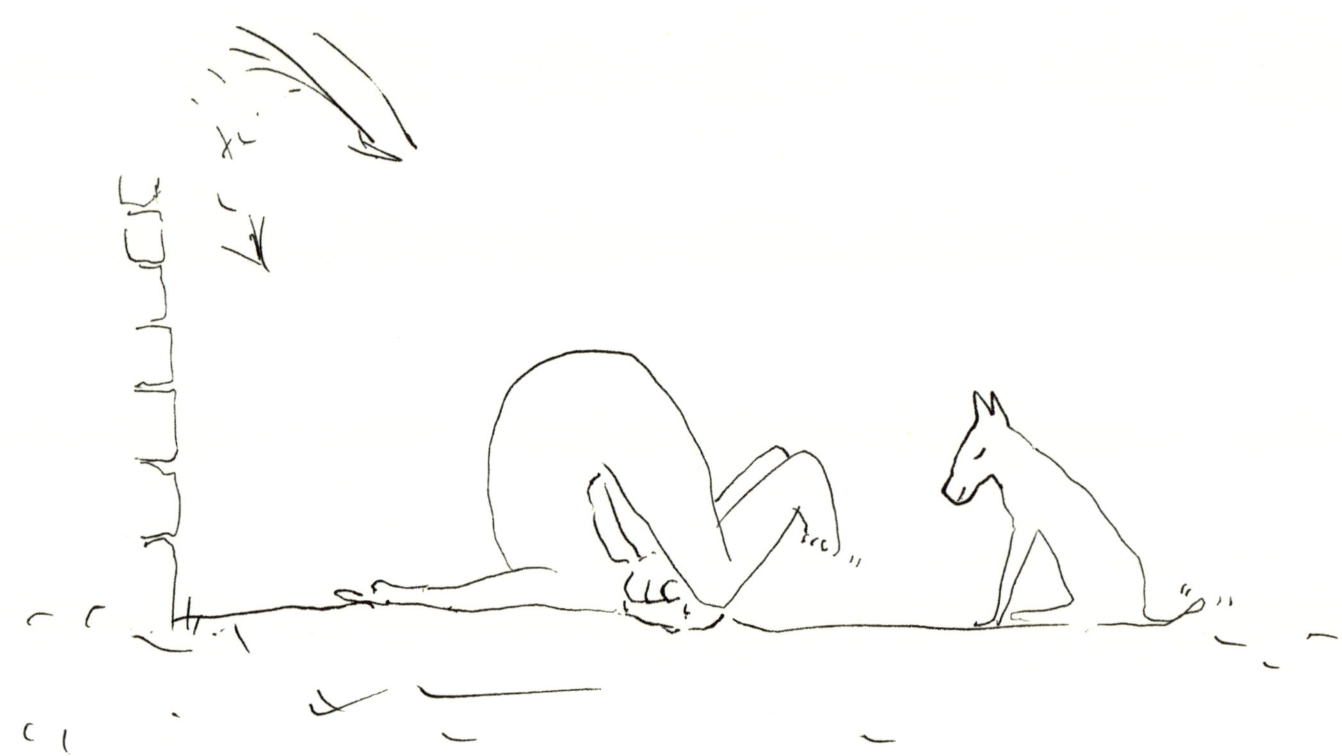

Torihiki shimasen
I don't deal
1977
8″ x 5″
Ink

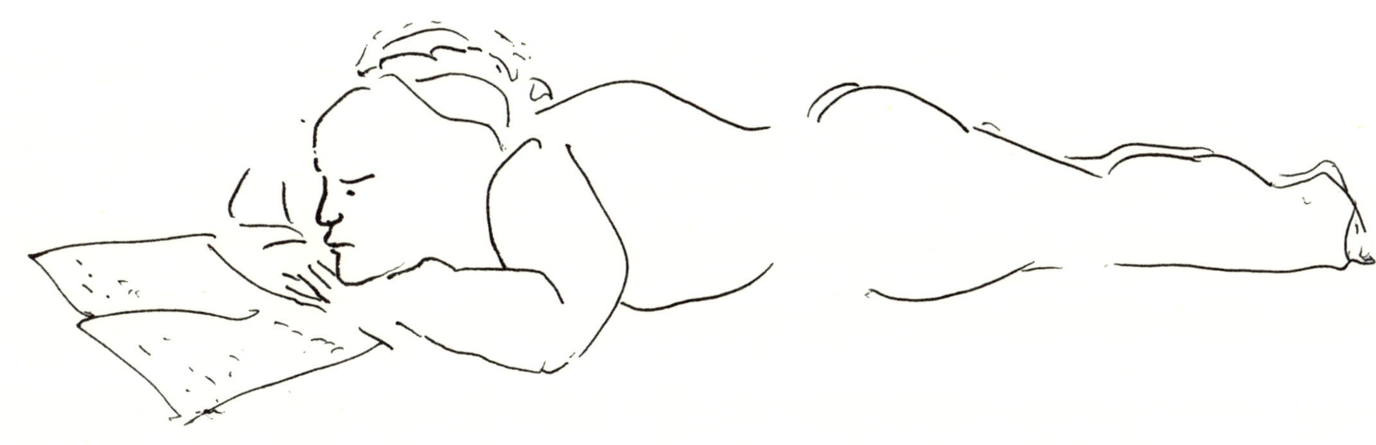

Zasshi o (yondeimasu)
Reading a magazine
1977
8″ x 5″
Ink

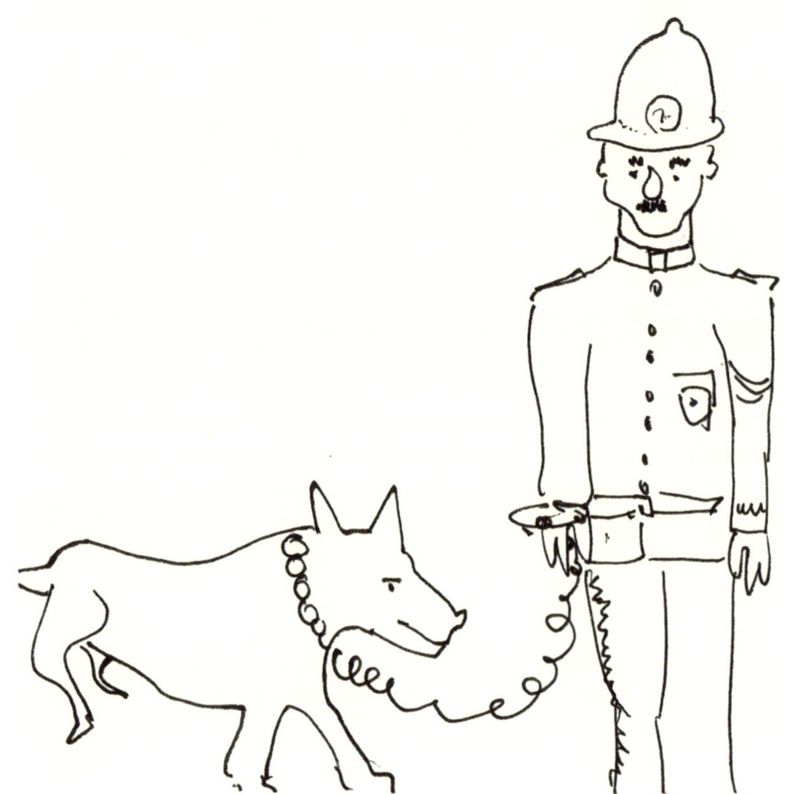

Omawari san (keikan)
Policeman
1977
8″ x 5″
Ink

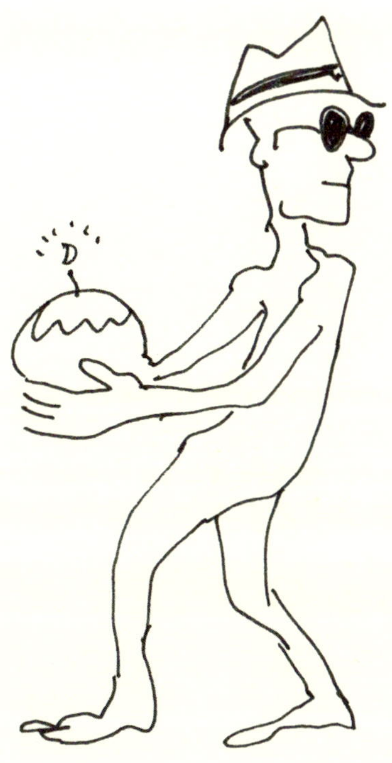

Taisetsu na nimotsu
Package
1977
8″ x 5″
Ink

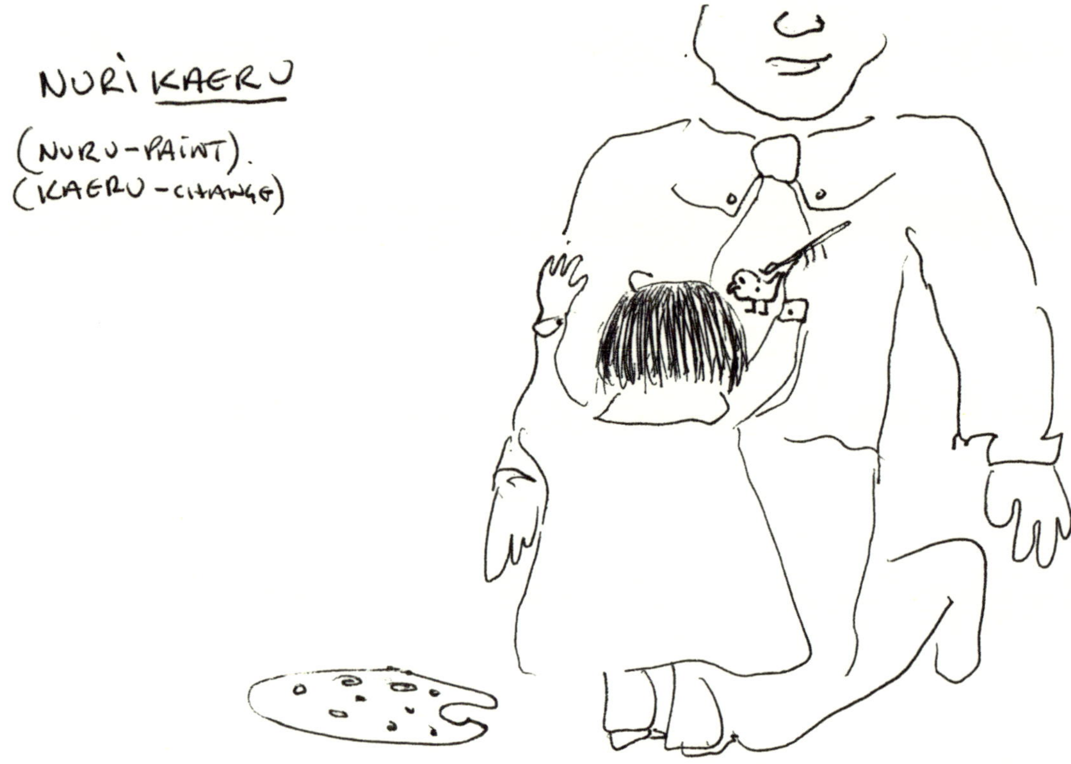

Nuri kaeru
Changing the paint
1977
8″ x 5″
Ink

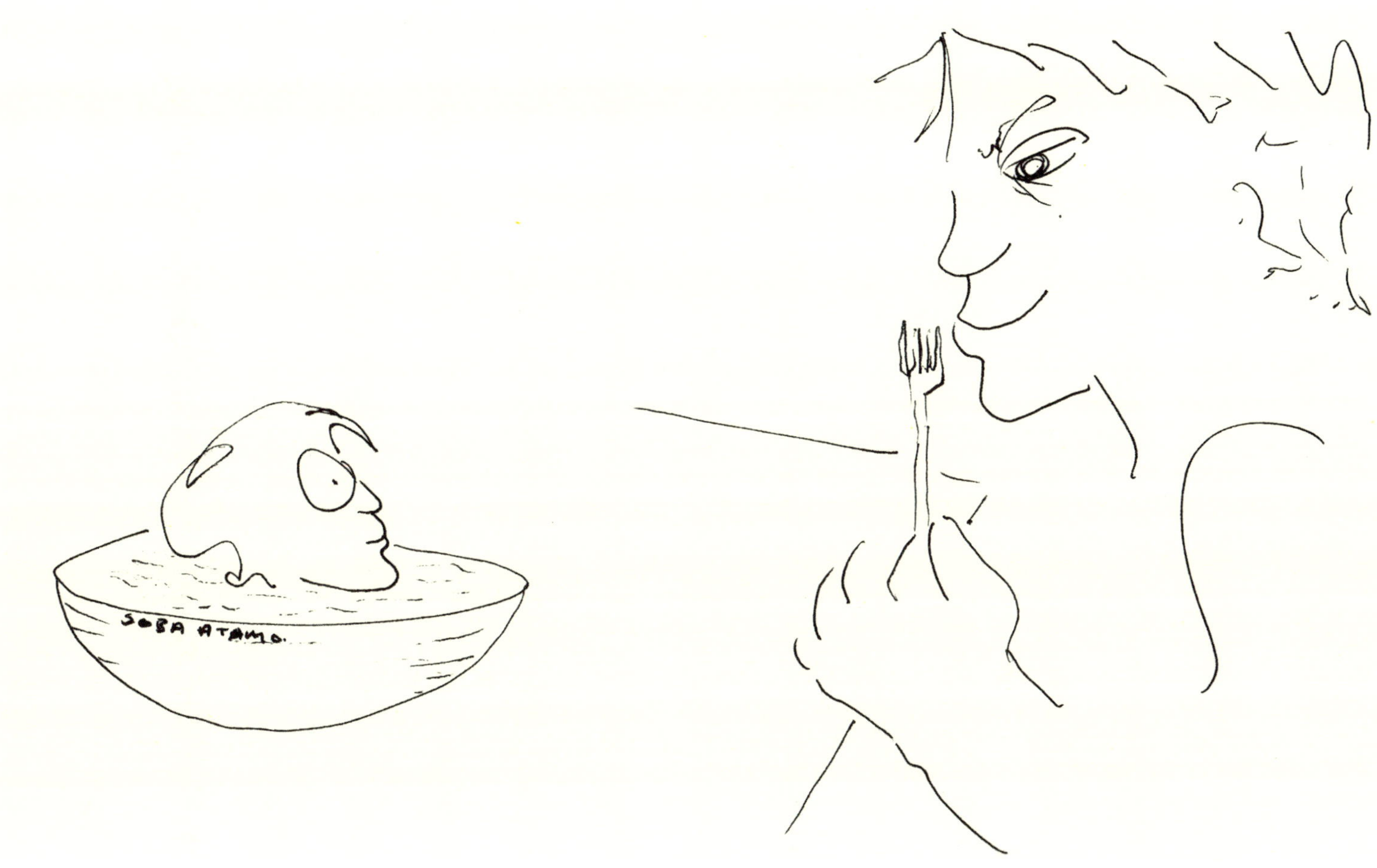

Soba atama
Noodlehead
1977
8″ x 5″
Ink

STAMP/O OSHIMASU

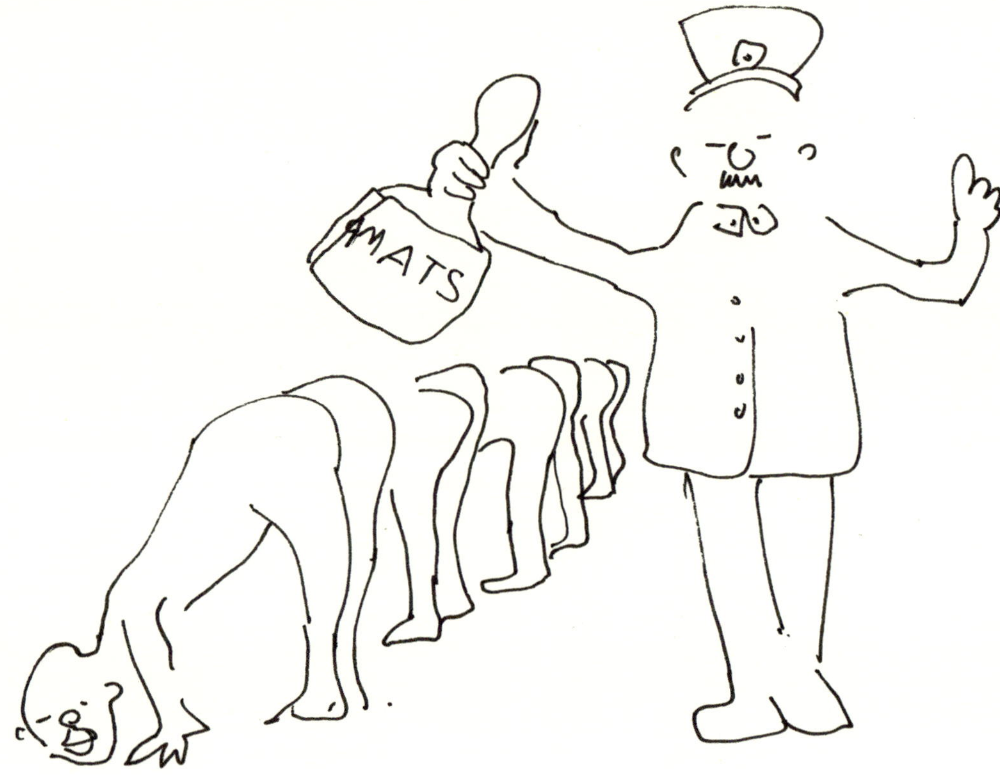

Oshimasu
To stamp
1977
8″ x 5″
Ink

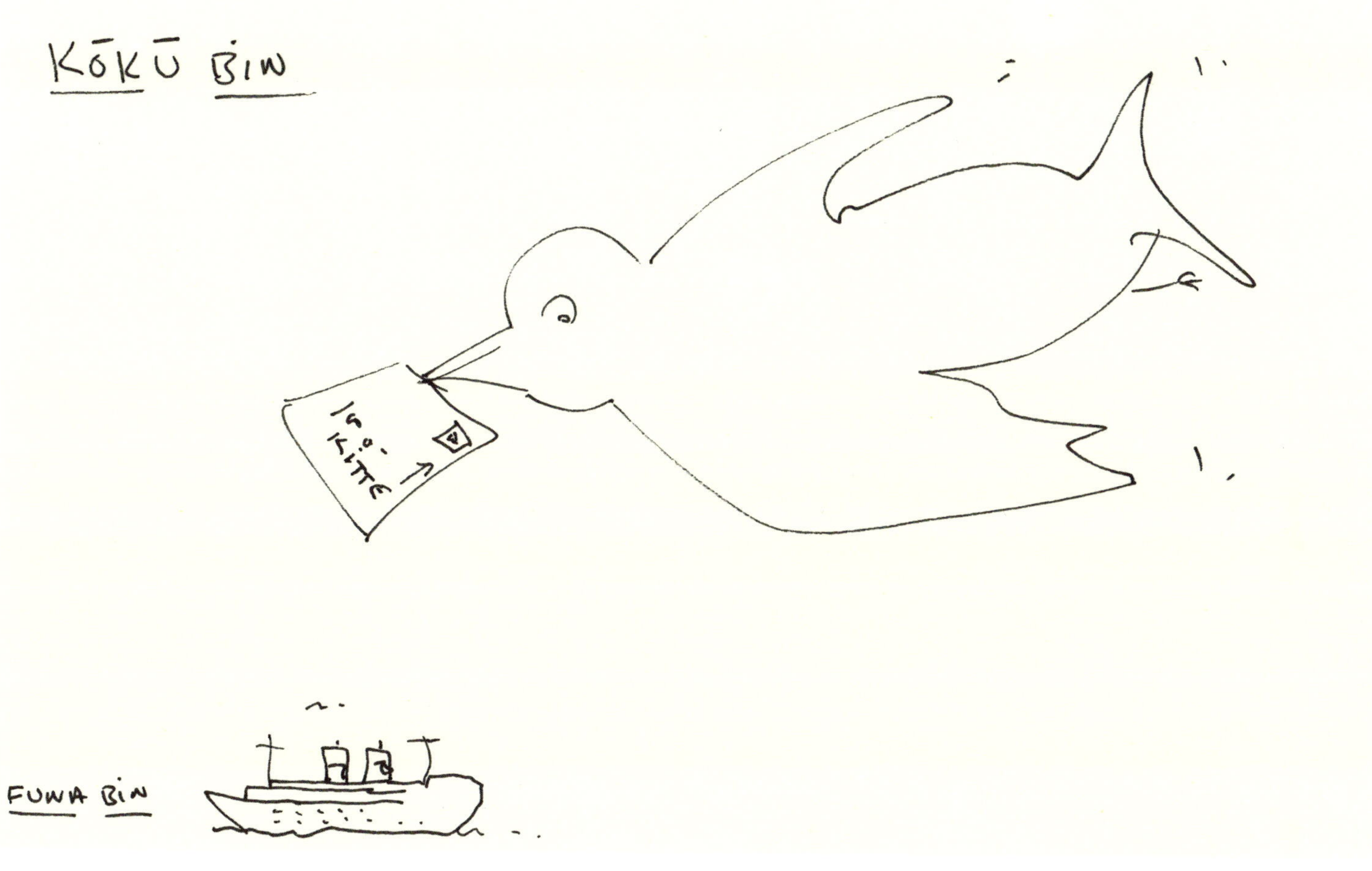

Kōkūbin – funa bin – kitte
Air mail – sea mail – stamp
1977
8″ x 5″
Ink

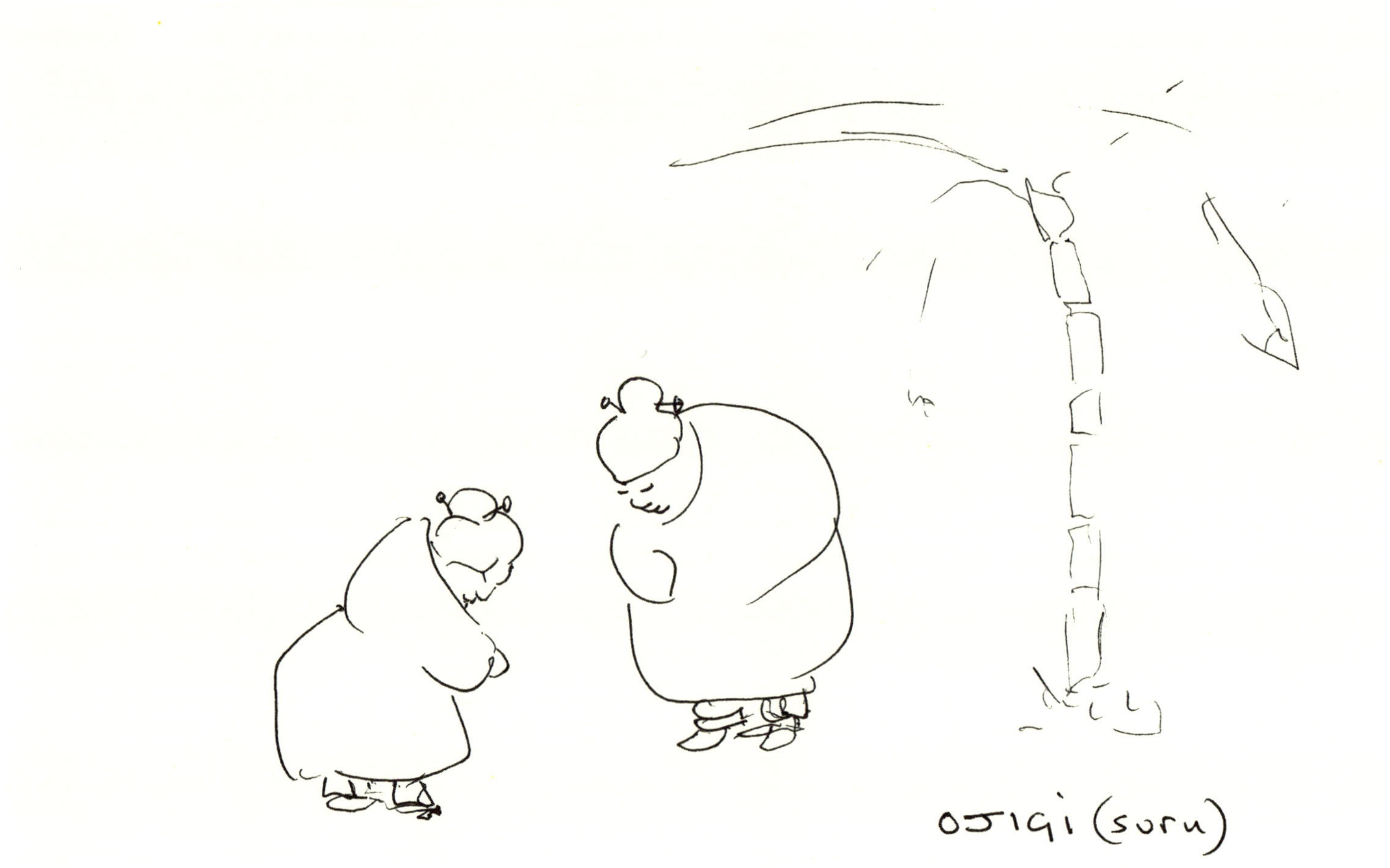

Ojigi (suru)
To greet
1977
8" x 5"
Ink

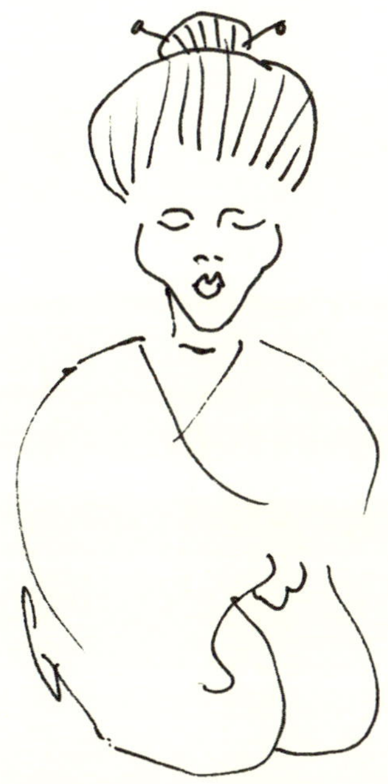

Geisha no nedan wa
agarimasu
The price of a geisha goes up
1977
8″ x 5″
Ink

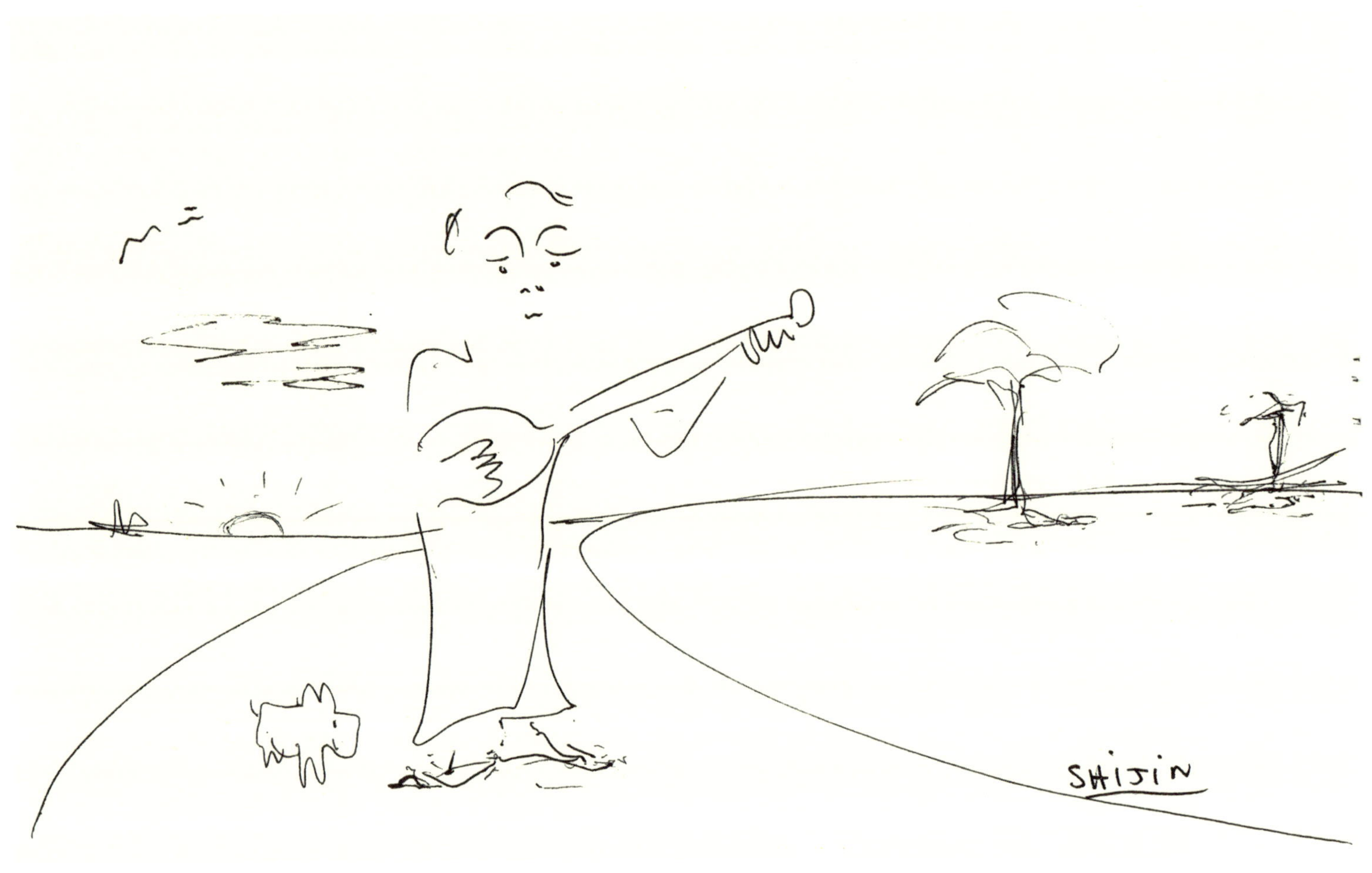

Shijin
Poet
1977
8″ x 5″
Ink

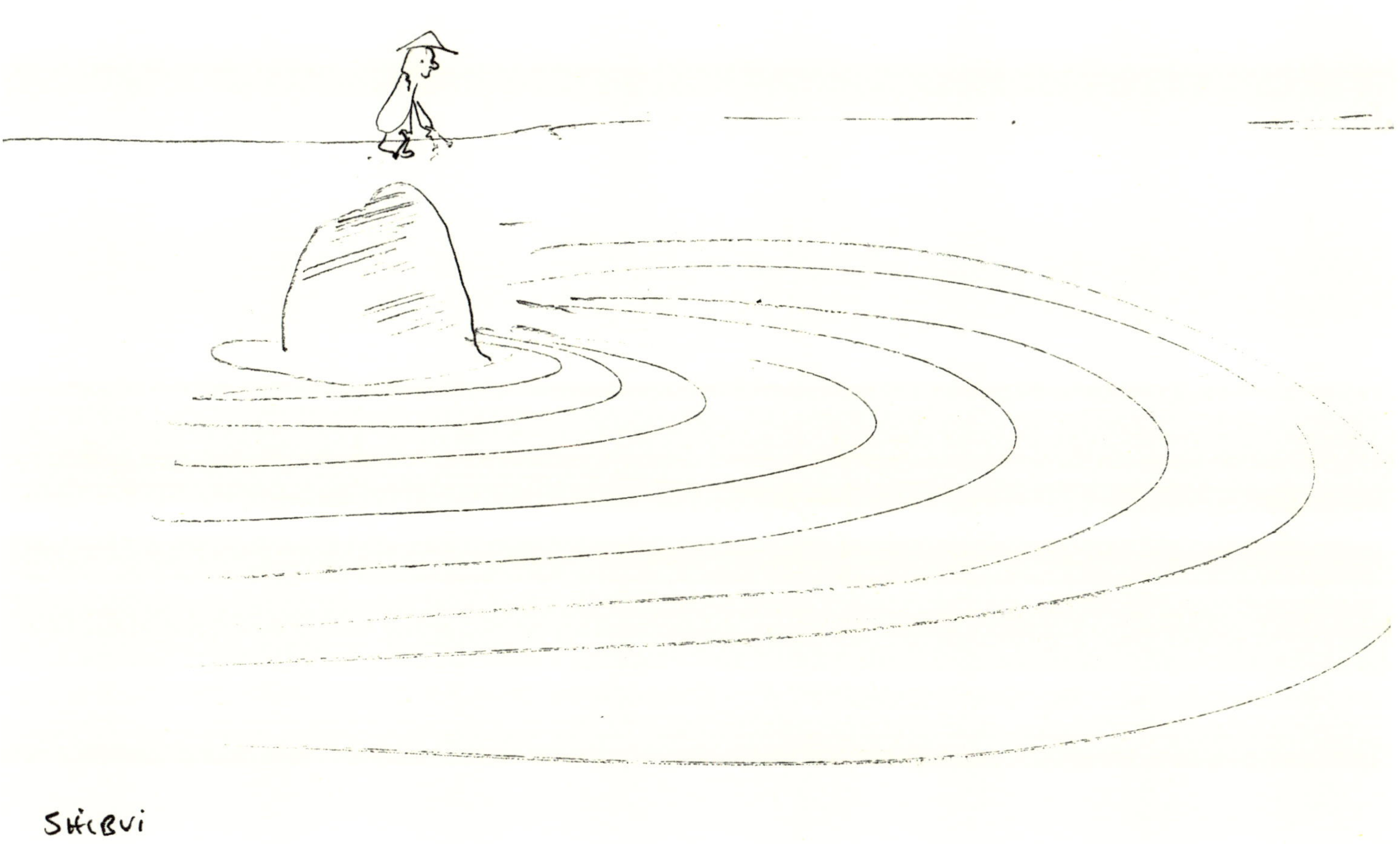

Shibui
1977
8" x 5"
Ink

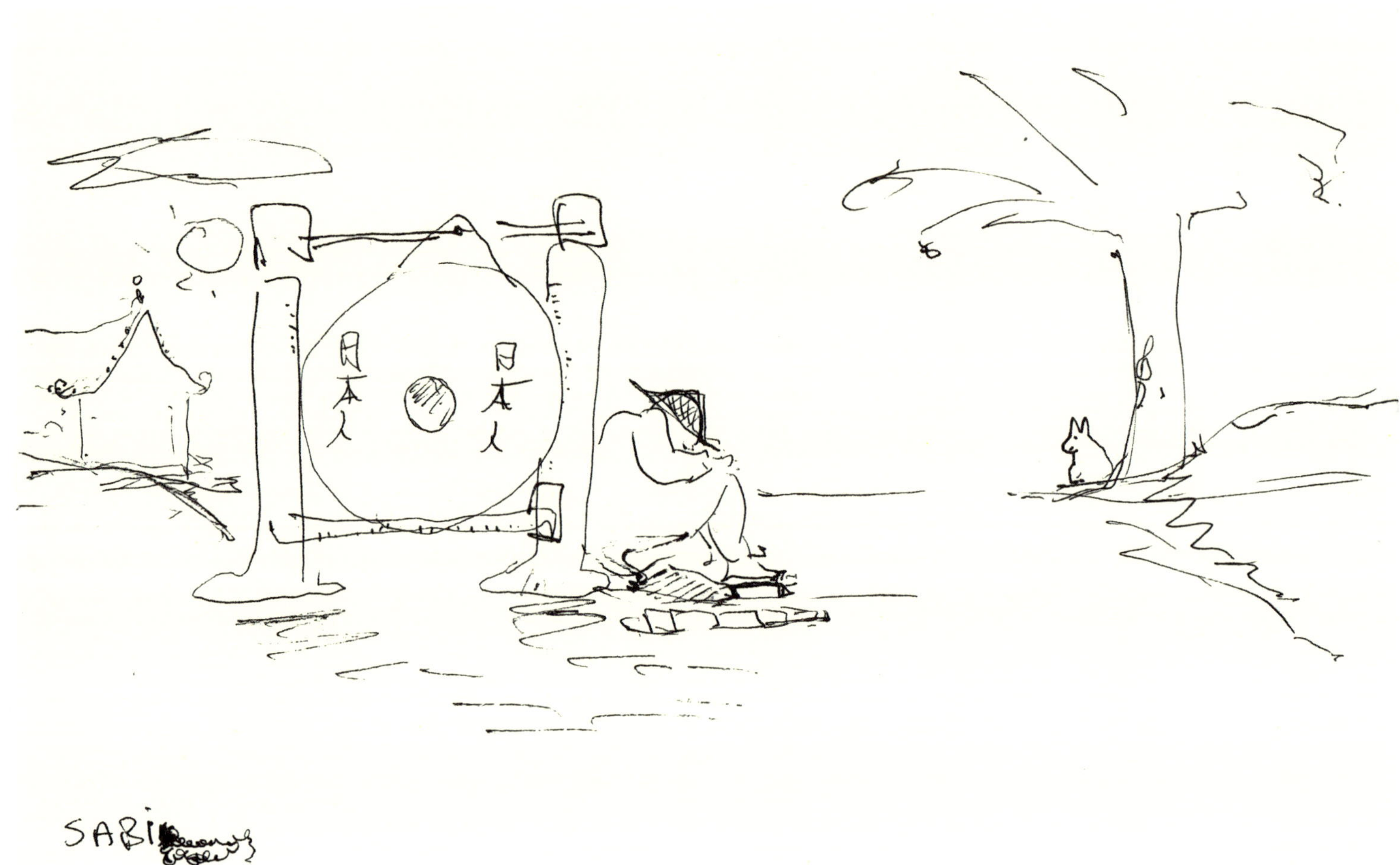

Sabi
1977
8" x 5"
Ink

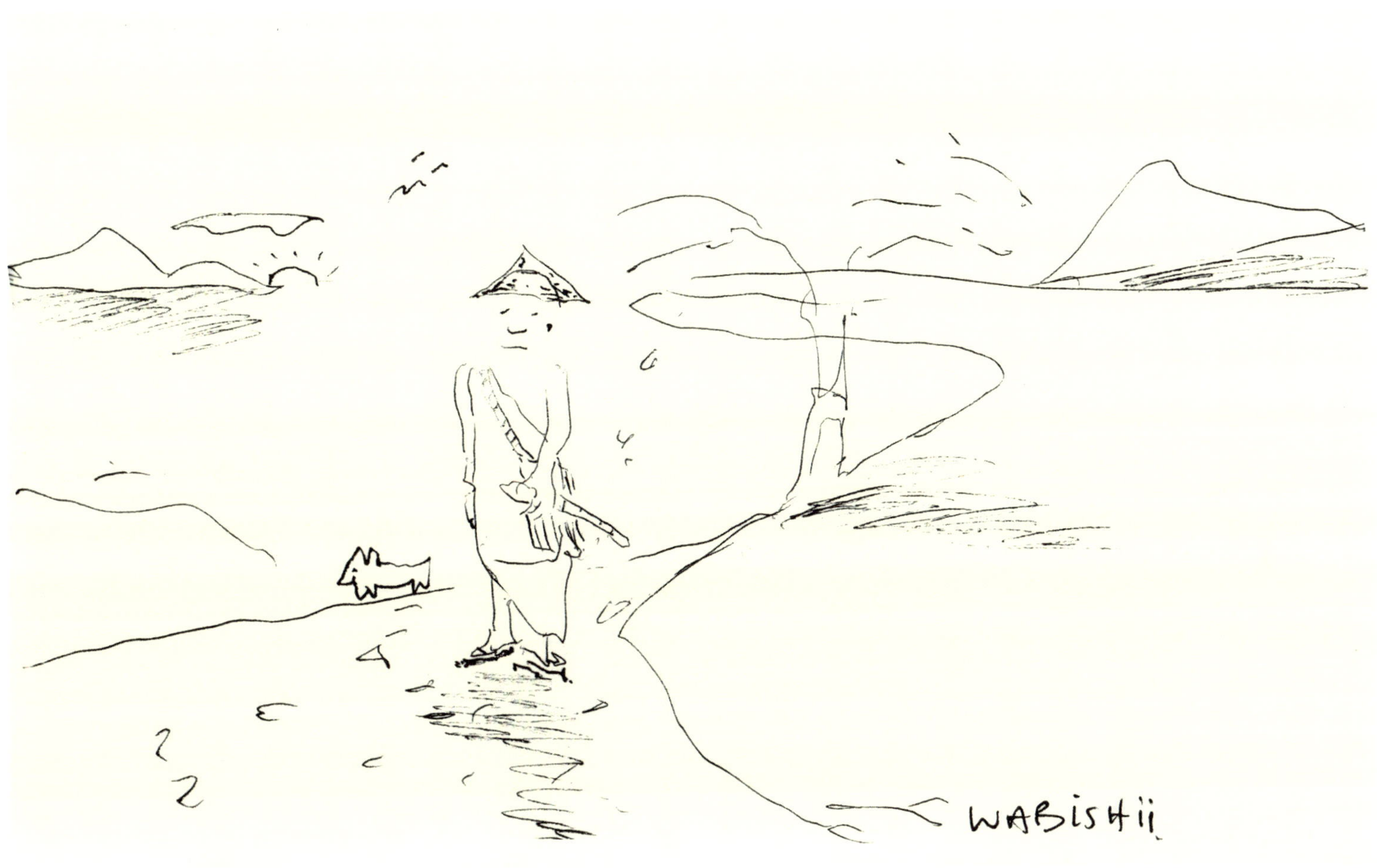

Wabishii
1977
8″ x 4¾″
Ink

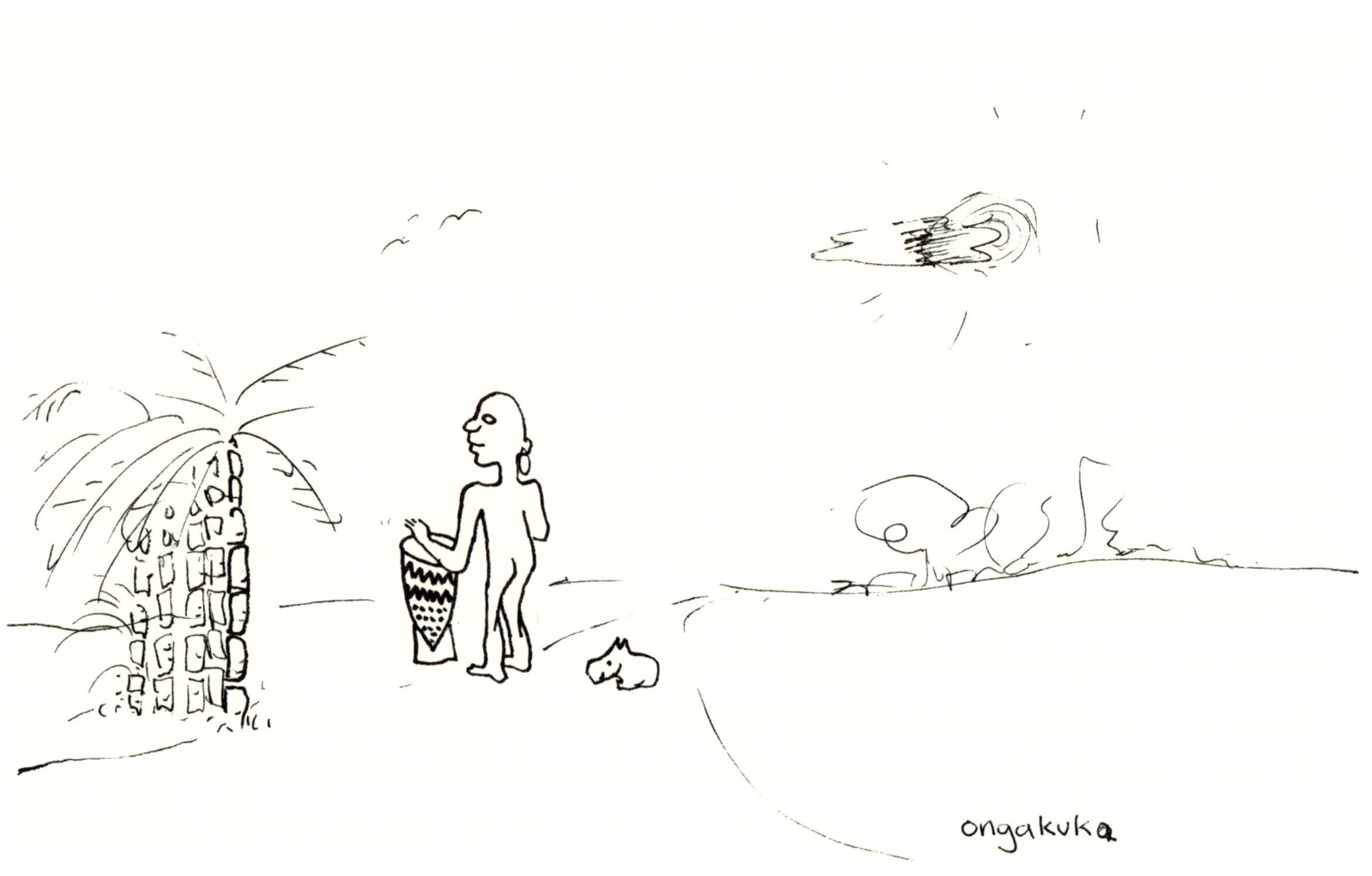

Ongakuka
Musician
1977
8″ x 5″
Ink

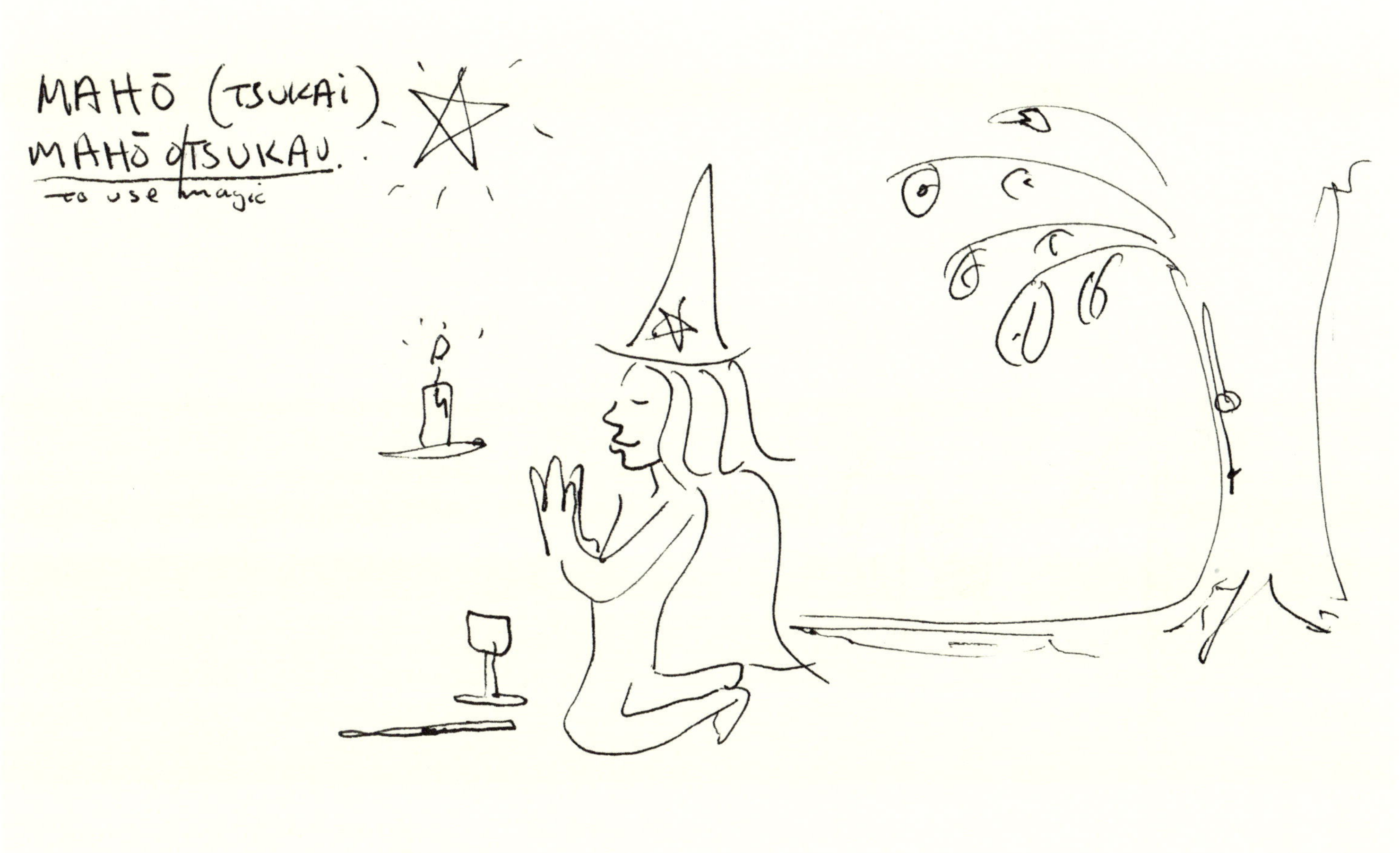

Mahō (tsukai)
To use magic
1977
8″ x 5″
Ink

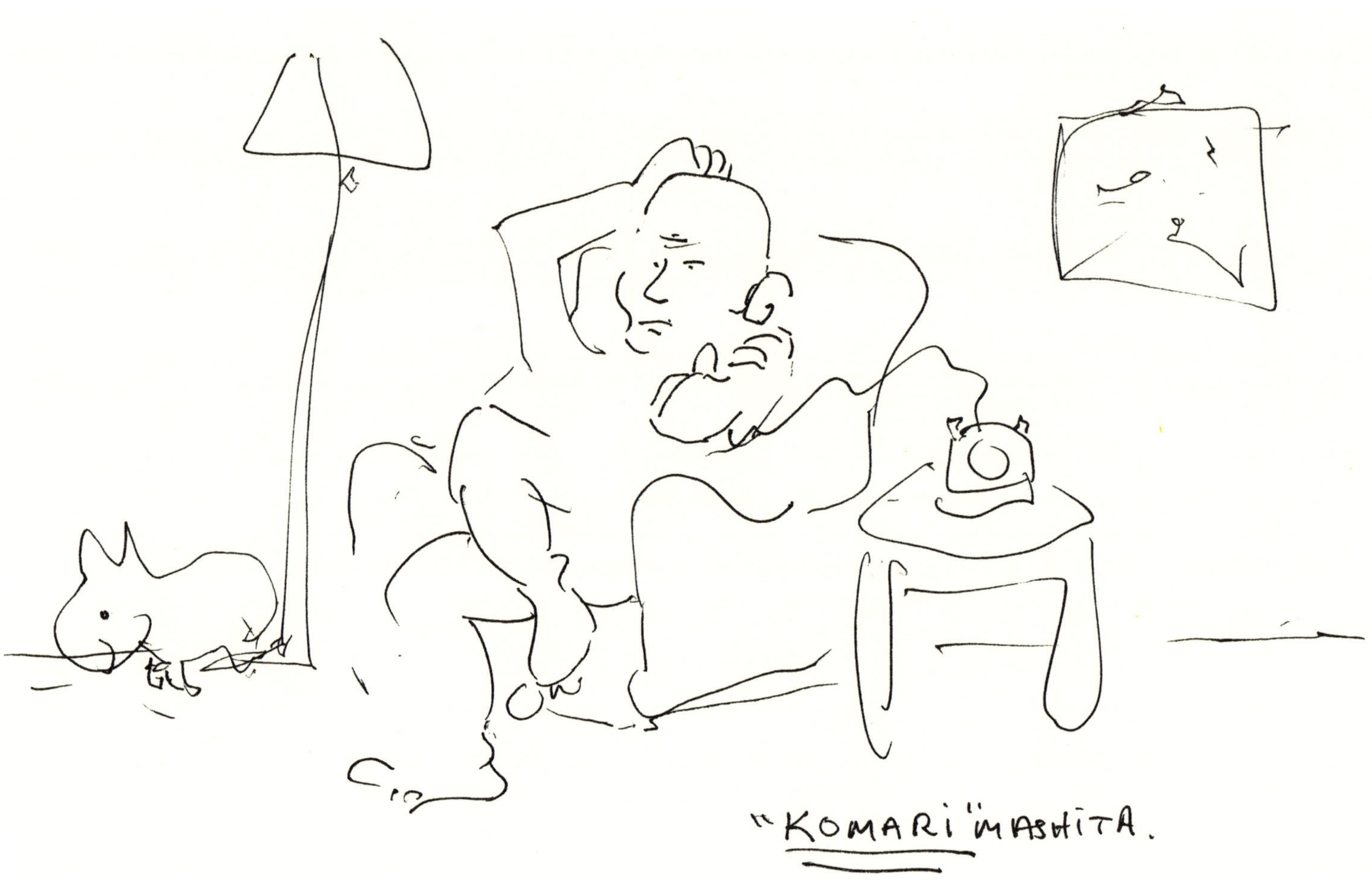

»Komari« mashita
It doesn't suit me
1977
8″ x 5″
Ink

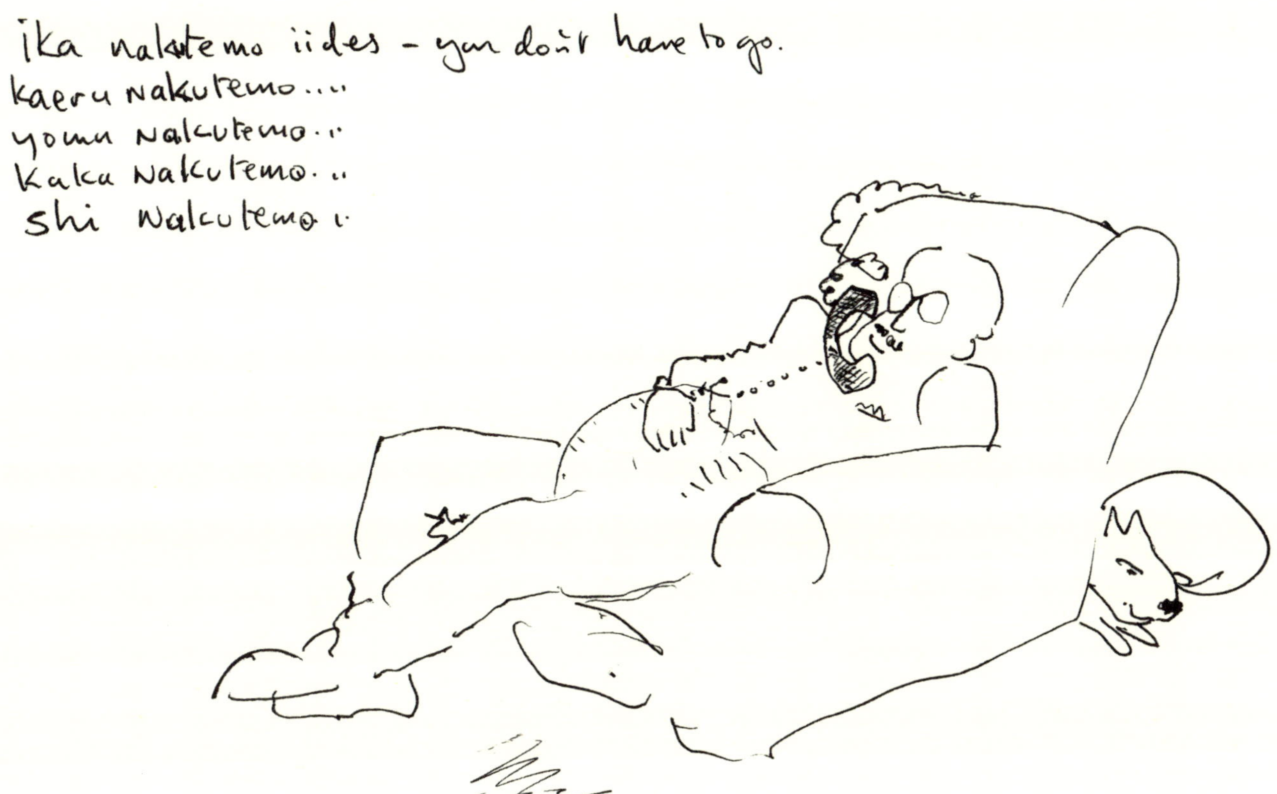

Ika nakutemo iides
You don't have to go
1977
8" x 5"
Ink

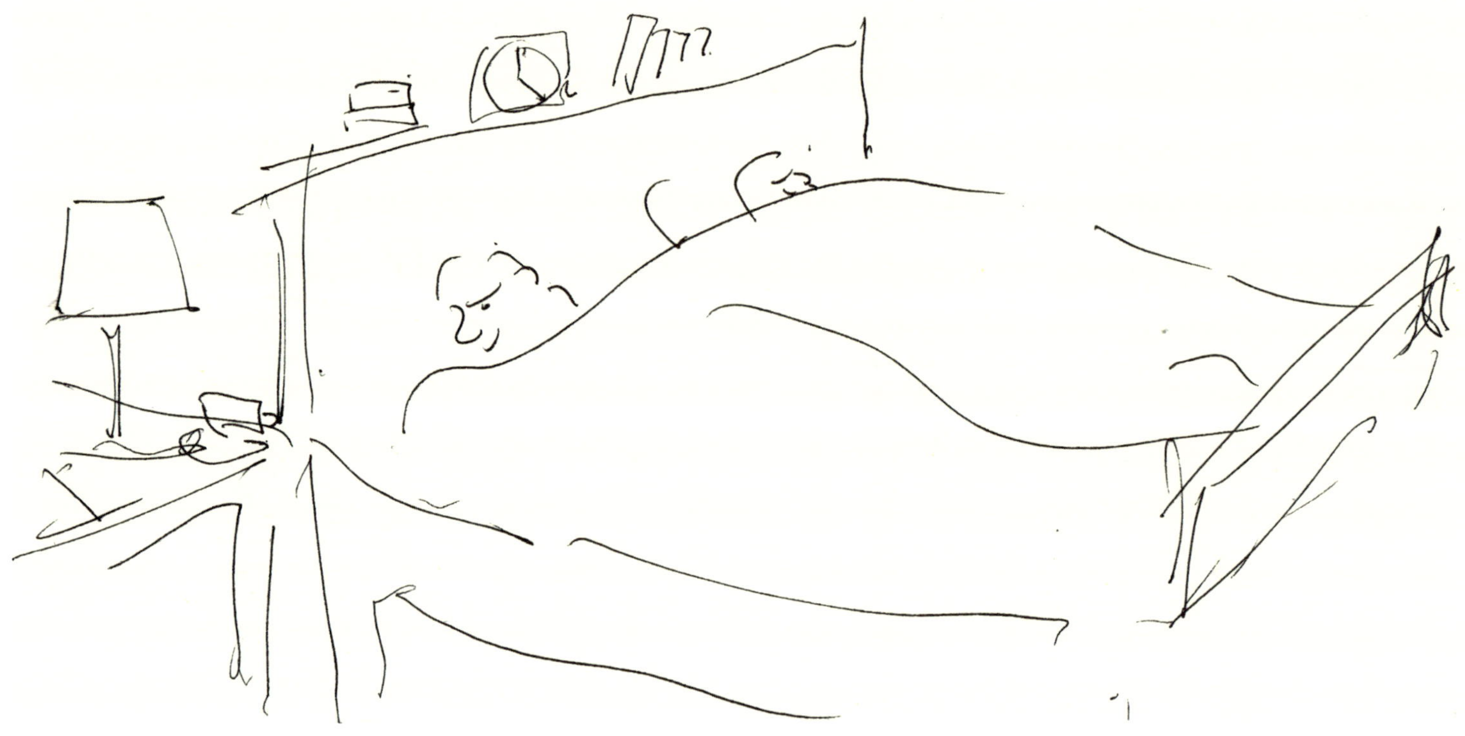

Mainichi umare kawarimasu
We are born anew everyday
1977
8″ x 5″
Ink

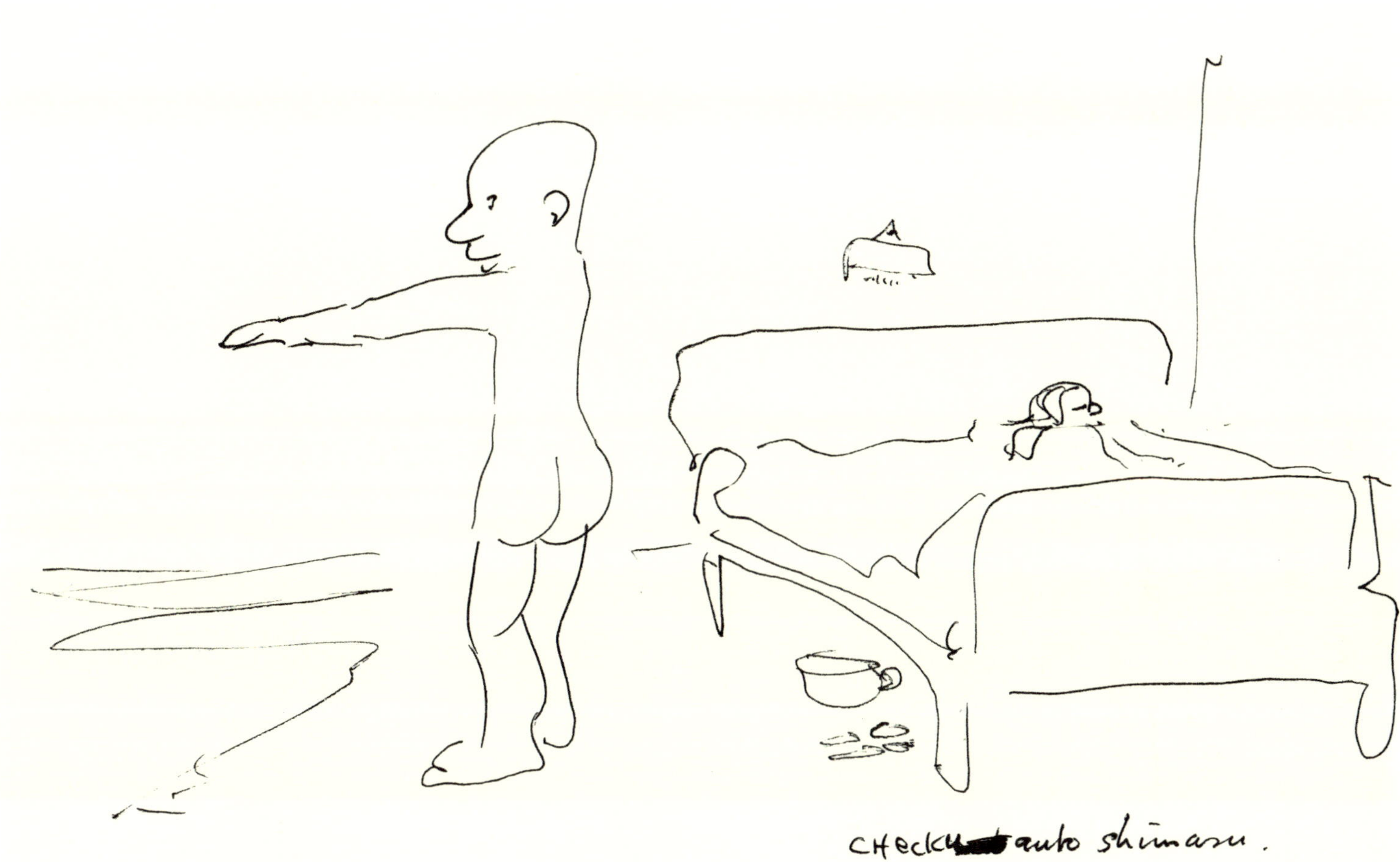

Checku auto shimasu
I'm checking out
1977
8″ x 5″
Ink

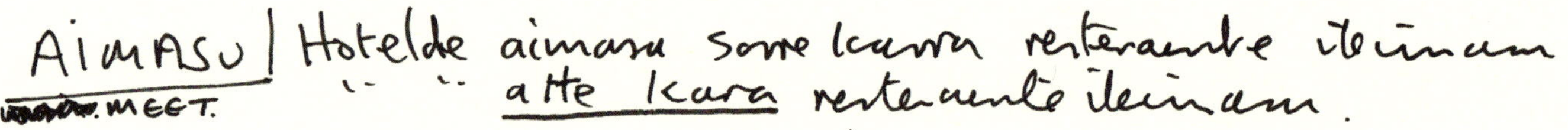

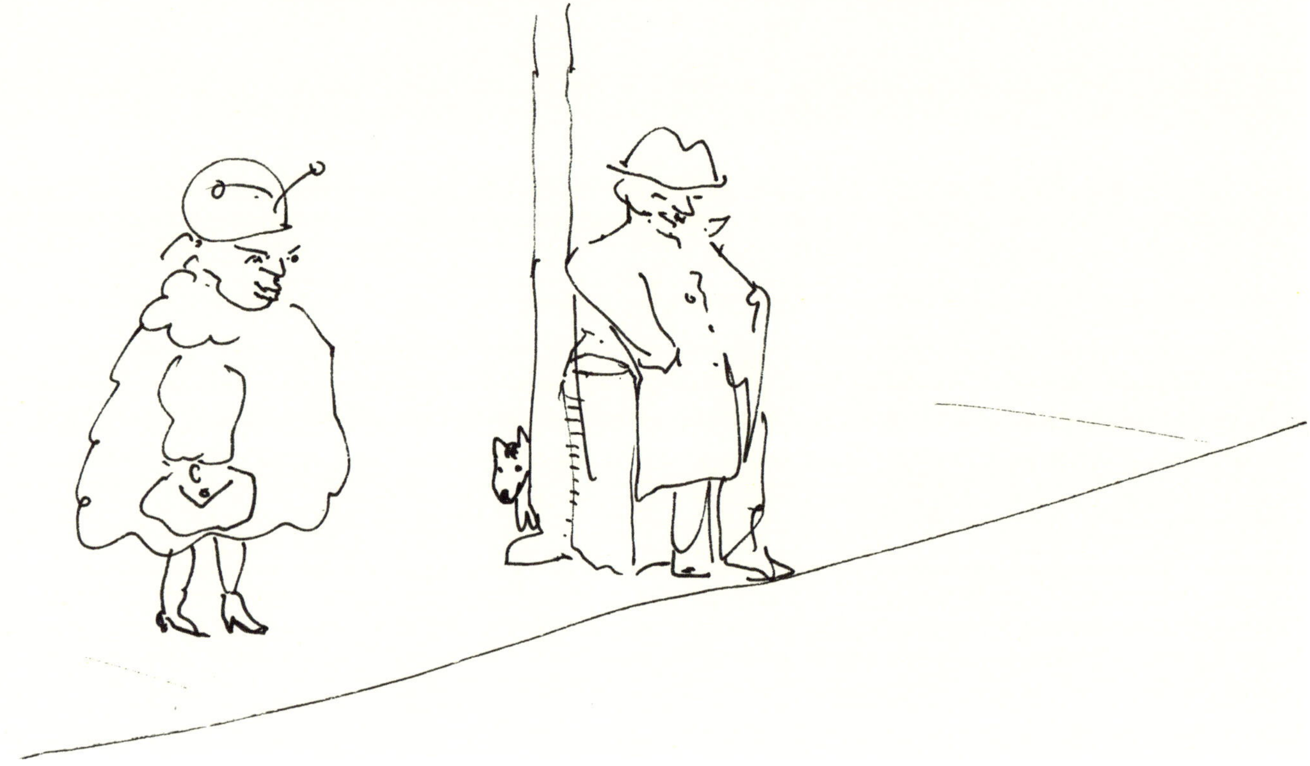

Aimasu
Meet
1977
8″ x 5″
Ink

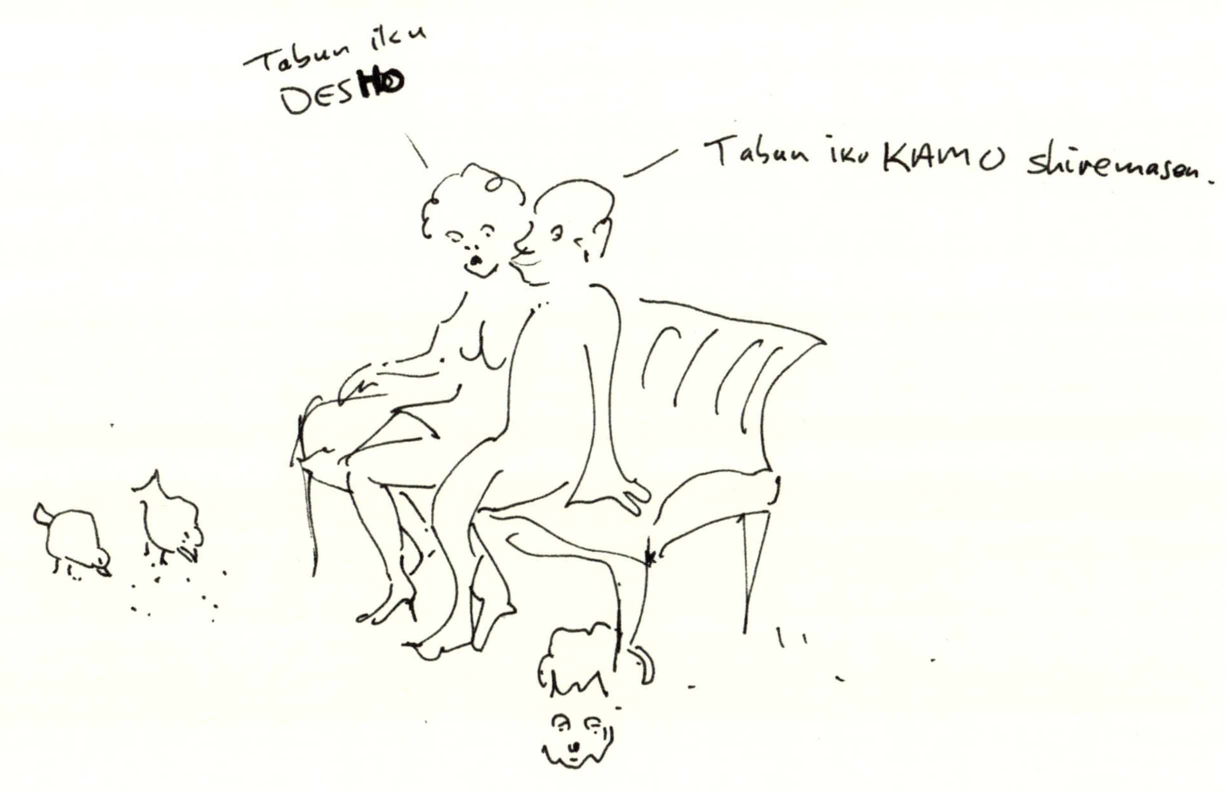

Tabun iku deshō
I'll probably go there
1977
8″ x 5″
Ink

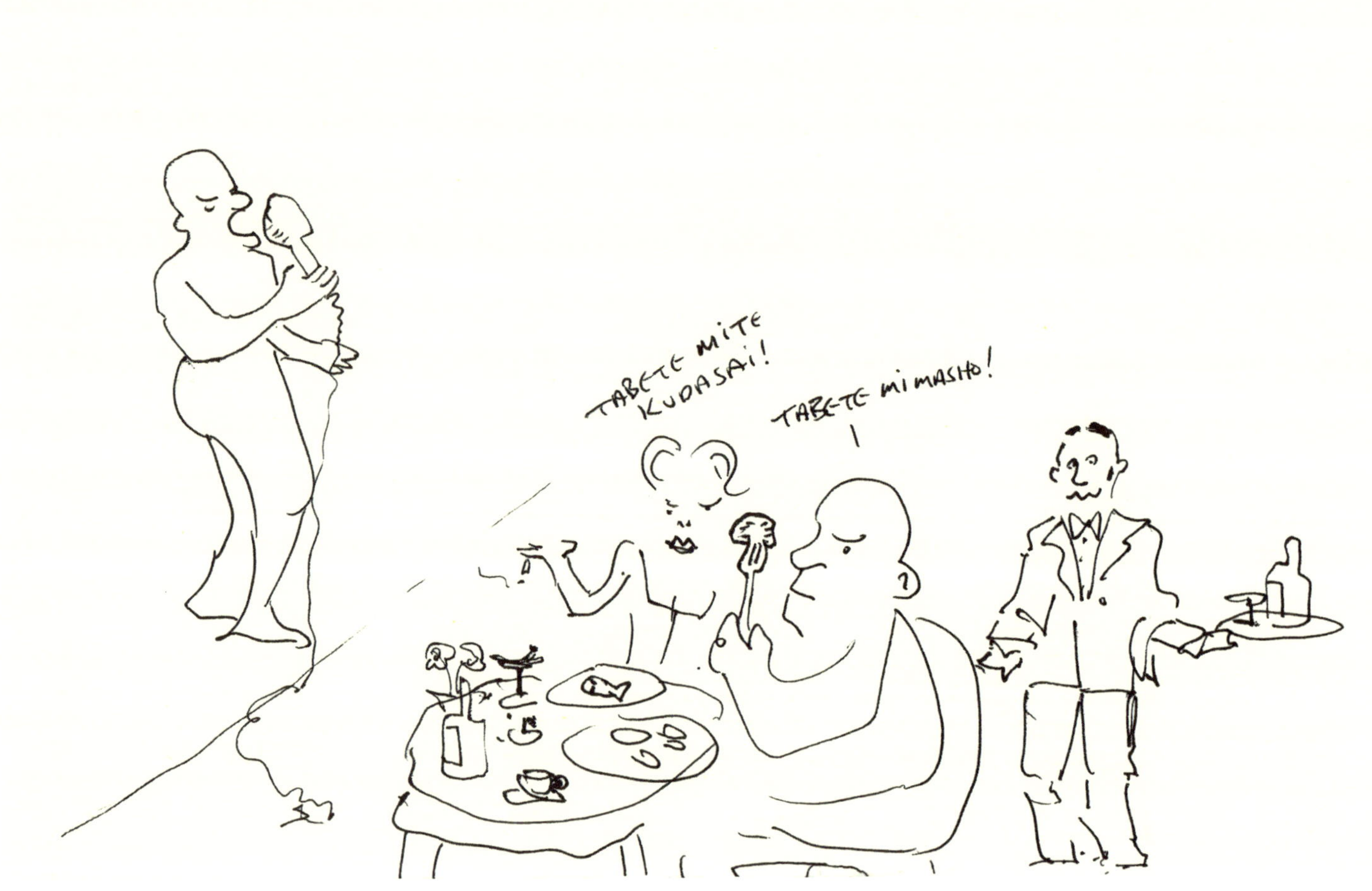

Tabete mite kudasai! –
Tabete mimasho!
Please taste this!
I'd try it!
1977
8″ x 5″
Ink

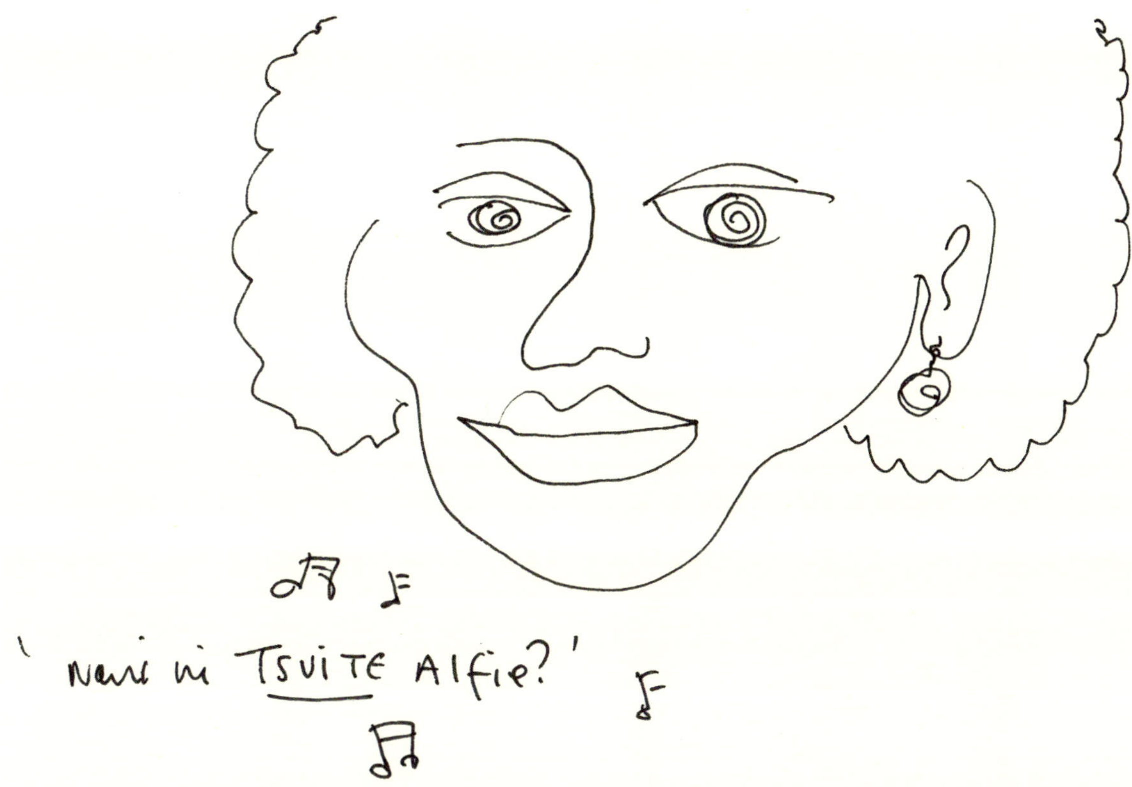

Nani ni tsuite Alfie?
About what, Alfie?
1977
8″ x 5″
Ink

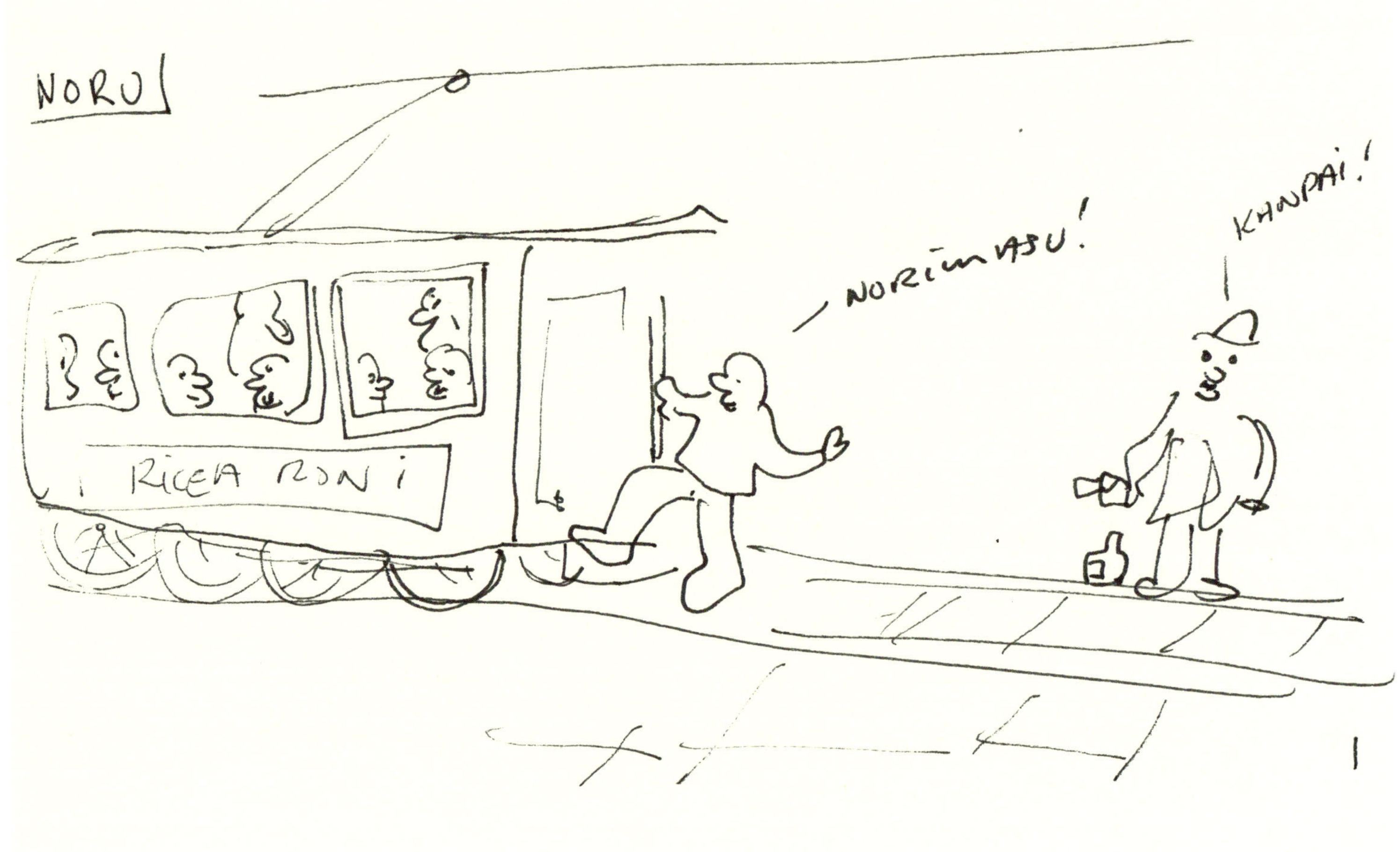

Norimasu!
Get on the train!
1977
8″ x 5″
Ink

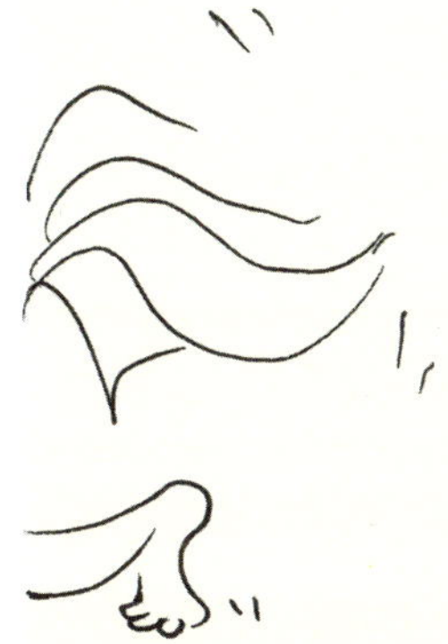

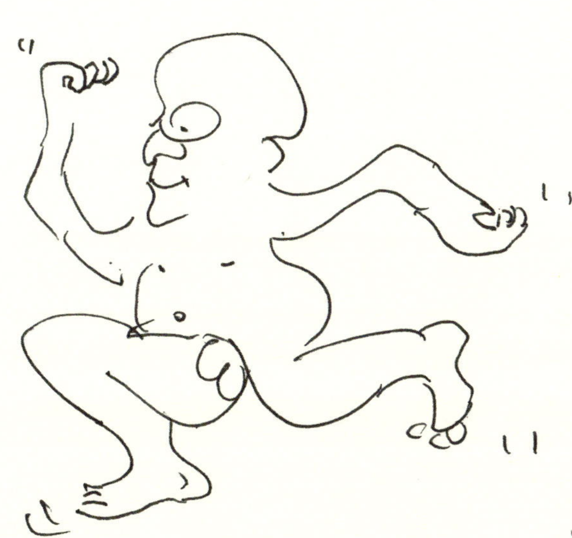

Kimono o osagashi
ni nate irassai masu.
Naze nara? Kimono
onokushi ni narimashita?
He's looking for a kimono.
Why? Has he lost his
kimono?
1977
8″ x 5″
Ink

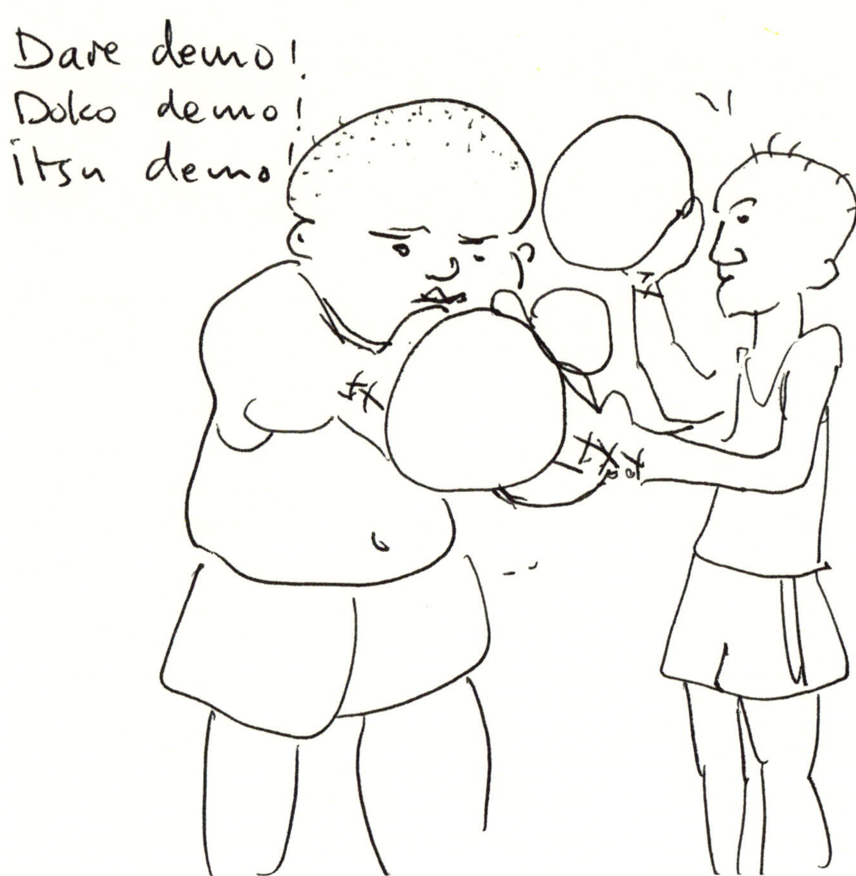

Dare demo! Doko demo!
Itsu demo!
Everyone! Everywhere!
At all times!
1977
8″ x 5″
Ink

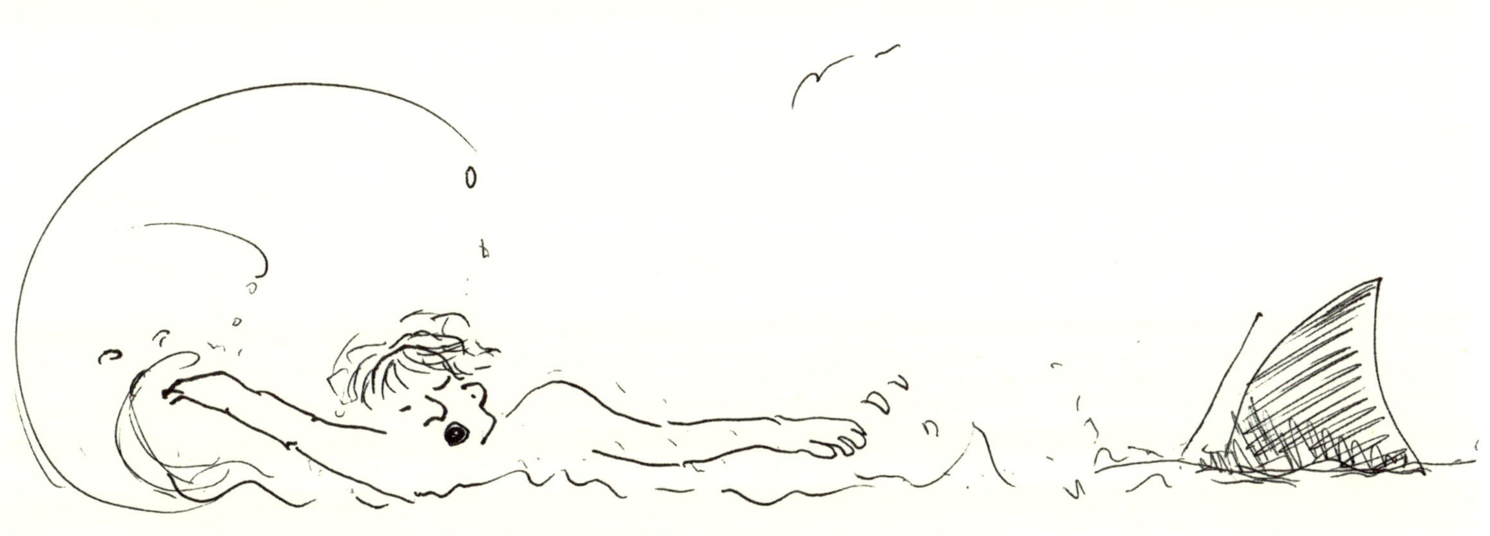

Oyogeba oyogu hodo,
karada ni ii desu.
The more you swim, the
better it is for your body.
1977
8″ x 5″
Ink

zeikin : TAX.   harau to pay   SEIFU: government

moshi camera o kaeby zeikin o harawa nakereba narimasen

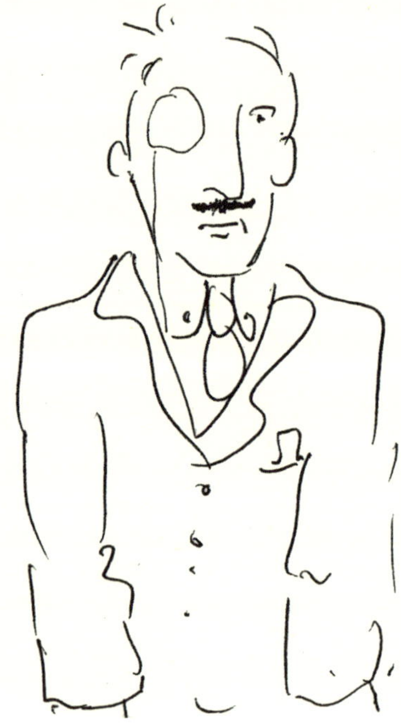
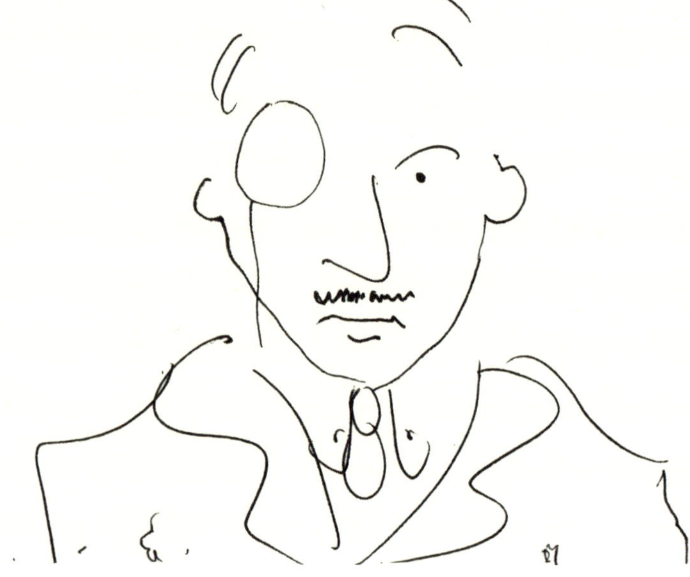

Moshi camera o kaeba,
zeikin o harawa nakereba
narimasen.
If you buy a camera, you
have to pay tax.
1977
8″ x 5″
Ink

moshi kai takereba okane o motte inakereba narimasen
if (to) buy would like money have (to) be must (ike masen)
(shopping) want

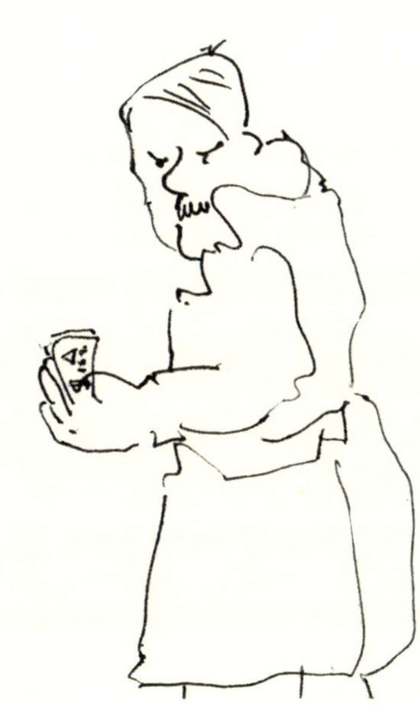

Moshi kai takereba ō-kane o
motte inakereba narimasen.
If you want to buy some-
thing you need money.
1977
8″ x 4¼″
Ink

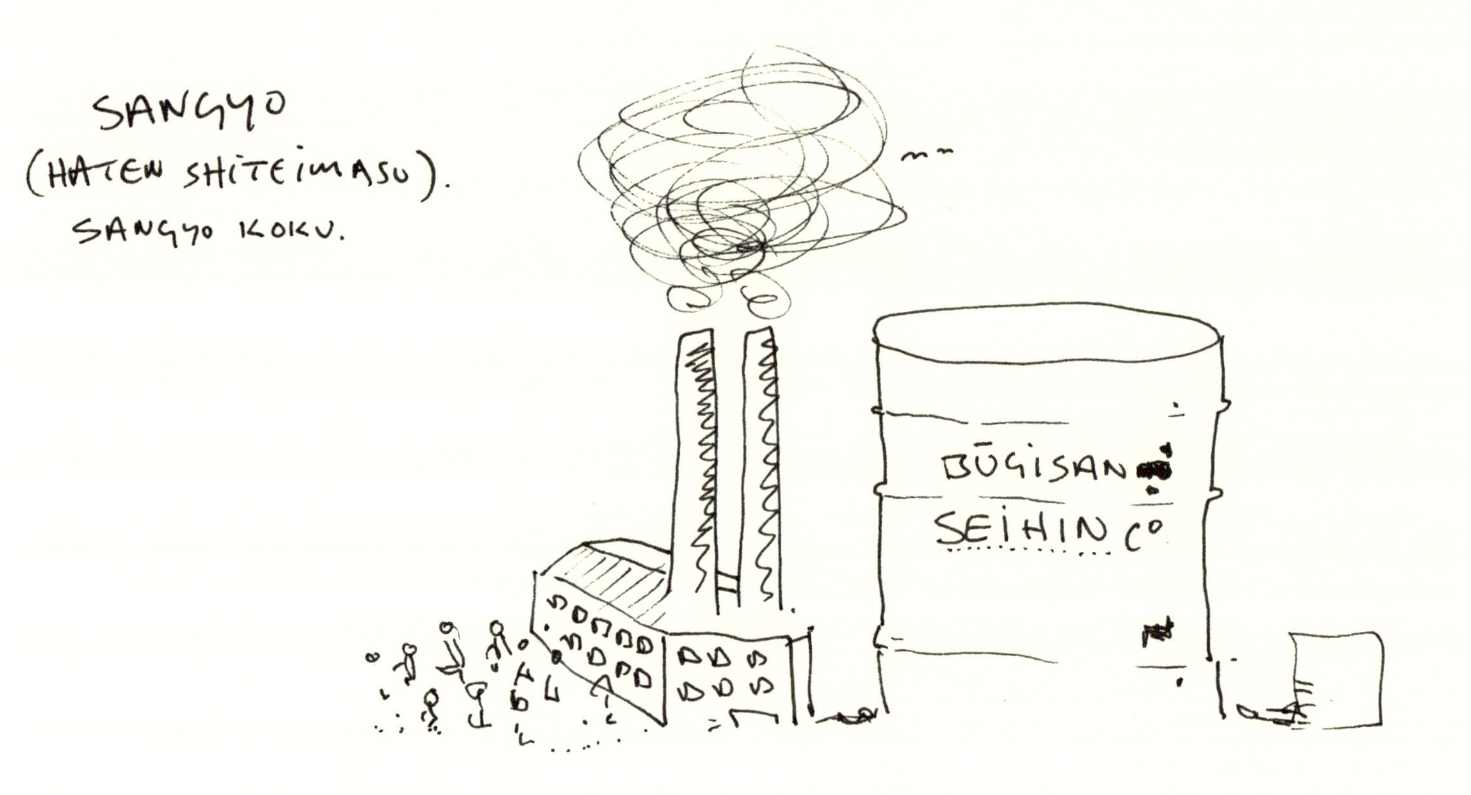

Sangyo
Industry
1977
8" x 5"
Ink

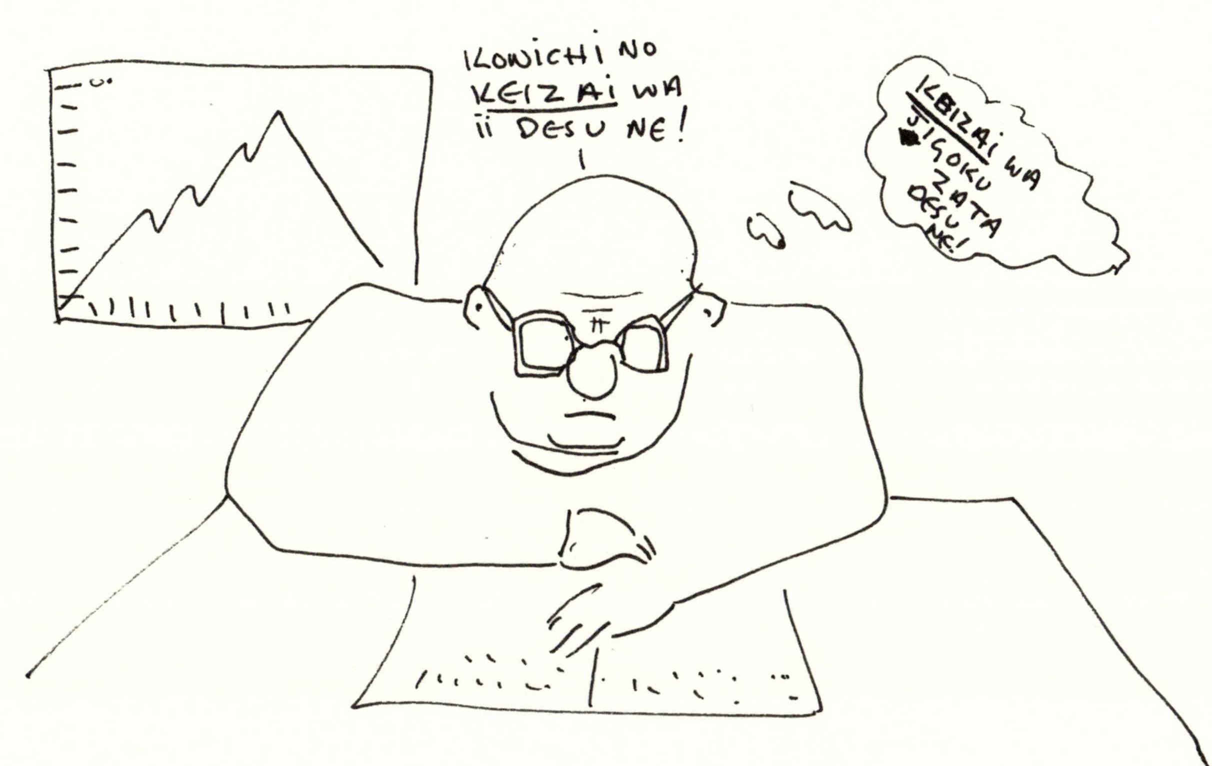

Konnichi no keizai wa ii
desu ne! – Keizai wa jigoku
zata desu ne!
Today's economy is good,
isn't it! – The economy is
hell, isn't it!
1977
8″ x 5″
Ink

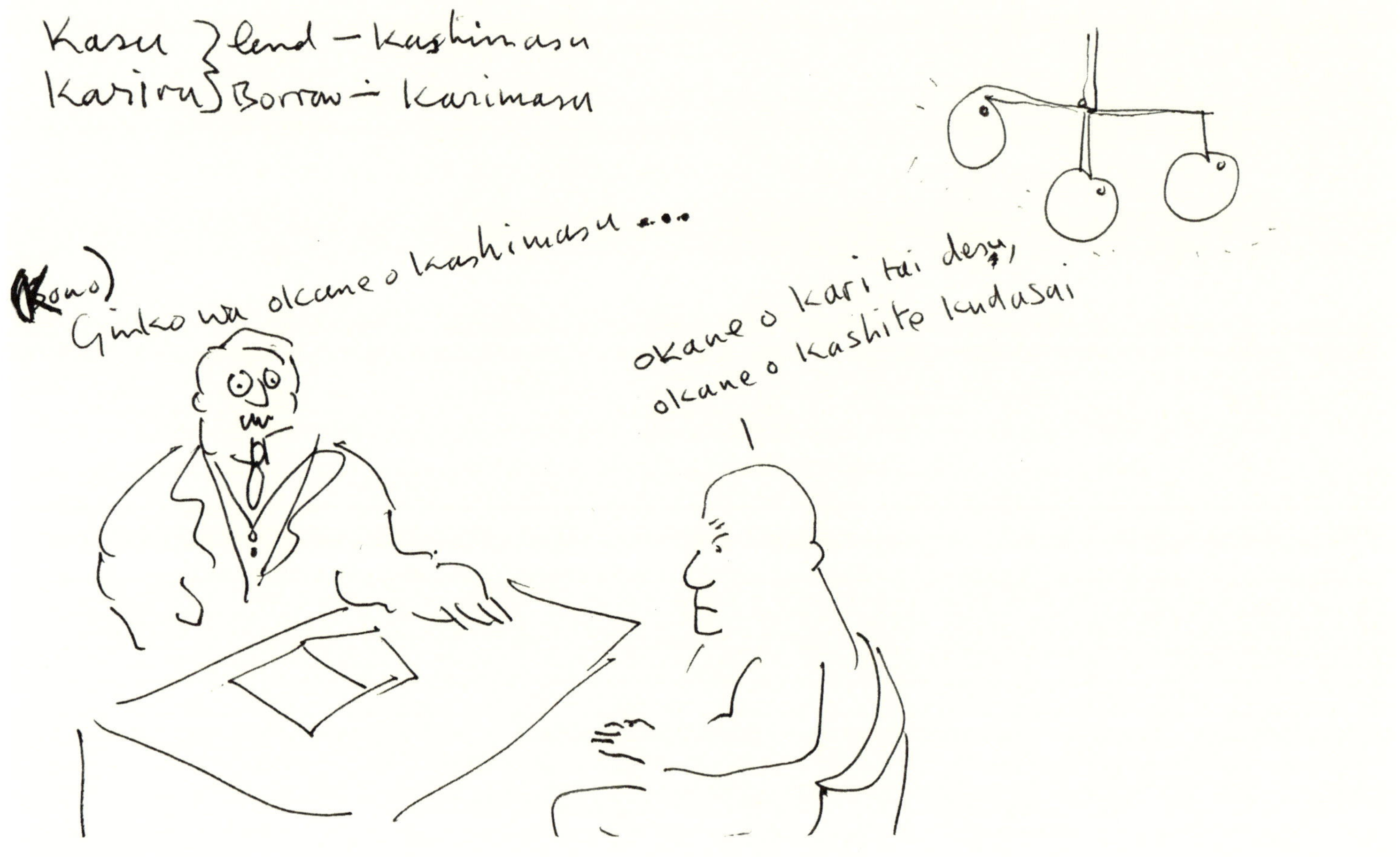

Kasu – kariru
To lend – to borrow
1977
8″ x 4¾″
Ink

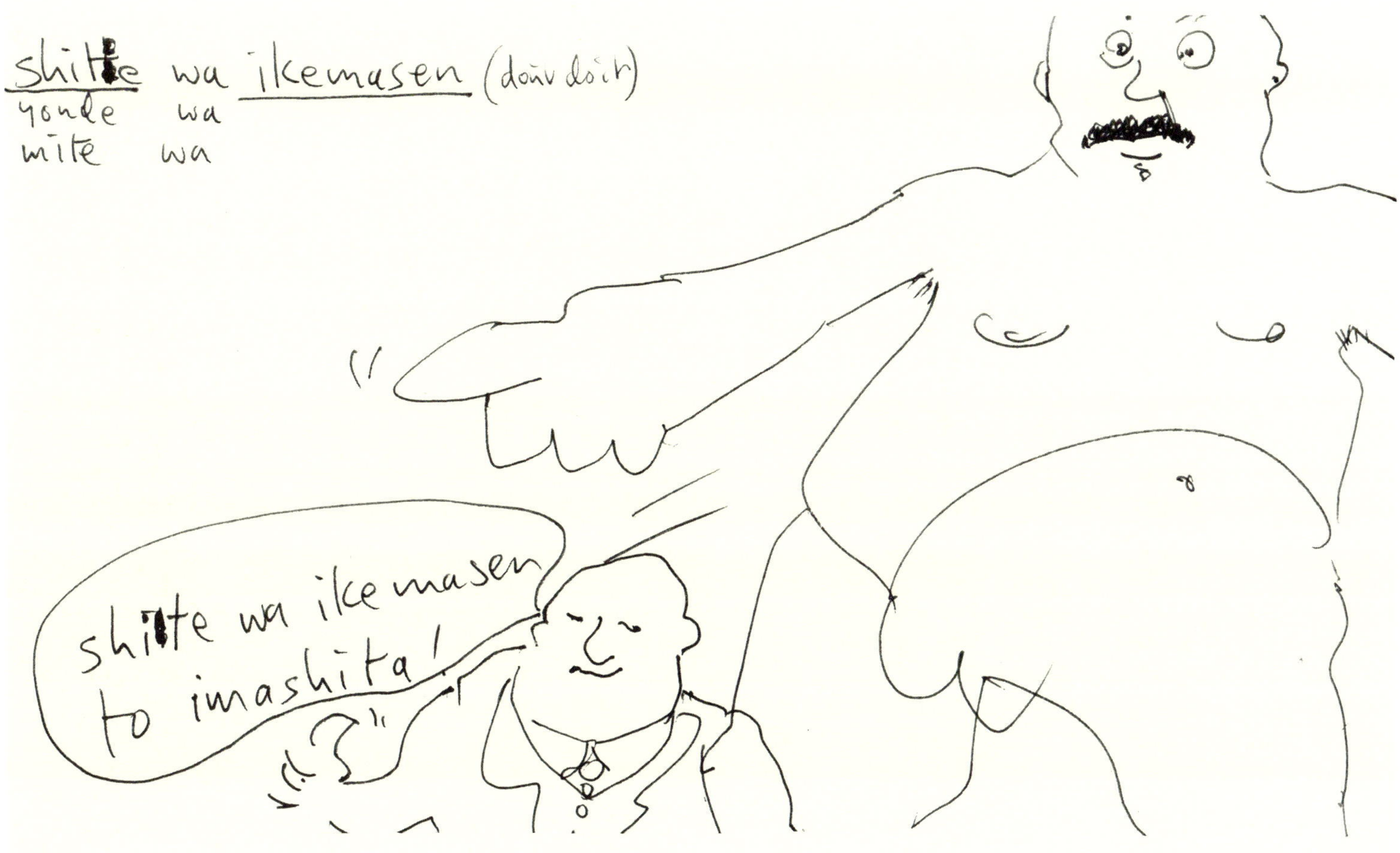

Shitte wa ikemasen
You must not do that
1977
8″ x 4¾″
Ink

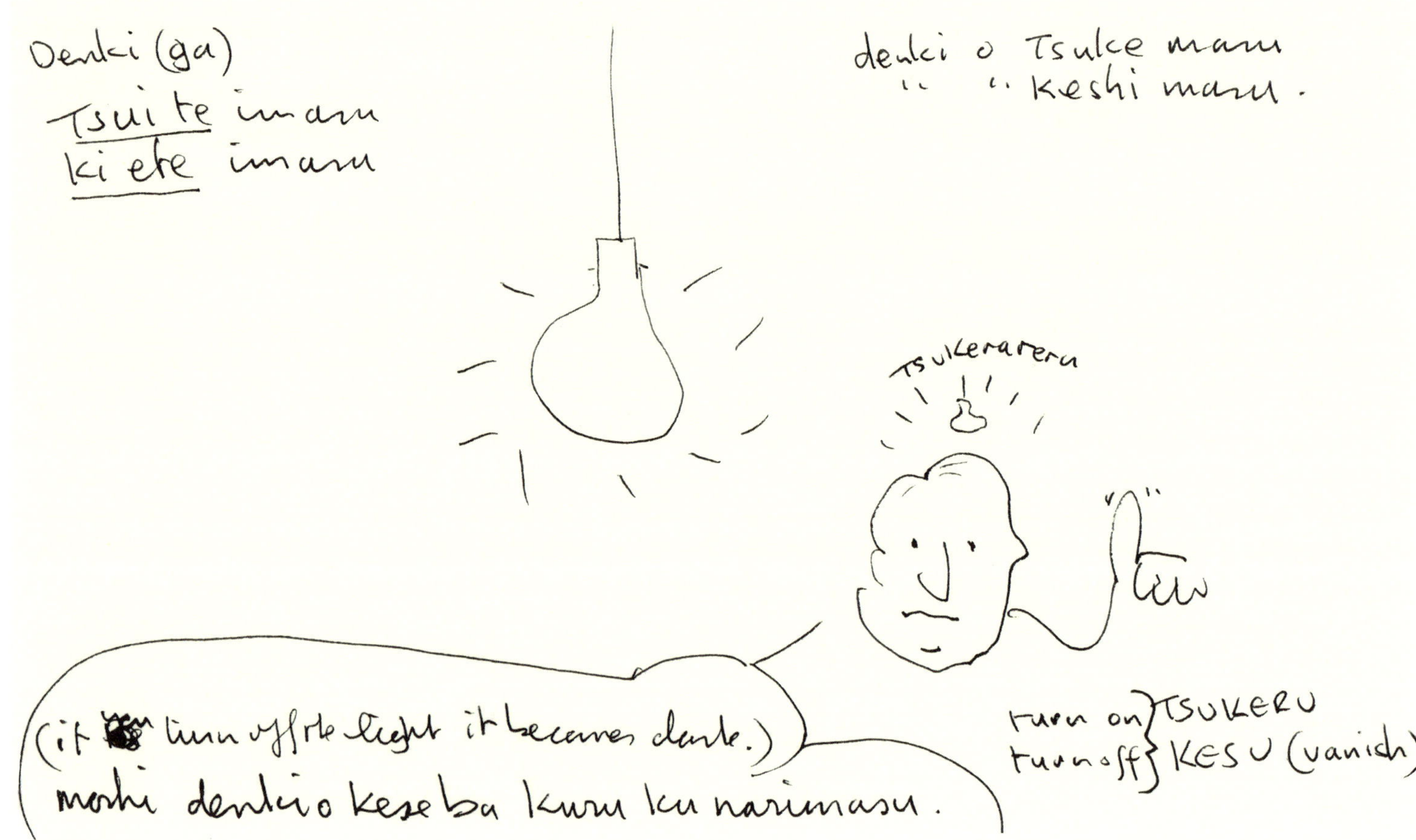

Denki(ga)tsuite imasu
The light is on
1977
8" x 4¾"
Ink

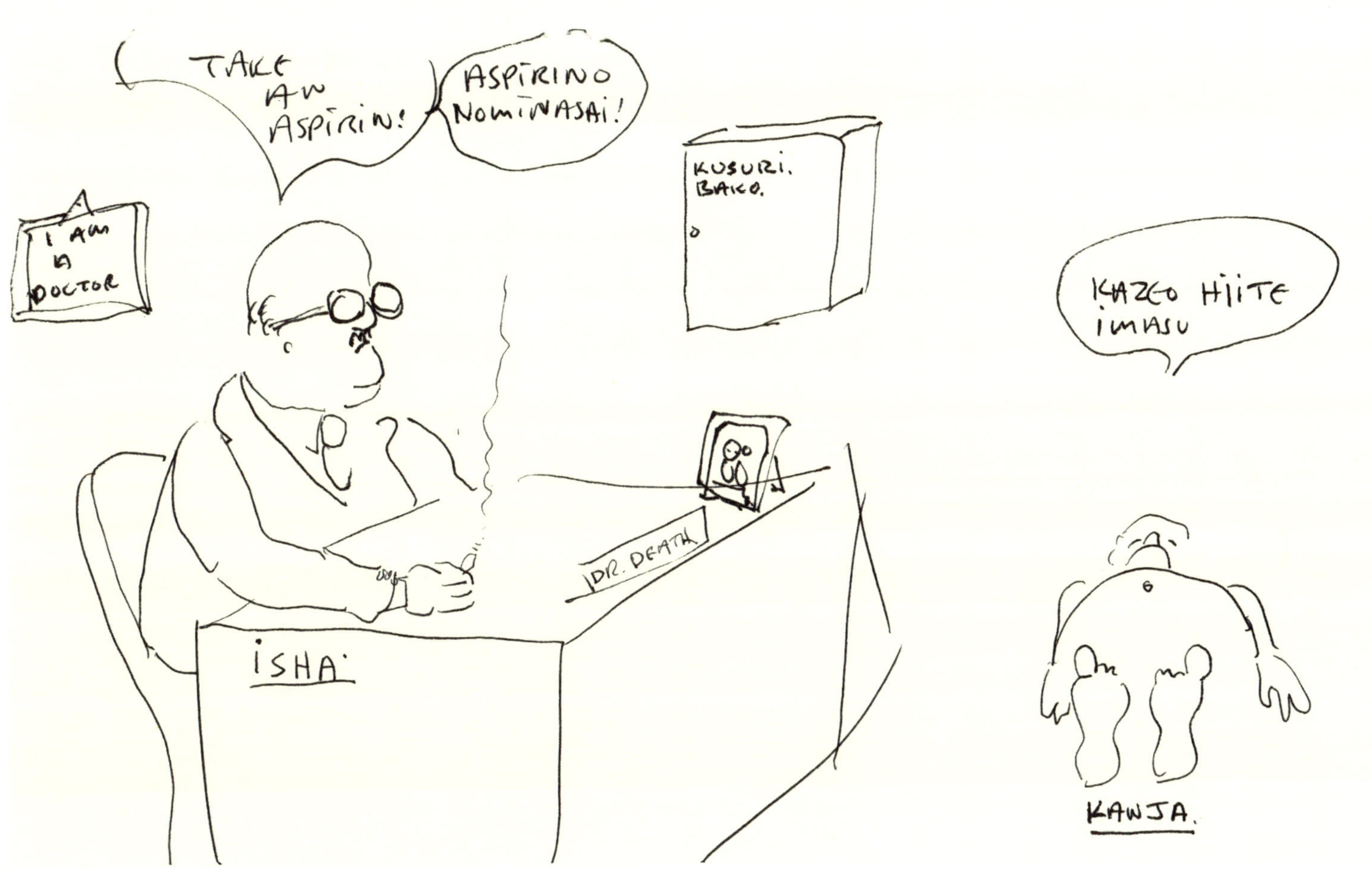

Kaze o hiite imasu. –
Aspirin o nominasai!
I have a cold. – Take an
aspirin!
1977
8″ x 5″
Ink

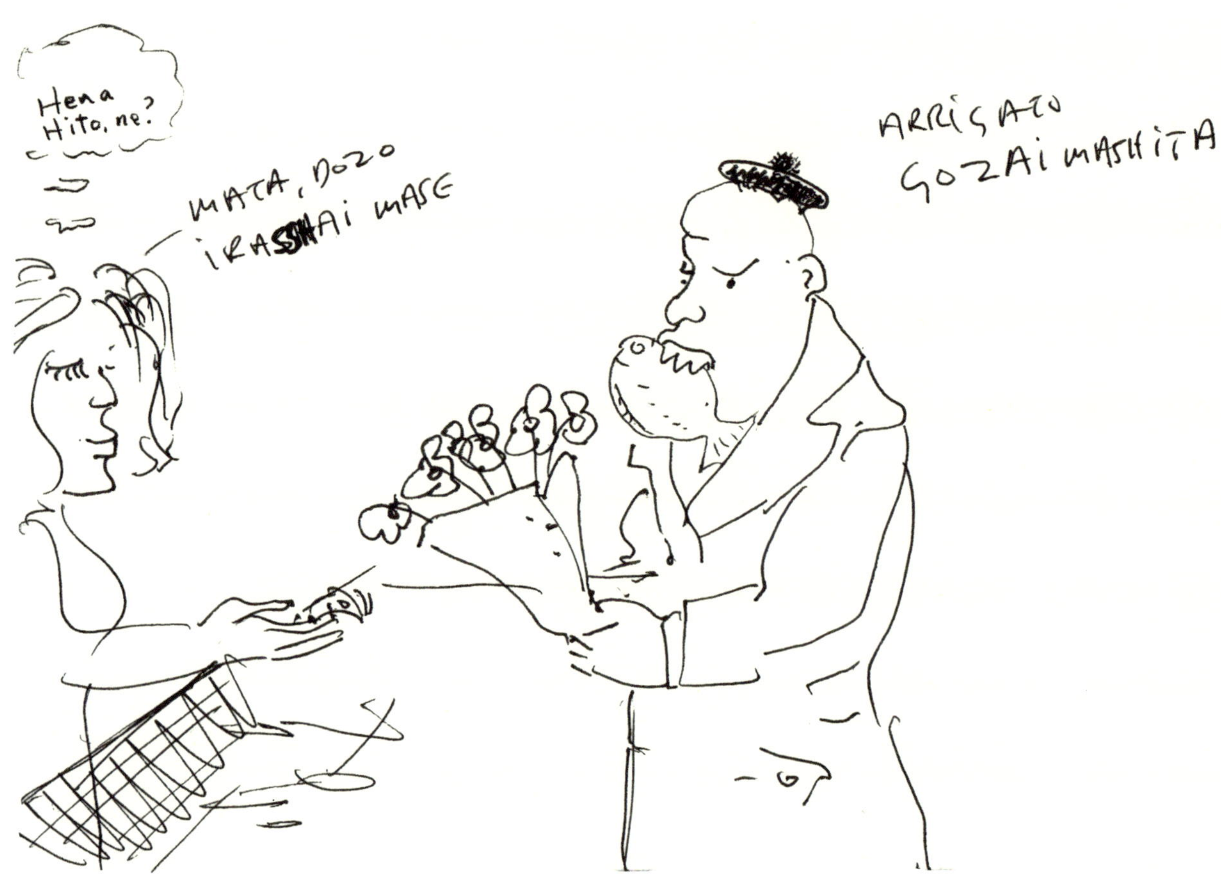

Mata dozo, irasshai mase –
Arigato gozai mashita – Hen
na hito ne?
Please come again – Thank
you very much – He's a
weirdo, isn't he?
1977
8" x 5"
Ink

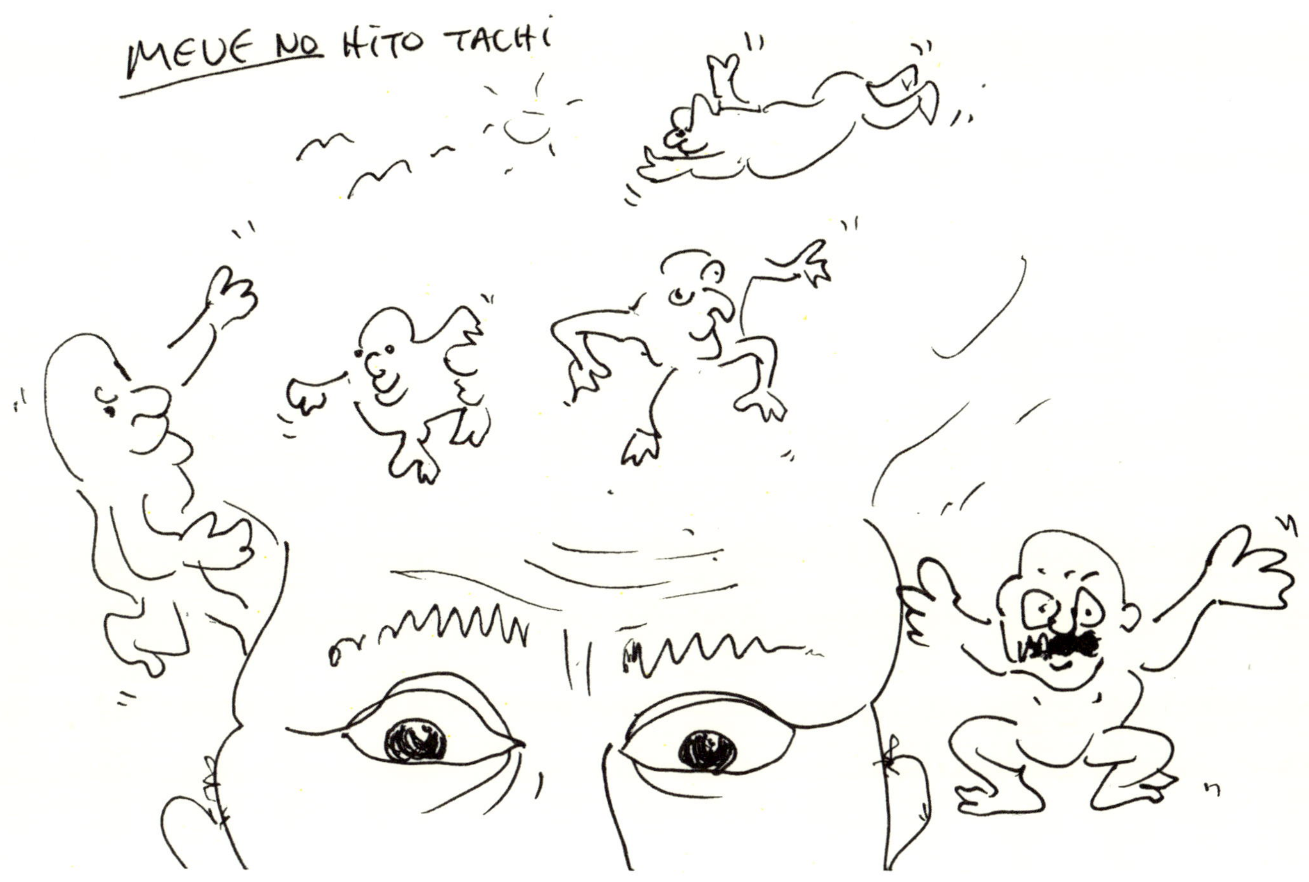

Meue no hito tachi
One's superiors
1977
8″ x 5″
Ink

atchie ittaka to omoimasu

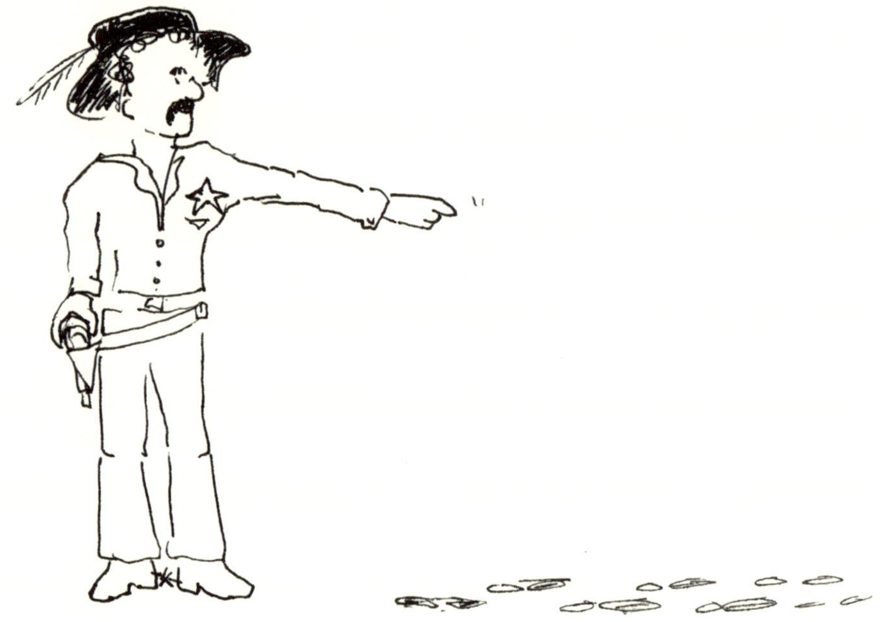

Atchie ittaka to omoimasu
I think he went there
1977
8" x 5"
Ink

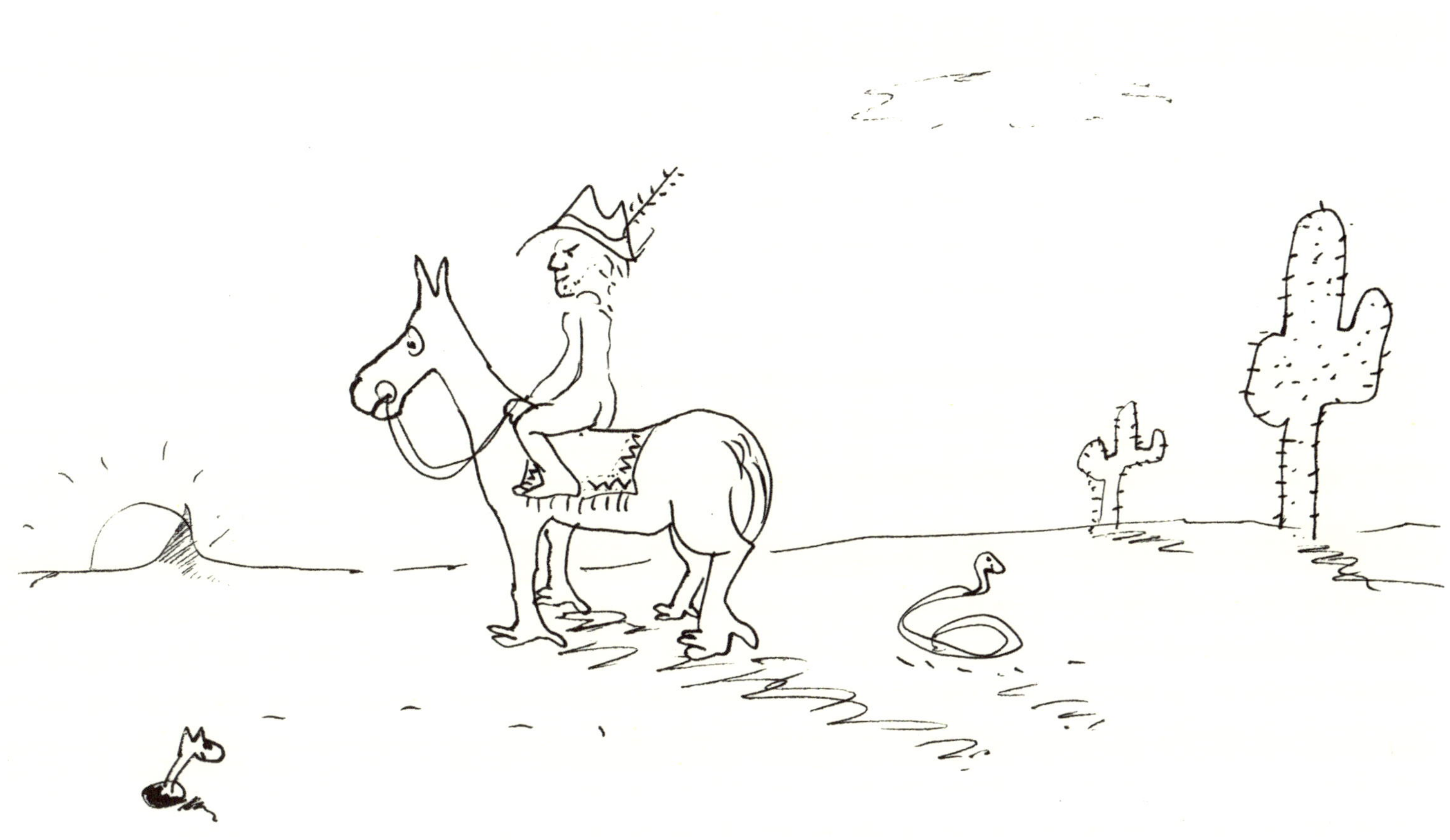

Untitled
1977
8″ x 5″
Ink

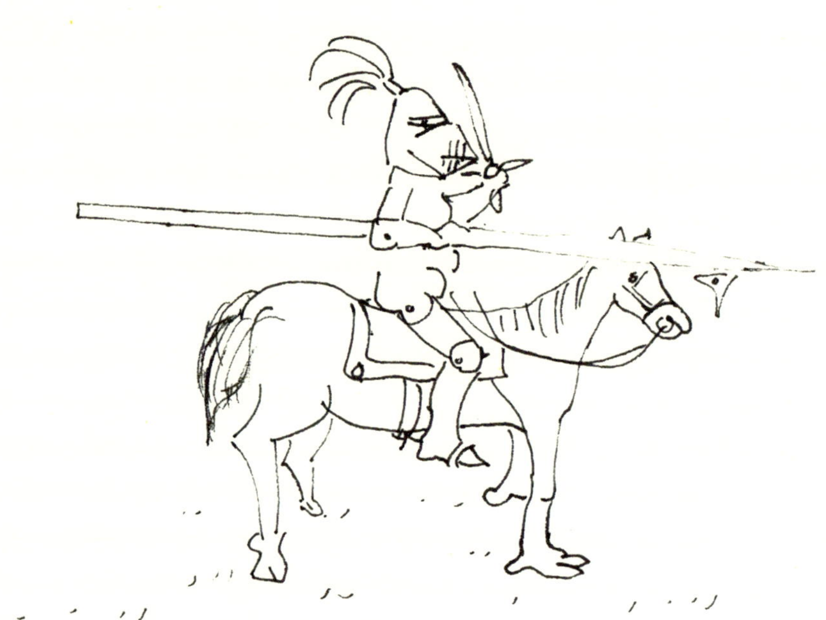

Untitled
1977
8″ x 5″
Ink

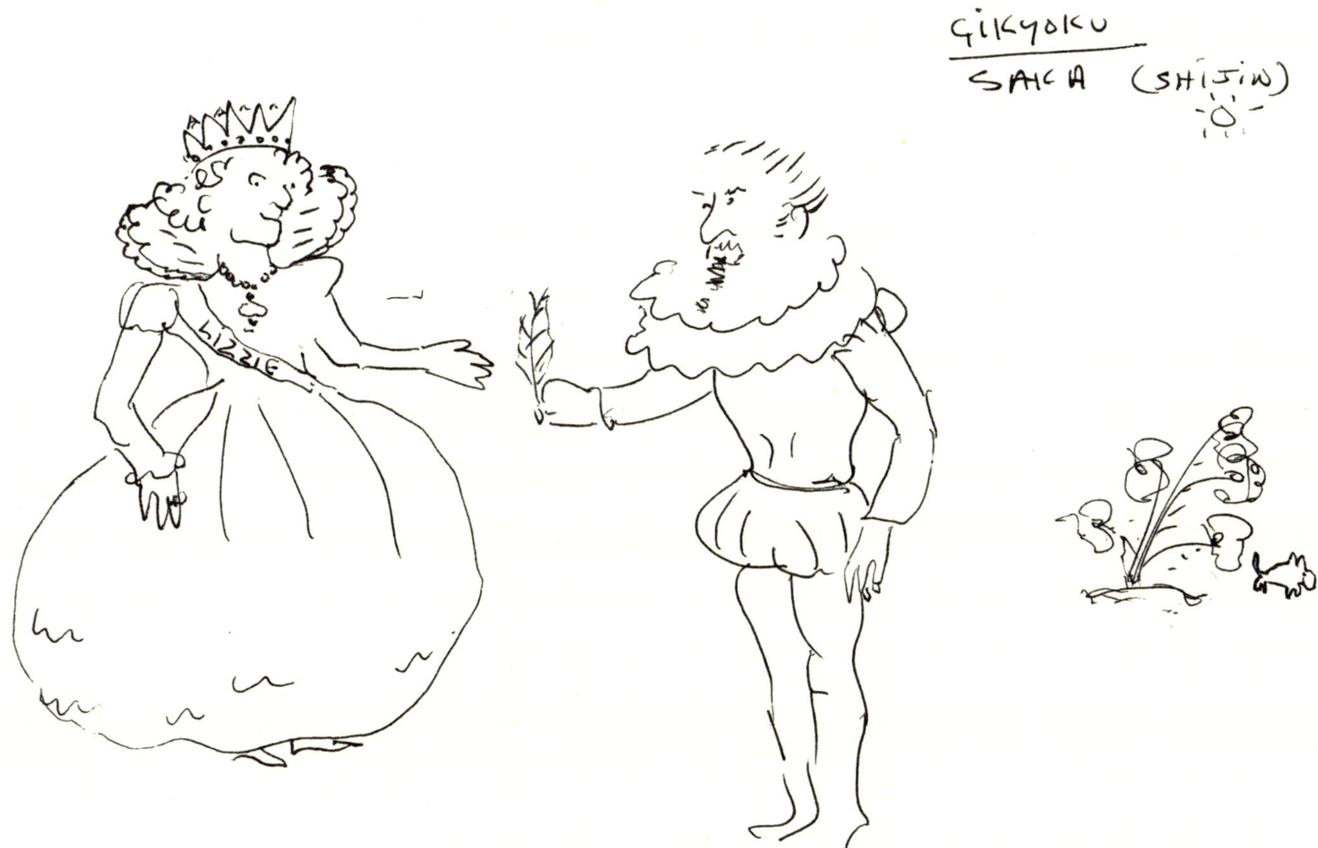

Gikyoku
Stage play
1977
8" x 5" x
Ink

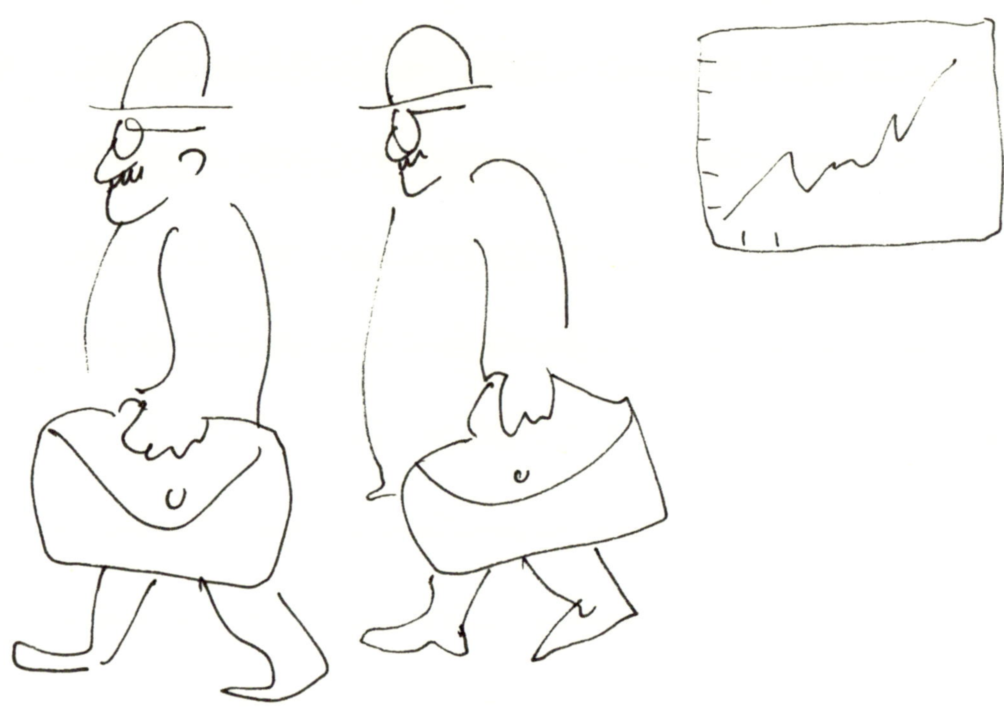

Experts are boomerang
rounding the world.
1977
8" x 5"
Ink

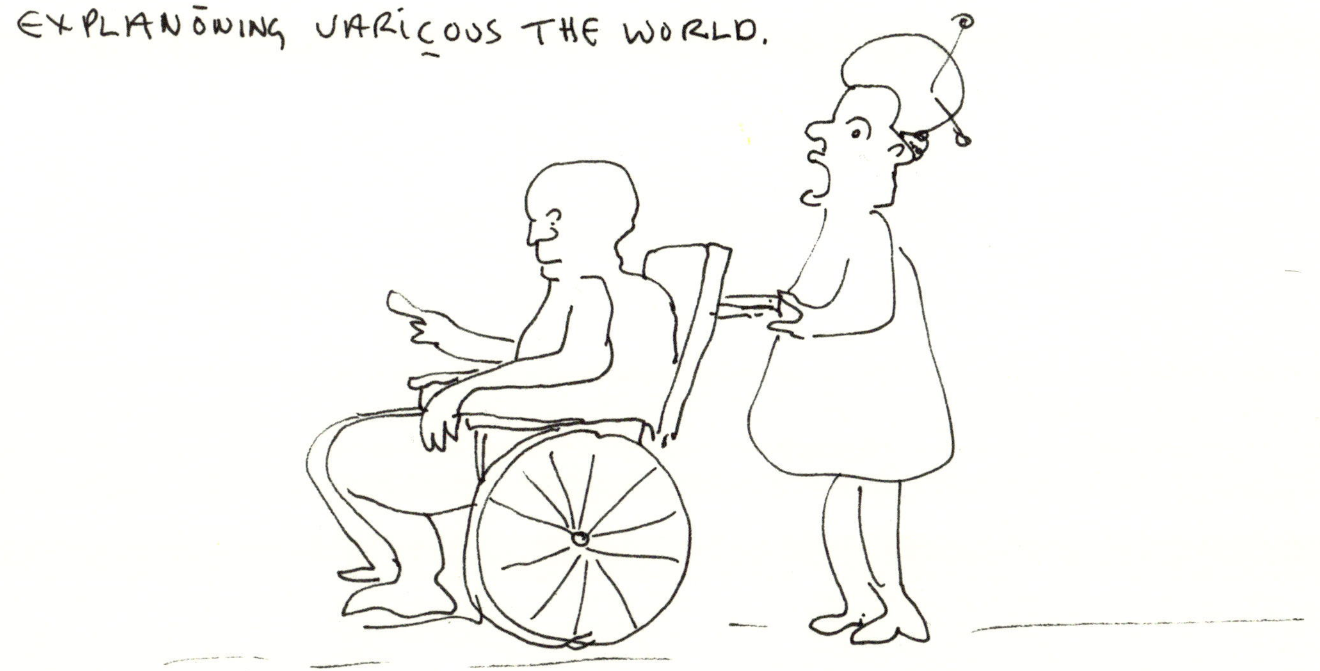

Explanowing varicous
the world.
1977
8″ x 5″
Ink

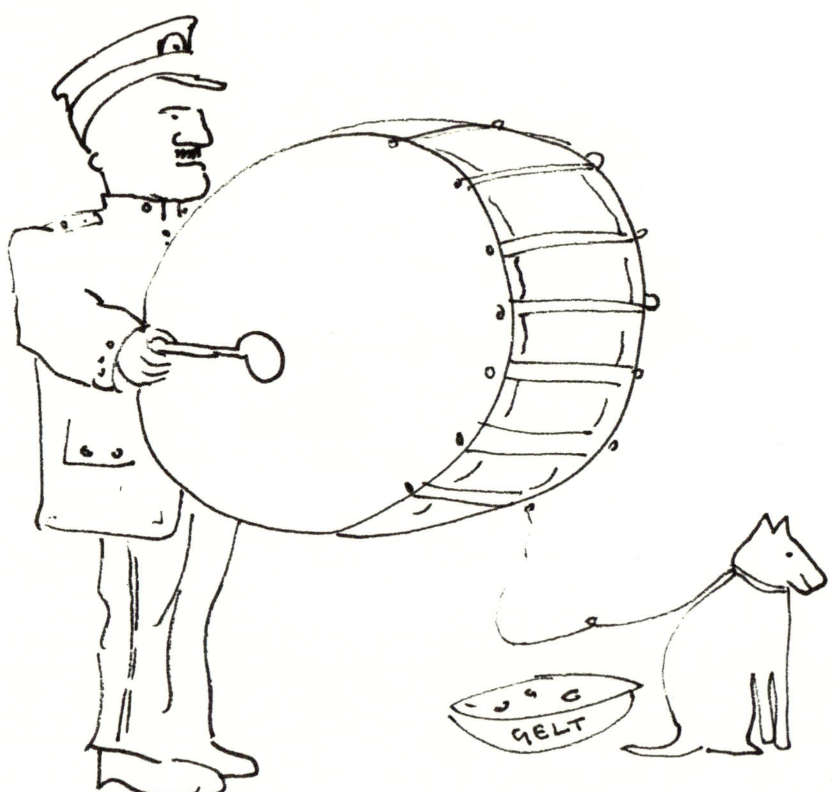

Untitled
1977
8″ x 5″
Ink

Bag One
A series of 15 original lithographs in a white plastic bag, 1970
Dorothee Hansen

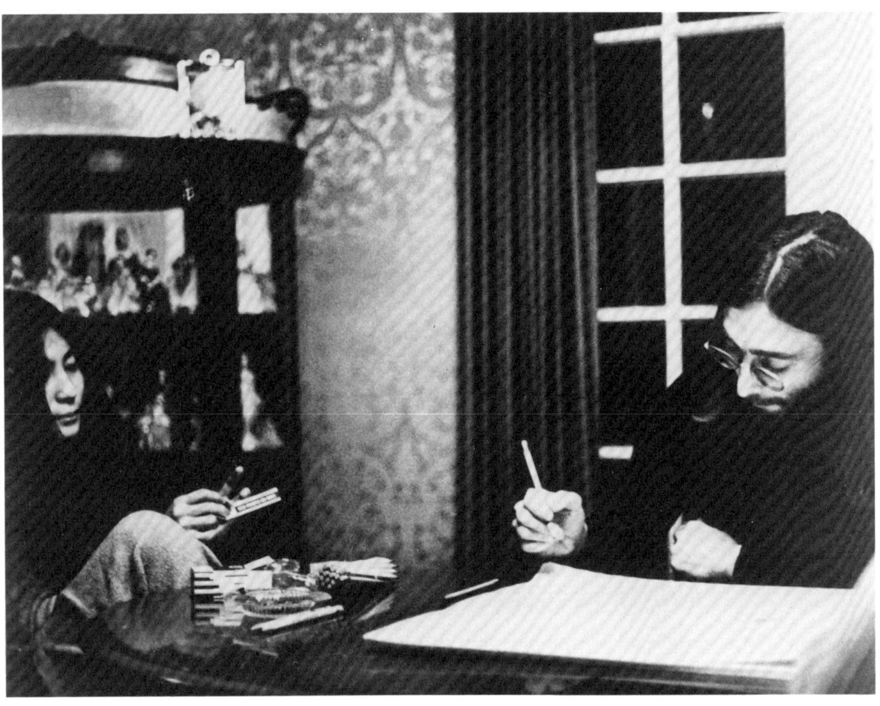

John Lennon with Yoko Ono signing the lithographs for the *Bag One* portfolio at Ronnie Hawkins' farm near Toronto, in December 1969. Photo: Ritchie Yorke Archives

45 prints, hors de commerce, each print signed by hand and numbered from HC I to HC VL
300 prints, each signed by hand and numbered from 1 to 300
Printed on BFK Rives paper

In 1968 Anthony Fawcett, who had collaborated for the first time with Lennon and Yoko Ono on the Acorn Event (see p. 158), suggested issuing a portfolio of lithographs. He showed Lennon, who had no experience of printing techniques, that working with litho paints and writing instruments on prepared paper was basically no different from the work he had done previously.

In 1968 and 1969 Lennon produced a large series of drawings using this technique, from which Fawcett and American prints publisher Ed Newman selected thirteen. The prints represented three scenes from the marriage in Gibraltar, one from the subsequent *Bed-In*, one showing the faces of Lennon and Ono, and eight erotic motifs. Lennon was delighted with the results of trial print runs by Aldo Crommylynck, who was Picasso's printer in Paris. However, as time was

short, printing was actually carried out at the Curwen studio in London. Lennon monitored the production precisely and added a sheet containing a poem, which he wrote straight onto the zinc plate at the printer's on 18 June 1969. What is more, with only a few strokes of the pen, he designed an additional fly sheet for the cover of the series showing himself and Yoko Ono embracing.

Parisian couturier Ted Lapidus designed a white plastic bag with a zipper as a portfolio for the sheets. At the end of December 1969, when Lennon was in Canada for an interview with Prime Minister Trudeau, he signed all of the 5175 prints at the farmhouse of singer Ronnie Hawkins near Toronto.

The *Bag One* portfolio was presented for the first time on 15 January 1970 at the London Arts Gallery in New Bond Street and went on sale for 550 pounds each. Next day, Scotland Yard officers confiscated the eight erotic prints. All the newspapers reported the scandal. Eugene Schuster, the American owner of the gallery, won the legal case involving the lithos on 27 April 1970. His defence counsel had cited the example of Picasso's erotic works, which had not been confiscated as pornography.

On 14 March, *Bag One* was shown in Germany for the first time at the denise rené hans mayer Gallery in Düsseldorf. In America, the Lee Nordness Gallery in New York was the first to show the 15 lithographs. The vernissage was attended by Salvador Dalí, whom Lennon and Yoko Ono had met in Paris on 24 March 1969. No prints were seized at any of these exhibitions, but at the Merrill Chase Gallery in Oak Brook near Chicago, on 28 March 1970, five prints were confiscated on grounds of alleged obscenity.

The title *Bag One* indicates that a second series was planned. It was to take as its theme the Chinese classic "The I Ching or Book of Changes". This project was never realised. At the same time, the title also suggests the bag perform-

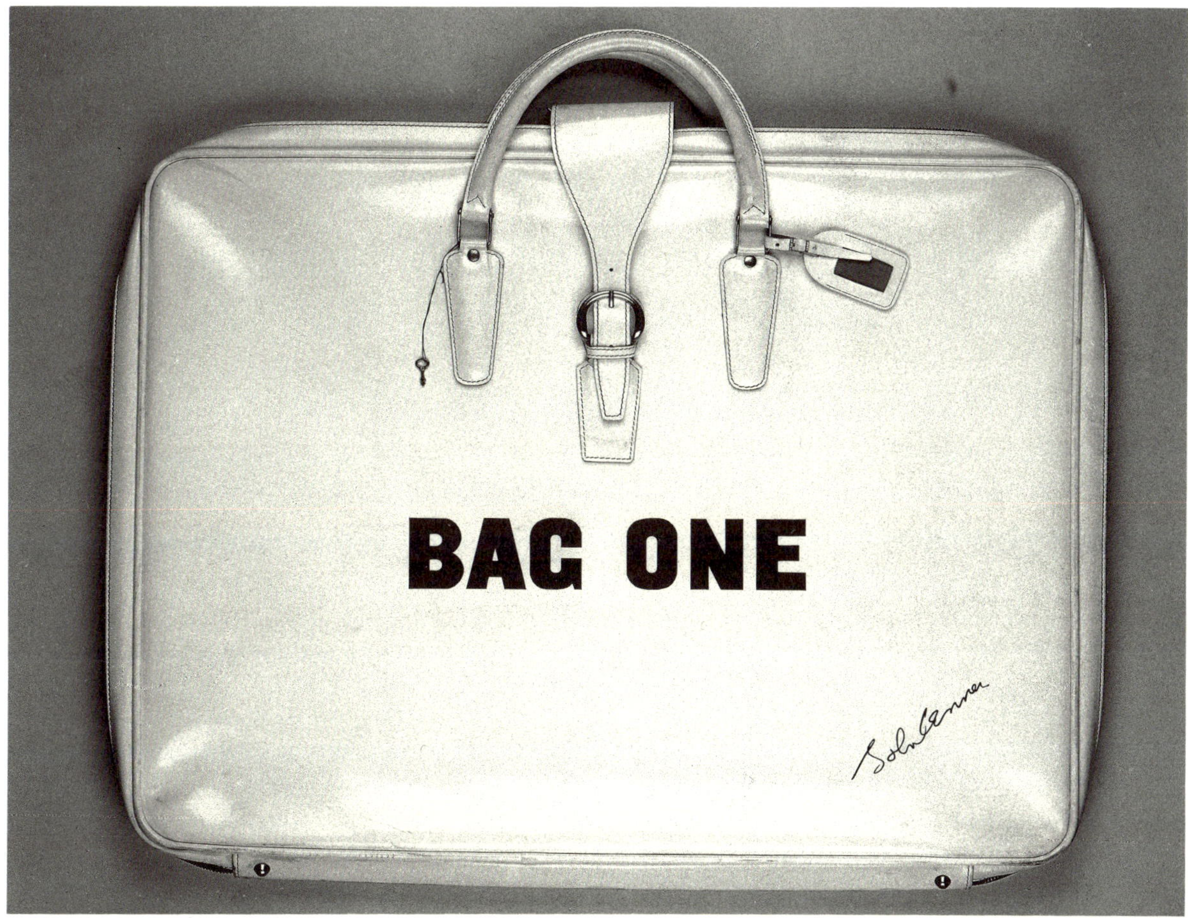

Bag One, 1970
The white plastic bag

ances at which Lennon and Ono appeared to the audience wrapped in a bag (see p. 176). The bag hides its contents. But that makes it all the more interesting for the audience. No sooner had the portfolio been opened and the prints publicly displayed at the London exhibition than the police seized them in the name of law and order. Once the press had described the erotic motifs, the curiosity of the public was aroused; all the more so because the pictures could no longer be seen.

In other words, *Bag One* was more than just a series of lithographs with motifs recalling the wedding and honeymoon of Lennon and Ono, but was also a multiple, revealing the prudery of society in dealing with love and sexuality. In her 1962 *Bag Piece*, Yoko Ono had already taken up this subject (see p. 176): together with her former husband Tony Cox, she had wrapped herself in a black bag. Inside the bag (the audience had been told) they would undress and dress again. Then they got out of the bag. The audience could see that they were moving inside the bag, but the interpretation of these movements was left entirely to their imagination.

Bag One, 1970
Cover sheet
23″ x 30″
Lithograph, black

John Lennon/bag one

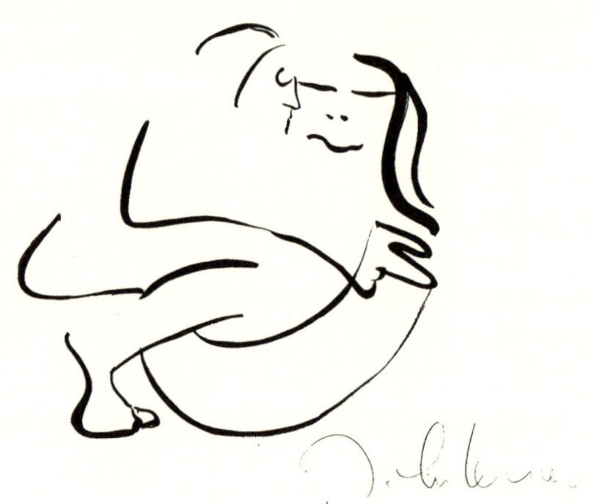

**Cinnamon Press
New York
1970**

Bag One, 1970
An Alphabeth (This is my
story both humble and true)
22¾" x 30"
Lithograph, black

A is for Parrot which we can plainly see.
B is for glasses which we can plainly see.
C is for plastic which we can plainly see
D is for Doris
E is for binoculars you'll get it in five
E is for Ethel who lives next door
G is for Orange which we love to eat when we can get them because
   they come from abroad.
H is for England and (Heather)
I is for monkey we see in the tree
J is for parrot which we can plainly see
K is for shoetop we wear to the ball
L is for larto because brown
M is for Venezuela where the oranges come from
N is for Brazil near Venezuela (very near)
O is for football which we kick about a bit
T is for Tommy who won the war
Q is a garden which we can plainly see
R is for intestines which hurt when we dance
S is for pancake or whole wheat bread
U is for Ethel who lives on the hill
P is arab and her sister will
U is for me
W is for lighter which never lights
X is easter — have one yourself
Y is a crooked letter and you can't straighten it
Z is for Apple which we can plainly see.

This is my story both humble and true
take it to pieces and mend it with glue

                    John Lennon 1969. Feb.

70/300

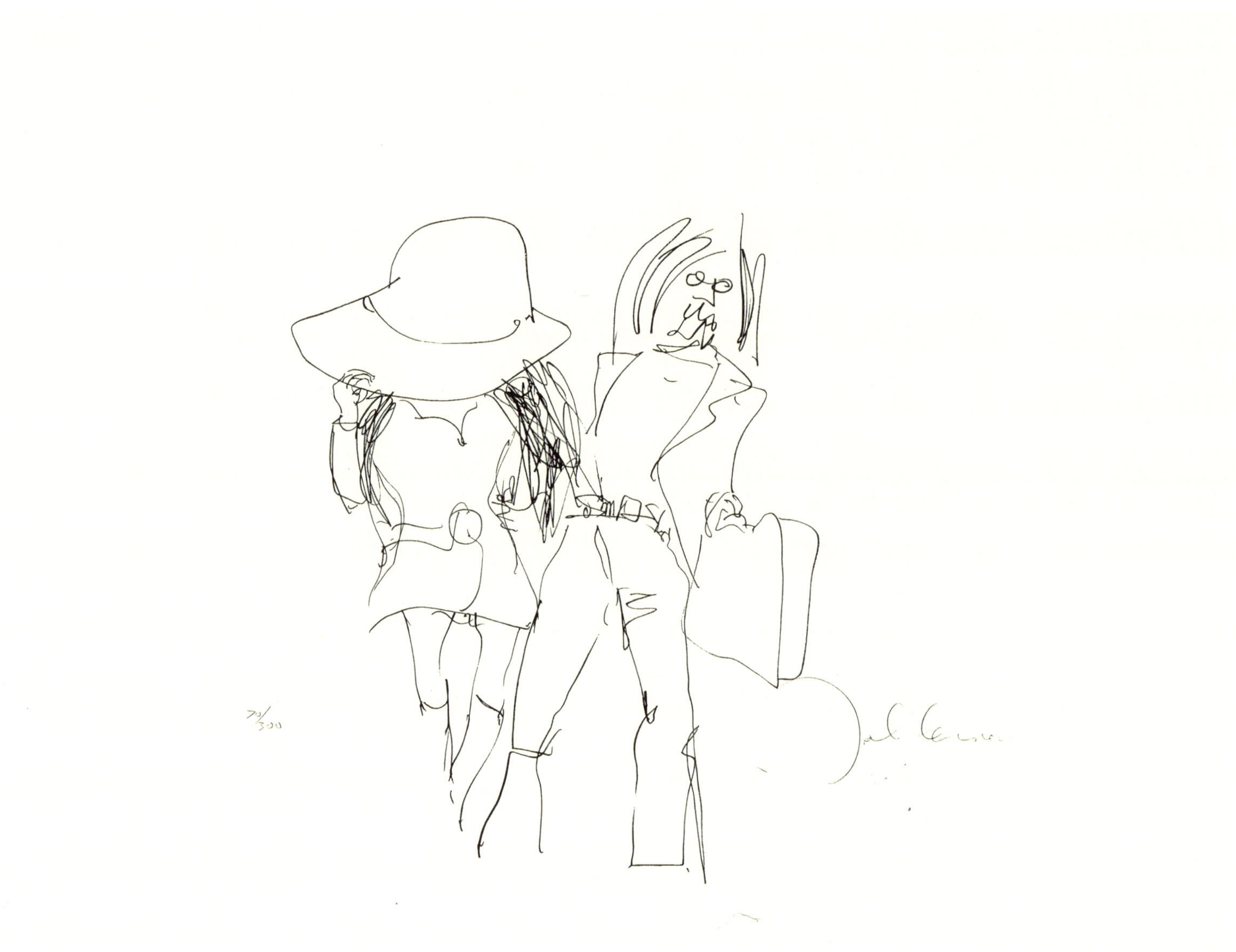

Bag One, 1970
The honeymoon
30″ x 22½″
Lithograph, black

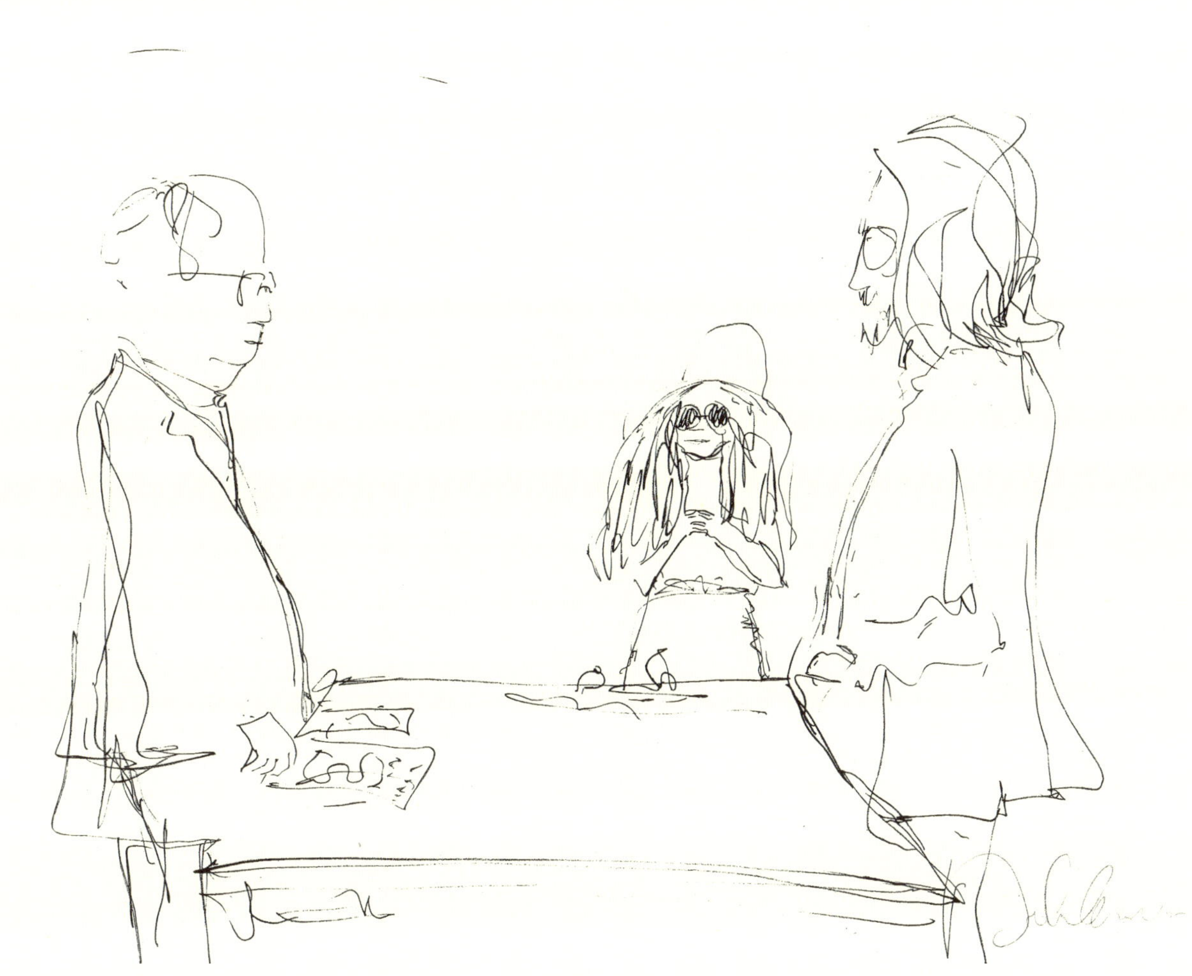

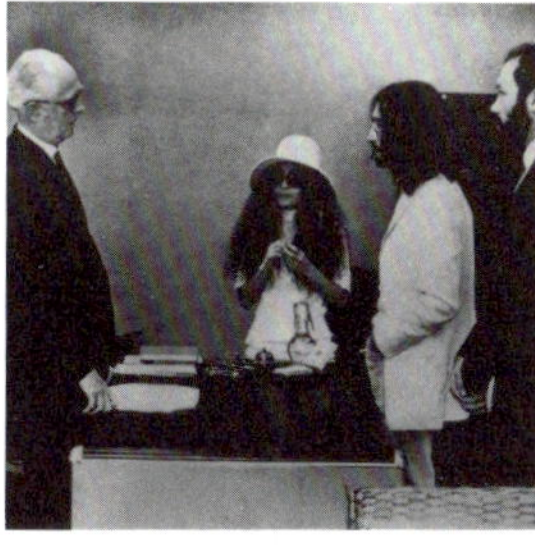

John Lennon and Yoko Ono
in front of the registrar in
Gibraltar, 20 March 1969.
Photo: David Nutter

Bag One, 1970
I do (in front of the registrar
in Gibraltar)
30″ x 22¾″
Lithograph, black

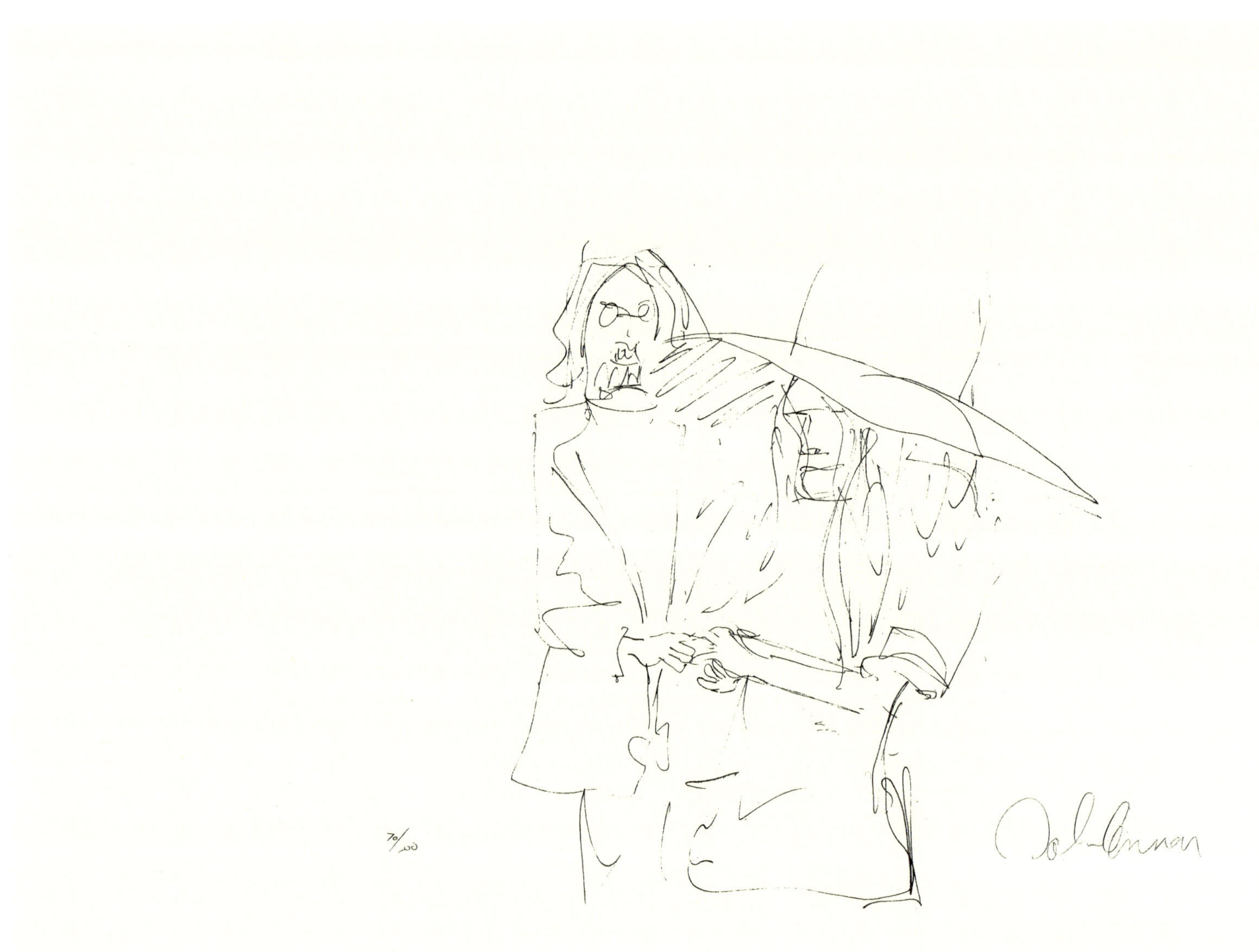

Bag One, 1970
Untitled (wedding ceremony
in Gibraltar)
30″ x 22¾″
Lithograph, black

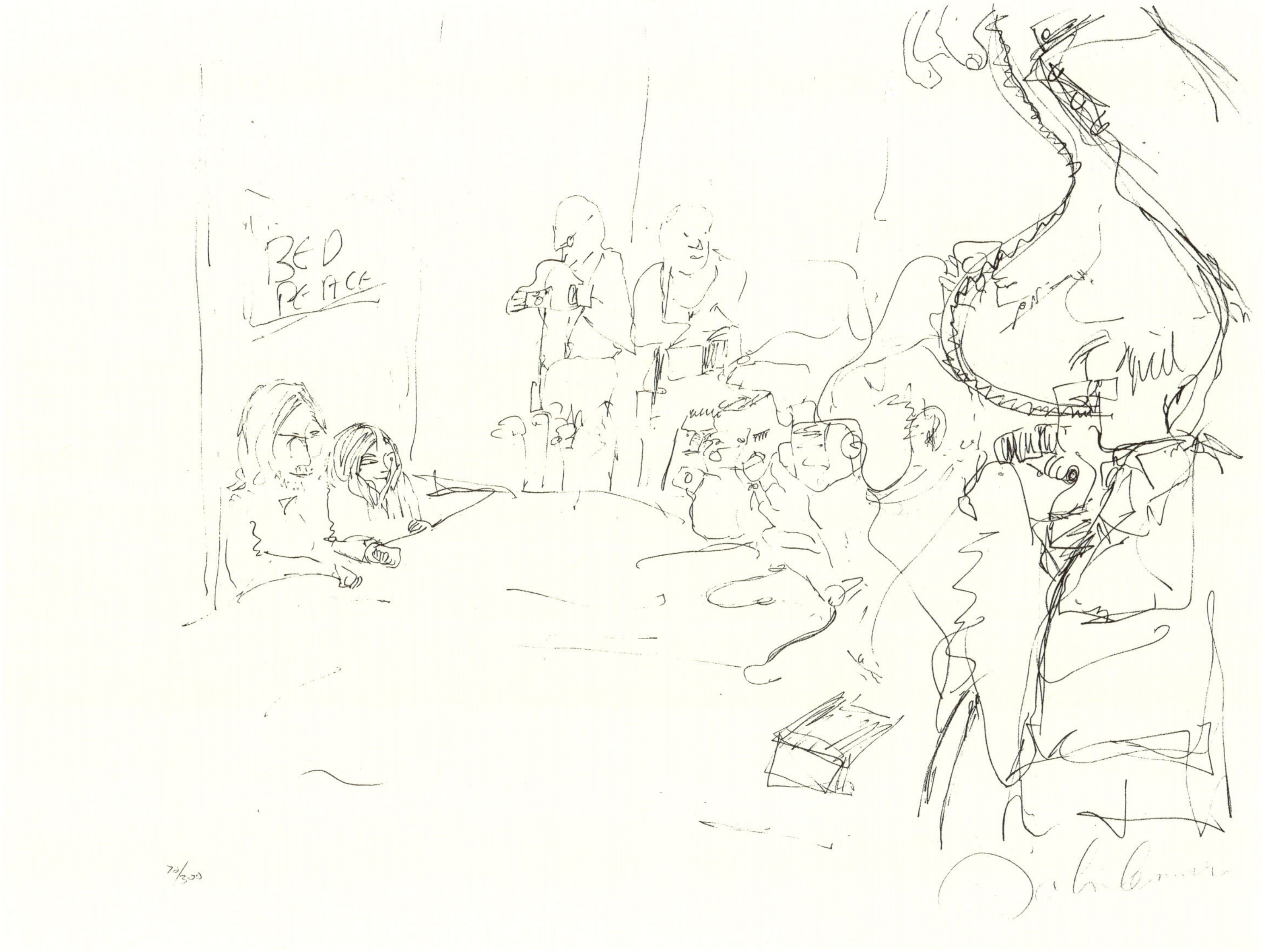

Bag One, 1970
Bed-In for Peace
30″ x 22¾″
Lithograph, black

Bed-In for peace at the
Amsterdam Hilton, in
March 1969.
Photo: Ruud Hoff

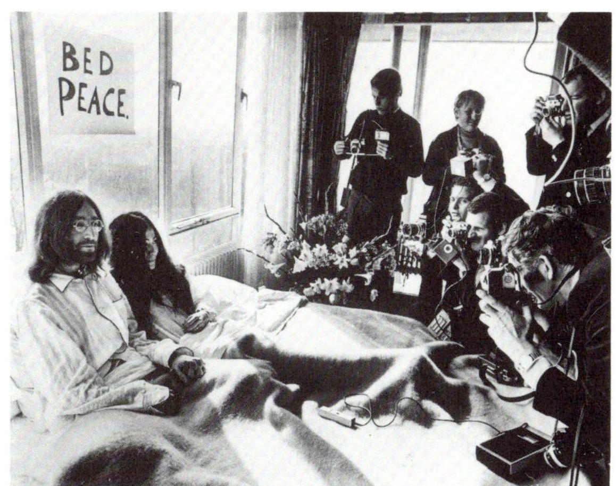

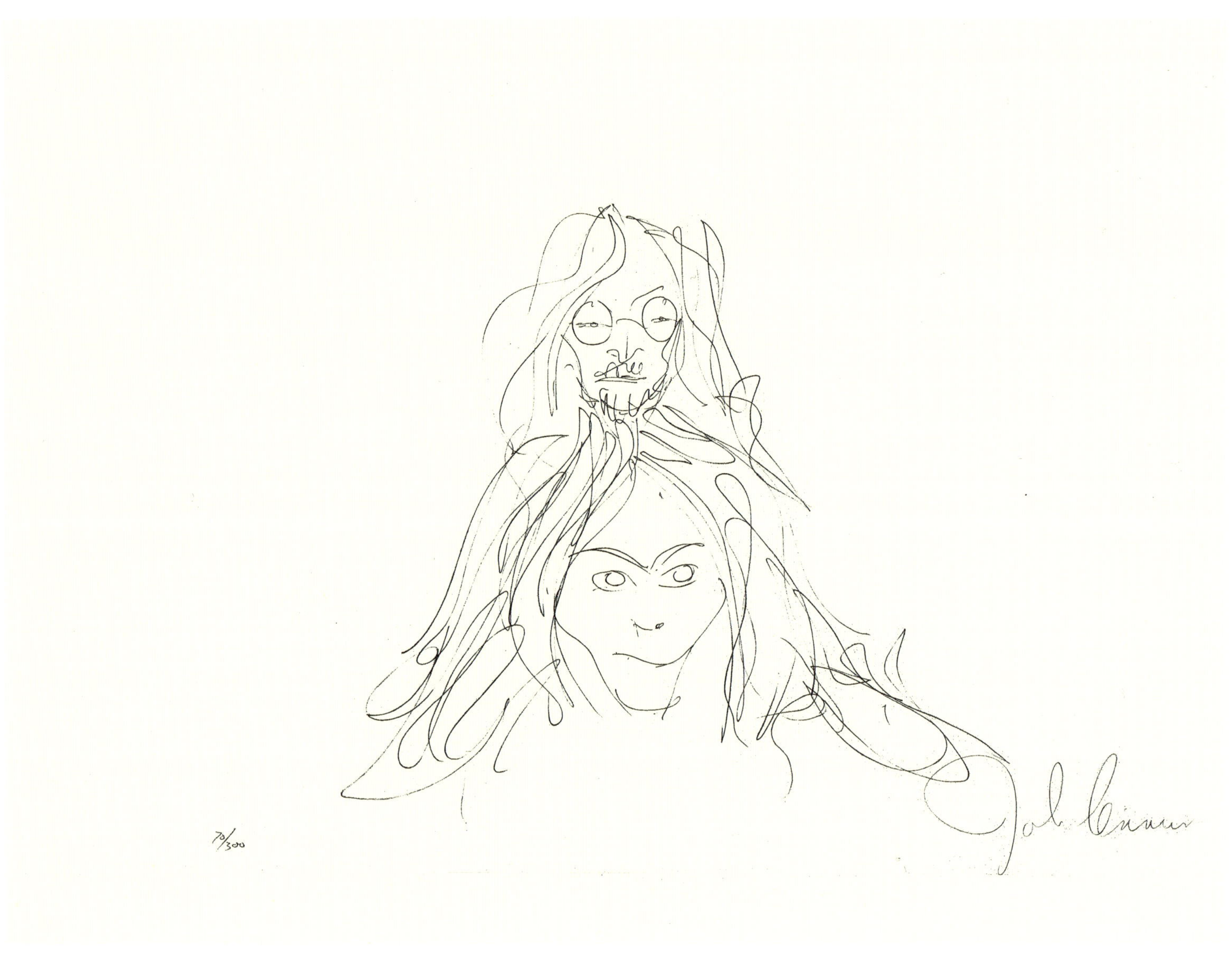

Bag One, 1970
John and Yoko
30″ x 22¾″
Lithograph, black

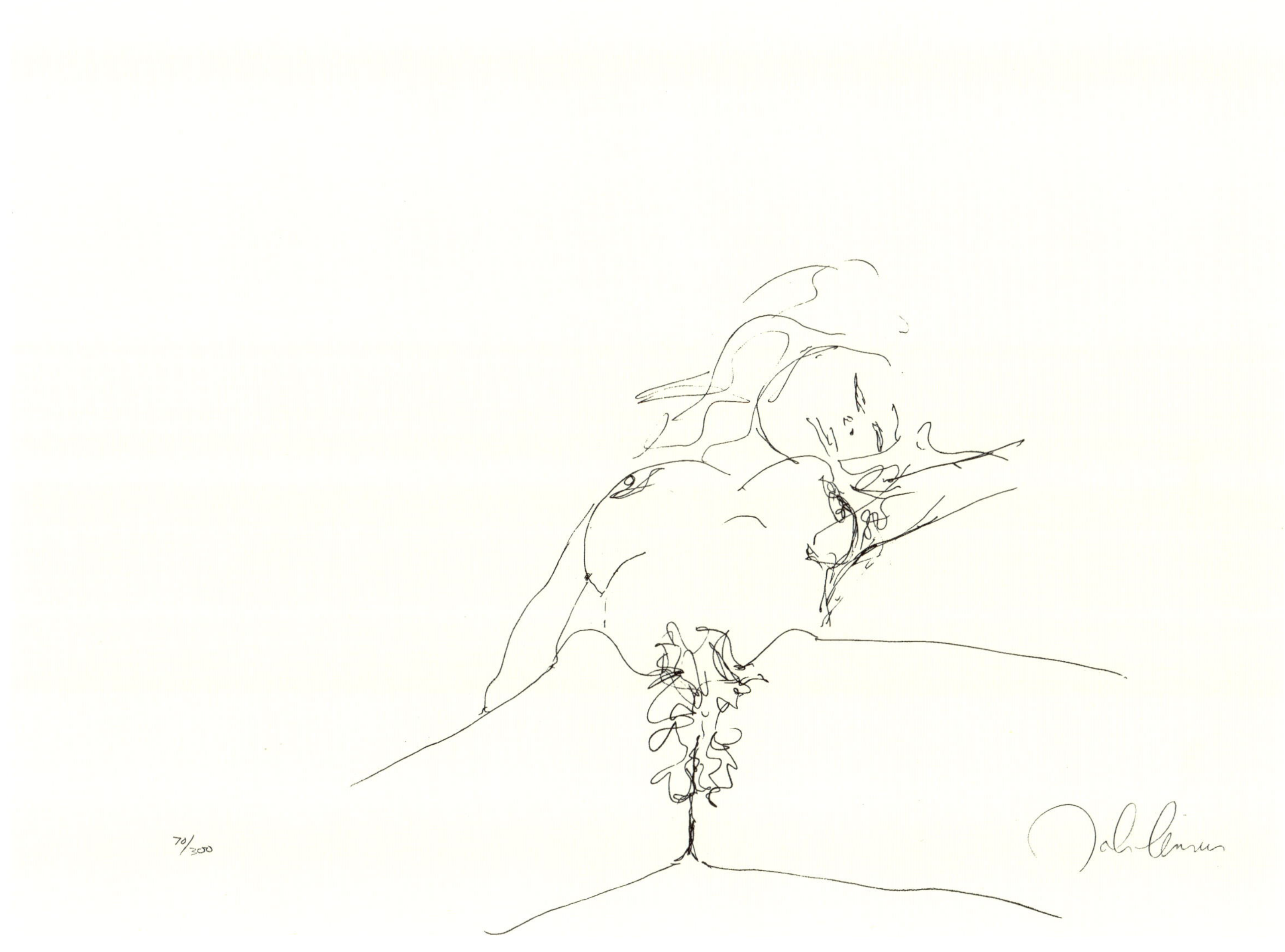

Bag One, 1970
Untitled
29¾" x 22¾"
Lithograph, brown

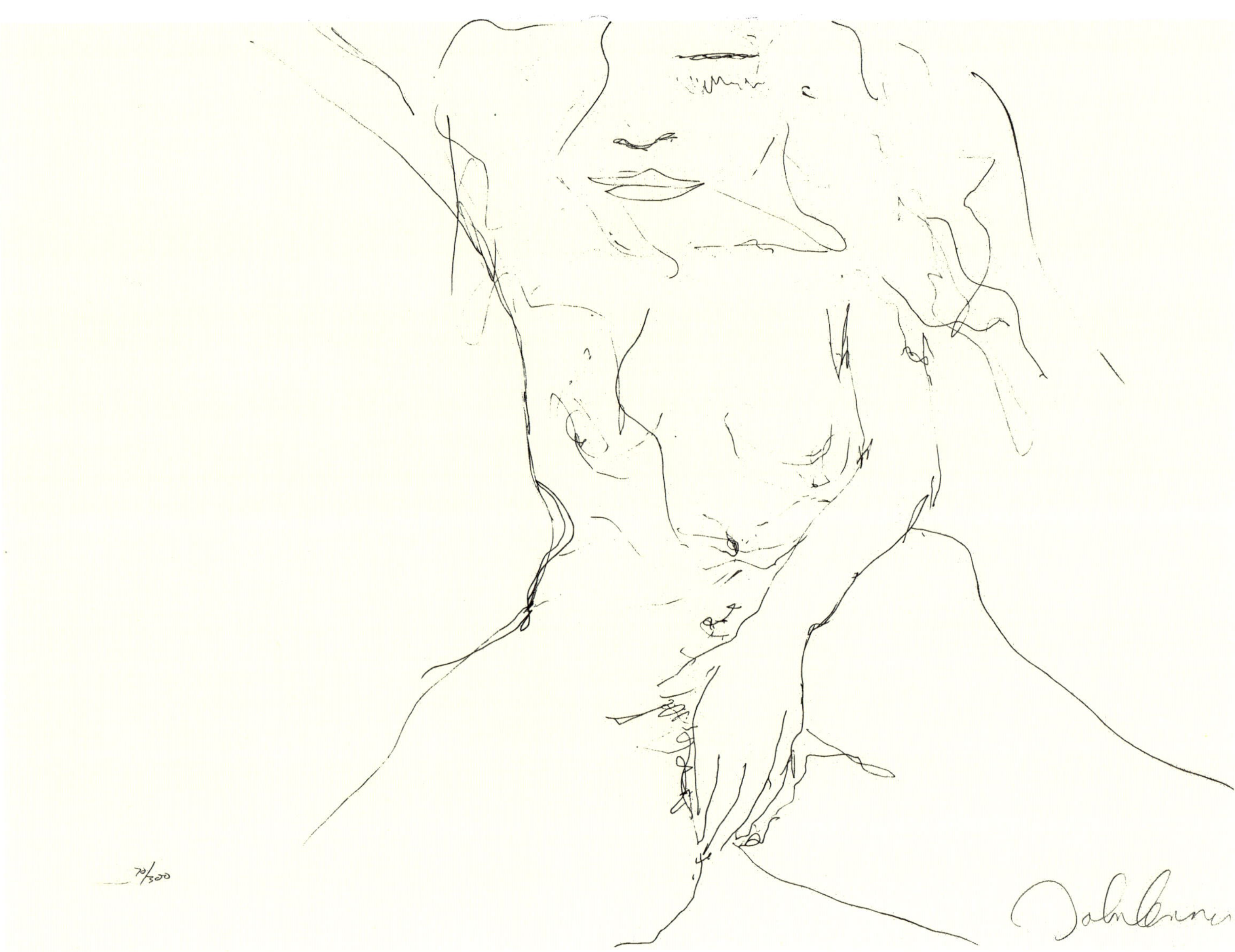

Bag One, 1970
Untitled
30″ x 22¾″
Lithograph, brown

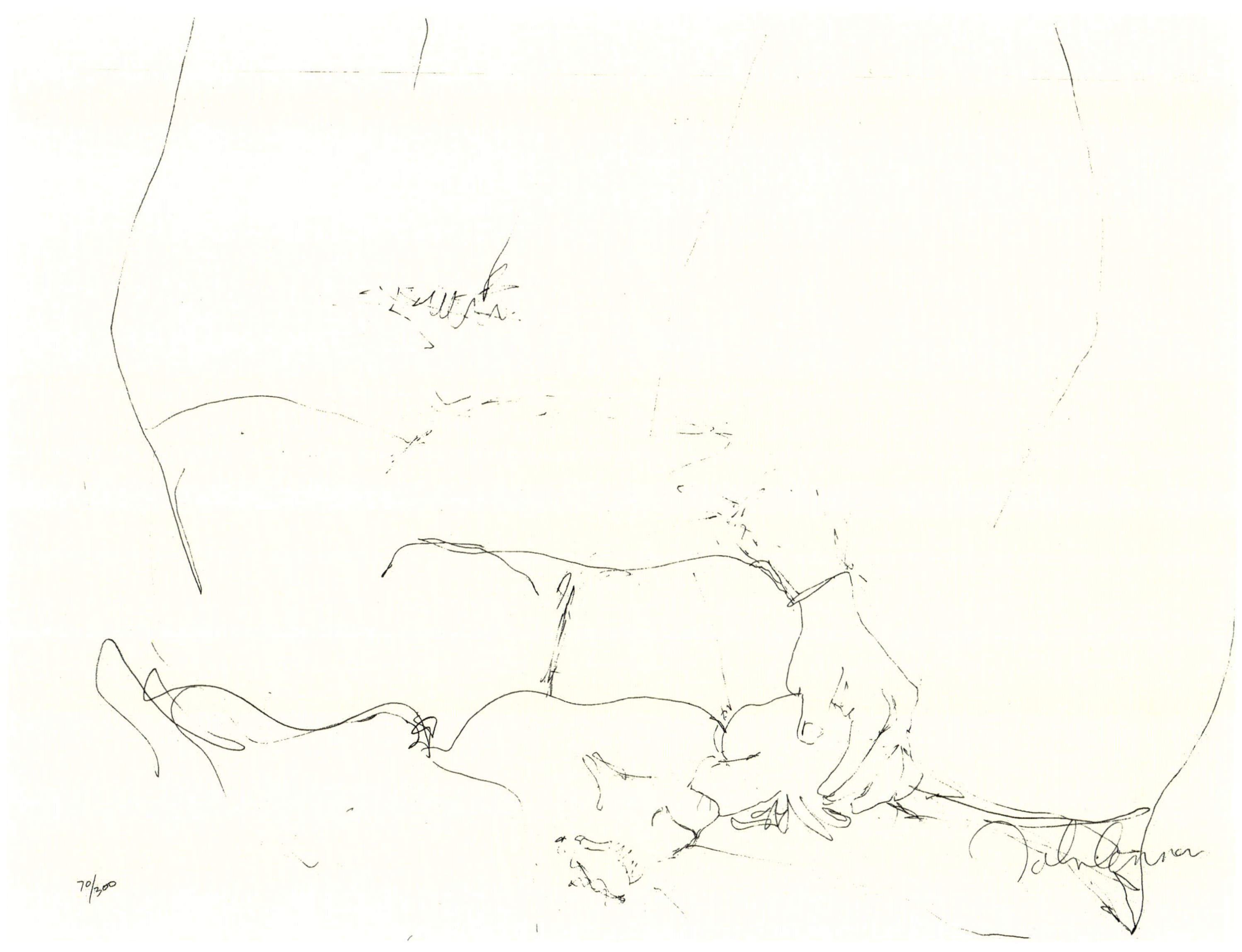

Bag One, 1970
Untitled
30″ x 22¾″
Lithograph, brown

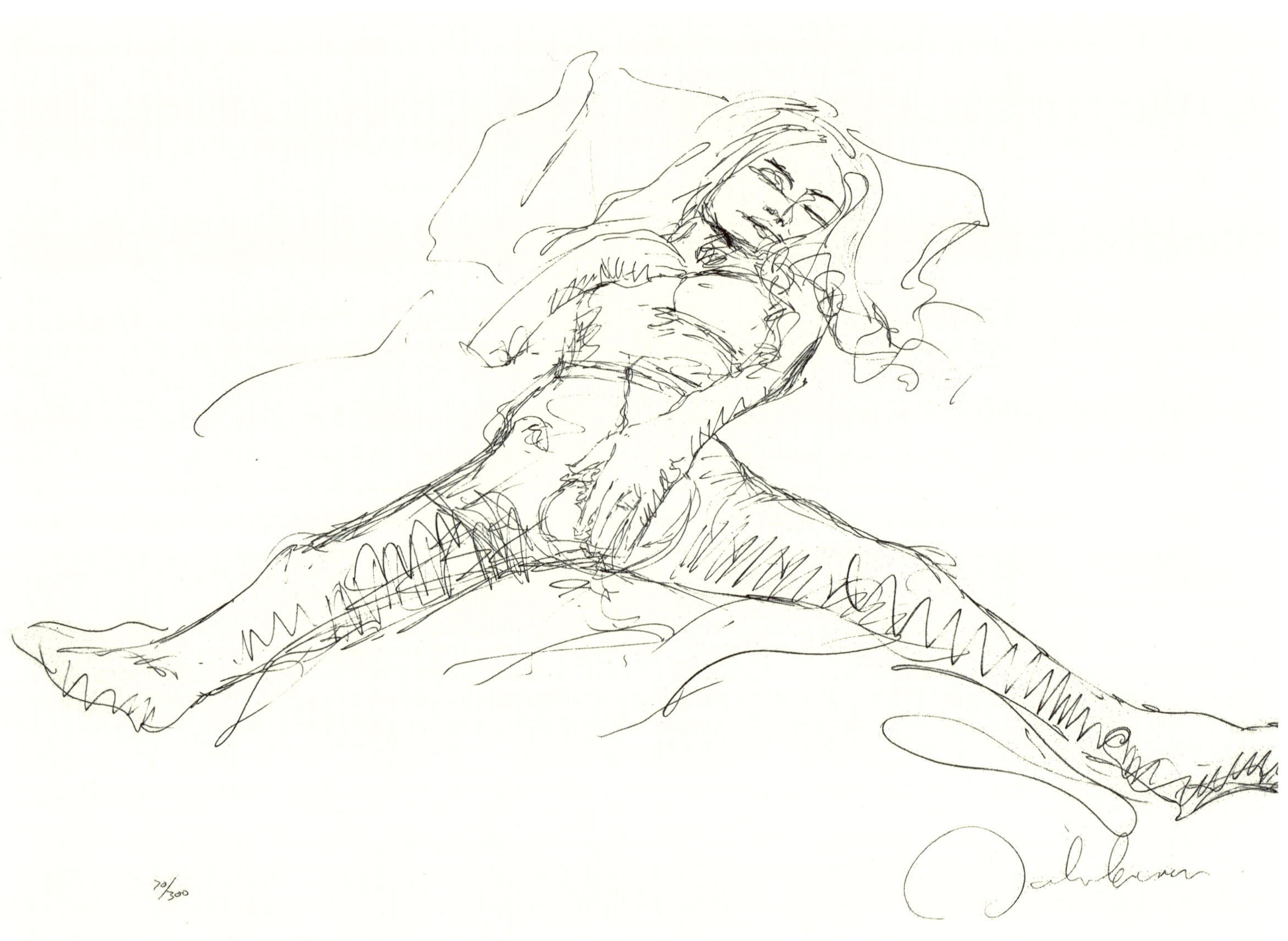

Bag One, 1970
Untitled
30″ x 22¾″
Lithograph, brown

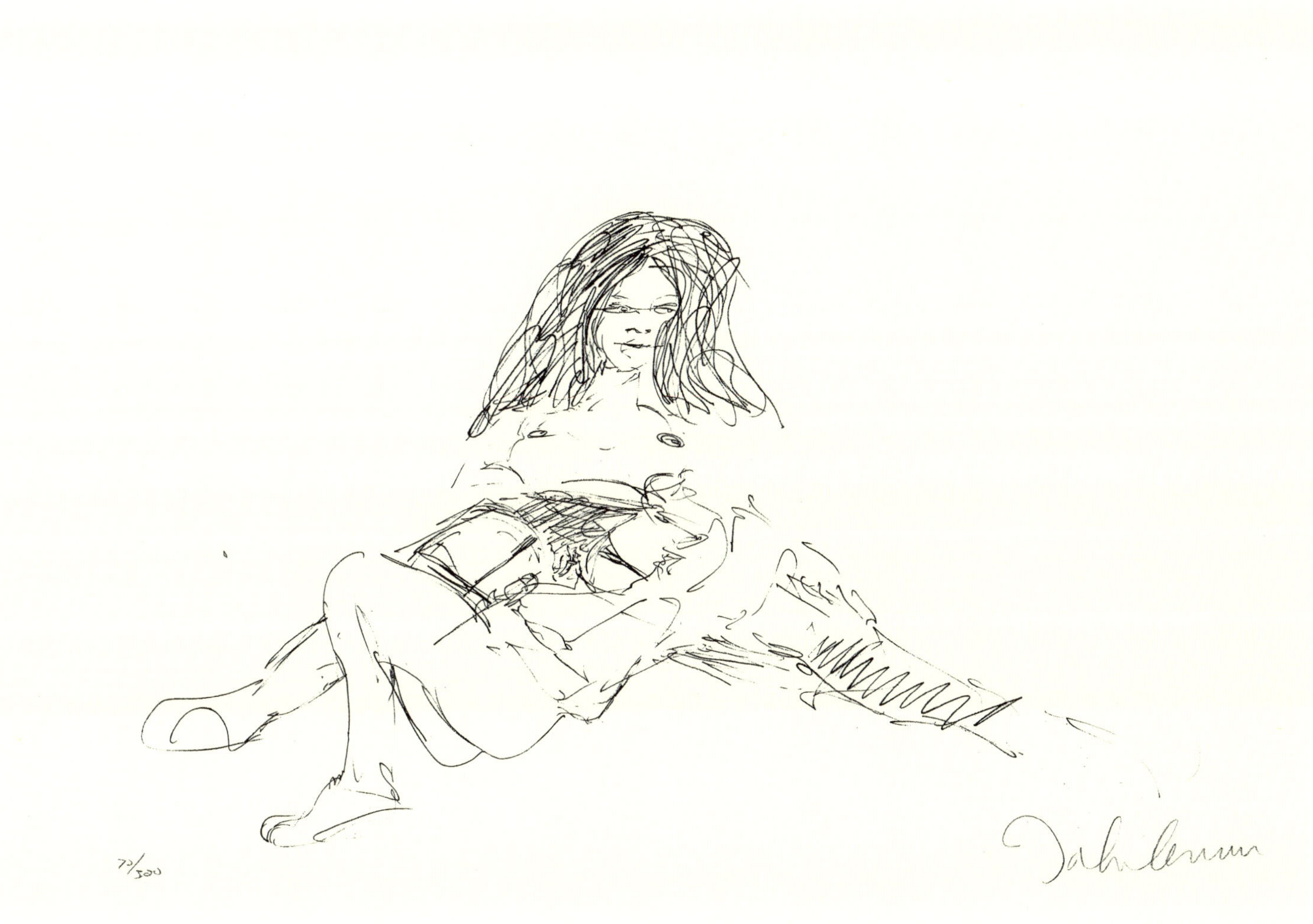

Bag One, 1970
Untitled
30″ x 22¾″
Lithograph, black

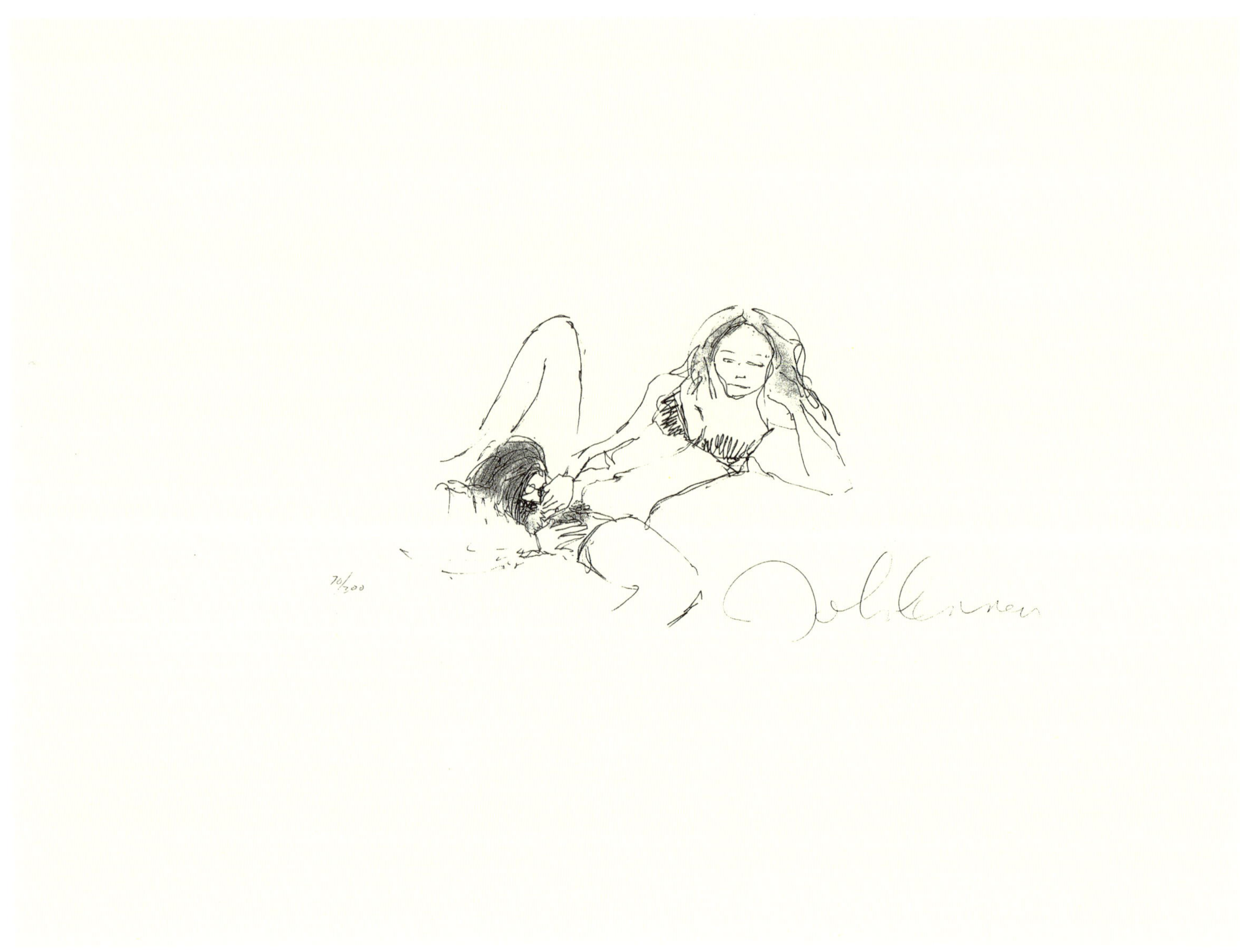

Bag One, 1970
Untitled
30″ x 23″
Lithograph, brown

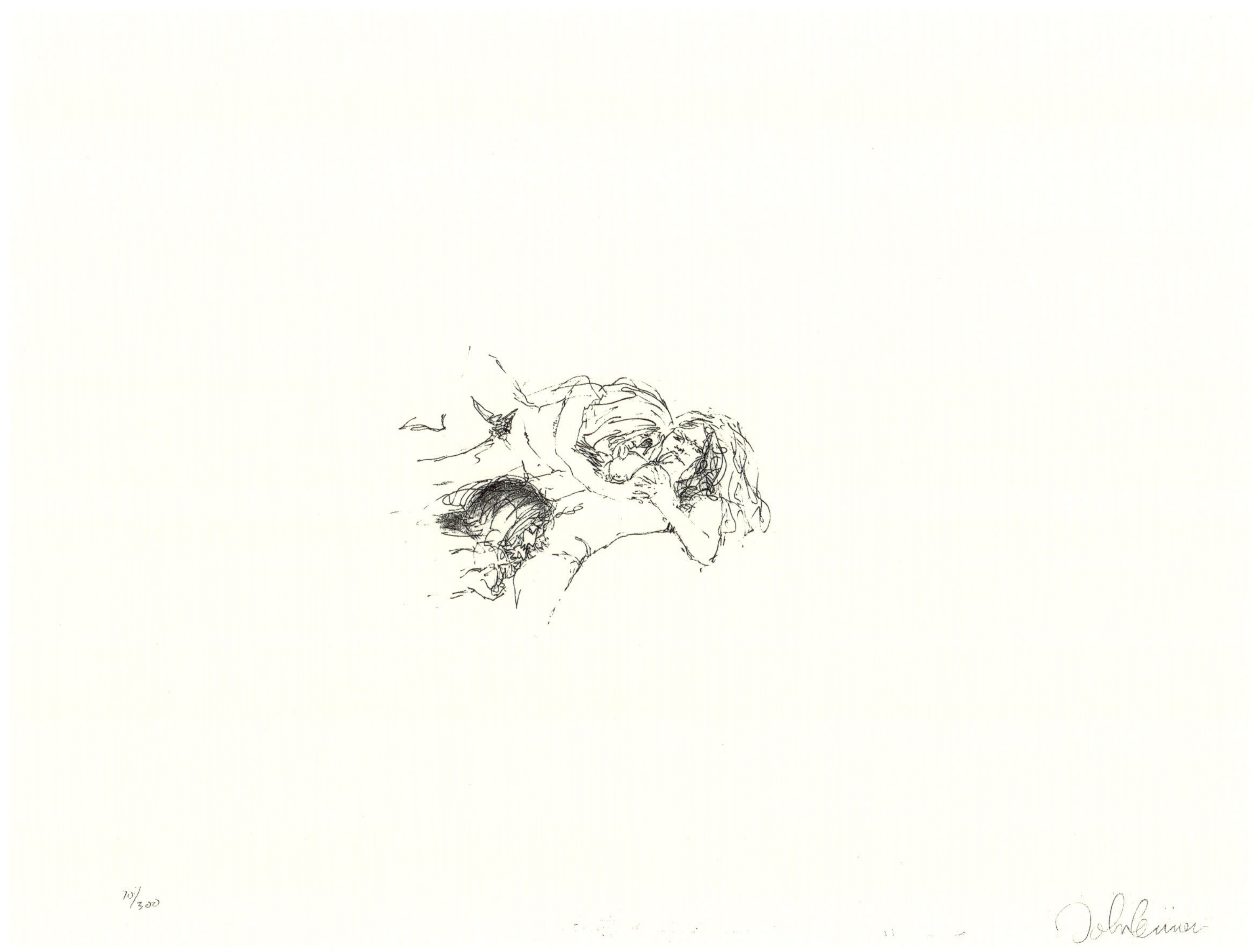

Bag One, 1970
Untitled
30″ x 23″
Lithograph, brown

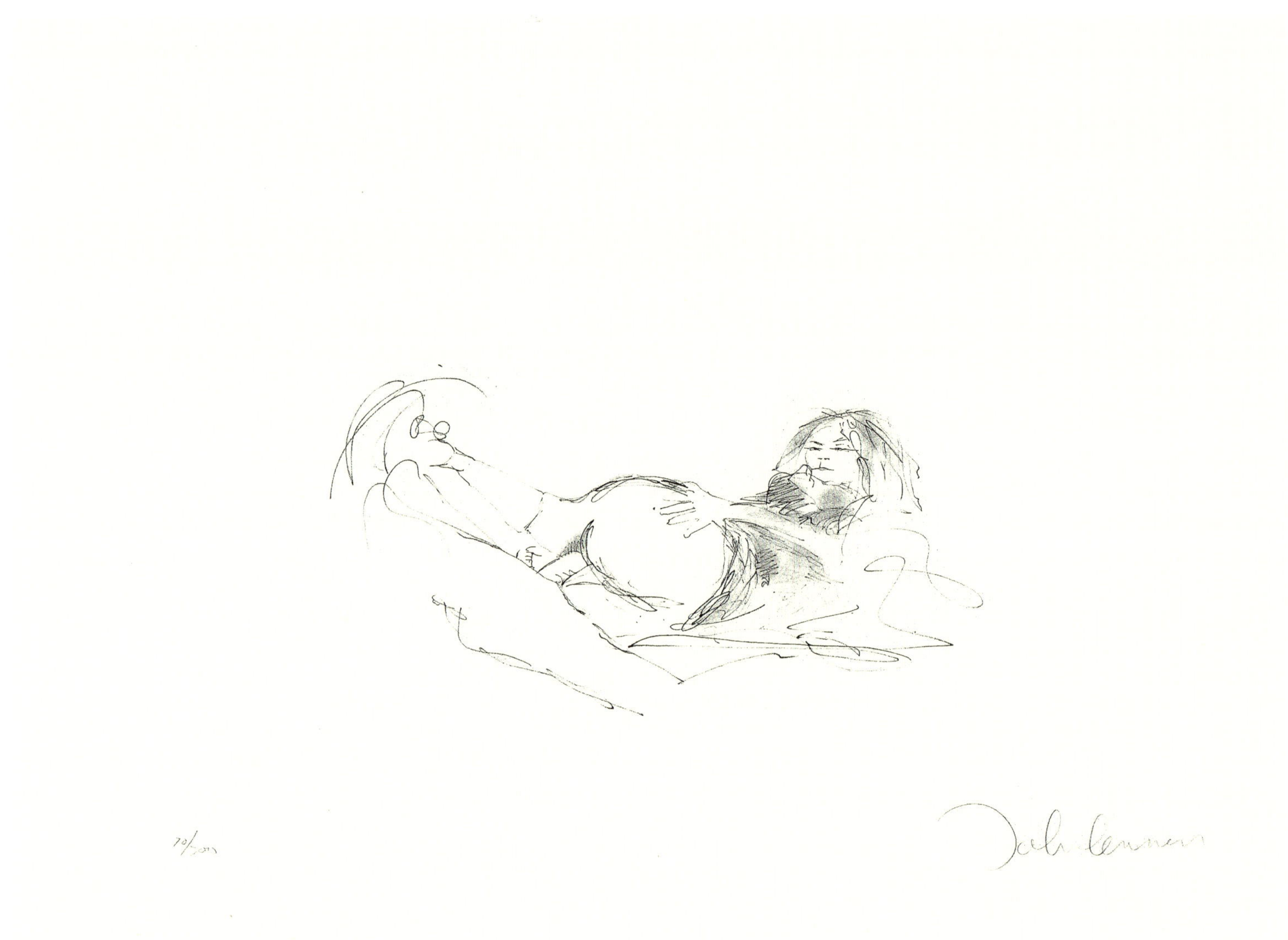

Bag One, 1970
Untitled
30″ x 23″
Lithograph, brown

Performances

"John" by Yoko Ono and "Yoko" by John Lennon
The Acorn Event in front of Coventry Cathedral on 15th June 1968
Dorothee Hansen

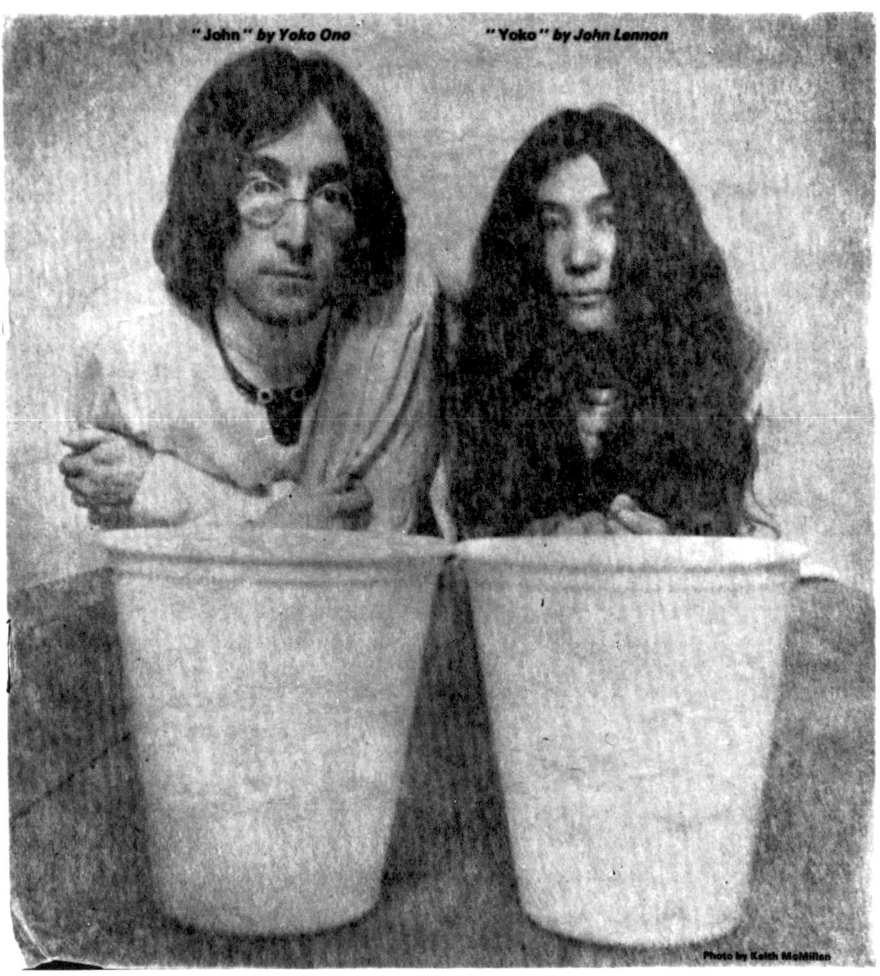

Catalogue of the *Acorn Event*. On the Japanese paper is the title of the work, the photo in the background shows John Lennon and Yoko Ono in front of the white plant pots with the acorns.
Photo: Keith McMillan

The first performance John Lennon and Yoko Ono carried out together was on the occasion of the *National Sculpture Exhibition* in 1968. Works by contemporary British sculptors, including Henry Moore, were exhibited in the ruins of the old cathedral of Coventry, which had been bombed in the Second World War. While most of the sculptures were in stone or bronze, the conceptual work by John Lennon and Yoko Ono was fundamentally different.

In the spring of 1968, Lennon and Yoko Ono had met Anthony Fawcett, one of the organisers of the exhibition. Although he lobbied the organising committee to allow their participation, their work was not permitted to appear in the official catalogue. Lennon and Ono then produced their own catalogue which was distributed free of charge.

They held their performance on 15 June 1968, the day of the exclusive exhibition preview. It was only at this point that Lennon and Ono discovered they were not to be allowed to plant their acorns on hallowed ground in the ruins of the old cathedral. After a heated discussion with the canon in charge, Stephen Verney, in which it became clear that Lennon and Yoko Ono's work was not regarded as a sculpture, it was decided that the performance should take place on a meadow in front of the new cathedral, where other works by younger sculptors were also displayed.

After precisely determining the compass directions, Lennon and Yoko Ono dug two holes on an east-west axis and placed a white plastic plant pot with an acorn in each of the holes. Before filling them in again with earth, Lennon expressed his hope that West and East would soon be united in peace.

Over the site where they had planted the acorns, they placed a round white garden bench of cast iron which they had specially brought along with them. This was meant to encourage visitors to take a seat and reflect on how the oaks grow. A large silver plaque bearing the title of the work was placed beside it on the ground:
"Yoko" by John Lennon
"John" by Yoko Ono
Some time in May, 1968

The acorns planted on an east-west axis stand for John Lennon and Yoko Ono who themselves represent the western and eastern cultures that have influenced them. The oaks will grow together and stand firm together. They are the symbol of love between two people and a sign of the peaceful unification of the eastern and western worlds.

As a catalogue, Lennon and Yoko Ono produced a folding leaflet inside a cover of Japanese paper. The two kinds of paper used also

Letter from John Lennon to
Canon Stephen Verney,
dated 28 June 1968.

28th June 1968.

Dear Canon Verney

Thank you for your Christian attitude.

I think the leaflet is explicit — Antony Fennell's notes are especially for 'puzzled people' — anyway do you have to explain an acorn? I don't understand why you can't issue our leaflet, unless you worry about gossip (cast the first stone etc.) The Christian Church does allow divorce doesn't it? Christians are supposed to stand for TRUTH. Christ stood for people — Yoko and I are people. — Of course the piece is about Yoko and me — it's also about YOU and me, and anyone else you care to mention — it's about EVERYONE and EVERYTHING. You talk about young people as if you know something about them — you obviously don't or you wouldn't be worried about our influence on them.

Jesus would have loved our piece for what it is.

Love*
John Lennon.

P.S. Could we not substitute something which is not worth stealing, instead of Coventry Cathedral, and which says quite simply. "Sit here, and think of a church growing into a bigger church." — Then we needn't bother to have clergy and everybody can enjoy THE idea.

* ♡

evoke the two cultures from which these artists originate. The title page shows Lennon and Yoko Ono sitting at a table. In front of them are the two white plant pots with the acorns. A strong perspectival distortion gives the impression that they themselves are growing directly out of the pots. The title written over their heads on the Japanese paper makes each of them a sculpture: "John" by Yoko Ono and "Yoko" by John Lennon.

Inside the leaflet, we find a poetic and enigmatic sentence repeated twice: "This is what happens when two clouds meet". Yoko Ono adds in brackets: "(the piece is John's idea but it was so good that I stole it)" – a clear indication of the active collaboration of Lennon, who was taking part in a performance for the first time. The sentence is directed at critics who might regard the performance as the idea of Yoko Ono's alone and who might be tempted to regard John Lennon as a mere sidekick intended to attract publicity. In this way, Yoko Ono shows the decisive significance of their collaboration, from which both Lennon and Ono herself benefit. Lennon had many creative ideas, but he had not produced works until now. It was Yoko Ono who motivated him to do so by introducing him to avant-garde art.

Canon Stephen Verney refused to display the leaflet in his church because he felt it had more to do with the adulterous love between Lennon and Yoko Ono than with the peace symbol of the growing acorns. He also complained that the acorns would be stolen within a week and that a keeper was needed to guard the bench and the plaque. Lennon wrote a letter to him turning the canon's arguments around and adding a postscript with a sarcastic suggestion: "Could we not substitute something which is not worth stealing, instead of Coventry Cathedral, and which says quite simply 'Sit here, and think of a church growing into a bigger church'. – Then we needn't bother to have clergy and everybody can enjoy THE idea."

It was in the Acorn Event that Lennon and Yoko Ono addressed the subject of peace for the first time. This was to become an increasingly important focal point in the period that followed, both in their performances and in Lennon's music. On 2 April, following the *Bed-In* in Amsterdam, Lennon announced the plan that was to be carried out in December 1969: Yoko Ono and he sent a pair of acorns each to leading politicians throughout the world, asking them to plant them for peace. Positive responses were received, among others, from the President of South Africa, Prime Minister Golda Meir of Israel, and King Hussein of Jordan.

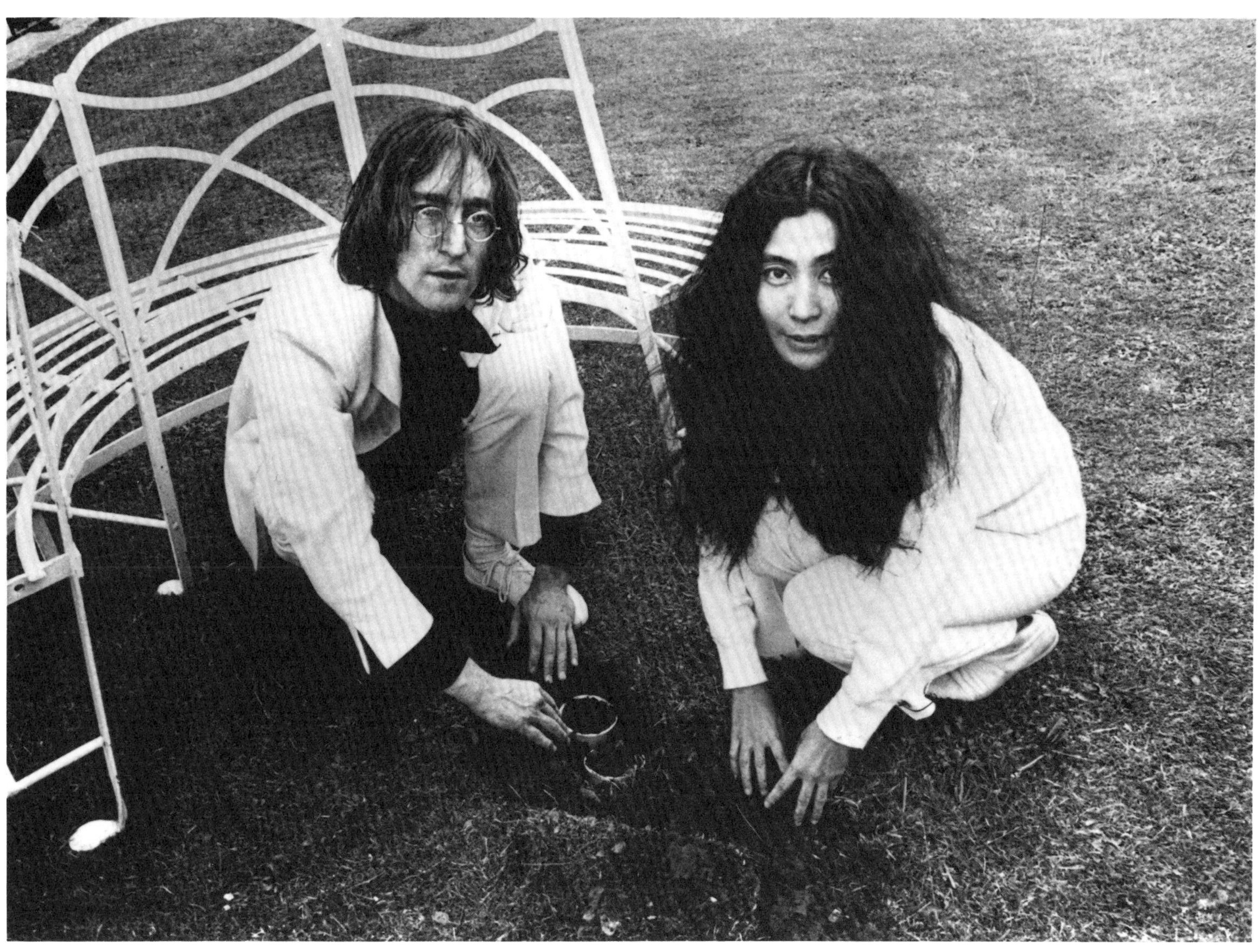

John Lennon and Yoko Ono
plant two acorns in front of
the new cathedral in
Coventry on 15 June 1968.
Behind them is one half of
the garden bench enclosing
the plant site.
Photo: Keith McMillan

You Are Here

Exhibition at the Robert Fraser Gallery, London, July 1968
Dorothee Hansen

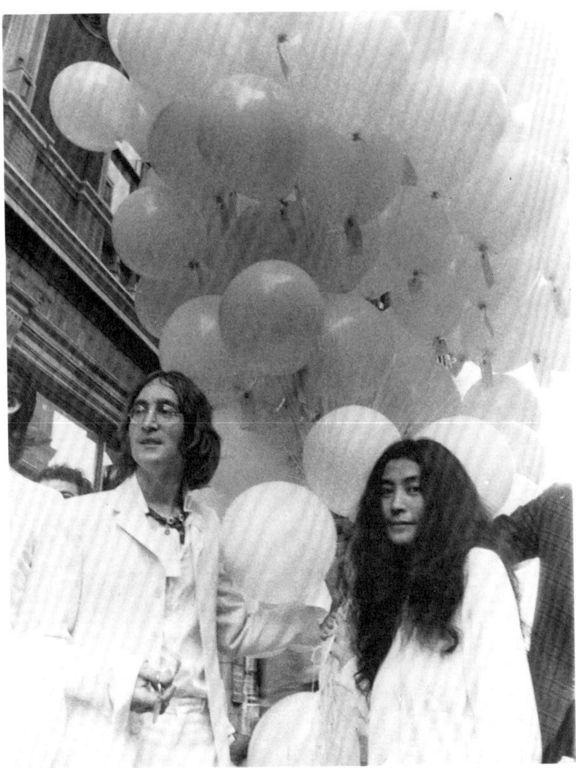

John Lennon and Yoko Ono release 365 white helium balloons at the inauguration of the *You Are Here* exhibition in the Robert Fraser Gallery, London, on 1 July 1968.
Photo: Keystone

On 1 July, the first exhibition of John Lennon's art, *You Are Here*, was opened at the Robert Fraser Gallery, 69 Duke Street, London.

Part of the exhibition space was dominated by a large, white, circular screen, in the centre of which Lennon had written the words "you are here." These words were aimed directly at the spectators, informing them that they were at Lennon's exhibition, in front of his round painting. Like the work of other concept artists of the sixties, it used extremely simple artistic devices to address complex questions of existence, time and space.

At the inauguration of the exhibition, John Lennon and Yoko Ono released 365 helium-filled balloons (one for each day of the year) with small notes attached saying "you are here" and requesting the finder to "write to John Lennon, c/o Robert Fraser Gallery, 69 Duke Street, London W1". The words "you are here" would be just as applicable to the situation of the finder, however far away, as they were to the exhibition

visitor, though they would be describing something else. After all, "you" can be anyone who reads these words and "here" can be anywhere the sentence is read. Here is always wherever I am.

Finally, the sentence "you are here" could also create a link between Lennon and the finder. By replying to the message, the finder would also be "here" at Lennon's exhibition. More than 100 of the tags were indeed returned – an astonishingly high response for an avant-garde event of this kind. They were then "here" at the Fraser Gallery, together with the names of the finders.

Lennon, who played with language and puns in his books, was now highlighting the way language and action interact. The white badges with the words "you are here", produced for the exhibition, function in this way. Pinned to a lapel, they would be carried from place to place and read by many people at different locations.

The other part of the exhibition was dedicated to found items (*objets trouvés*). Lennon had brought together a number of charity boxes used by various non-profit organisations to collect charitable donations. Some of them are colourful sculptures taking the form of the intended recipient of the donation: the cute WWF panda, children on crutches etc. In one corner of the gallery, he displayed the plainer collecting tins of the Red Cross and other charities.

Lennon had apparently been fascinated by cripples since his youth; he had not only deformed his teachers in the early "Daily Howl" sketchbooks, but later portrayed deformed characters in his books with biting sarcasm in word and image. Pity was certainly not the subject of this exhibition. He was clearly more interested in the variety of concerns reflected in the different forms of a charity boxes. He recognised these little sculptures as ready-mades.

Only two objects, which were not found items, were presented on white pedestals: a white hat, upside down, labelled "For the Artist. Thank

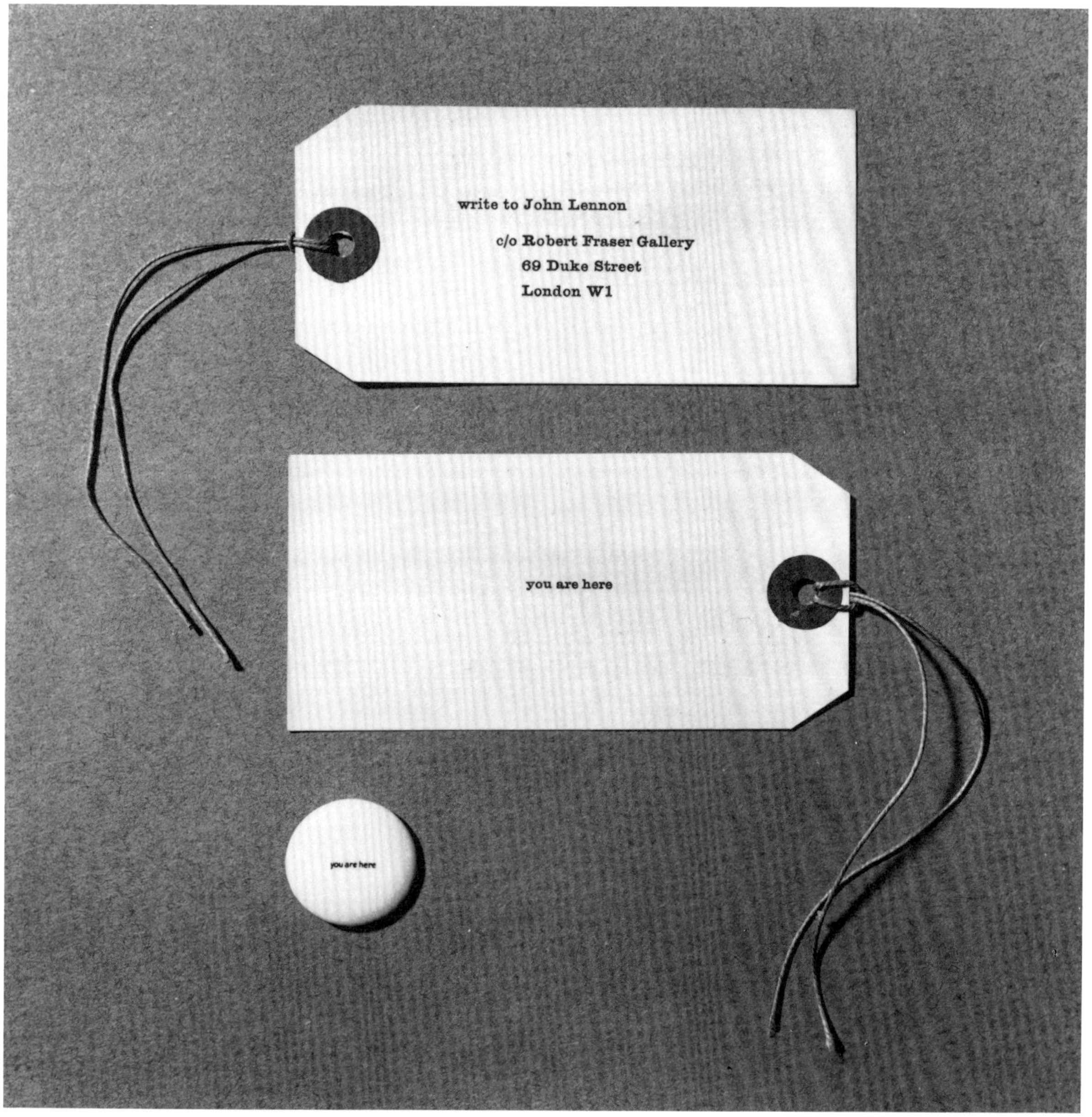

The tags attached to the balloons and the badges distributed at the exhibition bear the words *you are here*.
Photo: Iain Macmillan

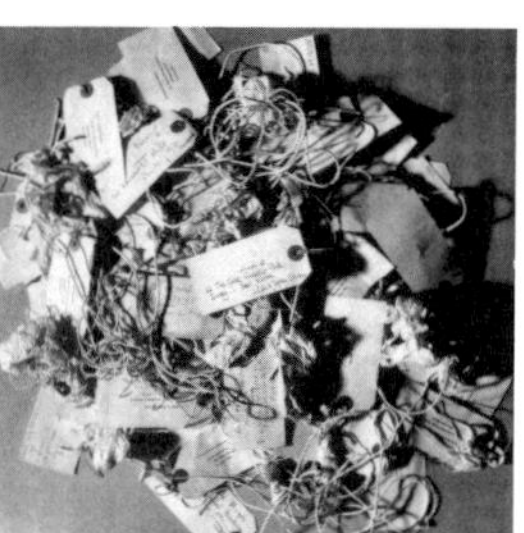

Returned balloons and tags with finders' addresses.
Photo: Iain Macmillan

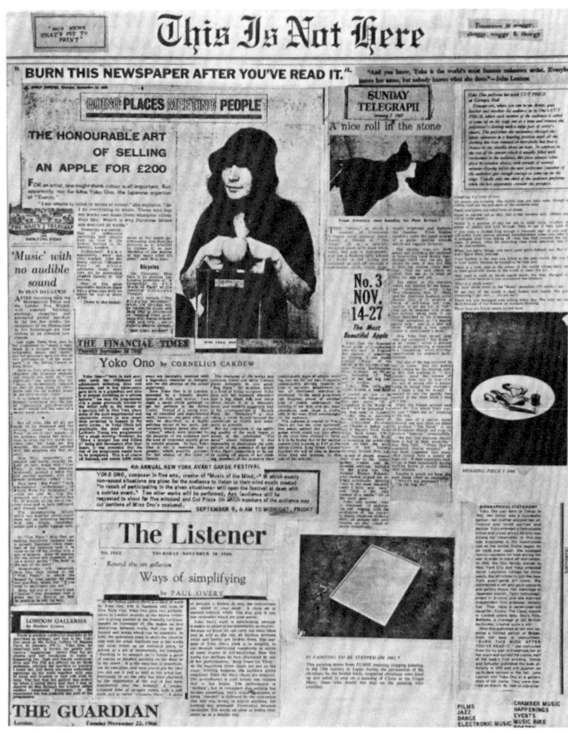

This Is Not Here, title page of the catalogue for Yoko Ono's exhibition at the Everson Museum, Syracuse, New York, October 1971, designed by John Lennon and Peter Bendry

you." and a glass containing the white lapel badges. The hat is Lennon's tongue-in-cheek comment on the many charity boxes. At first, it appears as a wealthy star's impertinent request for money – but then again, John Lennon had no income as a visual artist, and he was no star in the art world. At the same time, the hat indicates the simplest form of collecting, referring to the beggar in the street who has no sophisticated collecting box, but who presents his own cause personally.

In the exhibition of charity boxes, Lennon may well have been amused by another pun: he was collecting collecting boxes to exhibit them as an art collection, for which, as an artist, he collected with his hat.

In spite of its rich and complex approach to language and art, the exhibition went almost unnoticed. The art critics did not take it seriously because Lennon was a pop star, and his fans preferred to hear him sing. It was in reaction to this schematic categorisation, from which he was unable to escape all his life, that he and Yoko

Ono developed the concept of "bagism" (see p. 176).

John Lennon dedicated his exhibition *You Are Here* to Yoko Ono. She responded with her exhibition *This is Not Here*. This major retrospective exhibition at the Everson Museum of Art in Syracuse, New York, from 9 to 27 October 1971 was realised and organised by Fluxus artist George Maciunas. Yoko invited Lennon as "guest artist" – a gesture normally associated with pop concerts and virtually unknown in the art world.

Lennon not only presented some of his own works at this exhibition, but also designed the catalogue together with Peter Bendry. It took the form of a twelve-page newspaper, with the heading "This is not here" in the typeface of the *New York Times*. The content was a collage of newspaper cuttings about Yoko Ono and her work, intermixed with drawings, short texts and collages by her and Lennon. Lennon also applied this design principle to the *Wedding Album* insert and the record sleeve of *Some Time in New York City*.

This dialogue in the form of exhibitions shows that it was not only the individual works, but the overall concept of the exhibitions that interested Lennon and Yoko Ono. They took a similar approach to records which they released simultaneously, dedicating them to each other and quoting each other in the sleeve design and the music (see p. 190).

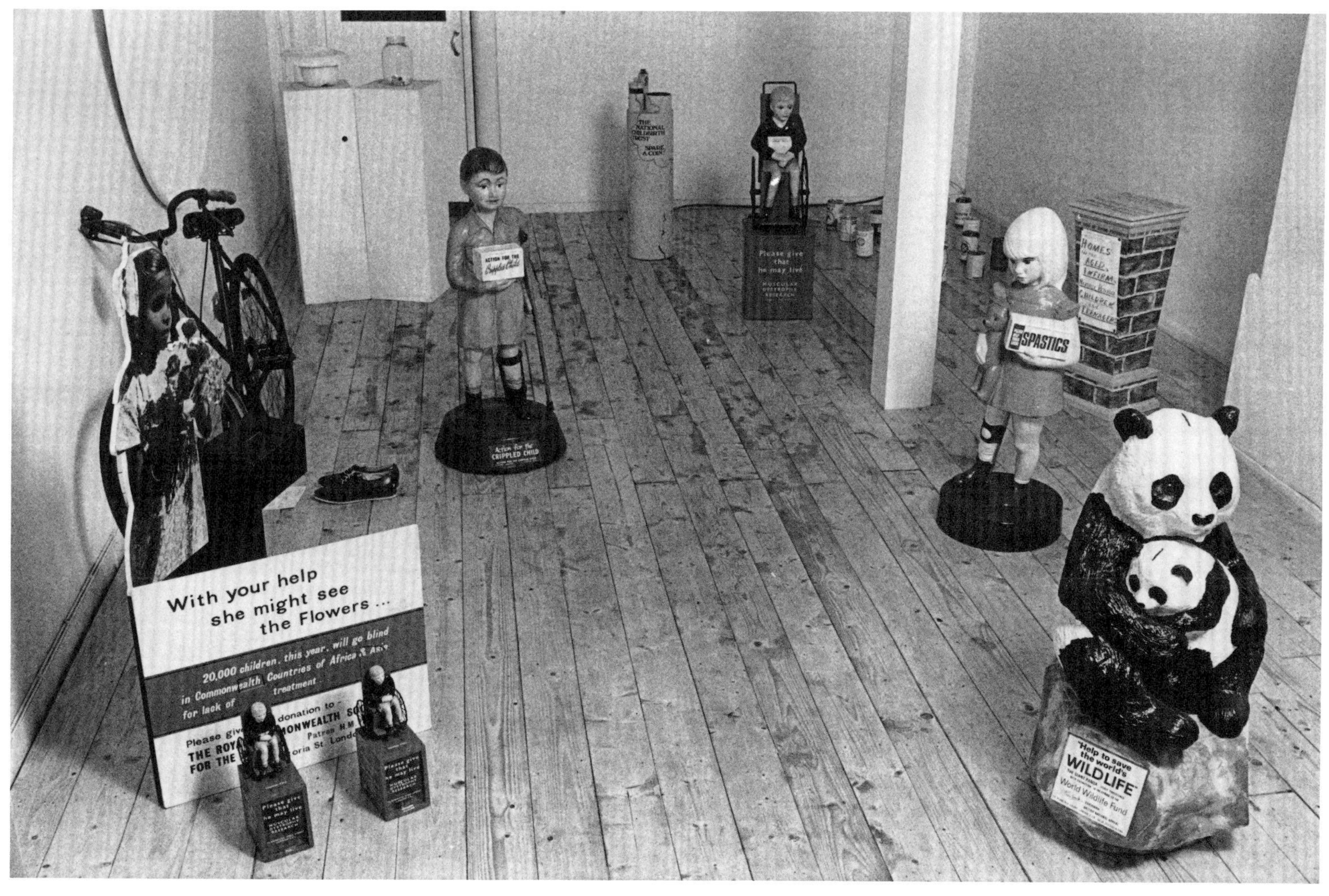

Charity boxes in John Lennon's exhibition *You Are Here* at the Robert Fraser Gallery, London, 1968.
Photo: Iain Macmillan

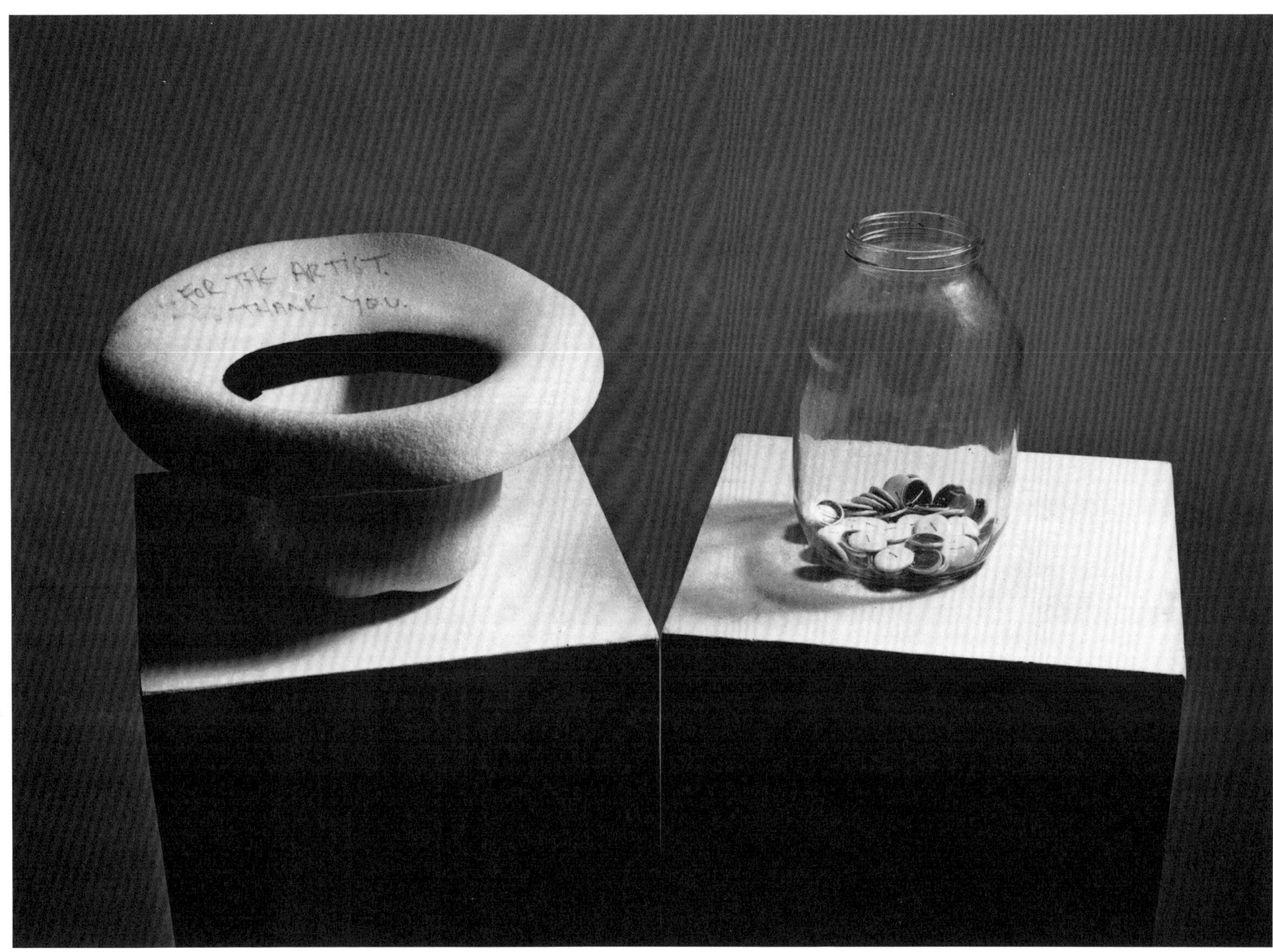

John Lennon, *For the Artist.*
Thank you, in the exhibition
You Are Here at the Robert
Fraser Gallery, London,
1968.
Photo: Iain Macmillan

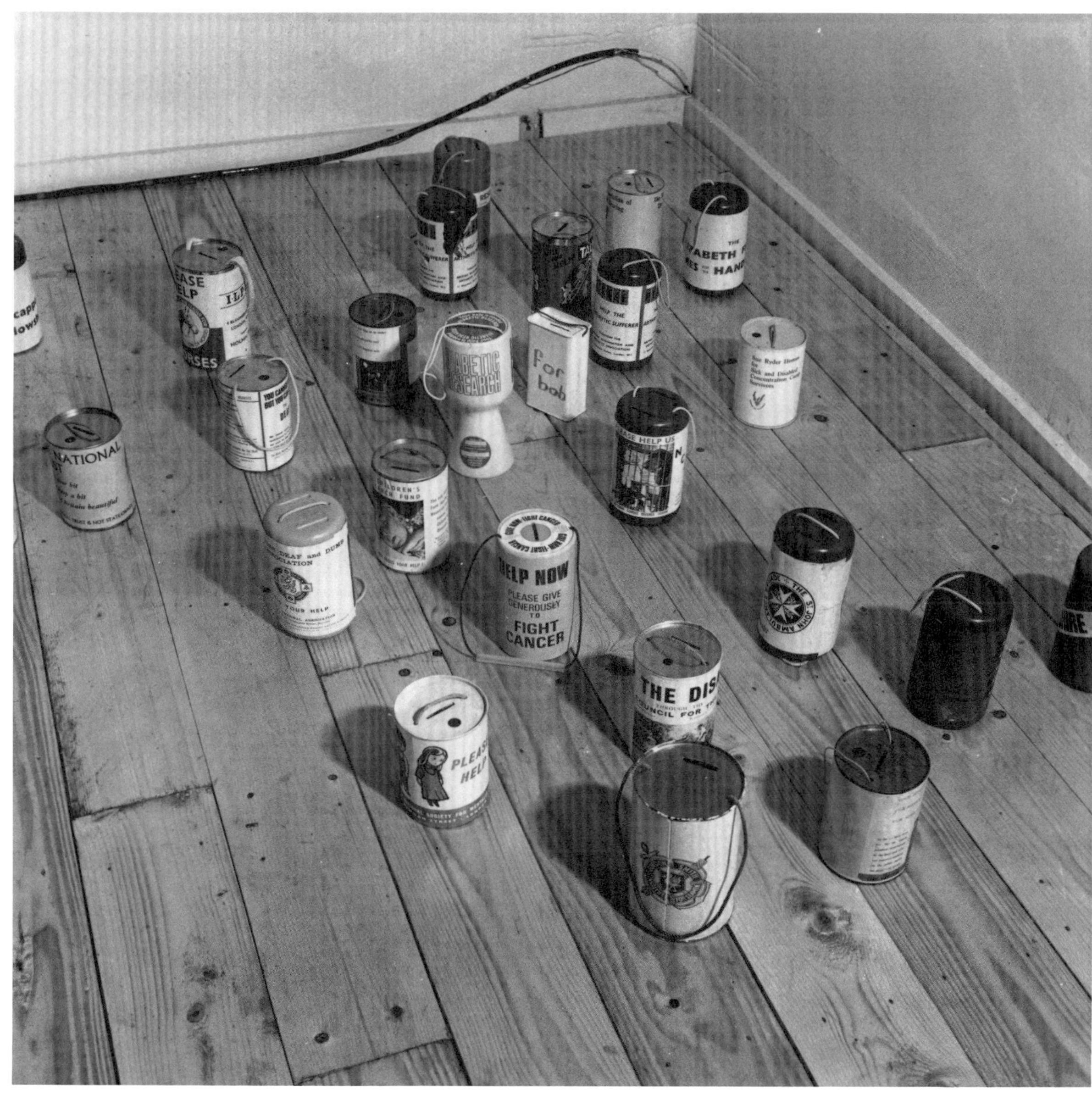

Charity boxes in John Lennon's exhibition *You Are Here* at the Robert Fraser Gallery, London, 1968.
Photo: Iain Macmillan

Bed-In for Peace
Performance at the Amsterdam Hilton, 1969
Dorothee Hansen

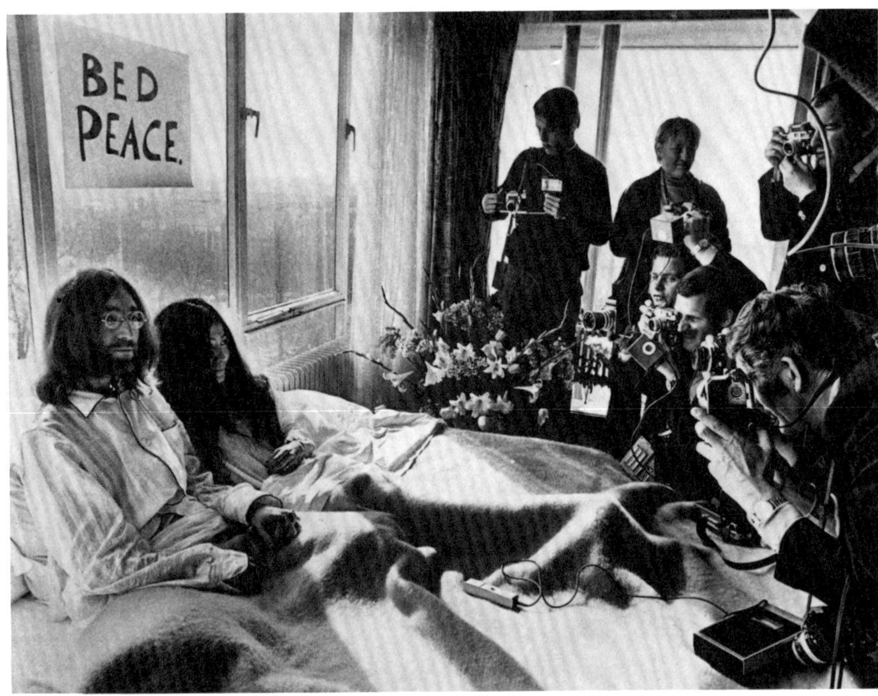

Bed-In for peace in
Amsterdam, Hilton Hotel,
March 1969.
Photo: Ruud Hoff

The *Bed-In* event is directly connected with the
marriage of John Lennon and Yoko Ono in
March 1969. From Paris, the couple flew to
Gibraltar on 20 March, where they were married
at the British Consulate. The wedding itself was a
performance. Lennon and Ono accepted this
traditional institution, disdained by the youth
culture of the day, as a public sign of their love.
At the same time, however, they called into
question its strict regulations by their behaviour
and their clothing: both were dressed all in white
– not in a suit and a bride's dress, but in cord
jeans, miniskirt, floppy hat and plimsolls – and
Lennon smoked during the ceremony. 70 minutes
later, they left Gibraltar and travelled to
Amsterdam via Paris.

As the press would have tracked them down
no matter where they spent their honeymoon,
they made the honeymoon itself a public event.
They exploited the media to campaign for their
political cause: peace. They planned to stay in bed
for a week and let their hair grow – an entirely
peaceful and meditative action as a demonstration against violence.

From 25 to 31 March they rented Presidential
Suite 902 on the seventh floor of the Amsterdam
Hilton and invited the press to discuss peace.
Lennon and Yoko Ono arranged the bedroom to
accommodate the crowd of reporters and photographers. They removed most of the furniture and
pushed the bed in front of the large window to
which they had stuck sheets of paper with their
messages: "Hair Peace" and "Bed Peace". All
over the walls there were further hand-written
posters calling for love, peace and freedom:
"I love John", "I love Yoko", "Stay in bed" and
"Grow your hair". The room was decorated for
the bridal couple with lavish bouquets of flowers
and an enormous gift basket. The bed, that most
private of places, became a public stage.

On the first day of the performance, Lennon
and Ono met the media in their pyjamas – more
than 50 journalists were there. They spent a total
of seven days in bed giving interviews. "Yoko and
I are quite willing to be the world's clowns," said
Lennon, "if by doing so it will do some good.
I know I'm one of these 'famous personalities'.
For reasons only known to themselves, people do
print what I say. And I'm saying peace... We're
trying to make Christ's message contemporary.
What would he have done if he had had advertise-
ments, records, films, TV and newspapers? Christ
made miracles to tell his message. Well, the
miracle today is communications, so let's use it."[1]

Lennon stressed that the performance had
been primarily Yoko's idea. It was both a political
demonstration and a theatrical scene. If Yoko
Ono was the producer of this scene, Lennon was
playing the leading role, because so many young
people admired him and took his messages seriously and because the media passed on his
messages so eagerly.

For Lennon and Yoko Ono, in addition to the
campaign for peace, mass communication and the
media itself were the theme. "Our name is known
and so we're using our fame and our money to
advertise for peace," Lennon explained in an

interview.[2] But this particular point came into the crossfire of criticism, because the argument was turned around and they were accused of wasting money for their own publicity when it could be used more sensibly for starving people in Biafra.

Lennon and Yoko Ono wanted to repeat the *Bed-In* in the USA. However, as Lennon was refused an entry visa, they headed for the Bahamas instead, but decided in the end to hold their second performance in Montreal, where they would have easy access to the North American media.

From 26 May to 2 June 1969, they held a *Bed-In* at the Queen Elizabeth Hotel, Room 1742, in Montreal. They gave more than 60 interviews. "The whole effect of our *Bed-In* has made people talk about peace. We're trying to interest young people into doing something for peace. But it must be done by non-violent means – otherwise there can only be chaos. We're saying to the young people – and they have always been the hippest ones – we're telling them to get the message across to the squares… The whole scene has become too serious and too intellectual."[3]

Irony and humour played an important role in the performance, not only because of the bizarre situation reminiscent of the *lever* at the court of Louis XIV, but above all in the replies to the interview questions. Lennon said there was so much violence in the papers that "the least Yoko and I can do is hog the headlines and make the people laugh. I'd sooner see our faces in a bed in the paper than yet another politician smiling at the people and shaking hands."[4] He felt that there was no point in fighting the establishment with violence, because "they know how to play the game of violence and it's easier for them when they can recognize you and shoot you. They don't know how to handle humor, peaceful humor, and that's our message, really."[5] In this way, the *Bed-In*, while it is very much in the tradition of Gandhi and Martin Luther King, differs from other peace campaigns, from demonstrations and political pamphleteering, in its exploitation of the media, in its visual slant and in its language.

At the end of the *Bed-In* in Montreal, the song *Give Peace a Chance* was recorded, which Lennon had composed during that week. The hotel room was full of visitors who sang as a choir, including "drug guru" Timothy Leary, former New York radio singer Rabbi Abraham L. Feinberg and the Canadian section of the Radha Krishna Temple. The song provided the brilliant finale to the performance and later continued to preserve the memory of the event. On 15 November, Vietnam Moratorium Day, almost half a million demonstrators sang the song that was to become the hymn of the peace movement.

The success of the *Bed-In* for peace is evident in the lively reaction of the media, collected and published by Lennon and Yoko Ono in a leaflet accompanying the *Wedding Album*. In spite of all the criticism it attracted, they had achieved their aim of having everybody talking about the performance and about peace.

1 Fawcett, *One Day at a Time*, p. 51.
2 Fawcett, *One Day at a Time*, p. 51.
3 Fawcett, *One Day at a Time*, p. 53.
4 Fawcett, *One Day at a Time*, p. 49
5 From the interview published with the *Wedding Album*.

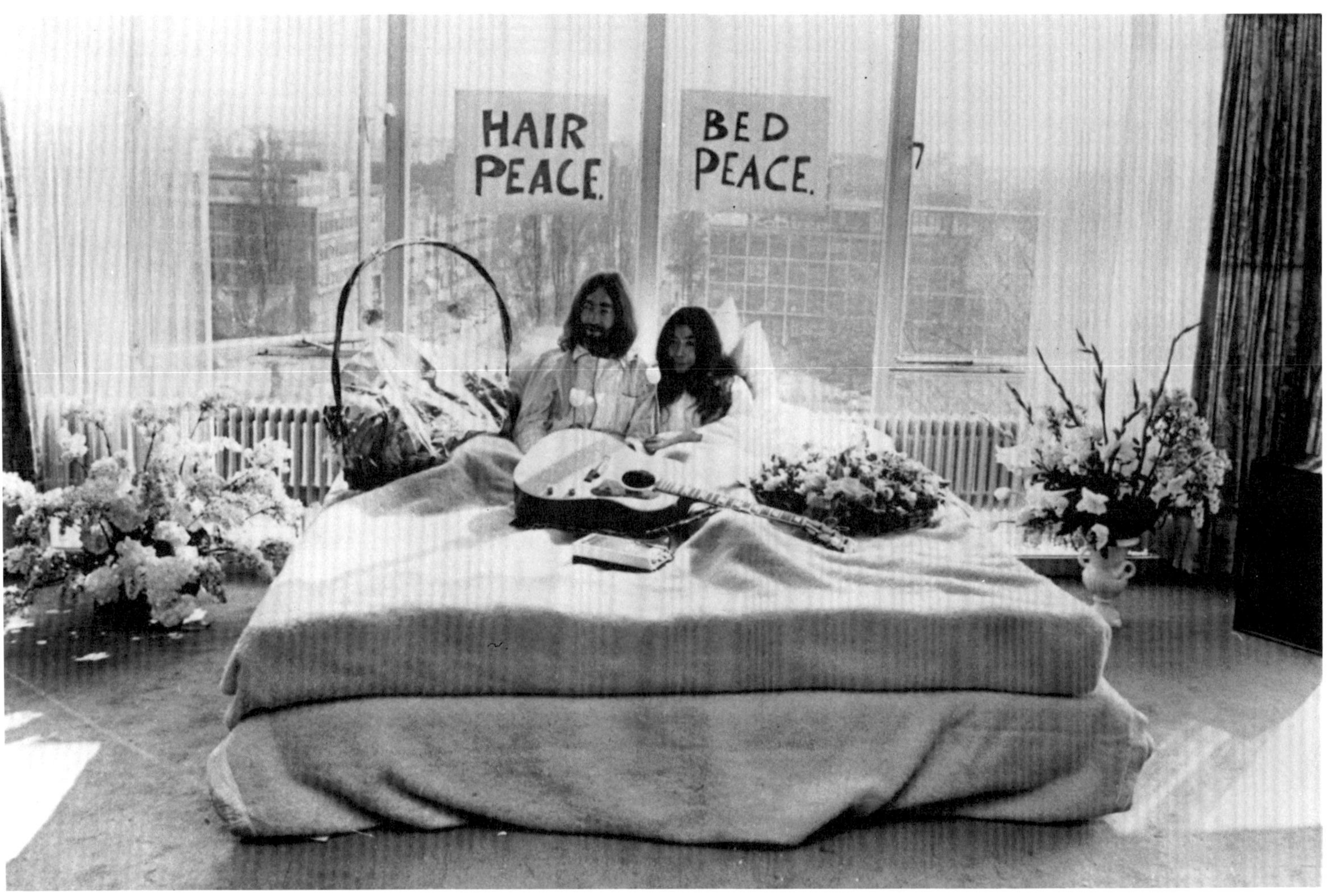

Bed-In for peace in
Amsterdam, Hilton Hotel,
March 1969.
Photo: Nico Koster

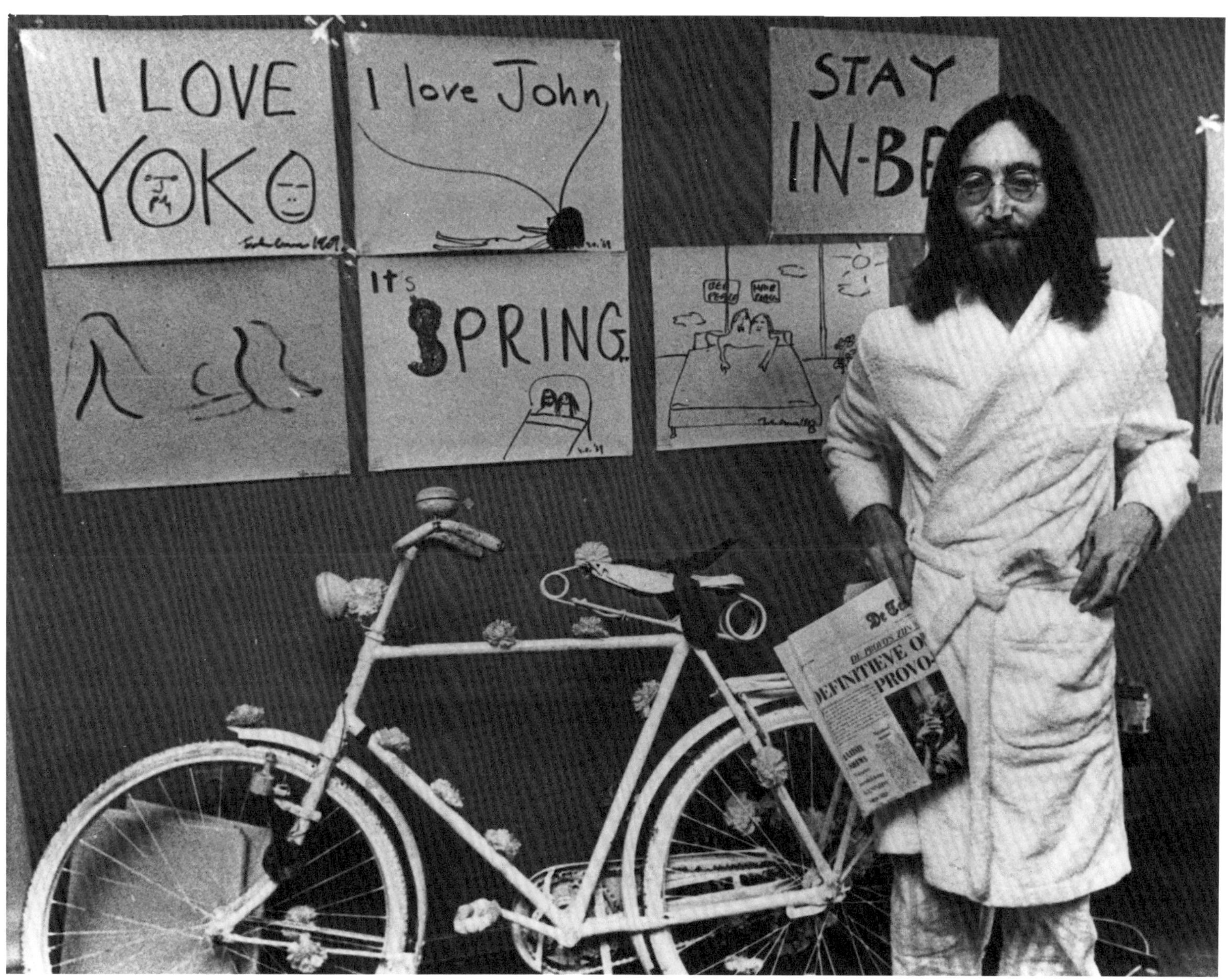

John Lennon during the
Bed-In for peace at the
Amsterdam Hilton,
March 1969, in front of
his drawings. The bicycle is a
wedding present. At the time
the city of Amsterdam had
municipally owned bicycles
distributed throughout the
city which could be used by
anyone who wanted to
borrow one.
Photo: Courtesy of
Lenono Photo Archive

War is over!
Worldwide poster action, December 1969
Dorothee Hansen

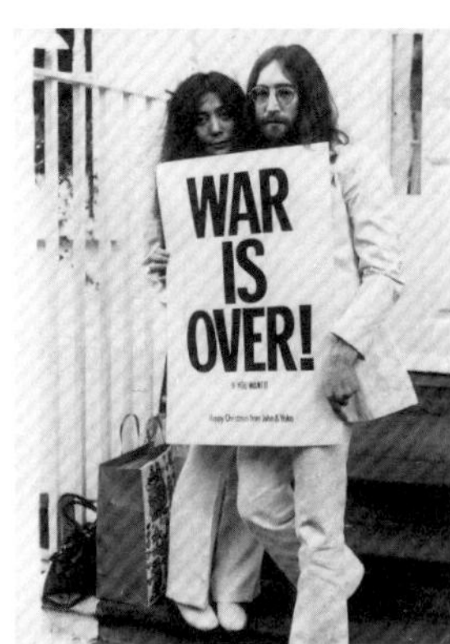

John Lennon and Yoko Ono
with the poster for their *War
is over!* peace campaign at
the entrance to the *Apple*
building in London,
15 December 1969.
Photo: Keystone

On 15 December 1969, John Lennon and Yoko Ono launched an international poster campaign in twelve cities: Athens, Berlin, Hong Kong, London, Los Angeles, Montreal, New York, Paris, Port-of-Spain (Trinidad), Rome, Tokyo and Toronto. The text of the poster, translated into the respective language of the country where it was displayed, read:
"WAR IS OVER!
IF YOU WANT IT
Happy Christmas from John & Yoko"
The poster was displayed in the most prominent locations. On the Champs-Elysées in Paris, London's Piccadilly Circus and Hollywood's Sunset Strip. The format varied, depending on the size of the advertising space available. It appeared on the oversized billboards on New York's Times Square, but was also displayed as a series of posters. Flyers were distributed with the same message as well.

To launch the campaign, Lennon and Yoko Ono held their *Peace for Christmas* charity concert for the benefit of UNICEF at the Lyceum Theatre in London on 15 December 1969. They performed with the *Plastic Ono Supergroup*, which included George Harrison, Eric Clapton, Klaus Voormann and Keith Moon of *The Who*. There were *War is over!* posters all over the stage, where Yoko Ono squatted at Lennon's feet in a white bag. When the song *Don't Worry Kyoko* began, she stood up, screamed and kept repeating "You killed Hanratty" (see p. 176). The following day, they flew to Toronto to campaign for peace in an interview with the Canadian Prime Minister Trudeau. Three days before Christmas Eve, on 21 December, they also ran a large *War is over!* ad in the New York Times.

The campaign slogan was also used in the Christmas song Lennon recorded in 1971 with children of New York's Harlem Community Choir: *Happy Xmas (War is over)*. The choir sang: "War is over if you want it".

In earlier performances such as the *Bed-In*,

which they had also instigated in the name of peace, John Lennon and Yoko Ono deliberately exploited Lennon's popularity as a Beatle whose very presence was enough to attract the attention of the press like a magnet. Television, radio and newspaper reporters repeated their message again and again; the media were turned into an instrument which could be targeted at will. With the huge advertising hoardings and posters, Lennon and Ono were now using a medium which had previously been the sole preserve of the ad world. For the first time, it gave them complete control of the message and the way it was spread, though professional use of this medium cost a great deal of money.

Apart from focusing on peace, Ono and Lennon also addressed the subject of the medium itself. "Henry Ford knew how to sell cars by advertising. I'm selling peace, and Yoko and I are just one big advertising campaign. It may make people laugh, but it may make them think, too. Really, we're Mr. and Mrs. Peace,"[1] Lennon said in 1969, and in an interview in 1971 with Jann Wenner of *Rolling Stone,* he summed up the poster action: "We got a big response. The people that got in touch with us understood what a grand event it was apart from the message itself."[2]

[1] Anthony Fawcett, *One Day at a Time,* p. 54.
[2] *Lennon Remembers –* The Rolling Stone Interviews by Jann Wenner, p. 178.

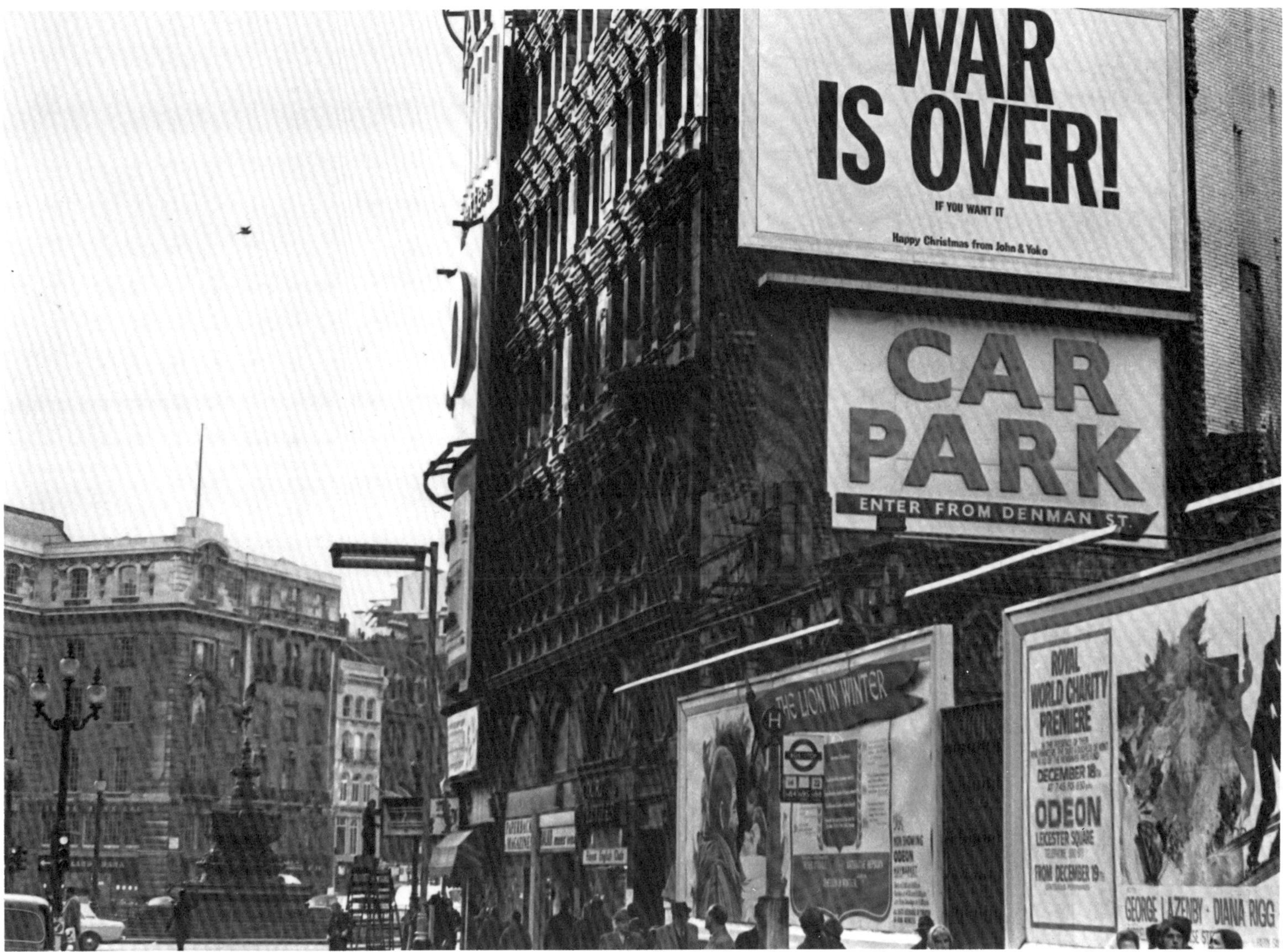

War is over! advertising
hoarding on Shaftesbury
Avenue near Piccadilly
Circus, London,
on 15 December 1969.
Photo: Associated Press

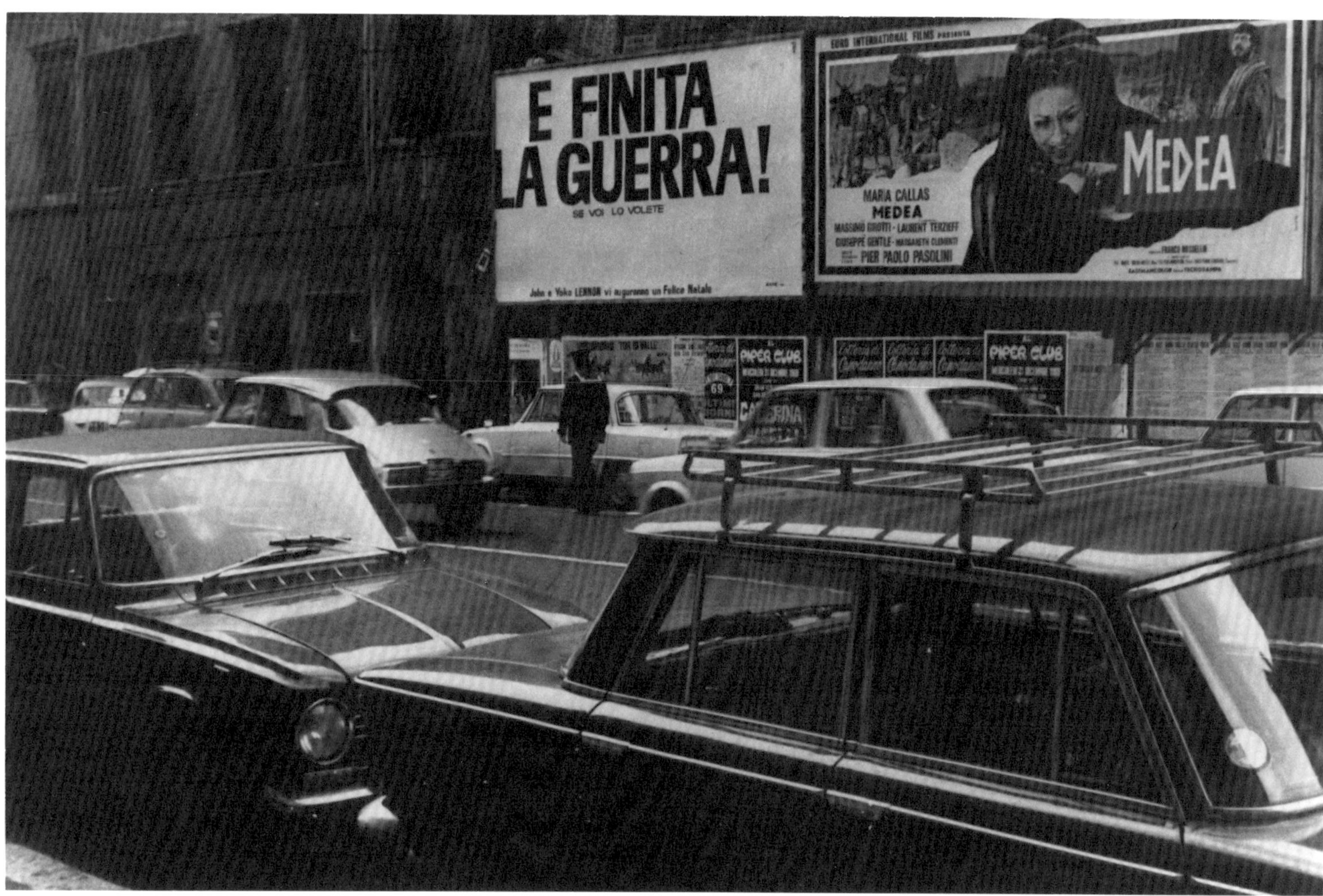

E Finita La Guerra! ad
hoarding on the Corso
Rinascimento in Rome,
in December 1969.
Photo: Courtesy of Lenono
Photo Archive

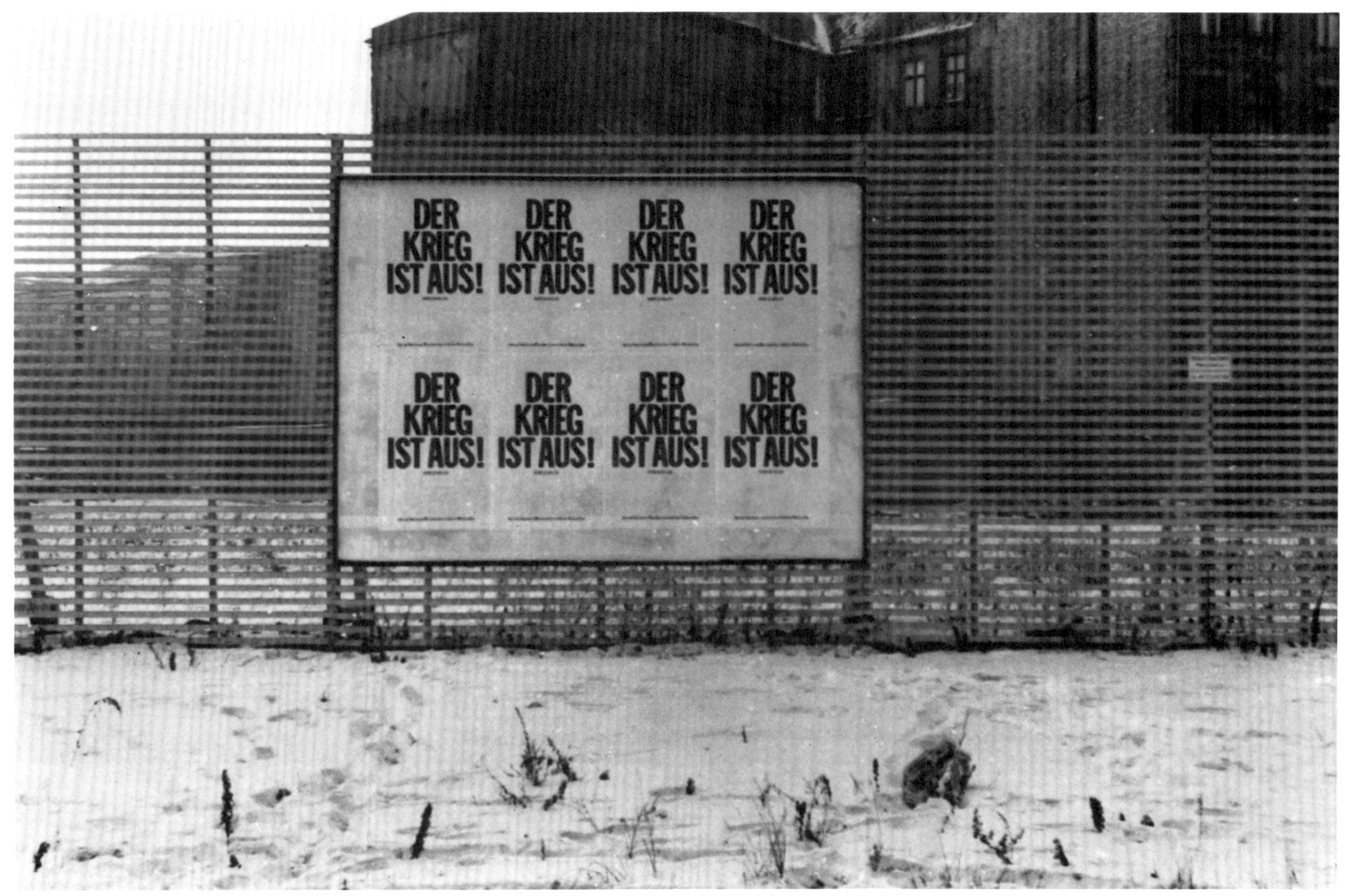

Der Krieg ist aus! posters in
Berlin, December 1969.
Photo: Erich Thomas

Bagism
A series of performances in which John Lennon and Yoko Ono wrapped themselves
in a bag, 1968–1971
Dorothee Hansen

18 December 1968
At the *Alchemical Wedding*, a Christmas
celebration for underground artists at the Royal
Albert Hall in London, John Lennon and Yoko
Ono take the stage in a white bag. They remain
inside the bag for 25 minutes, moving from time
to time. A man with a flute dances around them,
while the audience claps. A heckler in the
audience waves a Biafra flag and calls out,
"Do you care about that, John Lennon, do you
care about that?"

31 March 1969
Immediately after the Amsterdam *Bed-In*,
Lennon and Yoko Ono fly to Vienna for the
world premiere of her film *Rape*, to be screened
on Austrian TV that evening. They hold a press
conference in the Red Salon of the Sacher Hotel,
where they reply to journalists' questions from a
white bag. On the walls of the salon, there are
posters with the messages "Bagism", "Grow
your hair" and "Total communication".

1 April 1969
Lennon and Yoko Ono appear on the TV
programme *Today*. First of all, they squat in a
white bag labelled "Bagism", while interviewer
Eamonn Andrews waits in bed. Then, in reference
to the *Bed-In*, they get into bed with him.

10 September 1969
The New Cinema Club at the Institute of
Contemporary Arts in London screens films by
Lennon and Yoko Ono. Two people in a white
bag squat on the stage throughout the screening.
Nobody is sure whether the people in the bag are
Lennon and Ono. Bells ring from inside the bag,
while the audience drums rhythmically on baking
trays. The reactions of the audience are recorded
by hidden infrared cameras.

14 December 1969
A white bag containing two persons is labelled "A
silent protest for James Hanratty" and placed at
Speaker's Corner in Hyde Park. Hanratty's father
calls for a public inquiry into the wrongful
execution of his son in 1962. Later he hands in
a petition to Downing Street No. 10. Nobody
knows who was really sitting in the bag.

15 December 1969
Plastic Ono Supergroup concert on behalf of
UNICEF at the Lyceum Theatre in London. Yoko
Ono sits in a white bag on the stage at Lennon's
feet and calls out, "You killed Hanratty".

17 July 1971
Lennon and Yoko Ono are interviewed by
Michael Parkinson on BBC TV. They let
Parkinson get into a bag for a while during
the interview to ask his questions.

1972
In the musical film *Imagine*, a man in a black bag
walks through the town in the track *It's so hard*.
During the track *Mrs. Lennon*, one person in a
white bag and four people in black bags appear in
a cemetery. In the track *Gimme Some Truth*, the
same figures then appear in a church. On this
track, there is also a short excerpt from the
interview in which Michael Parkinson asks his
questions in a black bag.

Yoko Ono had already addressed the question
of wrapping. In 1962, she had invented a *Bag
Piece* which she performed with Tony Cox.
According to her instructions, they both got into
a black bag. They then undressed and dressed
again. After that, they got out of the bag and left
the stage. Because they were hidden from view,
they stimulated the imagination of the audience.
At the same time, Yoko Ono wanted to show that
the essence of the individual is not to be found in
his outward appearance, but is hidden deep
within him: wrapping the exterior opens up a
more direct access to inner reality.

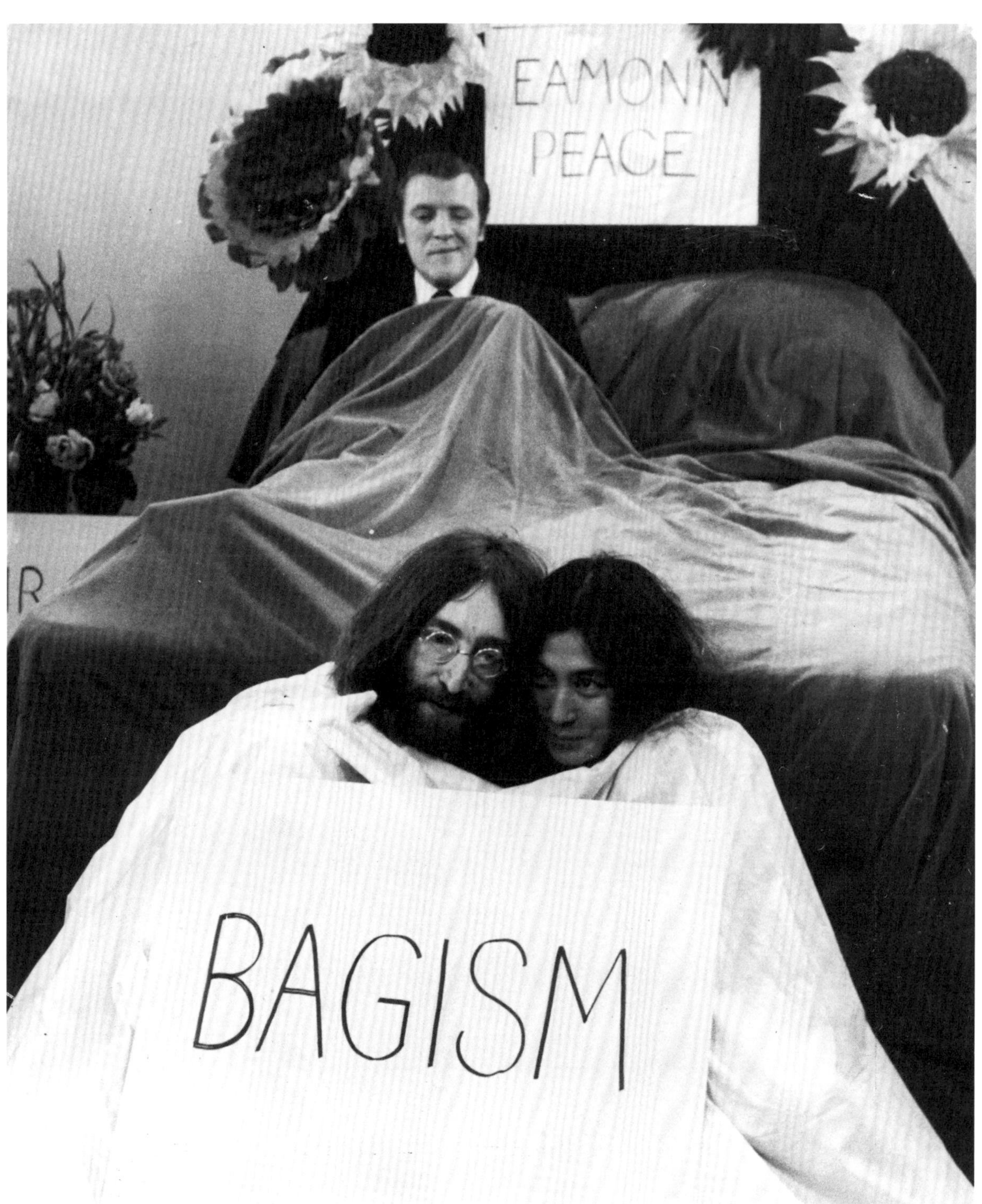

John Lennon and Yoko Ono in a bag on the BBC programme *Today* on 1 April 1969. They later got into bed with interviewer Eamonn Andrews.
Photo: Keystone

Charity concert at the Lyceum Theatre in London on 16 December 1969. Yoko Ono squats in a bag at John Lennon's feet. In the background on the right is George Harrison.
Photo: Keystone

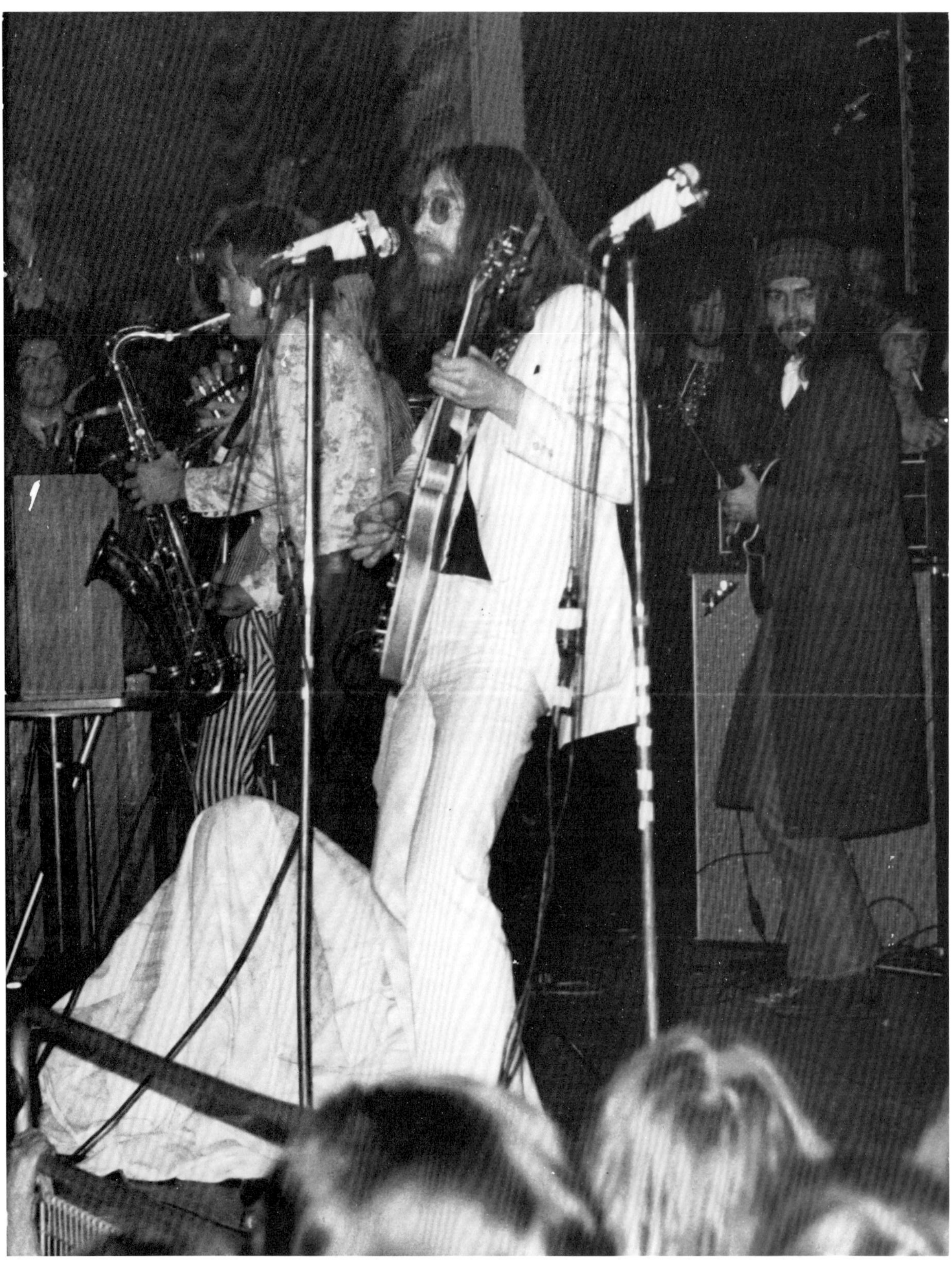

The first bag performance by John Lennon and Yoko Ono at the *Alchemical Wedding* was probably very similar. It is not clear whether it was already declared as a campaign for peace; the demonstrator in the audience, however, would appear to indicate this. *London Underground* was a group of artists, poets, mysticists and freaks. Lennon had several contacts with members of the group who regularly asked him what he did for peace. Encountering their ideas gave Lennon and Ono's large-scale peace campaign an important impetus.

The second *Bag-In*, at the Sacher Hotel press conference in Vienna immediately after the Amsterdam *Bed-In*, was clearly related to the peace campaign, as the similarity of the name suggests. "And we did the bed event in Amsterdam and the bag piece in Vienna just to give people an idea that there's many ways of protest and this is one of them. And anybody could grow their hair for peace or give up a week of their holiday for peace or sit in a bag for peace, protest against violence anyway, but peacefully, 'cause we think that peace is only got by peaceful methods."[1]

At the same time, the bag was a symbol of their wish for privacy. Lennon and Ono, who could never be sure of avoiding the press, had even turned their bedroom into a public room with the *Bed-In*. However, Lennon's drawing from the *Wedding Album* indicates that, when the reporters left at night, they enjoyed the peace and quiet which they described as "Bagism". The bedclothes became a "bag".

Above all, however, they criticised the media. On the one hand, Lennon used his fame to campaign for peace, but on the other hand he found that his message was not taken seriously because he was a pop star. If he was to have his voice heard, he had to hide. With the various bag performances, he and Yoko Ono wanted to show that it is the content of a message that is important, irrespective of the person who voices it. They railed against prejudices of all kinds based on external appearances, including, of course, racism: "Imagine if a black guy went for a job at the BBC and he had to wear a bag. They wouldn't know what coloured people were and there'd be no prejudice, for a kick-off!"[2]

The enormous amount of prejudice based on the external appearance of individuals is confirmed above all by the immense insecurity that occurs as soon as one is not quite certain *who* is in the bag. That person can no longer be categorised. This was exactly what Lennon intended to achieve, because he himself suffered from the same kind of categorisation, for which the bag was a synonym. "We're all in a bag," he said, explaining how they had invented the term "bagism" in the first place: he and his friends had all been in the "pop bag", while Yoko and her friends had been in their "avant-garde art bag". "And if you ask us what bagism is, then we say 'We're all in the same bag, baby'."[3]

1 From an interview published in the leaflet accompanying the *Wedding Album*.
2 Interview with Michael Parkinson in 1971, in: Coleman, Vol. II, p. 92.
3 Interview "Twenty-Four Hours", broadcast on 15 December 1969 by BBC. Quoted by Andrew Solt/Sam Egan, Imagine John Lennon, Munich 1989, p. 149.

Films
Record Sleeves
Writings

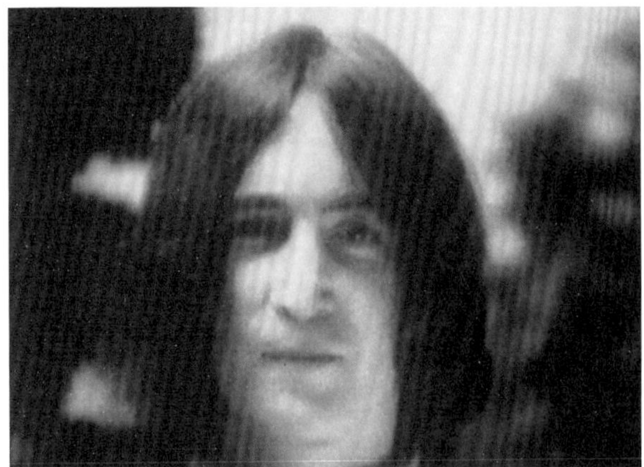

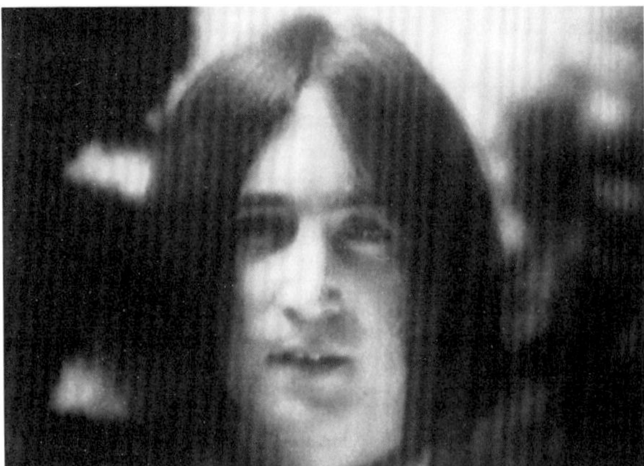

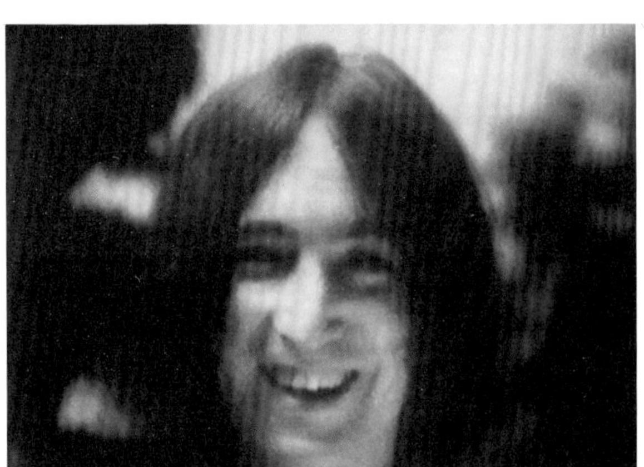

Film No. 5 – Smile, 1968
by Yoko Ono
Cast: John Lennon
Camera: William Wareing
Music: John Lennon
Light/location: garden
Instruction: Bring your own instrument
51 minutes
Premiere at the Chicago Film Festival 1968

A film portrait of John Lennon. For three minutes
Lennon's face was filmed with an ultra-high-
speed camera. By projecting this material at
normal speed it is stretched to a length of
51 minutes. The effect is that of extreme slow
motion.

Two Virgins, 1968
by John Lennon and Yoko Ono
Camera: William Wareing
Music: John Lennon and Yoko Ono from the
album *Two Virgins*
19:30 minutes

The faces of John Lennon and Yoko Ono are
superimposed over one another in slow motion
so that they partially blend. At the end there is
a longer sequence in which Lennon and Ono
embrace and kiss each other. The location is once
again Lennon's garden. The images are accompanied by sound experiments from the album of
the same name.

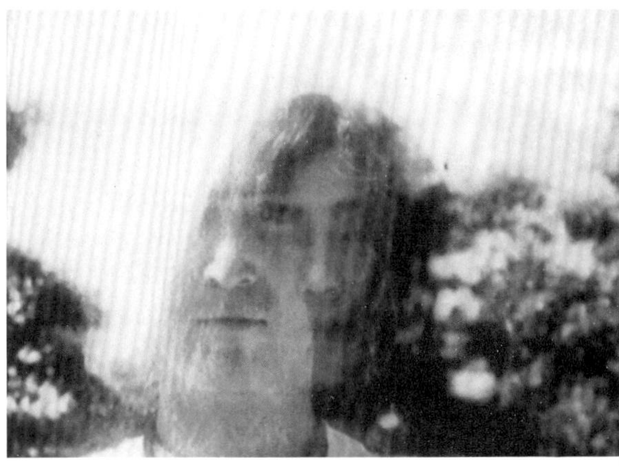

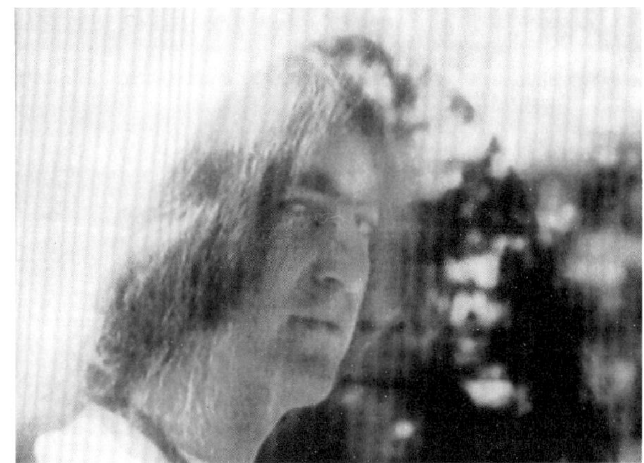

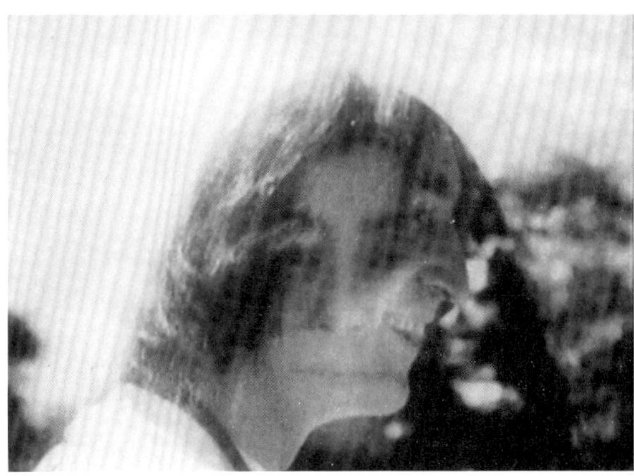

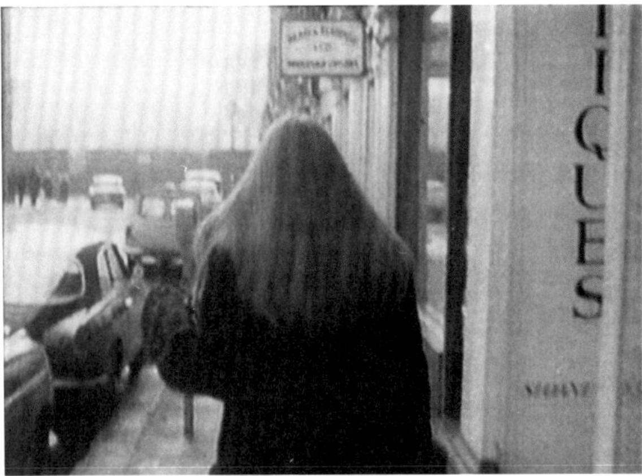

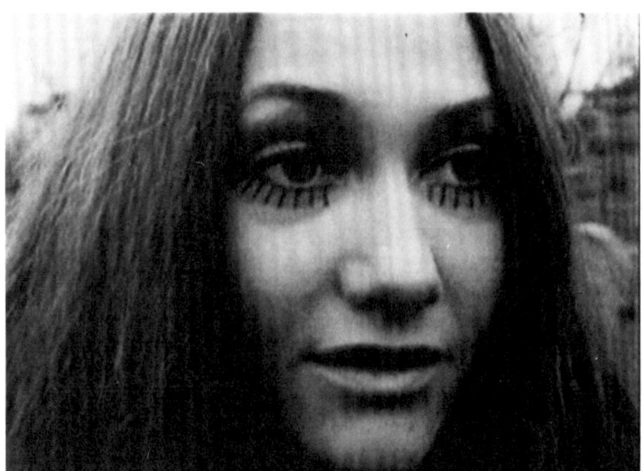

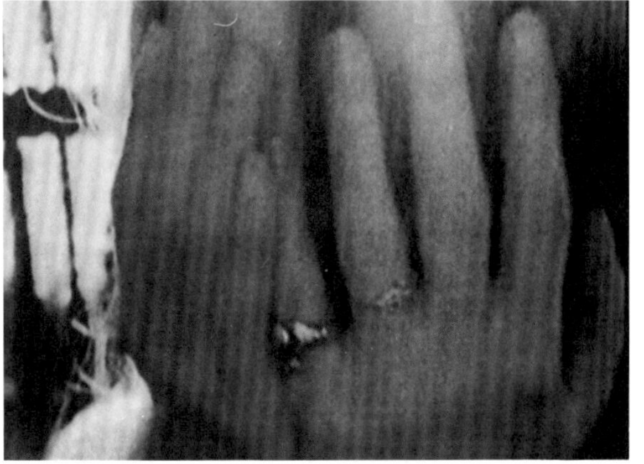

Rape, 1969
directed by John Lennon, Yoko Ono
Camera: Nic Knowland
Editing: John Lennon, Yoko Ono, Toni Trow
Music: John Lennon, Yoko Ono
76:30 minutes
Premiere on Austrian television on 31 March
1969

Cameraman Nic Knowland pursues an Austrian
tourist (Eva Majlath) in London with his camera.
The pursuit begins at a cemetery and is continued
in the streets of London on foot and by taxi. It
goes on for several days until the cameraman
finally enters her apartment and bolts the door
from inside so that the woman can no longer
avoid him.

The woman begs the cameraman time and
again to leave her alone. At first she is friendly
and surprised, then more annoyed and finally
desperate. She never receives a response; the
pursuit continues until the end.

The viewer becomes an accomplice of the
pursuer in that he sees the action through the eyes
of the cameraman, who is never shown in the
picture. Whenever the woman appeals to her
pursuer, she addresses the viewers directly, but
they can neither answer nor help her.

The merciless curiosity of the press and the
collaboration between the media and the
consumers are vividly illustrated in this film.

Erection, 1971
by John Lennon
Directed by John Lennon and Yoko Ono
Slides by Iain Macmillan
Lettering by George Maciunas
Music by Yoko Ono from her album *Fly*
18 minutes

Lennon commissioned photographer Iain
Macmillan to take slides of the construction of
the London International Hotel in North
Kensington at regular intervals from the same
vantage point. The material he gathered over
some 20 months was then filmed. In the film the
viewers see the building gradually being erected.

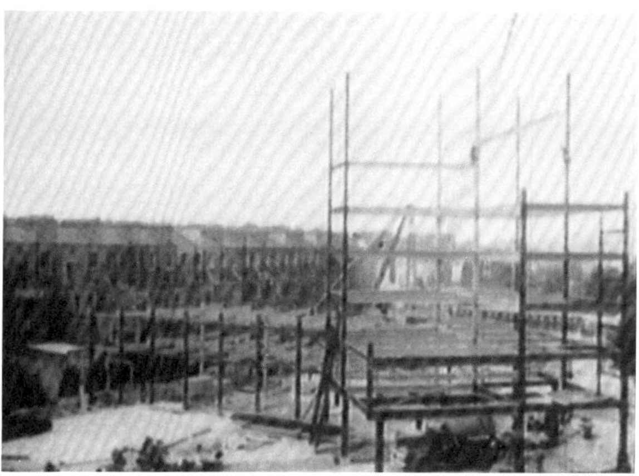

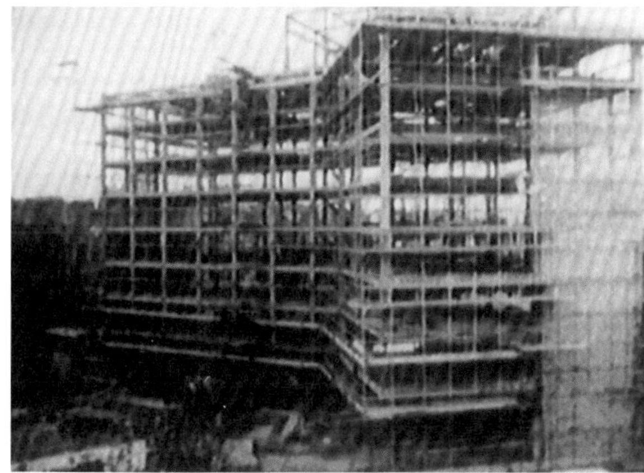

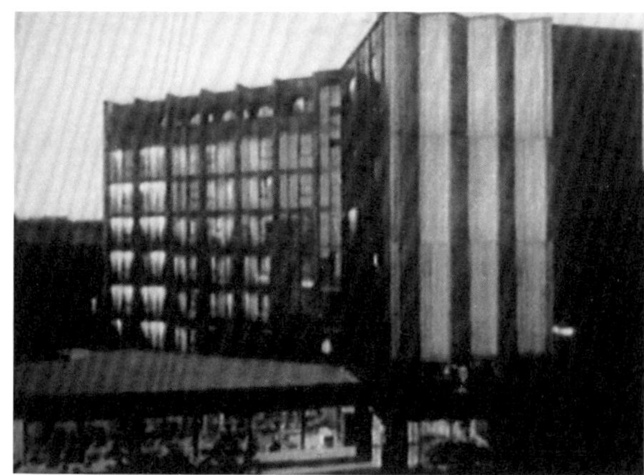

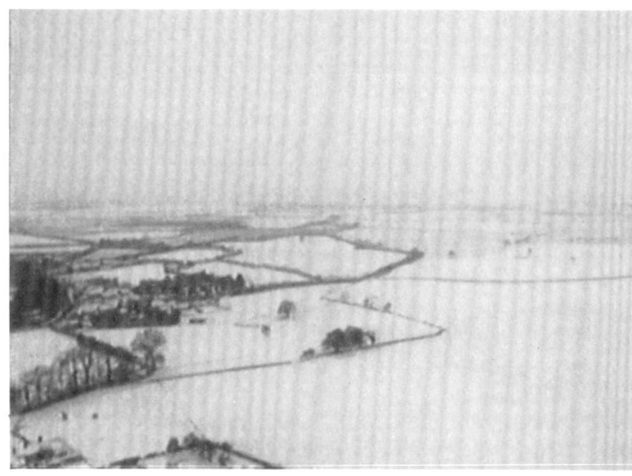

Apotheosis, 1970
by John Lennon
Directed by John Lennon and Yoko Ono
Camera: Nic Knowland
18:30 minutes
Premiere at the Cannes International Film
Festival 1971

The film shows the view from a hot-air balloon
that slowly rises over the grey, snow-covered
English countryside. As the balloon gradually
enters the dense cloud cover, the white of the
clouds blends in with the snow-covered landscape
so that it turns completely white for several
minutes. The balloon finally breaks through the
clouds, revealing the wide expanses of the sun.

The balloon can never be seen, so the viewers
get the impression that they themselves are rising
slowly and silently over the countryside. There is
no musical background. The silence in the air
above the landscape is interrupted only by two
shots.

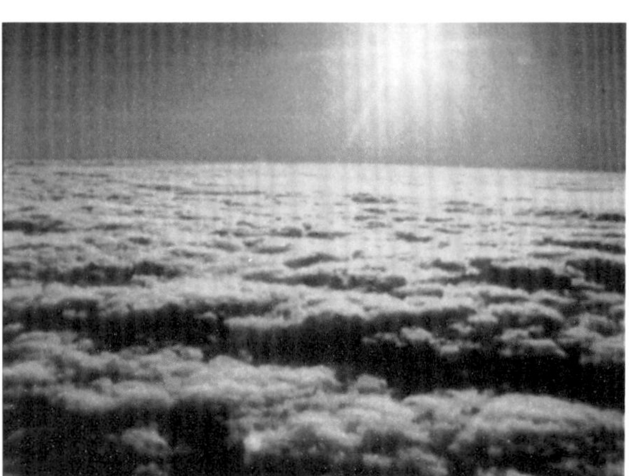

Imagine, 1972
by John Lennon and Yoko Ono
Directed by John Lennon and Yoko Ono
Music by John Lennon and Yoko Ono, produced
by Phil Spector
60 minutes

Music film with 13 pieces by John Lennon and
Yoko Ono (all songs are from Lennon's album
Imagine as well as *Don't Count the Waves* and
Mrs. Lennon by Yoko Ono and *Power to the
People* by Lennon/Ono).

Lennon and Ono have found personal images
to go with each song. In the way in which these
many different images are linked associatively,
the individual pieces resemble the structure of
modern video clips and anticipate, as it were, this
genre of music film. In addition to a number of
sequences from the park and their house in
Tittenhurst the pieces thus contain some very
surrealistic scenes, such as Lennon and Ono
with a white chessboard, made by Ono, whereby
Lennon eats the chess pieces in the end, or a scene
with Lennon and Ono playing a game of billiards
where they keep on changing their costumes and
finally appear with look-alikes. The *Bagism* motif
also occurs when a person goes through the
streets of London in a black bag.

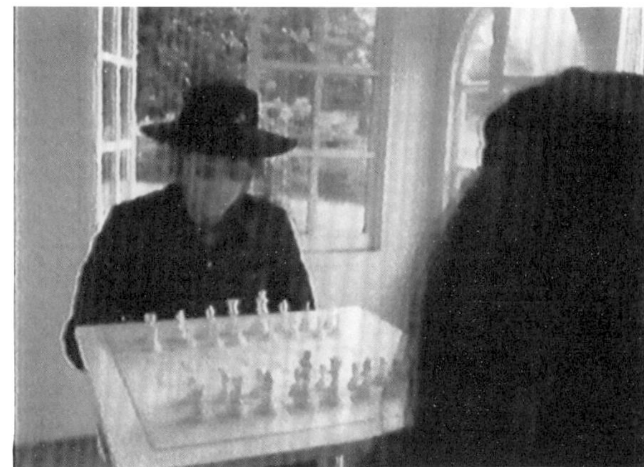

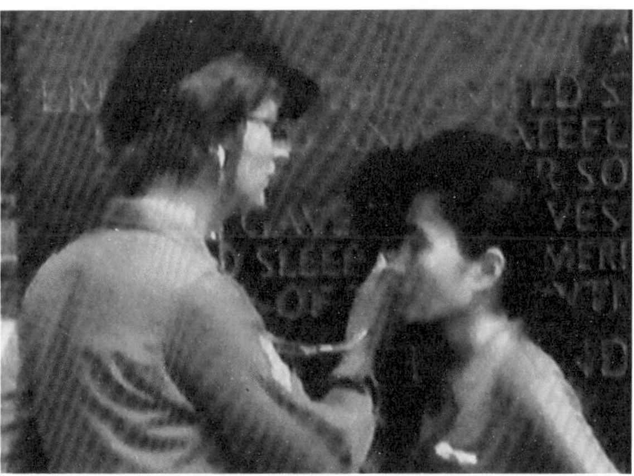

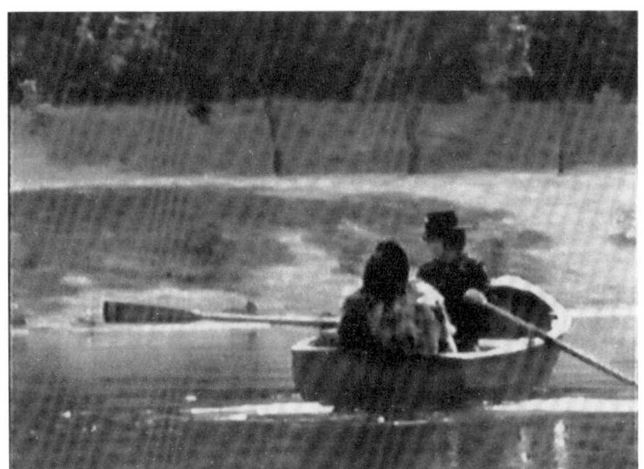

John Lennon's first solo album was released at the end of November 1968. The cover shows him and Yoko Ono naked – front and rear. The record sleeve was immediately censored and a court ruled that record shops wrap it in brown paper to hide the offensive photo. The music on the album was as experimental as the sleeve. Like Lennon's *Revolution No. 9* on the *White Album,* the entire recording was a collage of super-imposed tapes, distorted strains of piano and guitar, and Yoko Ono's brittle *a cappella* voice. The title, *Unfinished Music No. 1 – Two Virgins* is a reference to Yoko Ono's 1966 exhibition of *Unfinished Paintings and Objects* at the Indica Gallery in London in 1966. The cover concept of two figures in an open, undefinable space is also modelled on a portrait of the artist found in her exhibition catalogue.

Lennon used this as a vehicle to address the question of his identity as a Beatle. Instead of a painstakingly polished studio production, he released an improvised late-night home recording, and instead of a perfect colour print for the sleeve, he used a selftimer snapshot in black and white.

Another album followed in May 1969. *Unfinished Music No. 2 – Life with the Lions* has a slightly out-of-focus colour photo showing a rather melancholy Yoko Ono on a hospital bed, gazing pensively into the distance, with Lennon sitting on the floor on a sleeping bag. The image evokes an air of authentic and transfigured suffering, as does the black and white shot on the back cover showing them being led away from their home by police on charges of drug possession.

The oppressive atmosphere of the photos is also evident on the record itself. On the A side, a live concert recording is overlaid with Yoko Ono's abruptly aggressive vocal digressions and Lennon's screeching guitar riffs. On the B side, Yoko Ono tells of the problems relating to the censored *Two Virgins* album and her hospitali-sation due to complications in pregnancy. This is followed, logically enough, by *Baby's Heartbeat.* Then there is silence. In this context, the title *Two Minutes Silence* would seem to be a memorial for the child lost in a miscarriage. Like the two preceding tracks, the final track, *Radio Play,* is exactly what the title says it is: sounds from the radio.

Purely biographical explanations aside, the last two tracks are also variations on pieces by John Cage, whose famous silent composition *4:33* (1952) and slightly earlier *Imaginary Land-scape No. 4* for twelve radios are transformed here into a pop record. The very concept of *Unfinished Music,* in fact, evokes John Cage's aesthetic approach of not fixing all aspects of a work of art in order to prevent its precise repro-duction.

In his book *Notations* (1969), John Cage printed Yoko Ono's *Beat Piece,* derived from the appeal *Listen to a heartbeat.* On the *Life with the Lions* album, this written instruction takes the form of a documentary tape-recording, having already been presented as a performance in 1965 in New York.

This distinct transposition of artistic concepts to a wide variety of different media is a central tenet of Fluxus art. In keeping with the spirit of Fluxus, Lennon and Ono did not regard their joint recordings primarily as works of art intended for all eternity, but as documents recording fleeting moments of their current activities. Time and time again, we find visual and acoustic paraphrases of *Pieces* and *Events* which Ono had published in her book *Grapefruit.* For example, part of the *Sky Event* in that book – "wait until a cloud appears and comes above your head" – appeared on the cover of their fourth joint LP *Live Peace in Toronto,* featuring live recordings of the first concert by the Plastic Ono Band.

The first edition of the record contained a photo calendar for 1970, designed by Lennon and

Yoko Ono with texts and pictures. It not only includes Lennon's nonsense text *Jock and Yono,* but also brief and highly stylised autobiographies of them both. As well as recording such important events as the hospitalisation and the arrest, the photos present Lennon and Yoko Ono primarily as artists: at the *Acorn Event,* at the *You Are Here* exhibition and at a *Bag Piece.*

About one month before their *Live Peace in Toronto* LP, the elaborately designed *Wedding Album* was released in November 1969. It is a boxed album containing not only the LP in its own folding sleeve, but also a brochure of press cuttings on the wedding, drawings, photos, reproductions of the marriage certificate and a photo showing a piece of wedding cake.

This multimedia package, a multiple, may be regarded in the context of other projects of the late sixties, such as William Copley's *S.M.S.* edition – a series of 6 portfolios containing 73 multiples by various artists –, or *Aspen Magazine* (1965–70), the seventh issue of which was designed by John Cosh, the designer of the *Wedding Album.* Andy Warhol also demonstrated his strong interest in multimedia in his contribution to the third issue of *Aspen Magazine.* Warhol's own *Index Book* (1967) is a small *gesamtkunstwerk* in itself. It contains an interview text, full-page photographs, pop-up multiples and a record on which conversations of people leafing through the book can be heard.

The *Index Book* and the *Wedding Album* have more in common than their distinctly self-referential focus and multimedia form. Lennon and Ono's direct and undiluted translation of their personal lives into their art certainly brooks comparison with the way Warhol dealt with the reality around him. This is evident not only in the *Wedding Album*'s documentation of the Amsterdam Hilton *Bed-In,* complete with breakfast and room service, on one side of the LP (the other side is a further acoustic interpretation of the *Beat Piece*), but is also reflected in their

rapid and prolific output (3 LPs in 1969 alone). The *Wedding Album* also bears certain affinities to such Fluxus events as the 1967 wedding of Milan Knizak, or to Geoffrey Hendricks' 1971 *Fluxdivorce.*

These first four records by Lennon and Yoko Ono have gone virtually unnoticed right up to the present day because they are situated within a cultural no-man's-land between different target groups. Lennon fans failed to appreciate the intended cultural and social critique, while Cage devotees were sceptical about the proximity to the pop scene and Fluxus followers were more interested in the work of their official members.

Lennon and Yoko Ono then sought to combine their provocative candour with the prevailing pop idiom. They stopped recording together and, between 1970 and 1973, each released three solo albums. These LPs, issued simultaneously, possess conceptual and design parallels unique in the history of recording, right down to a joint variation on the Apple label.

The new direction they had chosen to take proved successful. With the 1970 LPs *John Lennon/Plastic Ono Band* and *Yoko Ono/Plastic Ono Band* they accomplished an extraordinary synthesis of primal therapy and rock music. At first glance, the record sleeves appear to be identical: a couple leaning against an oak tree with dappled light flooding through the foliage. On closer inspection, however, we see that Lennon's album sleeve shows Yoko Ono leaning against the tree, with Lennon in her lap, while Yoko Ono's album shows them the other way round. On the back of each album there is a childhood photo of Lennon and Yoko Ono respectively, while the inner sleeve with the lyrics bears a handwritten dedication to the partner.

The next two albums moved away from the uncompromisingly idiosyncratic musical approach of their predecessors. Here, as on all John Lennon's subsequent albums, the title and the artist are clearly visible on the sleeve. The sleeve designs for *Imagine* and for Yoko Ono's parallel release, *Fly*, show a double exposure of the respective artist's face. The back of the *Imagine* sleeve can be interpreted as a visual extension of Ono's *Sky Event*, which had been portrayed on the cover of *Live Peace in Toronto* at an earlier phase.

Imagine and *Fly* are connected with Yoko Ono's exhibition *This Is Not Here*. The LPs were released shortly before the exhibition opened on 9 October 1971. Fluxus founder George Maciunas, who had also been instrumental in organising the exhibition, was involved in the design. He created a photocollage for *Fly* and an inside sleeve for *Imagine*, stylistically related to the target-like Fluxus posters he designed. The first edition of *Imagine*, the title of which is also taken from *Grapefruit*, included a poster of John Lennon at the piano, and a postcard of John grabbing a pig by the ears, in reference to the cover of Paul McCartney's *Ram* (on which McCartney holds a ram by the horns).

In 1972, Lennon and Ono produced another joint album, *Some Time in New York City*, addressing the political events of the day. Lennon's cover design makes it clear that, for him, songs have a similar impact to newspaper articles. Formally, he refers to the catalogue he designed for Ono's exhibition *This Is Not Here*, while the typeface of both publications is that of the *New York Times*. Instead of a variation of the *Apple* motif on the label of the two records, this time there is a visual adaptation of their 1968 film *Two Virgins*. In a sequence of 5 photos, Lennon's face is gradually faded into Yoko Ono's face.

In their last twin production, *Mind Games* and *Feeling the Space* (both 1973), Lennon and Ono sought to return to the lyricism of *Imagine*. The record sleeves are photomontages with similar colouring. The *Mind Games* design, by Lennon himself, is clearly adapted to prevailing taste. Between 1972 and 1975, many record sleeves had used photomontage or photo-realistic painting to produce unexpected and surrealistic visual effects – the Pink Floyd albums *A Nice Pair* (1973) and *Wish You Were Here* (1975) spring to mind, as does Jackson Browne's *Late for the Sky* (1974).

The object-like gimmick cover for Lennon's next release, *Walls and Bridges*, was hardly unusual in the early seventies amongst artists with commercial potential. The front cover cites three early watercolours by Lennon. Two horizontal printed strips, printed with photographic details on the back, make the cover variable in a way that is reminiscent of the surrealist *cadavre exquis* experiments.

This concept is not actually by Lennon, but by art director and designer Roy Kohara, who also designed the typography for the next two releases. For the cover of the following LP, *Rock'n'Roll*, he designed lettering made of neon tubing, which he then superimposed on a photo of Lennon taken in Hamburg in 1961 by Jürgen Vollmer.

Shaved Fish, John Lennon's next release, was a compilation of his singles and appeared in 1975, the same year as *Rock'n'Roll*. The eleven tracks on the album are presented on the cover in a surreally photo-realistic series of images with certain stylistic affinities to the work of Belgian painter René Magritte. Draughtsman Michael Bryan transposed and varied existing cover motifs and photos for the sleeve. James Whistler's 1871 portrait of his mother was used to illustrate the track *Mother*.

John Lennon contributed more to the cover design of his last LP, *Double Fantasy* (1980). The black and white cover photo reiterates motifs from the *Wedding Album* sleeve in a self-citation that rekindles the myth of John and Yoko.

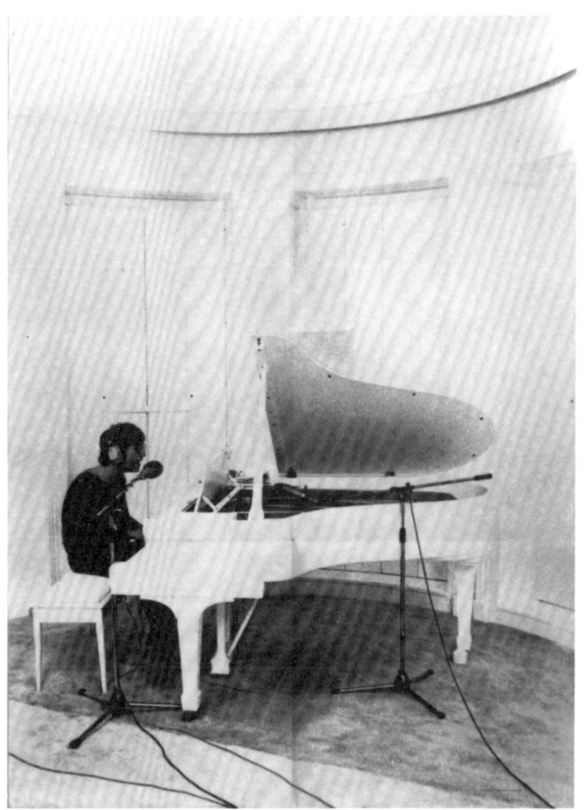

John Lennon at the piano in Tittenhurst Park. Poster from the *Imagine* album, 1971

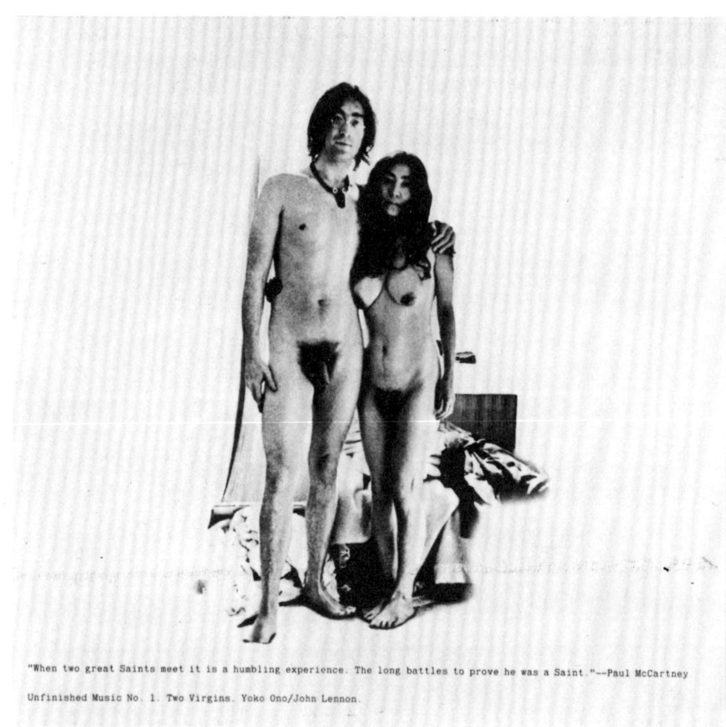

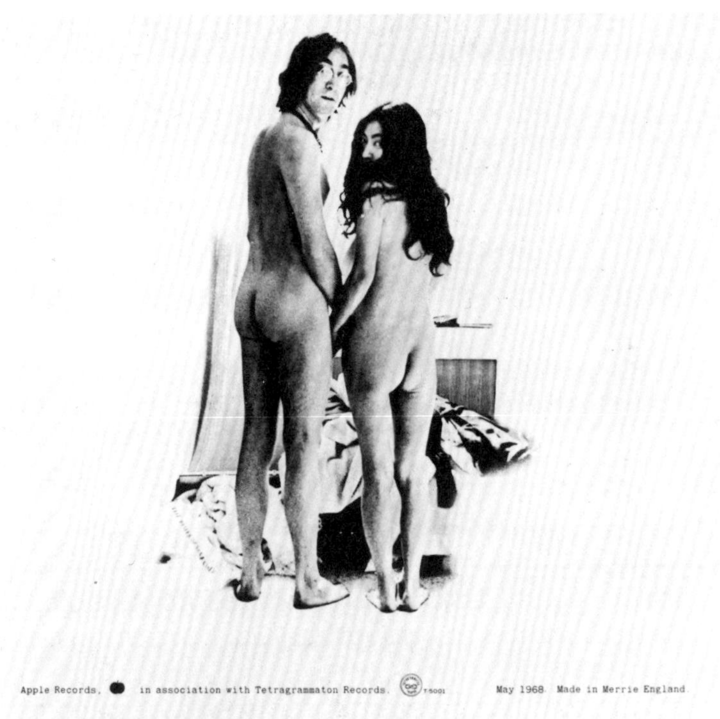

*Unfinished Music No. 1 –
Two Virgins,*
John Lennon and
Yoko Ono.
Released: 29 November
1968.
Front and rear uncensored.

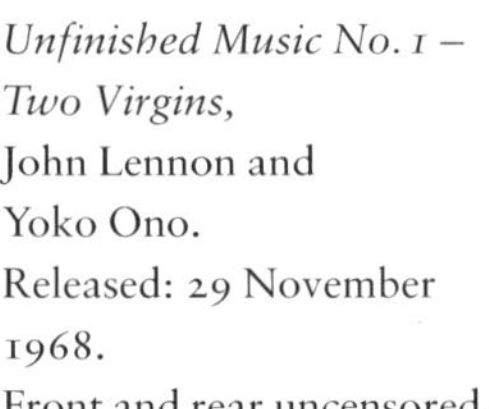

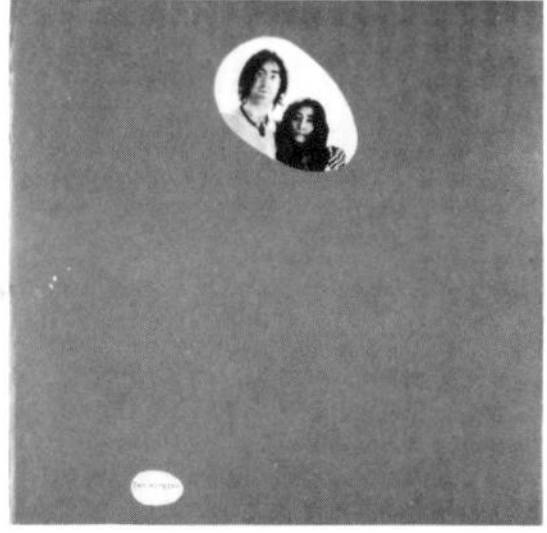

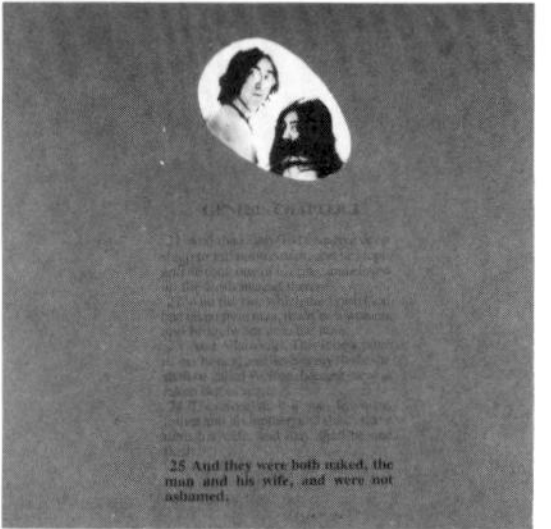

Front and rear sides, covered
over with paper by order of
the censors.

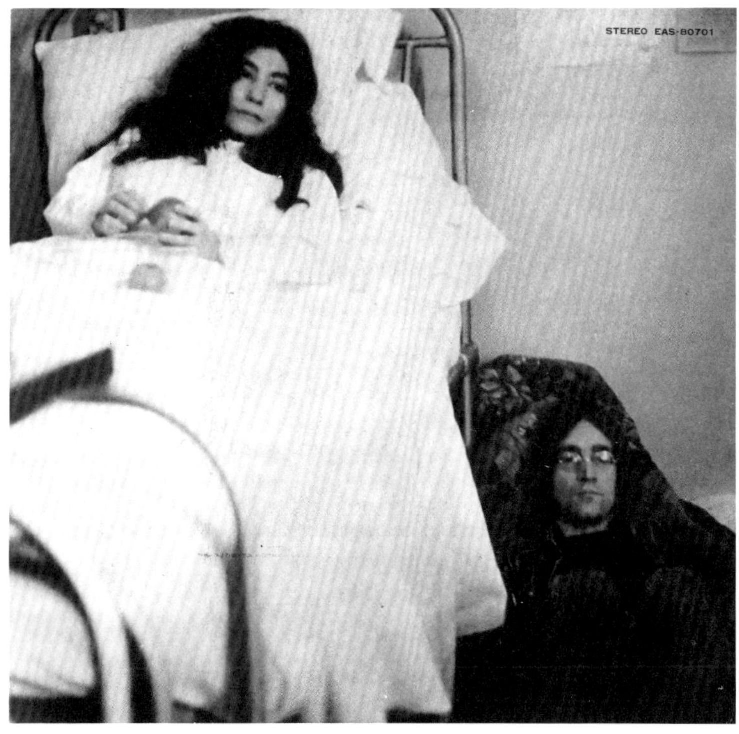

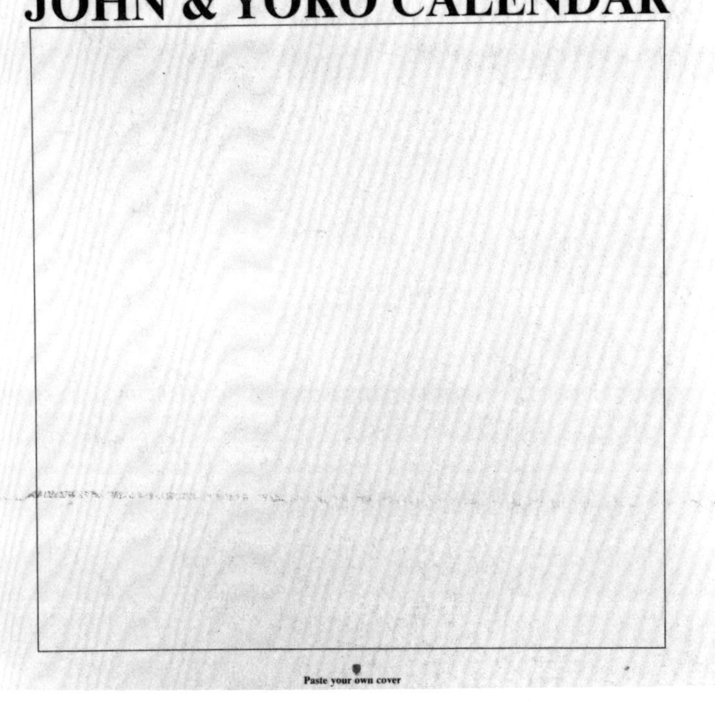

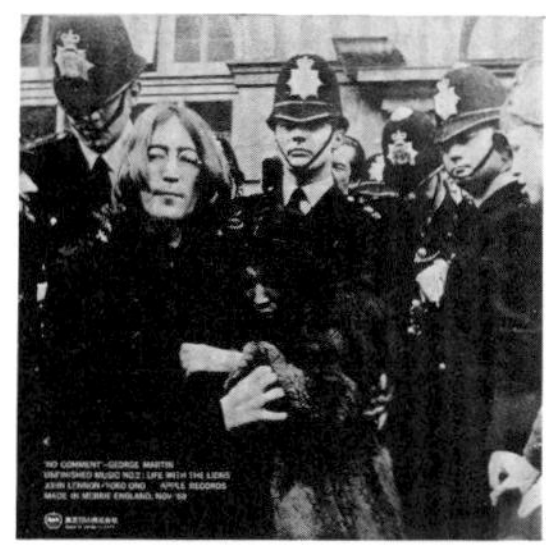

*Unfinished Music No. 2 –
Life with the Lions,*
John Lennon and
Yoko Ono.
Released: 9 May 1969.

Front: Lennon on his
sleeping bag keeping watch
at Yoko Ono's bedside in
hospital.

Rear: Lennon and Yoko
Ono arrested by police in
London for drug possession.

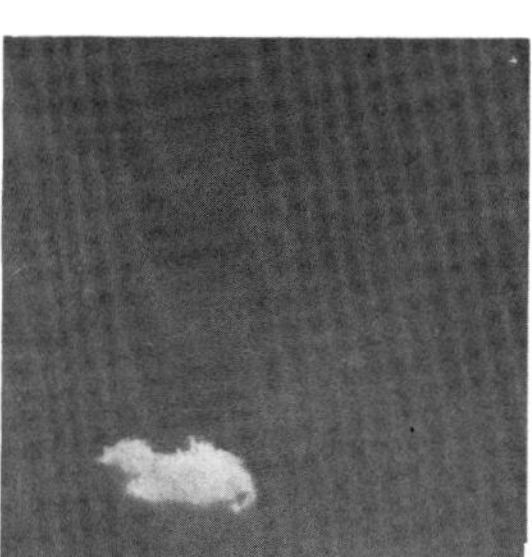

A calendar designed by
Lennon and Yoko Ono was
enclosed with the record

*The Plastic Ono Band – Live
Peace in Toronto,*
John Lennon, Yoko Ono,
Eric Clapton, Klaus
Voormann, Alan White.
Released: 12 December
1969.

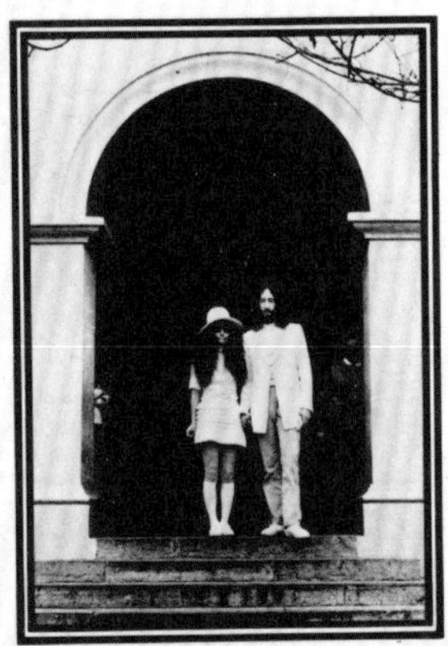

Wedding Album,
John Lennon and Yoko Ono.
Released: 7 November 1969
The *Wedding Album* is a collection of souvenirs of the marriage, the *Bed-In* and the subsequent *Bag* Events, documented here as a series of related performances. It contains the reproduction of the marriage certificate, a series of four passport photos, a postcard from the *Bed-In* in Amsterdam, a press kit with cuttings, a poster printed on both sides called "The Wedding", a poster printed on both sides with drawings by Lennon and Ono, the text of an interview as well as the record.

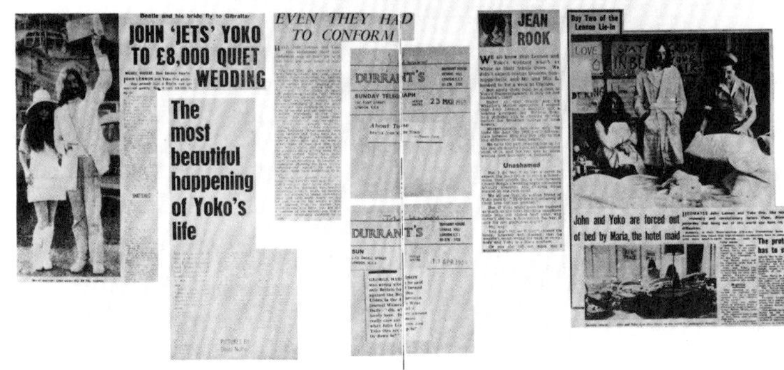

Press kit with cuttings (texts, photos, caricatures) about the wedding, the *Bed-In* and *Bagism*.

Photo of a piece of wedding cake.

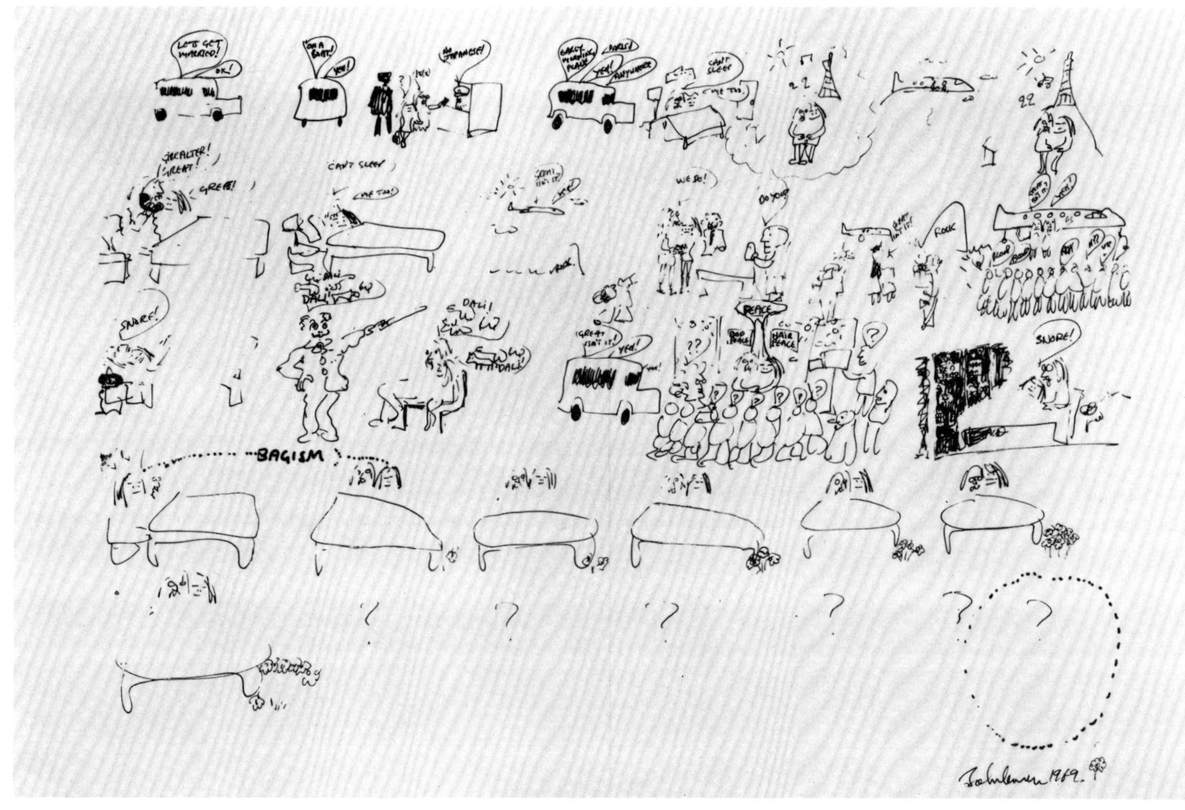

Drawing by John Lennon from the *Wedding Album*.

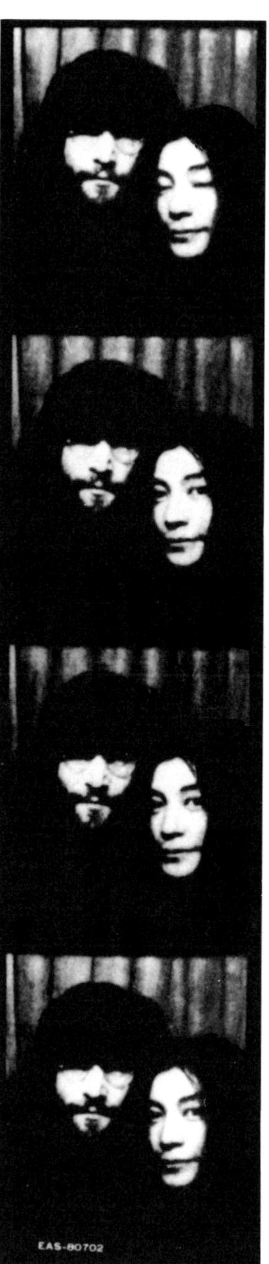

Four photo-booth shots of John Lennon and Yoko Ono, from the *Wedding Album*.

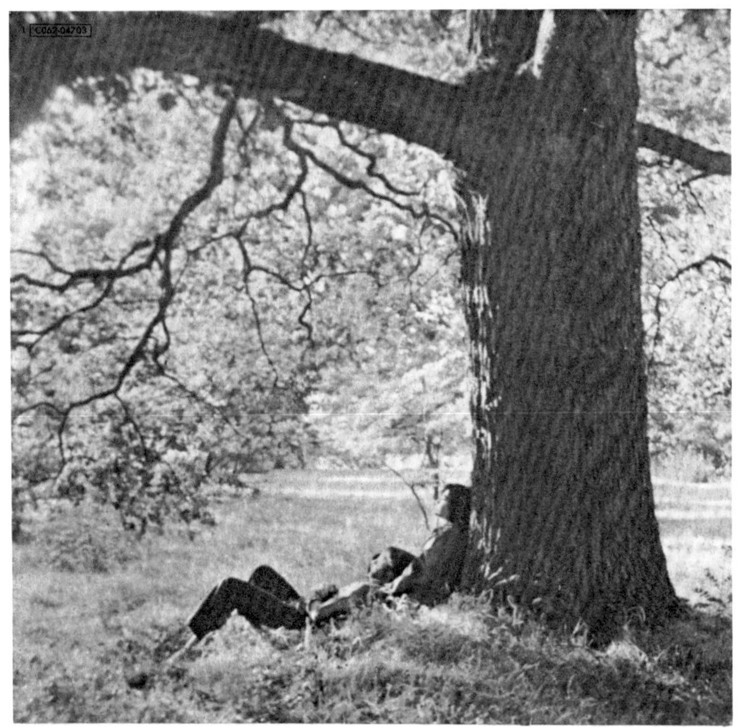

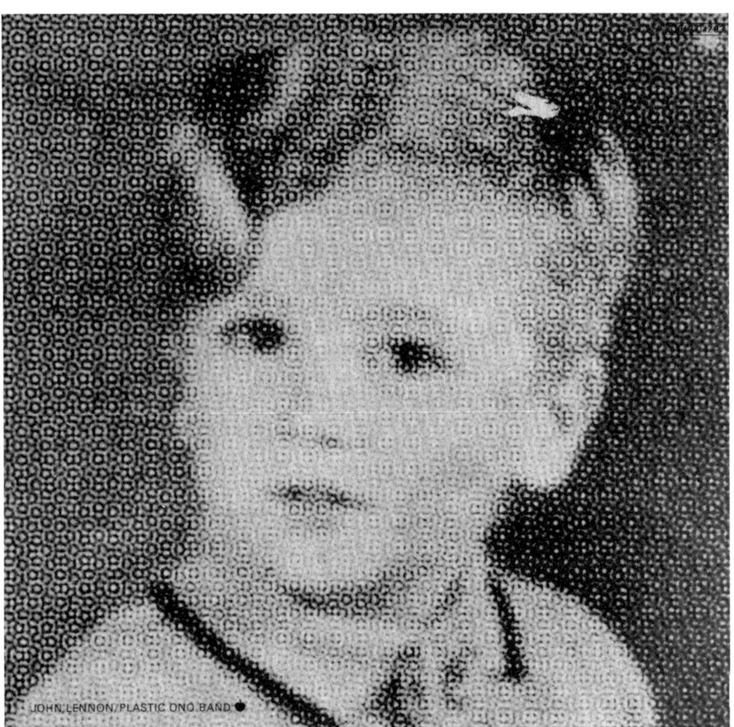

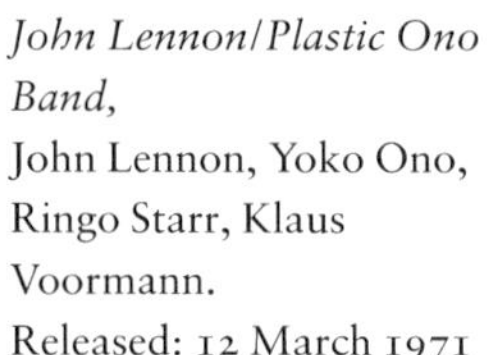

John Lennon/Plastic Ono Band,
John Lennon, Yoko Ono,
Ringo Starr, Klaus
Voormann.
Released: 12 March 1971

Rear: Photo of John Lennon
as a child

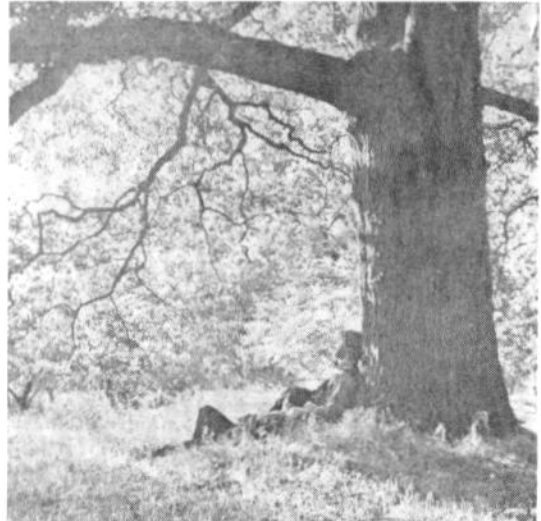

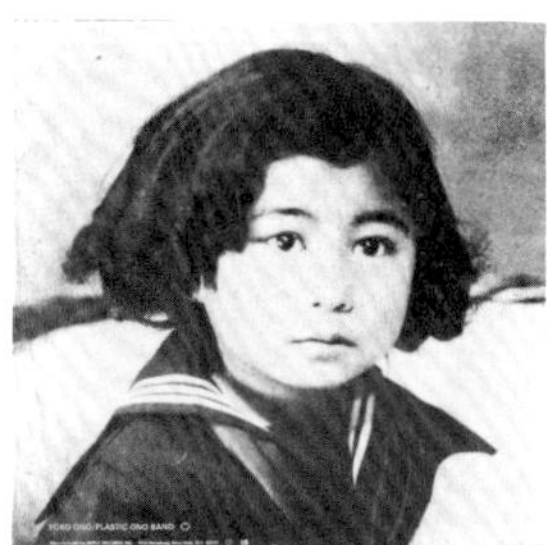

The counterpart: *Yoko Ono/
Plastic Ono Band,* 1971

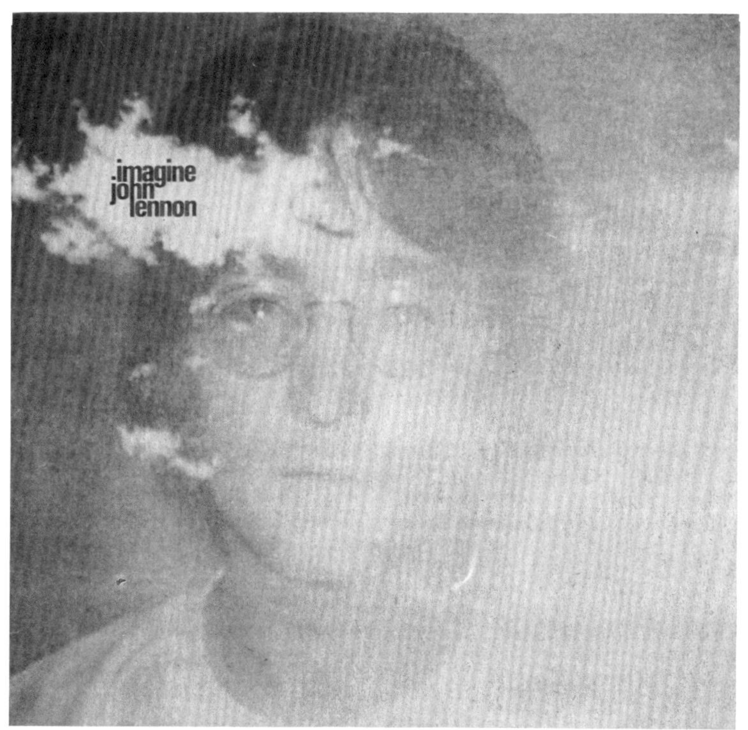

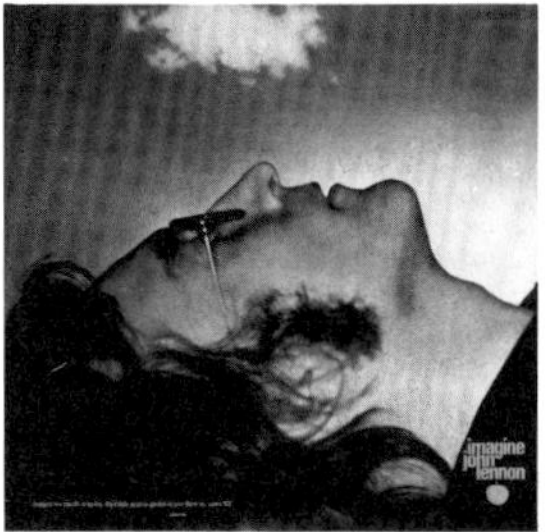

Imagine,
John Lennon/Plastic Ono
Band (with the flux fiddlers)
Released: 7 September 1971
(USA)

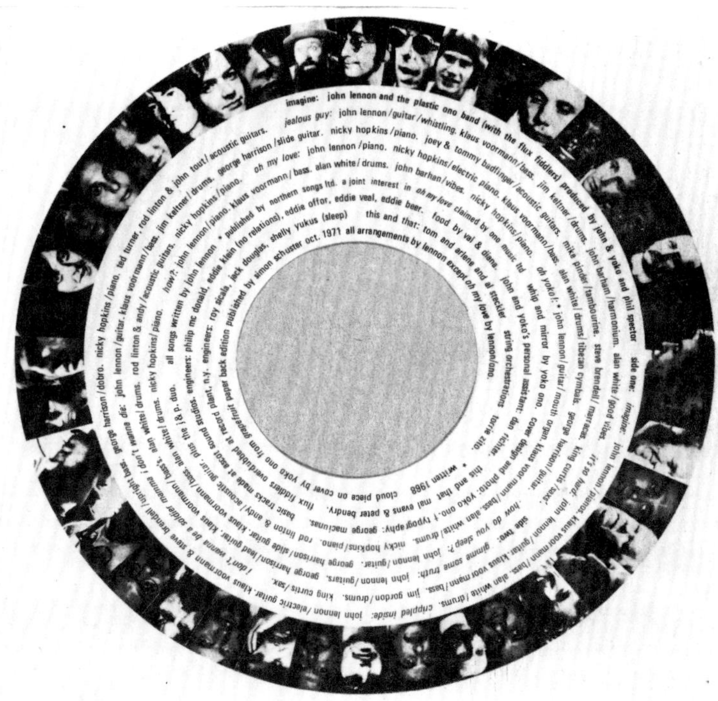

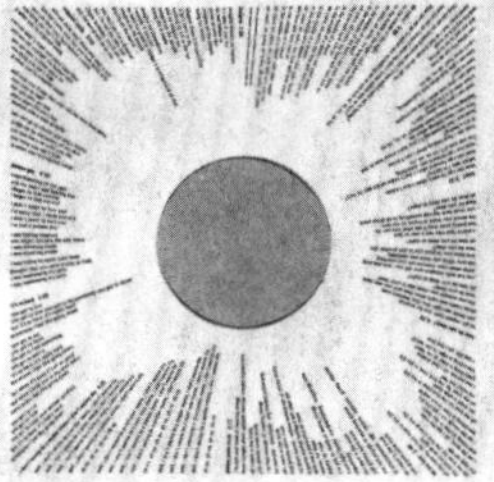

Inside cover with track titles
and credits and the texts of
the lyrics.

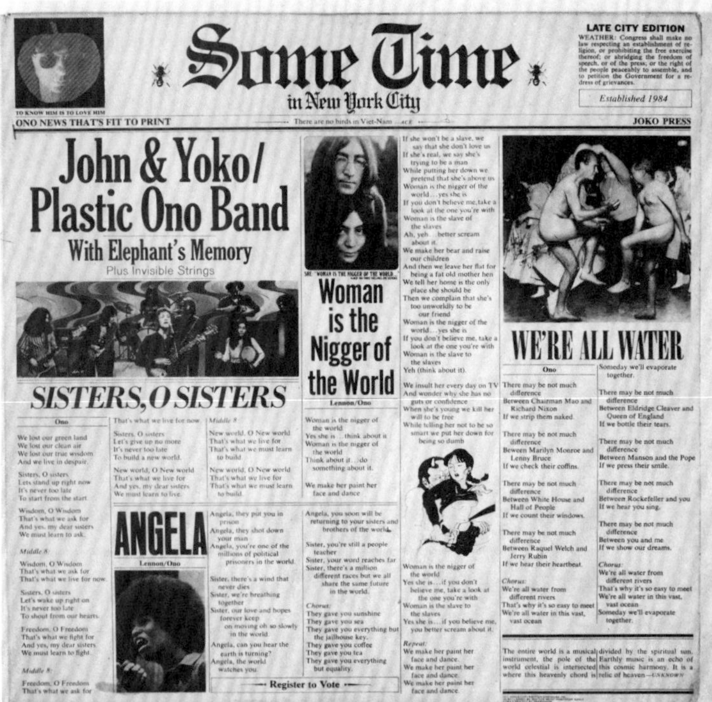

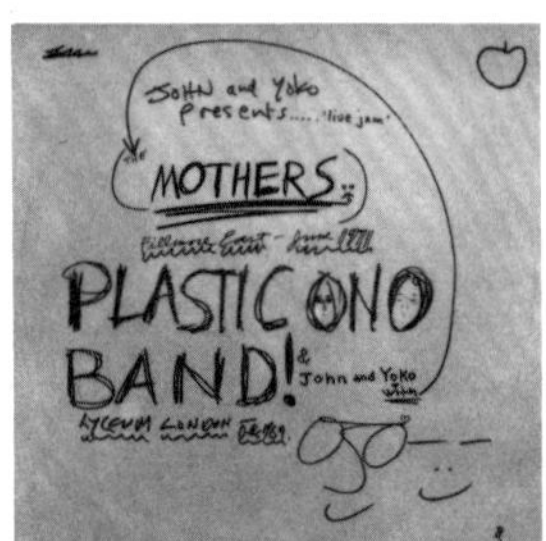

*Some Time in
New York City,*
John & Yoko/Plastic Ono
Band with Elephant's
Memory Plus Invisible
Strings (sides 1 and 2).
John Lennon and Yoko Ono
with the Plastic Ono Super-
group (side 3).
John Lennon and Yoko
Ono, Plastic Ono Band with
Frank Zappa and The
Mothers of Invention
(side 4).
Released: 12 June 1972
(USA).

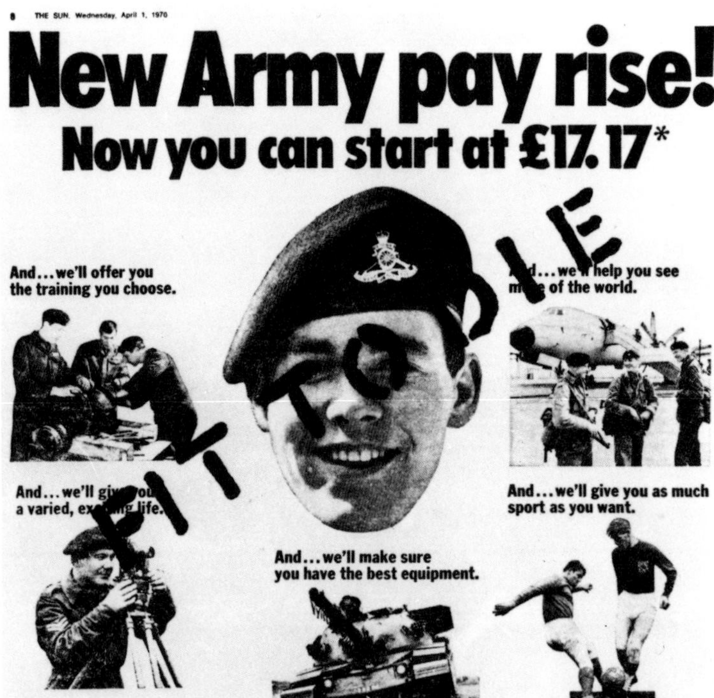

British army recruitment
leaflet reworked by John
Lennon.
Insert to the album *Some
Time in New York City.*

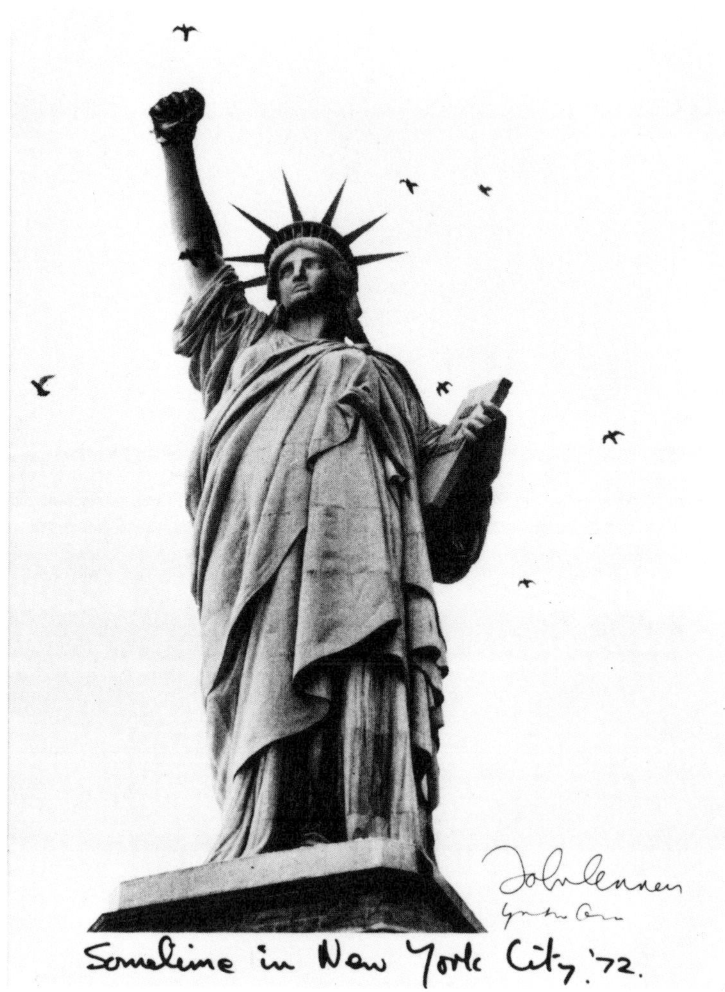

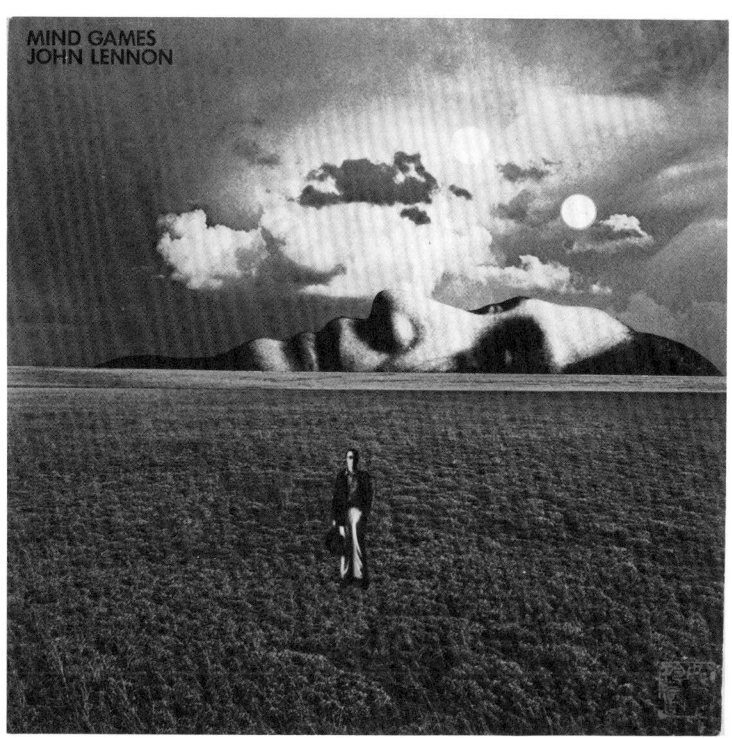

Mind Games,
John Lennon and the Plastic
U.F. Ono Band.
Released: 16 November
1973

The Statue of Liberty with a
clenched fist,
collage by John Lennon.
Postcard enclosed
in the album *Some Time in
New York City*.

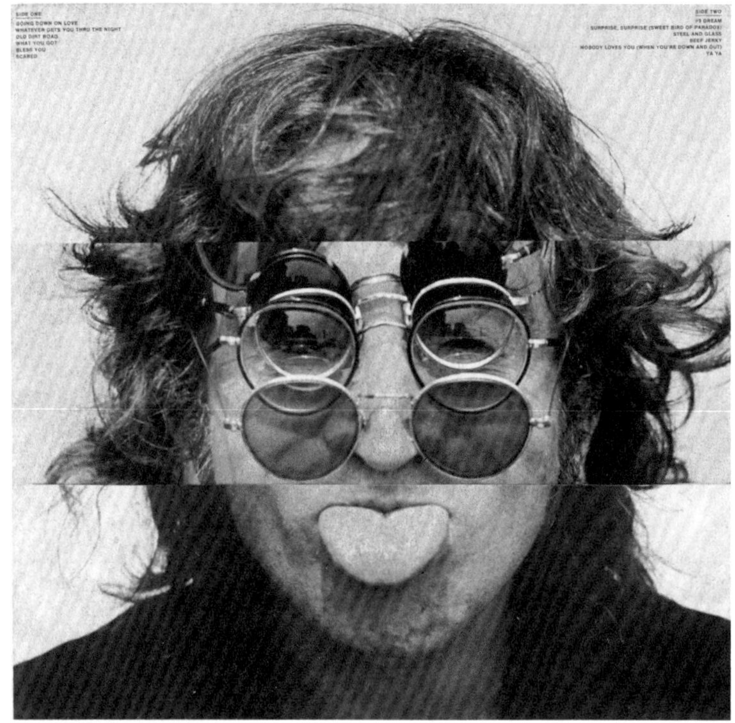

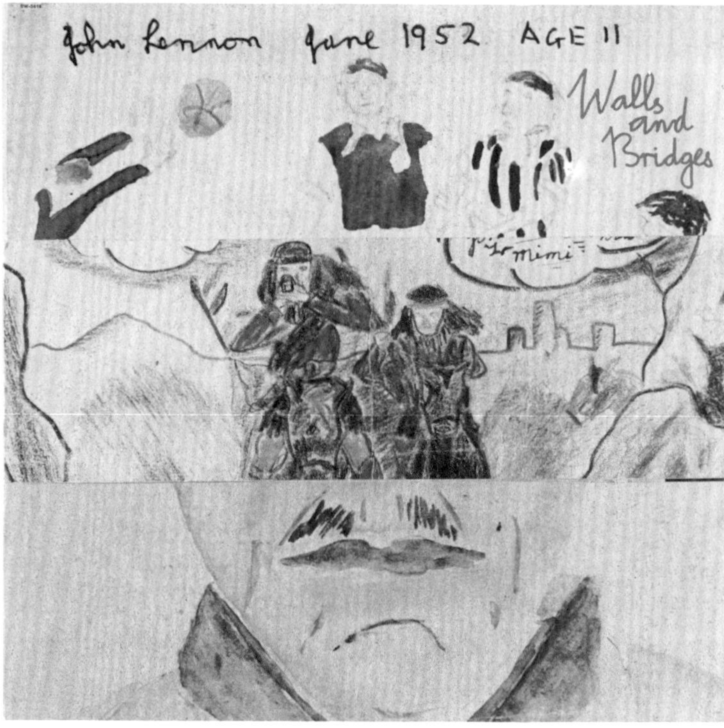

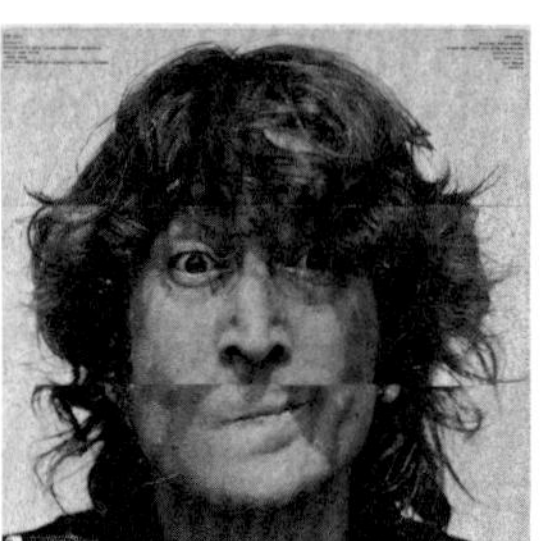

Walls and Bridges,
John Lennon and The Plastic
Ono Nuclear Band.
Released: 4 October 1974
Front: Lennon's face can be
varied by two moveable
strips.

Rear: watercolour by
11-year-old John Lennon.
This side can also be varied
by the moveable strips.

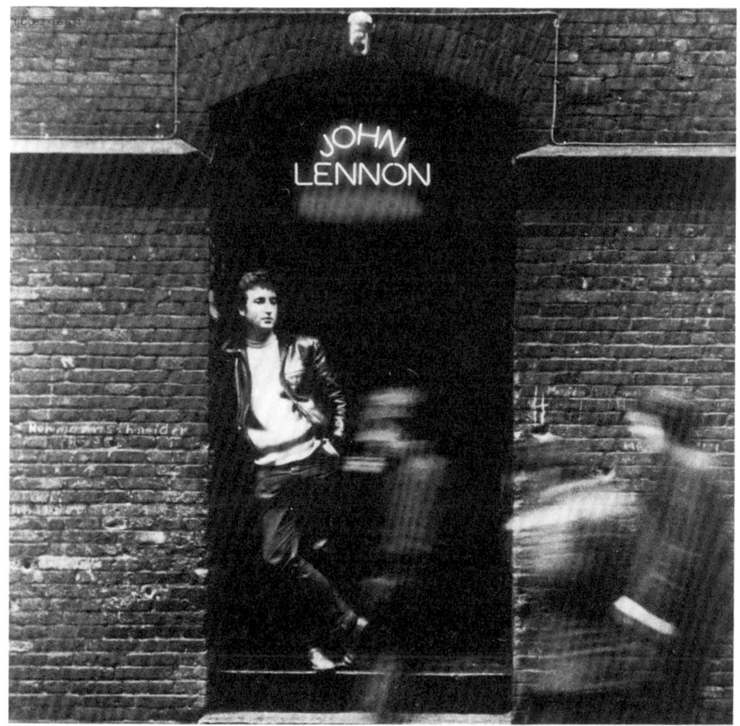

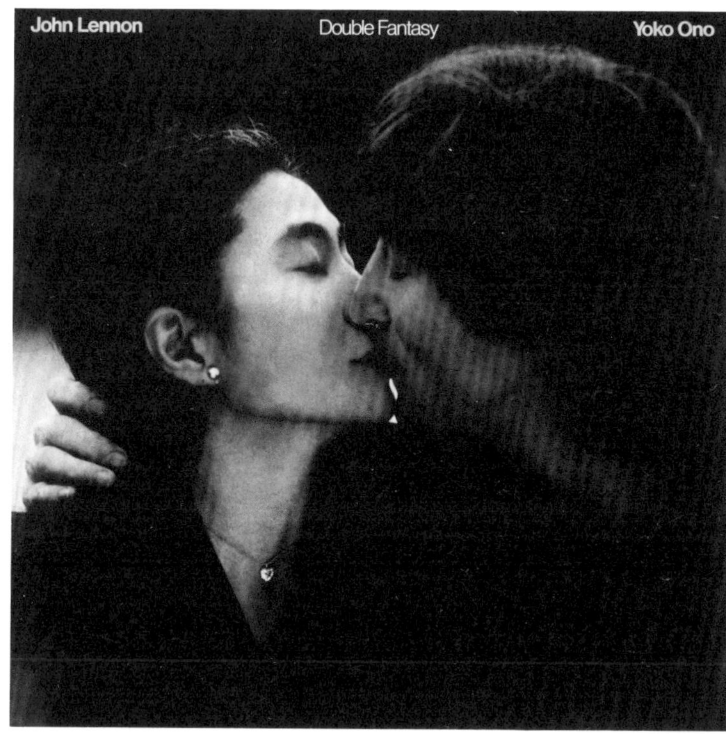

Rock'n'Roll,
John Lennon.
Released: 21 February 1975.
Front with photo of John
Lennon by Jürgen Vollmer.

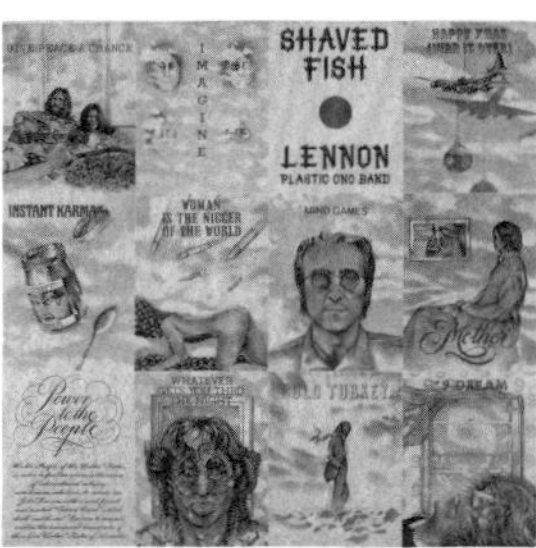

Shaved Fish,
John Lennon/Plastic Ono
Band, Collection of tracks
released as singles.
Released: 24 October 1975.
Front: the individual images
take reference to the singles
sleeves.

Double Fantasy,
John Lennon/Yoko Ono.
Released: 16 November
1980.
Front: the kiss motif
reiterates the Wedding
Album sleeve.

John Lennon as a Writer: Shun the Punman![1]
Jörg Helbig

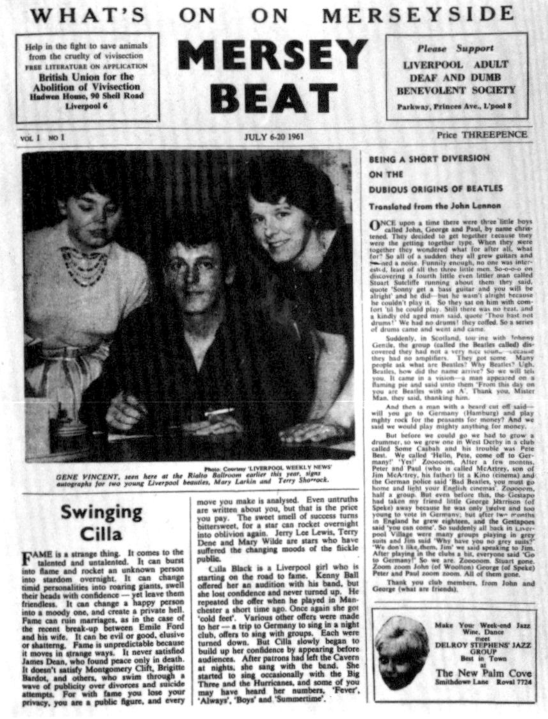

WHAT'S ON ON MERSEYSIDE

MERSEY BEAT

Help in the fight to save animals from the cruelty of vivisection
FREE LITERATURE ON APPLICATION
British Union for the Abolition of Vivisection
Hadwen House, 90 Sheil Road
Liverpool 6

Please Support
LIVERPOOL ADULT DEAF AND DUMB BENEVOLENT SOCIETY
Parkway, Princes Ave., L'pool 8

VOL 1 NO 1 — JULY 6-20 1961 — Price THREEPENCE

BEING A SHORT DIVERSION ON THE DUBIOUS ORIGINS OF BEATLES

Translated from the John Lennon

ONCE upon a time there were three little boys called John, George and Paul, by name christened. They decided to get together because they were the getting together type. When they were together they wondered what for after all, what for? So all of a sudden they all grew guitars and formed a noise. Funnily enough, no one was interested, least of all the three little men. So-o-o-o on discovering a fourth little even littler man called Stuart Sutcliffe running about them they said, quote 'Sonny get a bass guitar and you will be alright' and he did—but he wasn't alright because he couldn't play it. So they sat on him with comfort 'til he could play. Still there was no beat, and a kindly old aged man said, quote 'Thou hast not drums!' We had no drums! they coffed. So a series of drums came and went and came.

Suddenly, in Scotland, touring with Johnny Genile, the group (called the Beatles called) discovered they had not a very nice sound because they had no amplifiers. They got some. Many people ask what are Beatles? Why Beatles? Ugh, Beatles, how did the name arrive? So we will tell you. It came in a vision—a man appeared on a flaming pie and said unto them 'From this day on you are Beatles with an A'. Thank you, Mister Man, they said, thanking him.

And then a man with a beard cut off said— will you go to Germany (Hamburg) and play mighty rock for the peasants for money? And we said we would play mighty anything for money.

But before we could go we had to grow a drummer, so we grew one in West Derby in a club called Some Casbah and his trouble was Pete Best. We called 'Hello, Pete, come off to Germany!' 'Yes!' Zooooom, After a few months, Peter and Paul (who is called McArtrey, son of Jim McArtrey, his father) lit a Kino (cinema) and the German police said 'Bad Beatles, you must go home and light your English cinemas'. Zooooom, half a group. But even before this, the Gestapo had taken my friend little George Harrison (of Speke) away because he was only twelve and too young to vote in Germany; but after two months in England he grew eighteen, and the Gestapoes said 'you can come'. So suddenly all back in Liverpool Village were many groups playing in grey suits and Jim said 'Why have you no grey suits?' 'We don't like them, Jim' we said speaking to Jim. After playing in the clubs a bit, everyone said 'Go to Germany!' So we are. Zooooom. Stuart gone. Zoom zoom John (of Woolton) George (of Speke) Peter and Paul zoom zoom. All of them gone.

Thank you club members, from John and George (what are friends).

Photo: Courtesy 'LIVERPOOL WEEKLY NEWS'
GENE VINCENT, seen here at the Rialto Ballroom earlier this year, signs autographs for two young Liverpool beauties, Mary Larkin and Terry Shorrock.

Swinging Cilla

FAME is a strange thing. It comes to the talented and untalented. It can burst into flame and rocket an unknown person into stardom overnight. It can change timid personalities into roaring giants, swell their heads with confidence — yet leave them friendless. It can change a happy person into a moody one, and create a private hell. Fame can ruin marriages, as in the case of the recent break-up between Emile Ford and his wife. It can be evil or good, elusive or shattering. Fame is unpredictable because it moves in strange ways. It never satisfied James Dean, who found peace only in death. It doesn't satisfy Montgomery Clift, Brigitte Bardot, and others, who swim through a wave of publicity over divorces and suicide attempts. For with fame you lose your privacy, you are a public figure, and every move you make is analysed. Even untruths are written about you, but that is the price you pay. The sweet smell of success turns bittersweet, for a star can rocket overnight into oblivion again. Jerry Lee Lewis, Terry Dene and Mary Wilde are stars who have suffered the changing moods of the fickle public.

Cilla Black is a Liverpool girl who is starting on the road to fame. Kenny Ball offered her an audition with his band, but she lost confidence and never turned up. He repeated the offer when he played in Manchester a short time ago. Once again she got 'cold feet'. Various other offers were made to her — a trip to Germany to sing in a night club, offers to sing with groups. Each were turned down. But Cilla slowly began to build up her confidence by appearing before audiences. After patrons had left the Cavern at nights, she sang with the band. She started to sing occasionally with the Big Three and the Hurricanes, and some of you may have heard her numbers, 'Fever', 'Always', 'Boys' and 'Summertime'.

Make Your Week-end Jazz Wine, Dance meet
DELROY STEPHENS' JAZZ GROUP
Best in Town at
The New Palm Cove
Smithdown Lane   Royal 7724

Anyone closely studying the English literature of the last three decades will come across a surprisingly frequent number of references to the Beatles. The legendary British band is to be encountered in work from Graham Greene to David Lodge, from Anthony Burgess to Hanif Kureishi. The reason is, of course, that their mythological cult status and omnipresent music made the Beatles a cultural institution clearly influencing the collective world view of today's generation of readers and writers.

For the field of literature, though, another significant factor is that one of the Beatles, John Lennon, was in fact a man of considerable literary talent whose work was observed by other authors with interest and curiosity. Lennon was considered to be rooted in the tradition of British nonsense literature, and John Wain even compared the style of the "writing Beatle" with that of James Joyce. Most recently, Hanif Kureishi still seemed to think it adequate to reduce the London youth scene's literary education of the early seventies to the lyrics of a single John Lennon song: "We were proud of never learning anything except the names of footballers, the personnel of rock groups and the lyrics of 'I am the Walrus'."[2] How can it be explained that Lennon's lyrics have the power to fascinate even those young people who otherwise refuse to have anything to do with literature?

In 1961 when Bill Harry, Liverpool art student and founding editor of *Mersey Beat*, asked his friend John Lennon to write a biographical sketch of Liverpool's leading band for the magazine's first edition, he most probably had a conventional text in mind. But what Lennon delivered was a travesty, a deliberate deconstruction of the stereotyped biographical form. *Being a Short Diversion on the Dubious Origins of Beatles* blends the familiar language of the Bible with that of fairytales, rendering a grotesquely comical genesis of the Beatles. Its publication marks the moment of John Lennon's birth as a writer in the public arena.

Encouraged by the positive response to his article, Lennon (alias Beatcomber) willingly provided *Mersey Beat* with further bits of short prose and poetry between 1961 and 1964, among which was the elegy *I Remember Arnold* and the two nonsensical poems *The Tales of Hermit Fred* and *The Land of Lunapots*.

Lennon incorporated several of these into his first book, *In His Own Write*, the title of which plays on the homonymy of "write" and "right" and refers to Lennon's independence from the Beatles as well as his unconventional literary style. The book immediately became a bestseller upon its publication on March 23, 1964. Lennon's unconventional texts met with a receptive and sensitised audience, for they arrived at a time in which public literary interest was focused on the Beat generation authors, led by American writers Allen Ginsberg and Jack Kerouac, who used literary means to rebel against established cultural values. In keeping with this trend, the numerous reviews of the book proved

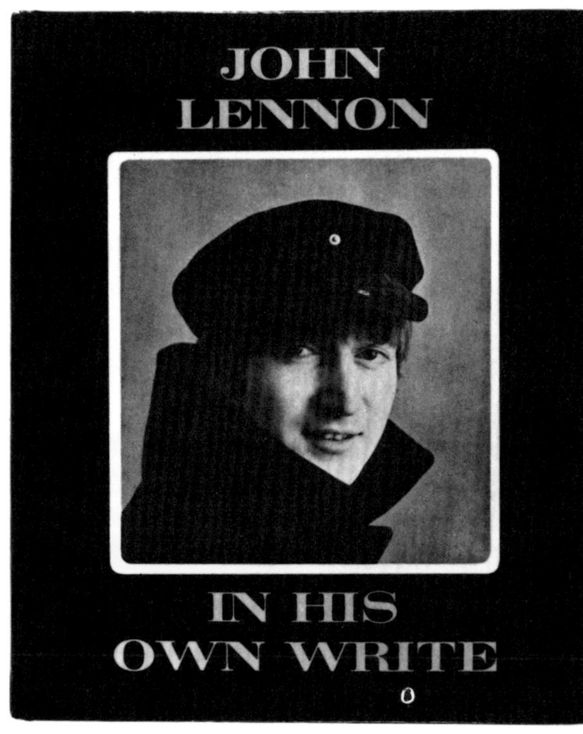

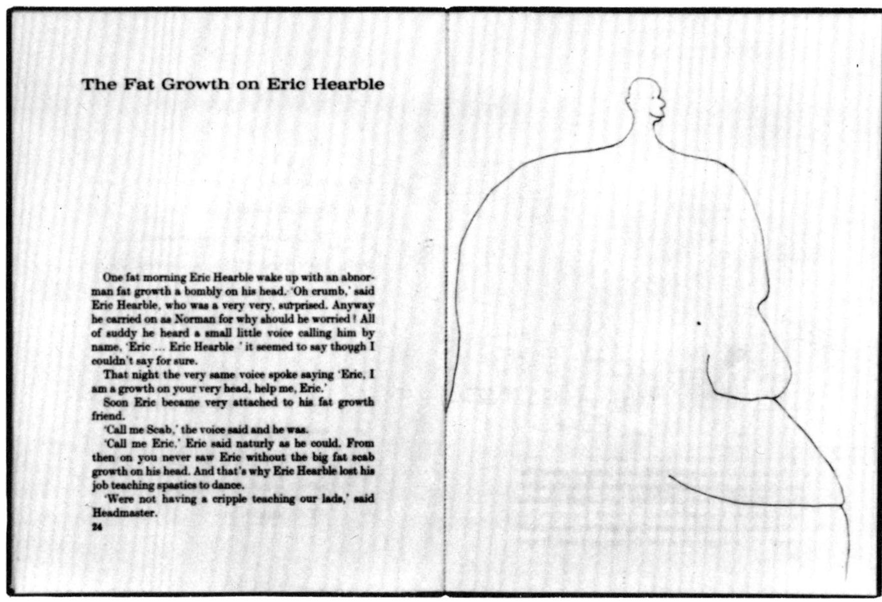

The Fat Growth on Eric Hearble

One fat morning Eric Hearble wake up with an abnor-man fat growth a bombly on his head. 'Oh crumb,' said Eric Hearble, who was a very very, surprised. Anyway he carried on as Norman for why should he worried ? All of suddy he heard a small little voice calling him by name, 'Eric … Eric Hearble ' it seemed to say though I couldn't say for sure.

That night the very same voice spoke saying 'Eric, I am a growth on your very head, help me, Eric.'

Soon Eric became very attached to his fat growth friend.

'Call me Scab,' the voice said and he was.

'Call me Eric,' Eric said naturly as he could. From then on you never saw Eric without the big fat scab growth on his head. And that's why Eric Hearble lost his job teaching spastics to dance.

'Were not having a cripple teaching our lads,' said Headmaster.

24

overwhelmingly positive, not only drawing parallels to James Joyce, but also suggesting that Lennon's work was modelled on Edward Lear, Lewis Carroll and James Thurber.

In His Own Write is a compilation of 23 prose texts, eight poems and 26 drawings. Clad in the ever-changing guise of a wide variety of genres and immersed in black humour, the texts deal with the subjects of death, vulnerability, violence, disability and decay. Yet the common ground linking them all is their anarchic use of language. Processes of disintegration, dissimulation and interpenetration join together in a bizarre *jeu d'esprit* with the semantics of the English language. To increase the complexity and wealth of association in his texts, Lennon makes express use of that method described by Lewis Carroll's Humpty Dumpty character as portmanteau words, also appearing in similar form in the works of James Joyce when several terms are fused into one ambiguous word (which he calls polyhedrony). Several signifiers are combined to form one semantically compressed word, like

parchment that has been written on and rubbed out time and again (palimpsest) – or (to borrow an image from John Lennon) as seen through a glass onion. In the short story *On Safairy with Whide Hunter,* for example, the morphological term "hippoposthumous" refers to the post-humous nature of the prey (a hippopotamus). In addition, Lennon intensifies the subtle play of semantic nuance by adding further layers of language; how this works using Latin grammar is illustrated in a passage from *Alec Speaking:*

He is putting it lithely when he says
Quobble in the Grass,
Strab he down the soddieflays
Amo amat amass;
Amonk amink a minibus,
Amarmylaidie Moon,
Amikky mendip multiplus
Amighty midgey spoon.[3]

Lennon's second book, *A Spaniard in the Works,* was published on June 24, 1965. It was commissioned by the London publisher Jonathan Cape and contains twelve prose texts, six poems and 33 drawings.

John Lennon,
In His Own Write, London 1964.
Cover of the first edition with a photo by Robert Freeman

John Lennon, *The Fat Growth on Eric Hearble,* from: *In His Own Write,* 1964

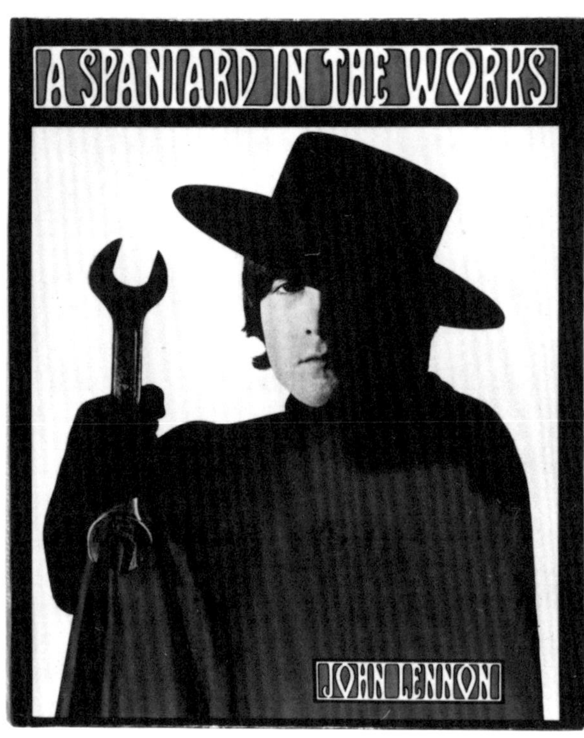

John Lennon, *A Spaniard in the Works*, London 1965. Cover of the first edition with a photo by Robert Freeman

Nearly all reviews were unanimous in their view that *A Spaniard in the Works* had not achieved the lightness and imaginative strength of the first book. This scepticism can be primarily traced to three obvious differences to *In His Own Write*. Firstly, most of the texts are considerably longer, making the book appear altogether less adept and varied. Secondly, Lennon based the pieces more closely on specific literary sources, partially transferring the unlimited wealth of subject matter in the first book into the more limited arena of an intertextual dialogue. The longest text in the collection, *The Singular Experience of Miss Anne Duffield*, is thus conceived as a parody of Conan Doyle's Sherlock Holmes stories, and *Snore Wife and some Several Dwarts* is an ambiguous persiflage of Snow White and the Seven Dwarfs. Thirdly, Lennon's second book is distinguished by a more distinct element of satire. The satirical treatment of political and religious institutions, the media and current events gave the book, in part, a bitter tone lacking its predecessor's carefree charm. Such sweeping

criticism of *A Spaniard in the Works* cannot be justified, however, as the volume contains some of Lennon's most mature texts, for instance in the short fervent prayer from the story *Silly Norman:*

"Goody Griff, which artery in HEFFER harold by thy norm! is these not thet enid of the worm? Surely to goosestep I am nit that larst man on earn?" he fell suddy to the ground weefy and whaley crizeling tuber Lawn aboove to savfre him or judge spare a friend or to. "I wilf give of awl my wordy posesions, awl me foren stabs, awl me classicow rechords, awl me fave rave pidgeons of Humpty Littlesod thee great nothing. All these oh wondrouse Sailor up above, I offer ye if only yer will save me!"[4]

If this short story is at least partially reminiscent of *Finnegans Wake*, other texts, such as *The Wumberlog (or the Magic Dog)*, a poem in three stanzas, clearly reveal a reference to Lewis Carroll, whose books *Alice's Adventures in Wonderland* and particularly *Through the Looking-Glass and What Alice Found There* were Lennon's most important source of literary inspiration. This source was not sufficient, however, to sustain a third book which Lennon was to have submitted to Jonathan Cape in February 1966. His waning interest in the subject was presumably not least of all due to the fact that he increasingly poured his tried and tested linguistic strategies of alienation into his lyrics, which had previously shown little trace of their author's literary talent. Lennon's style now switched from the straight rock'n'roll lyrics of his early songs to more experimental ones, such as *I'm only Sleeping, She Said, She Said* and *Tomorrow Never Knows*. Yet it was not until 1967 that the album *Sgt Pepper's Lonely Hearts Club Band* found an enthusiastic audience with *Lucy in the Sky with Diamonds*, whose lyrics cautiously tie in with Lennon's literary texts. In *I am the Walrus, Glass Onion, Happiness is a Warm Gun, Come Together* or *Across the Universe*, which appear on subsequent Beatles albums, Lennon writes lyrics filled with

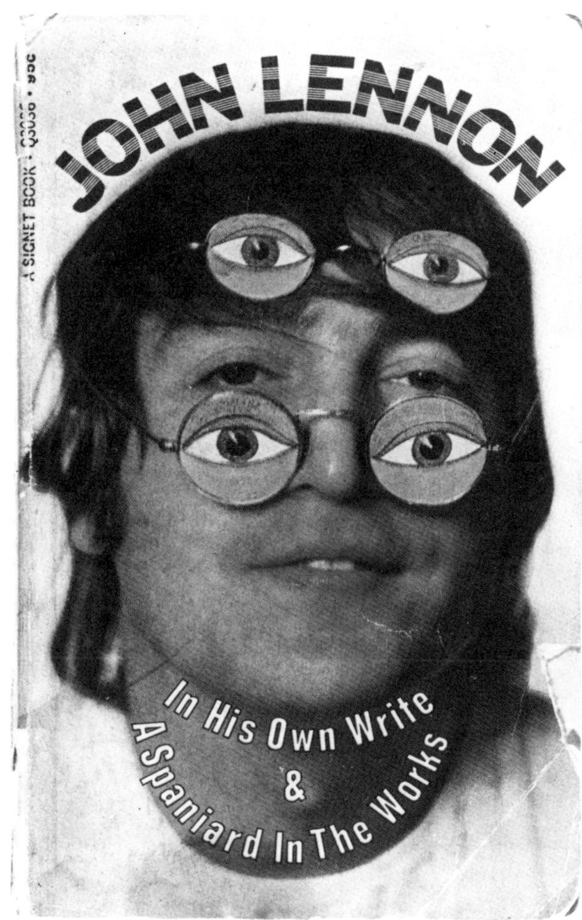

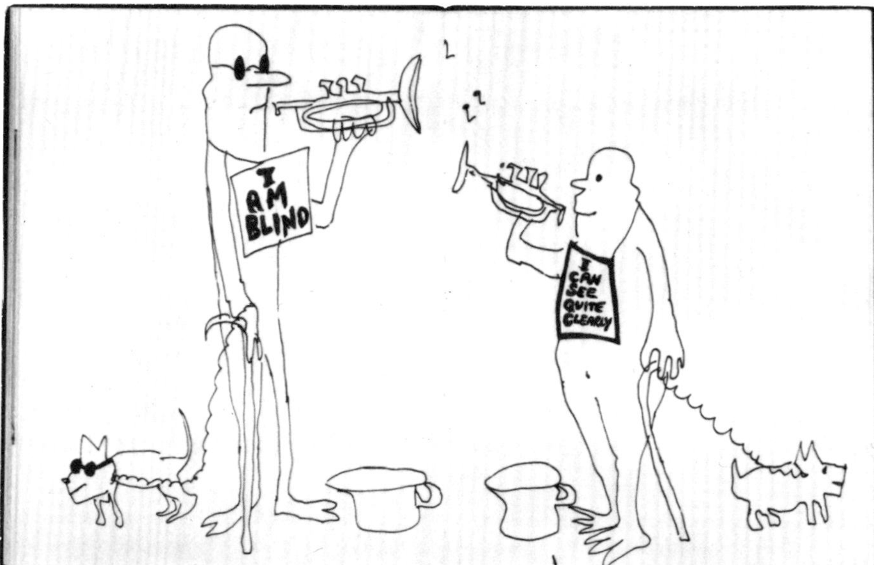

surrealist images persistently resisting any attempt at stringent deciphering. As with his books, Lennon incorporated a wide variety of texts into his songs. He used everything from newspaper articles, circus posters and advertising slogans to the Tibetan *Book of the Dead* and *The I Ching,* including the lyrics of other song-writers such as Bob Dylan and Chuck Berry. Taking up all available material, he even included references to his own Beatles lyrics, fusing them into building blocks for his labyrinth of language. As "the girl with kaleidoscope eyes", Alice finds her way into the "Wonderland" of Lennon's songs. Close parallels exist particularly between *Lucy in the Sky with Diamonds* and *Through the Looking-Glass,* in which Alice hallucinates as she drifts downstream in a rowboat "under trees… frowning over their heads."

Whereas the combination of text and illustration in Lennon's books merely hints at his talent for embracing a variety of media in his art, it is fully revealed in his songs. This aspect is best expressed in *I am the Walrus,* where Lennon not only blends various literary and non-literary elements in the final product (adding film and video in the *Magical Mystery Tour*), but also incorporates theatre and radio, included in this synthesis of the arts with the insertion of a production of *King Lear.* The complex and progressive combination of media and linguistic disorientation – way ahead of its time – in *I am the Walrus* stands as a high point of Lennon's most avant-garde lyrics.

True to the role of anti-elite rock musician of the people he favoured his whole life, John Lennon temporarily moved away from any form of linguistic experimentation in the early seventies. Only during a musically inactive period in the middle of the decade did his insatiable need for artistic activity give rise to numerous new texts and illustrations. However, as their author doubted their quality, they were never published. A compilation of these works only appeared post-humously in a volume entitled *Skywriting by Word of Mouth,* which contained other texts

John Lennon, *I am blind – I can see quite clearly,* from: *A Spaniard in the Works,* 1965

John Lennon, *In His Own Write & A Spaniard in the Works,* Paperback edition, New York, n.d.

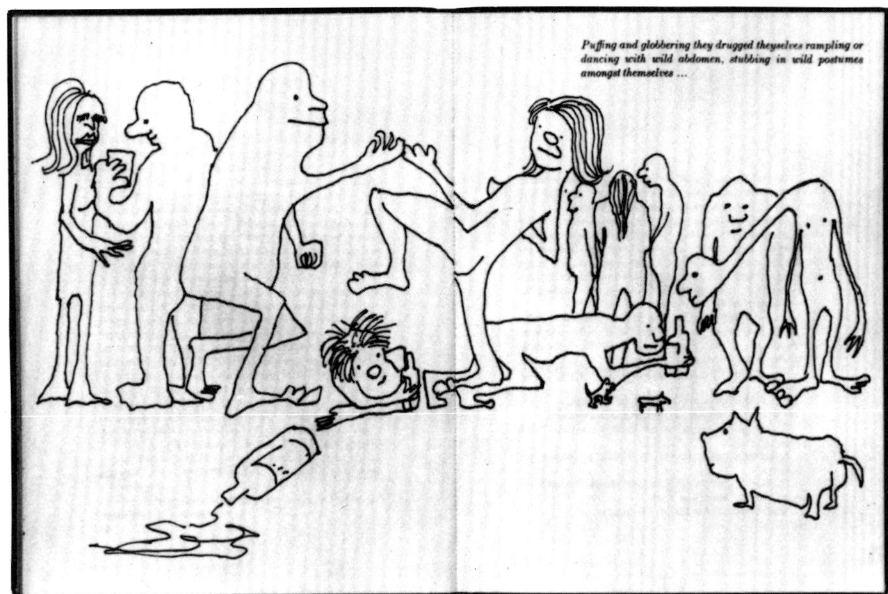

John Lennon, *Puffing and globbering they drugged theyselves rampling or dancing with wild abdomen, stubbing in wild postumes amongst themselves…*
from: *In His Own Write*, 1964

1 From: James Joyce, *Finnegans Wake.*
2 Hanif Kureishi, *The Buddha of Suburbia,* p. 178.
3 John Lennon, *In His Own Write*, 1964, p. 50.
4 John Lennon, *A Spaniard in the Works*, p. 68.

from a much earlier period as well. Although the selection (highly divergent in respect to both quality and content) leaves an incoherent and haphazard impression of the book, several texts in the collection are among the best that Lennon ever wrote. Here, too, the wealth of literary allusion is most pronounced. In referring to William Shakespeare, Guy de Maupassant, F. Scott Fitzgerald, Oscar Wilde, James Joyce, Truman Capote or Max Frisch, Lennon presents us with an illustrious parade of international authors, giving this book, in particular, numerous moments of brilliance. Seen in this light, it has been to the immense profit of English literature that John Lennon refused, as Leslie Fiedler phrased it, to become a prisoner of his musical talent, and so searched for alternative forms of artistic expression.

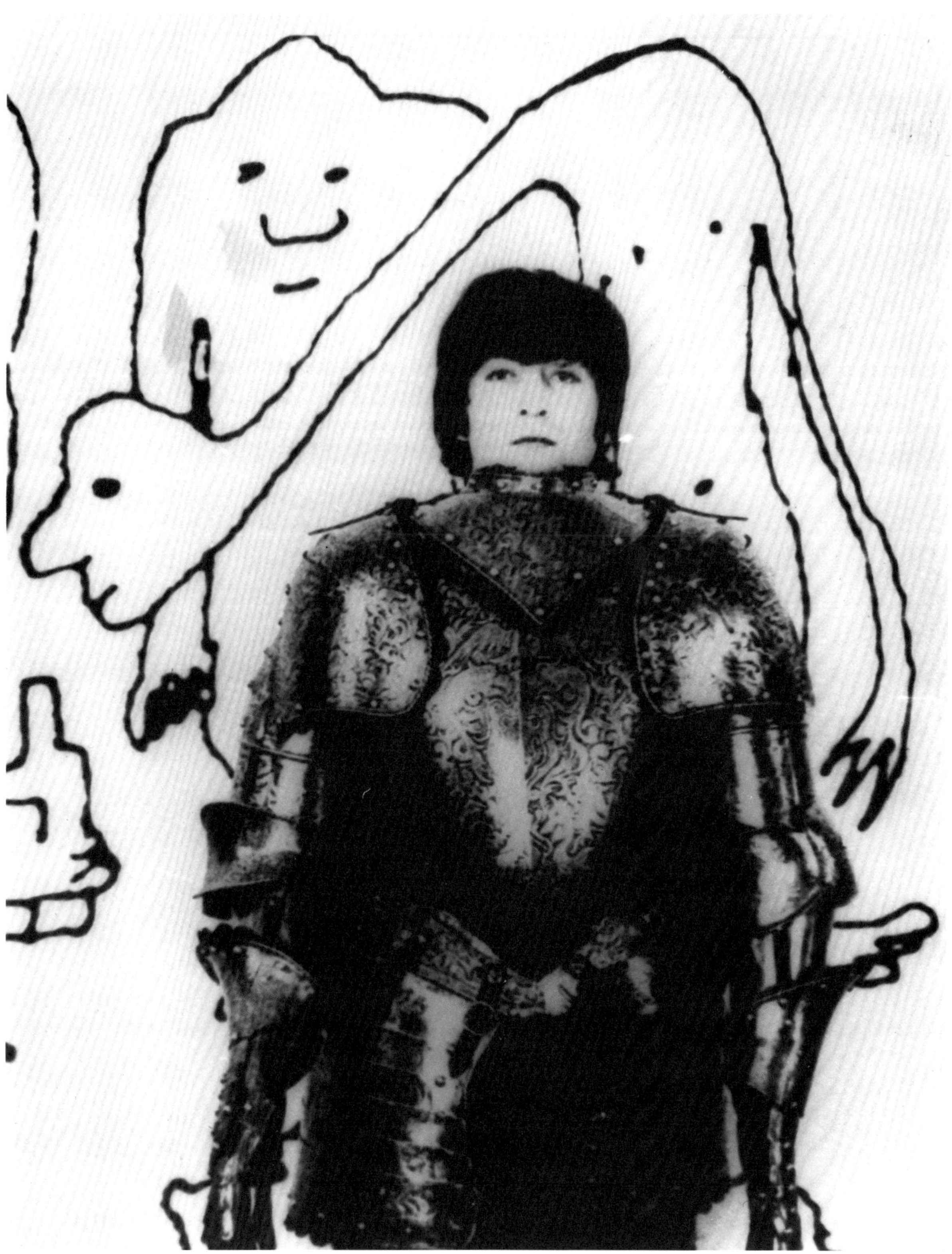

John Lennon behind a suit of armour in the hallway of his Weybridge home, 1964. In the background is a drawing from *In His Own Write*. Photo: Robert Freeman, © Apple Corps. Ltd.

Biography
Bibliography

Biographical Notes
John Lennon: The Visual Artist
Matthias Höllings

9 October 1940

John Winston Lennon is born in Liverpool's Oxford Street Hospital to Fred and Julia Lennon (née Stanley). He later describes this event in his first book *In His Own Write*, as follows: *"I was bored on the 9th of October 1940 when, I believe, the Nastics were still booming us led by Madalf Heatlump (Who only had one). Anyway they didn't get me…"*

1941

Julia Lennon places her son in the care of her sister Mary Smith (Aunt Mimi) and brother-in-law George.

1942

Fred Lennon leaves the family. Julia Lennon sets up home with her new lover.

1946

Lennon's father, who has been away at sea, turns up in Liverpool and takes his son to Blackpool. Julia follows them and asks her 5-year-old son to choose between his mother and his father. John chooses to stay with his mother, but on returning to Liverpool, she leaves him with his Aunt Mimi. This traumatic separation marks him for life.
As a schoolboy, his love of Walt Disney films and the annual Christmas pantomime inspires him to write stories himself. One of his earliest works, entitled *Sport and Speed Illustrated*, consists of cartoons, jokes and photos of film stars and football players pasted into a notebook. He is so taken with *Alice in Wonderland* that he draws all the characters. He asks his Aunt Mimi to keep the pictures and stories because, he says, he is going to be famous one day. Aunt Mimi, a strict guardian, does not always do so.
As an adult, Lennon recalls: *"People like me are aware of their so-called genius at ten, eight, nine… I always wondered, 'Why has nobody discovered me?' In school, didn't they see that I'm cleverer than anybody in this school? That the teachers are stupid, too? That all they had was information that I didn't need."*

1957–1960

Lennon forms a skiffle band (The Quarrymen). He meets Paul McCartney and later invites him to join the band. Shortly afterwards, Lennon enters Liverpool College of Art, where he meets Cynthia Powell and Stuart Sutcliffe.
Lennon turns out to be an eccentric and unconventional loner who rarely does what is expected of him and often swims against the tide. For example, in one life study class, instead of drawing the nude, he sketches the only item the model is wearing: a watch. John seems to have a fascination with disability, and frequently includes people with crutches in his drawings. Later, he also imitates spastic movements on stage during Beatles concerts.
In his *Daily Howl* sketchbook, Lennon caricatures his teachers and fellow pupils, and comments on the drawings with dry humour. Although a talented visual artist, he is equally attracted to music. Elvis Presley, Chuck Berry, Little Richard and Buddy Holly, who dies in a plane crash in 1959, are his idols. Lennon's mother is killed in a road accident in 1958. Lennon seeks refuge in black humour.

July 1960

John Lennon leaves Liverpool College of Art. He persuades his friend Stuart Sutcliffe to join him and his band *The Beatles* (with guitarists Paul McCartney and George Harrison and drummer Pete Best) on an engagement to play a Hamburg nightclub.

According to photographer Astrid Kirchherr, *"…John was the worst. He sang like a god. He sang like a pig. He stood with his legs wide apart. He pushed his knees and hips forward. He held his guitar like a soldier with a machine gun, and hit out with it. He had set his microphone so high that he could hardly reach it to sing. John never sang. He screamed and purred and spat like an animal, he cried, he begged forgiveness and then insulted his audience. 'Get on with the show!' his audience would yell, and he would yell back 'Heil Hitler! Who are you anyway? And do you know who we are? Okay, we're the Beatles. And you? You're idiots, Hamburg idiots!'"*

1961

Tony Sheridan's single *My Bonnie*, accompanied by the Beatles, is released in Germany. In Liverpool, the first issue of Bill Harry's *Mersey Beat* appears on the news stands. John's satirical parody *Being a Short Diversion on the Dubious Origins of the Beatles* is printed on the front page. In the following three years, Lennon continues to write for the *Mersey Beat* under the pseudonym Beatcomber.

28 October 1961

Brian Epstein, who runs a record store in Liverpool, sees the band at a *Cavern Club* gig in Liverpool and offers to be their manager.

10 April 1962

John is devastated when his best friend, Stuart Sutcliffe, dies of a brain tumour in Hamburg.

9 May 1962

The Beatles sign their first major recording contract with EMI in London. Producer George Martin is in charge of all their recordings at the Abbey Road studios from now until 1970.

16 August 1962

Drummer Pete Best leaves the Beatles at the request of producer George Martin.

18 August 1962

Richard Starkey (Ringo Starr) joins the Beatles as drummer. What follows is music history. The second single, *Please, Please Me* tops the UK charts. In the years that follow, the group travels the world, and Beatlemania takes hold. The unique and hitherto unprecedented marketing strategy pursued by manager Brian Epstein makes the Beatles victims of their own success. They are under instructions to make no comments on politics.

23 August 1962

After a long break John Lennon, aka Beatcomber, publishes a humorous short story, *Small Sam*, in the *Mersey Beat*. This text is not included in either of his later books. On the same day, John Lennon marries Cynthia Powell at Liverpool's Mount Pleasant registry office. The Beatles have a gig in Chester that evening.

6 September 1962

Another text by Beatcomber appears in the *Mersey Beat*. According to Lennon, Paul McCartney collaborated on this text, *On Safari with Whide Hunter*. It begins with the words *"in the jumble, the mighty jumble, whide hunter sleeps tonight…"* – a parody of the *Tokens'* hit – and features such characters as Elephoon Bill and Jumble Jim. Together with Buffalo Bill, these characters reappear almost six years later in the *White Album*, on the track *The Continuing Story of Bungalow Bill*.

8 April 1963

John and Cynthia Lennon's son John Charles Julian is born in Liverpool.

4 November 1963

At the *Royal Command (Variety) Performance* at the Prince of Wales Theatre, Coventry Street, London, in the presence of the Queen and Princess Margaret, John Lennon announces: *"For this numer we'd like to ask your help. Will the people in the cheaper seats clap your hands? All the rest of you, if you'll rattle your jewellery."*

9 February 1964

Beatlemania is in full swing. Before the start of their US tour, the Beatles have their first appearance on American TV as guests of the *Ed Sullivan Show*. More than 70 million viewers tune in.

27 February 1964

Two nonsense poems of Lennon's not later published in his books appear in the music magazine *Mersey Beat: The Tales of Hermit Fred* and *The Land of Lunapots*.

23 March 1964

In His Own Write – John Lennon's first book – is published. The first edition of 50,000 (UK) and 90,000 (US) copies sells out quickly. With the publication and success of the book, Lennon unwittingly bridges the gap between the Beatles fans and intellectual admirers – a hitherto inconceivable cultural border-crossing.

19 June 1964

Conservative MP Charles Curran claims in Parliament that the book *In His Own Write* is proof of the poor standards of education in Liverpool schools, and that the author is certainly illiterate.

6 July 1964

The Beatles' first feature film, *A Hard Day's Night*, opens in London. The film is shot in black and white because of the production company's fears that box office revenue would not cover the cost of a colour production.

19 September 1964

In the run-up to Christmas, various commercial organisations and charities ask Lennon to design Christmas cards. Lennon draws a round robin and donates it to Oxfam, who do a print run of 500,000.

13 April 1965

The recording of *Help,* with lyrics by John Lennon as the title track of the film, proves to be a turning point in his life. In 1965, Lennon felt he was in a rut. His work with the Beatles was starting to bore him, and he had become introverted. In this song, Lennon expresses his sense of emptiness, describing how he feels and how he sees himself. His songs start to take on a new and more personal quality.

24 June 1965

Jonathan Cape publishes Lennon's second book, *A Spaniard in the Works*. Originally, the contract had stipulated that the book was to appear for Christmas 1964, but Lennon did not meet the deadline. Whereas his first book received critical acclaim, the second was generally a flop.
Even Lennon had to admit that it was very difficult to maintain a certain level of creative output during the Beatles tours and the shooting of their films.
"I wrote it with a bottle of Johnnie Walker," he said in a 1980 interview.
In spite of his difficulties and the tight schedule, he signed a contract for a third book to appear in February 1966.

19 July 1965

The Beatles' second feature film, *Help,* is released and premieres in London.

26 October 1965

The Beatles are awarded an MBE at Buck-
ingham Palace in recognition of the
contribution made by their concerts and
record sales to Britain's export trade. In
protest at this award for the pop group,
several MBEs are returned.

December 1965

As John Lennon has written only one poem
for his third book so far, the project is
dropped. Lennon sells the poem *The Toy Boy,*
about a boy and his toys each denying the
other's existence, to *McCall's* magazine.

1966

In July, the Beatles play Manila. The group
has to leave the country in a hurry, because the
wife of President Marcos feels insulted by
them.

29 July 1966

A quote that had appeared in the *London
Evening Standard* on March 4th is reprinted,
completely out of context, in the American
magazine *Datebook,* causing an uproar.
Lennon's misquoted remark about the Beatles
being more popular than Jesus and Christ-
ianity dying out triggers a wave of record-
burning in various American cities.

29 August 1966

The Beatles give their last live concert in Can-
dlestick Park, San Francisco. They capitulate
before the masses and their Beatlemania. The
fans' screams drown out the music. John
Lennon has been suffering for some time due
to the relentless Beatlemania.

5–7 September 1966

John Lennon, bored, frustrated and curious to
see what will happen, launches into the
shooting of Richard Lester's anti-war film

How I Won the War, filmed on location in
Germany (Celle) and Spain (Carbonaras).
The script has a touch of typical British
humour: a detachment of recruits is sent on a
mission to set up a cricket pitch behind enemy
lines. Lennon takes on a leading role as Private
Gripweed.
It changes Lennon's appearance considerably.
Not only does his role as a WW II soldier
require him to cut his hair – an unforgivable
affront to Beatles fans worldwide –, but he
also adopts for many years to come Gripweed's wire-rimmed glasses as a signature
accessory that is acceptable in intellectual
circles as well.
Paul McCartney frees himself by composing
film music, George Harrison learns to play the
sitar. The Beatles as a unit no longer exist.

27 October 1966

John Lennon admits he is unable to fulfil the
contract for his third book. It is decided that
the first two books should be published by
Penguin in a single volume as *The Penguin
John Lennon.*

9 November 1966

The era of Swinging London is at its height,
with galleries and boutiques everywhere.
Lennon turns increasingly to art and starts
experimenting with LSD.
John Dunbar, ex-husband of singer Marianne
Faithfull and owner of the Indica Gallery in
Mason's Yard, Piccadilly, invites John to a
happening where Japanese artist Yoko Ono
is to perform in a bag.
Lennon later described this fateful meeting:
*"John Dunbar introduces me to this strange-
looking Japanese woman… She gives me a
little card. And it just says 'Breath' on it… I
see this thing called* Hammer and Nail, *and it's
a board with a chain and a hammer hanging
on it, and a bunch of nails at the bottom. I said*

– Well, can I hammer a nail in? she says no. So John Dunbar whisks her away and says – You know who that is? That's a millionaire. She didn't know who I was, you know. Well, whatever, she came over and said, You can hammer one in for five shillings. I said, Are you… I'll give you an imaginary five shillings and hammer an imaginary nail in. All right? And that's when we fell… But it was eighteen months to two years before we really got together."

Early November 1966

John Lennon makes his first home demos of his composition *Strawberry Fields Forever*.

November 1966 – April 1967

Recording of Beatles album *Sgt Pepper's Lonely Hearts Club Band*. Yoko Ono gives John Lennon her book *Grapefruit* with concepts and stage directions for her performances.

As Lennon said in a 1970 interview: *"(…) sometimes I'd get very annoyed by it; it would say things like 'paint until you drop dead' or 'bleed' and then sometimes I'd be very enlightened by it, and I went through all the changes that people go through with Yoko's work…"*

Late 1966

John Lennon uses various tape recorders in his private studio to create increasingly bizarre sound collages and begins experimenting with film as a medium as well, using an 8mm Canon.

1 June 1967

Sgt Pepper's Lonely Hearts Club Band is released: a milestone in music history.

27 August 1967

Beatles manager Brian Epstein is found dead in his flat in Chapel Street, London.

August – November 1967

The Beatles record *I am the Walrus* for their *Magical Mystery Tour* album. Lennon later describes the track as his favourite, perhaps because its surrealistic word plays link up with his two books. He took his inspiration from several sources: Lewis Carroll's *The Walrus and the Carpenter*, George Harrison's *Hare Krishna* chant, the refrain "I'm crying" from the soul classic *Ooh Baby Baby* by the Miracles, the image of *Lucy in the Sky* (as Lennon told the press) from his son Julian, "I am he as you are he…" from Buddhist and Taoist writings, and partly from Shakespeare's *King Lear*.

11 September – November 1967

Shooting of the film *Magical Mystery Tour*.

11 October – 14 November 1967

John Lennon sponsors Yoko Ono's exhibition *Half-a-Wind Show* at the Lisson Gallery in London to the tune of 5000 pounds. The exhibition opens on Lennon's 27th birthday. In 1970, he said of the exhibition: *"There was half a bed, half a room, half of everything, all beautifully cut in half and all painted white. And I said to her, 'Why don't you sell the other half in bottles?', having caught on by then what the game was, and she did that – this is still before we'd had any nuptials – and we still have bottles from the show, it's my first. It was presented as 'Yoko Plus Me' – that was our first public appearance. I didn't even go to see the show, I was too uptight."*

18 October 1967

The world premiere of *How I Won the War* takes place in London.

4 December 1967

John Lennon visits the Royal Institute Gallery in Mayfair to see the *large and colourful works* exhibition by his former school friend Jonathan Hague. The exhibition is sponsored by Lennon and McCartney.

26 December 1967
The BBC premieres the Beatles' third film, *Magical Mystery Tour.* It is never released on the cinema circuit and is still considered to have been a commercial flop.

20 May 1968
While his wife Cynthia and son Julian are on holiday in Greece, Lennon invites Yoko Ono to his home. He plays his multitape sound collages for her. Ono improvises with voice accompaniment. They later release this sound experiment as an album entitled *Unfinished music No. 1 – Two Virgins.* From now on, Lennon and Ono are a couple.

15 June 1968
Lennon and Ono perform their Acorn Event in front of the new cathedral in Coventry as part of the National Sculpture Exhibition.
In a follow-up event, they send acorns to heads of state throughout the world, asking them to plant them for peace.
They receive a positive response from many countries.

July 1968
Lennon's first exhibition, entitled *You Are Here,* is opened in London at the Robert Fraser Gallery.
Outside the gallery, Lennon and Ono release 365 white helium balloons with reply cards saying "You Are Here – please write to John Lennon". Lennon had the idea because he had been so excited as a child at finding a balloon with a message in a field.
The press attributed the idea for the exhibition to Yoko Ono, but she said that it was John's idea.

17 July 1968
The Beatles' cartoon film *Yellow Submarine* premieres in London.

August 1968
Yoko Ono shoots her *Film No. 5 – Smile* with John Lennon performing. It shows Lennon's face turning – in slow motion – into a smile. It premieres at the Chicago Film Festival that year.

August – September 1968
Lennon produces the 16mm film *Two Virgins* in which images of Lennon and Yoko Ono are superimposed and faded into each other. Like *Smile,* this film is also screened at the Chicago Film Festival.

October 1968
Every Christmas, the Beatles have surprised their fan clubs with greetings from all four on a flexidisc. In 1968, they each issue their own separately, for the first time.
Lennon and Ono record two texts in the style of his books: *Jock and Yono* and *Once Upon a Pool Table.*

18 October 1968
Lennon and Ono are arrested in a police raid on Ringo Starr's home at 34 Montagu Square, London W1, and charged with possessing eleven grams of cannabis.

19 October 1968
John Lennon and Yoko Ono are released on bail at Marylebone Magistrate's Court.

7 November 1968
In the interview book *Lennon Remembers,* John Lennon shows his ability to laugh at himself by publishing his cartoon of himself and Yoko Ono referring to the nude photos on the cover of their *Two Virgins* album.

The cartoons were originally drawn for the macrobiotic magazine *Harmony*. Around this time, Lennon begins adding little caricatures of himself and Yoko Ono to his autographs.

27 November 1968

Lennon sleeps on the floor of Queen Charlotte's Maternity Hospital in Hammersmith, London W6, next to Yoko Ono's bed. She has had a miscarriage. A photo of Lennon and Ono in the hospital room is used for the cover of the album *Unfinished Music No. 2 – Life with the Lions*.

28 November 1968

John Lennon pleads guilty to possessing cannabis and is fined 15 pounds by Marylebone Magistrate's Court. It is a relatively lenient punishment with disastrous consequences; his criminal record is later the reason for a delay of four years in granting Lennon permanent residency in the USA.

29 November 1968

Unfinished Music No. 1 – Two Virgins is released. The sleeve causes such a scandal that sales are prohibited unless it is wrapped in an additional paper cover.
EMI chairman Sir Joseph Lockwood recalls that Lennon and Ono, supported by Paul McCartney, came to his office: *"John said to me, 'Well, aren't you shocked?' 'No,' I say, 'I've seen worse than this.' 'So it's all right then, is it?' 'No, it's not all right – I'm not worried about the rich people, the duchesses and those people who follow you. But your mums and dads and girl fans will object strongly. You will be damaged and what will you gain? What's the purpose of it?' Yoko said: 'It's art!'"*
John Lennon and Yoko Ono insist on the record sleeve design. Sir Joseph Lockwood hits on a compromise with EMI pressing the

album and Apple being responsible for distribution.

December 1968

What is now the British Academy of Film and Television (BAFTA) then housed the Royal Institute Gallery where Lennon and Ono visit the exhibition *Guildford Minus 40*, showing the work of 40 part-time teachers made redundant from the Guildford School of Art. Lennon mounts a small stage there and distributes squares of paper with the message: "Fold it nine times – John Lennon 1968". (Try it).

December 1968

Lennon and Ono produce their *Film No. 6 – Rape*. With his camera, cameraman Nic Knowland pursues a woman running away from him. It is screened to critical acclaim on Austrian TV in March 1969 and six months later in London. A similar 45-minute film, *Rape Part 2* is produced some time later.

18 December 1968

At the underground Christmas party *Alchemical Wedding* at the Royal Albert Hall, various artists protest against Britain's military involvement in Biafra. Lennon and Ono take the stage in a bag. The audience is disappointed.
Further bag-ins follow over the next few months. The performance is to give its name to the Bag Productions company founded by John Lennon and Yoko Ono.

2 January 1969

The Beatles spend one month recording a huge amount of material at Twickenham Film Studio for their subsequent LP *Let It Be* and the film of the same name. Amongst the many songs, there is another protest by John Lennon. In *Gimme Some Truth* he picks up where he left off with the *Jock and Yono* Christmas greeting in October. However, he reworks the song, which has to wait two years to be released – on Lennon's solo LP *Imagine*.

3 January 1969
In New Jersey/New York 30,000 copies of the LP *Two Virgins* are confiscated because the cover is allegedly pornographic.

30 January 1969
The Beatles give a concert on the roof of their Apple offices in Savile Row for the film *Let It Be*. It is their last live performance; it takes place without an audience.

2 March 1969
Lennon and Ono give an avant-garde jazz concert at Cambridge University's Lady Mitchell Hall. For Yoko Ono, this was routine, but for Lennon it was terra incognita. Ono makes long, atonal sounds, screaming, moaning and clucking. She is accompanied by Lennon, who sits in the semidarkness using his guitar to produce howling feedback. It is a new experience for John Lennon, far removed from the harmonious tones of the Beatles songs.
The Cambridge concert is released as one side of the *Life with the Lions* album in May 1969.

20 March 1969
Lennon and Ono fly from Paris to Gibraltar, where they are married at the British Consulate by registrar Cecil Wheeler. They fly back to Paris two hours later.

25–31 March 1969
Lennon and Ono hold their famous *Bed-In* for peace. The newly-weds spend seven days in bed in Room 902 (Presidential Suite) at the Amsterdam Hilton, receiving journalists and giving countless interviews.

John Lennon (1980): *"The point of the Bed-In in a nutshell was a commercial for news about peace instead of war, which was there every day in the newspaper. What the Bed-in was was seven days when the press can ask anything – no secrets, you know, no time limit."*
The Amsterdam bed-in was the start of John Lennon and Yoko Ono's peace campaign. Lennon, who had previously sung of love, now turned his attention to peace. With the bed-in, Lennon and Ono made life and art inseparable. Some recordings of the bed-in were included in the *Wedding Album* released in November 1969.
Documentary footage of the events in the hotel room, filmed by their ever-present assistants in accordance with strict directions, was later incorporated in their one-hour film *Honeymoon*.

31 March 1969
John Lennon and Yoko Ono fly direct from the Amsterdam Hilton to Vienna to present their film *Rape*, which is to be broadcast on Austrian TV that evening. They hold the press conference at Hotel Sacher, sitting in a bag on a table.
John Lennon (1980): *"We came down the elevator in the bag, and we went in and got comfortable, and they were all ushered in. It was a very strange scene because they'd never seen us before, or heard our voices – Vienna is a pretty square place.
A few people were saying, 'C'mon, get out the bags.' And we wouldn't let 'em see us. They all stood back saying, 'Is it really John and Yoko?' and 'What are you wearing and why are you doing this?' We said, 'This is total communications with no prejudice.' It was just great. They asked us to sing and we sang a few numbers. Yoko was singing a Japanese folk song."*

14 April 1969

Shooting of *The Ballad of John and Yoko*. Based on the premise "we are art", Lennon and Ono film a trailer for the Beatles song *The Ballad of John and Yoko*, comparable to today's video clips. Though entirely John's own work, the song is credited as a Lennon/McCartney composition.

The film contains just one brief Beatles sequence, and otherwise consists entirely of existing clips featuring John and Yoko, indicating that his work with the Beatles is no longer Lennon's top priority.

22 April 1969

Lennon takes his wife's name. From now on, he calls himself John Ono Lennon. (Only in his official application for permanent residency in the USA does he later use the name John Winston Lennon one more time.) The change is registered by a civil servant on the roof of the Apple building.

9 May 1969

Unfinished Music No. 2 – Life with the Lions by John Lennon and Yoko Ono is released on the Zapple label (a derivative of Apple). The sleeve shows Yoko Ono in hospital and John on the floor beside her bed. *Life with the Lions* was Lennon's favourite radio programme as a child.

24 May 1969

Lennon and Ono plan another seven-day bed-in at the Sheraton Oceanus on the Bahamas, but change their minds and fly to Canada the same day.

26 May – 2 June 1969

Their bed-in for peace in Room 1742 of Montreal's Queen Elisabeth Hotel turns into a media spectacle far exceeding the Amsterdam bed-in.

John Lennon: *"One problem with what we're doing is that we'll never know how successful we are. With the Beatles, you put out a record and either it's a hit or it's a miss. I don't expect the prime ministers or kings and queens of the world to suddenly change their policies just because John and Yoko have said, 'Peace, brother'. It would be nice! But it's youth we're addressing. Youth is the future. If we can get inside their minds and tell them to think in favour of non-violence, we'll be satisfied. What's the point of getting fame as a Beatle and not using it?!"*

1 June 1969

During the Montreal bed-in, John Lennon has an 8-track reel-to-reel tape recorder brought to their room, invites a few friends to join in and records the song *Give Peace a Chance*. This live recording session is also filmed. The song becomes an international hit and the anthem of the peace movement. The promotional claim "You are all the Plastic Ono Band" heralds the band name used in the future for a wide variety of projects.

August 1969

Shooting of the film *Self-Portrait*. A renewed attempt to loosen his ties to the Beatles goes even further than the nude self-portrait of *Two Virgins*. Like *Smile*, *Self-Portrait* is filmed with an ultra-high-speed camera. Projected at normal speed, the material is extended to 15 minutes; it shows John's semi-erect penis. The film is premiered on 10 September and screened only for small gatherings and private film clubs.

Early September

Shooting of the film *Apotheosis*.

10 September 1969

An evening of films by Yoko Ono and John

Lennon is held at the Cinema Club of the ICA in London, featuring *Smile, Honeymoon, Two Virgins, Rape* and the premiere of *Self-Portrait*.
Throughout the screening, an unidentified couple sits on the stage in a white bag. Two Hare Krishnas are said to have stood in for Lennon and Ono.

13 September 1969
Concert and shooting of *Sweet Toronto*. The Plastic Ono Band, consisting of Eric Clapton (guitar), Klaus Voormann (bass), Alan White (percussion), Yoko Ono (sounds and vocals) and John Lennon (guitar and vocals), perform at a music festival in Toronto's Varsity Stadium. The first half of their performance features several rock classics and Beatles hits as well as the new Lennon composition *Cold Turkey*. In the second half, over an improvised sound collage, Yoko Ono drives her vocal powers to an unheard-of pitch in a performance so compelling and disturbing that the audience simply stands awe-struck. Although the entire festival is actually filmed, the video does not include the performance of the Plastic Ono Band; it is not released until 20 years later. Excerpts from the concert are released on the LP *Live Peace in Toronto 1969*, in a sky blue sleeve with a little white cloud.

12 October 1969
Yoko Ono has a second miscarriage and is admitted to King's College Hospital, London.

Early October 1969
Shooting of *Apotheosis 2*. Nic Knowland films Lennon and Ono ascending in a hot-air balloon at dusk, lit by fireworks.
This material is then combined with footage shot from a helicopter for the first film *Apotheosis*.

7 November 1969
The *Wedding Album* is released as an elaborately designed package.

25 November 1969
John Lennon returns his MBE with the statement: *"Your Majesty, I am returning this MBE in protest against Britain's involvement in this Nigeria-Biafra thing, against our support of America in Vietnam and against* Cold Turkey *slipping down the charts. With Love, John Lennon of Bag."*

26 November 1969
John Lennon holds a press conference at which he reads his letter to the Queen and claims: *"Of course my action was a publicity gimmick for peace. I always squirmed when I saw M.B.E. on my letters. I didn't really belong to that sort of world. I think the Establishment bought the Beatles with it. Now I am giving it back, thank you very much. Investitures are a waste of time. It's mostly hypocritical snobbery and part of the class system. I only took it to help the Beatles make the big time. I know I sold my soul when I received it, but now I have helped to redeem it in the cause of peace. When we thought of that we were screaming with laughter, and*

so a few snobs and hypocrites got very upset about mentioning Cold Turkey *with the problem of Biafra and Vietnam, but that saved it from being too serious and being another Colonel protesting! You have to try and do everything with humour, and keep smiling."*

4 December 1969
Recording of *Item 1* and *Item 2*. Lennon and Ono work on a soundtrack for a BBC TV documentary on their artistic output, using material from their earlier sound collages. Intended as a fourth LP, but never released.

9 September 1969

In 1962, James Hanratty was hanged for a murder, though he had always claimed he was innocent. His parents ask Lennon and Yoko Ono to help clear his name. The Apple office announces that Lennon and Ono will finance a documentary proving his innocence. The film is screened at St. Martin-in-the-Fields, London, on 17 February 1972.

14 December 1969

A white Rolls Royce drives to Speaker's Corner in Hyde Park, from which a big white bag bearing the words "A silent protest for James Hanratty" emerges. Hanratty's father, who is calling for a public enquiry into the miscarriage of justice, is also present.
John Lennon (1970): *"For Hanratty, yes, we did a sort of bag event, but it wasn't us in the bag, it was somebody else."*

15 December 1969

Plastic Ono Supergroup plays in a *Peace for Christmas* concert at the Lyceum in London. Proceeds go to UNICEF. The musicians include: John Lennon, Yoko Ono, George Harrison, Eric Clapton, Billy Preston, Keith Moon.

16 December 1969

Lennon and Ono underline the peace message of their bed-in events by billboarding their message "WAR IS OVER! IF YOU WANT IT. Happy Christmas from John & Yoko" in 12 cities, in the respective language of the country.
John Lennon (1970): *"We got a big response. The people that got in touch with us understood what a grand event it was apart from the message itself. We got just thank you's from lots of youths around the world – for all the things we are doing – that inspired them to do something. We had a lot of response from other than pop fans, which was interesting, from all walks of life and age."*

18 – 20 December 1969

John Lennon spends some time on the farm of Canadian singer Ronnie Hawkins, near Toronto, where he signs 5175 sheets of his *Bag One* portfolio of erotic lithographs. According to organiser Anthony Fawcett, Lennon was undaunted by the amount, and calmly set to work while Hawkins presented his new rock'n'roll album.

24 December 1969

John Lennon and Yoko Ono stage a sit-in at Rochester Cathedral, Kent, to fast for peace and protest against famine. Critics claim it is easy to demonstrate against hunger when you can drive around in a Rolls Royce.
John Lennon: *"Would they want me to walk here? The people who criticise us have cars. If they give up theirs, first, for peace, I'll give up my Rolls."*

15 – 28 January 1970

The *Bag One* exhibition of 15 lithographs opens at the London Arts Gallery in New Bond Street. Lennon is not there. He and Yoko Ono are holidaying in a small Danish village near Aalborg.
On 16 January, Scotland Yard confiscates eight of the lithographs as obscene publications under the 1839 Metropolitan Act. On 25 January the gallery director is summonsed. On 1 April, the Lennon lithographs are compared in court with erotic drawings by Picasso.
On 27 April, the London Arts Gallery wins the case and the eight confiscated lithographs are returned.
The opening of the *Bag One* exhibition at the Lee Nordness Gallery in New York in February is attended by Salvador Dalí and

luminaries of the New York art scene. The lithographs are also shown at the Denise René Gallery in Paris. In March they are shown in Amsterdam and Düsseldorf. In reply to the question why he made the lithographs in the first place John Lennon states: *"Because somebody said do some lithographs, and I was in a drawing mood – and I drew them."*

4 February 1970

At 95–99 Holloway Road in North London, John Lennon and Yoko Ono have a meeting with Trinidad-born black power leader Michael X. They ceremoniously exchange their shorn hair for the bloodstained shorts of Muhammad Ali, intending to auction them to raise funds for their peace campaign. On 1 February 1974, Michael X is found guilty of a double murder in Trinidad. Lennon seeks a reprieve, raising funds for three appeals. Michael X is executed in Trinidad on 16 May 1975.

17 April – 12 June 1970

Joe Jones, member of the New York Fluxus movement, invites fellow Fluxus member Yoko Ono to design the Canal Street *Fluxfest*. Ono and Lennon work together to develop various projects, creating a motto for each week:
Week 1: *Do-it-yourself by John and Yoko,* including *Two Eggs by John Lennon*
Week 2: *Tickets by John Lennon* for *Fluxtours*
Week 3: *Measure by John and Yoko*
Week 4: *Blue Room by John and Yoko* including *Three Spoons by John Lennon* and *Needle by John Lennon*
Week 5: *Weight and Water by John and Yoko*
Week 6: *Capsule by John and Yoko*
Week 7: *Portrait of John Lennon as a Young Cloud*

Week 8: *The Store by John and Yoko*
Week 9: *Exam by John and Yoko*

Late April 1970

John Lennon and Yoko Ono fly to Los Angeles for a four-month primal therapy session with Arthur and Vivian Janov.

10 April 1970

Paul McCartney announces that he has left the band, marking the break-up of the Beatles.

December 1970

Shooting of *Fly* and *Up Your Legs Forever*, two projects by Yoko Ono. *Up Your Legs Forever* shows the legs of 300 members of the New York art scene. The 75-minute film ends with a shot of the bare buttocks of John Lennon and Yoko Ono.
In *Fly*, the camera follows the movements of a fly on the naked body of a woman. The soundtrack consists of Yoko Ono's vocal improvisations and John Lennon's guitar accompaniment played backwards. *Fly* premieres on 15 May 1971 at the Cannes film festival, attended by Lennon and Ono.

11 December 1970

Plastic Ono Band, John's first solo album, is released. It owes much to his four-month primal therapy with Arthur Janov, especially evident in the track *Mother*, which is like a cry for help from his childhood.

Early Summer 1971

Shooting of *Erection*, a film about the construction of London International Hotel (now Swallow Hotel) at 147 Cromwell Road, London.

6 July 1971

John Lennon and Yoko Ono appear in concert with Frank Zappa at New York's Fillmore

East. A live recording of this session can be heard on the double album *Some Time in New York City.*

July 1971
Within the space of just one week, John Lennon records his *Imagine* album at his home in Tittenhurst Park. The title track is now regarded as a Lennon classic, though he later admitted it was strongly influenced by Yoko Ono's book *Grapefruit* and that she really should have been credited as co-author. John Lennon (1980): *"It was right out of* Grapefruit, *Yoko's book, where there's a whole pile of pieces about imagine this and imagine that... I just put Lennon, because, you know, she's just the wife and, you know, you don't put her name on, right? ... And I have given her credit now long overdue."* The track *Imagine* is not released as a single for another four years.
Lennon and Ono also make their 85-minute film *Imagine,* but find no distributor. It is first screened in late 1972 on American TV in an abridged version. A version re-edited by Yoko Ono appears later as a video in the mid-80s. This film was made to fit the music, rather than vice versa.

September 1971
Shooting of *Clock.* John Lennon and Yoko Ono film an hour passing on the clock hanging on the wall of their room at the St. Regis Hotel in New York. The musical accompaniment consists of Lennon on acoustic guitar, playing his favourite 1950s songs. At the same time, Yoko Ono makes telephone calls enquiring about exhibits she requires for a projected exhibition at the Everson Museum of Arts.

Autumn 1971
Lennon and Ono are invited to contribute a film to the forthcoming Chicago film festival. John creates a one-minute film by scratching the message *Freedom* direct onto the film material. Yoko Ono creates a short film to music by Lennon on electric keyboards in which she tries to unfasten her bra.

8 October 1971
John Lennon's album *Imagine* is released.

9–27 October 1971
The Yoko Ono retrospective exhibition *This Is Not Here* opens at the Everson Museum of Art, Syracuse, New York, on Lennon's 31st birthday. The recently completed film *Clock* is shown in the foyer.

11 December 1971
John Lennon and Yoko Ono appear at a concert in Ann Arbor, Michigan, organised as a rally to free left-wing author John Sinclair, jailed in 1969 for possession of two joints of marihuana.

13 December 1971
55 hours after the concert, John Sinclair is freed. Lennon dedicates a song to him on his album *Some Time in New York City.*

6 March 1972
The provisional extension of Lennon's visa for the USA is cancelled. The reason stated is his previous conviction for drug possession. A four-year struggle for permanent residency begins.

Early April 1972
For the first issue of the arts-and-politics periodical *SunDance* Lennon creates a series of pencil drawings of women in everyday situations. Yoko Ono writes an article about the problems of working women, *What a Bastard the World Is.*

Spring 1972

John contributes a drawing of a naked man sitting on a cloud, together with a limerick, to *The Gay Liberation Book,* an anthology of gay writing:
Why makes it so sad to be gay?
Doing your own thing is OK
Our bodies are our own
So leave us alone
So play with yourself – today

11 May 1972

As a guest on the *Dick Cavett Show,* Lennon claims he is being tailed by government agents and that his phone is being tapped.

12 June 1972

The LP *Some Time in New York City* by John Lennon and Yoko Ono is released. On it, both of them take a stance on the current political situation.
The double album also includes live recordings of the Fillmore East concert with Frank Zappa.

23 December 1972

The film *Imagine,* originally scheduled to coincide with the release of the album on 8 October 1971, is premiered on American TV.

23 March 1973

Lennon is ordered to leave the country within 60 days. Yoko Ono is permitted to retain her permanent residency in New York and need not leave.

October 1973

John Lennon and Yoko Ono separate. Lennon goes to Los Angeles for 18 months with his girlfriend May Pang, records a new album and attracts much negative publicity due to his heavy drinking.

16 November 1973

John Lennon's album *Mind Games* is released.

17 July 1974

John Lennon is again ordered to leave the country within 60 days. He files an appeal again.

4 October 1974

John Lennon's album *Walls and Bridges* is released, containing a booklet of lyrics with several childhood drawings by Lennon.

January 1975

John Lennon returns to the Dakota Building in New York to live with Yoko Ono. He describes the 18-month separation as his "lost weekend".

9 October 1975

After three miscarriages, Yoko Ono (42) gives birth to Sean Taro Ono Lennon in a New York hospital on John Lennon's birthday.

21 December 1975

Lennon's album *Rock'n'Roll* is released. The cover photo by Jürgen Vollmer shows John Lennon as a young man in Hamburg.

Spring – Summer 1976

A number of song lyrics and short stories, word plays and a manuscript with the title *Skywriting by Word of Mouth* are created in early 1976. Lennon cannot bring himself to publish any of it. Some of the texts are later published by Yoko Ono in 1986 under the same title, with drawings he made mostly in 1979. The book is published by Pan Books in collaboration with Jonathan Cape, publisher of Lennon's first two books.

27 July 1976

After a long, hard struggle, John Lennon is

finally granted permanent residency (Green
Card No. A 17-597-321).

October 1976

John Lennon withdraws from the public eye to
become a househusband looking after his son
Sean. In the following five years, the Lennons
travel a lot, including an extended stay in
Japan.

1977

Lennon starts learning Japanese and draws his
Japanese dictionary sketches.

Mid-1978

John Lennon and Yoko Ono had planned to
write a Broadway musical about their life
together. Lennon creates *The Ballad of John
& Yoko* in the form of a play. This time, he
does not use his typical word plays, writing his
autobiographical text in lucid prose. This text
is also published in the book *Skywriting by
Word of Mouth,* which appeared in 1986.

June 1978

John Lennon, Yoko Ono and Sean spend five
months in Japan.

Late 1978 – early 1979

Lennon draws a series of self-portraits, some
of which are published in *Skywriting.*

17 November 1980

Lennon and Ono's joint album *Double
Fantasy* is released to unprecedented critical
acclaim for Yoko Ono: she is applauded for
contributing the best tracks.

8 December 1980

John Lennon is shot in front of his New York
home.

Texts by John Lennon

Mersey Beat, Reprint, edited by Bill Harry, Thetford 1977

In His Own Write, London 1964

A Spaniard in the Works, London 1965

The Penguin John Lennon, London 1966 (paperback version of the first two books)

Skywriting by Word of Mouth, London 1986

Gimme Some Truth – Das komplette John Lennon Songbook. The complete songs of John Lennon together with a German translation, translated and edited by Thomas Rehwagen, Bielefeld 1990

Books and Essays

Ai. Japan Through John Lennon's Eyes. A Personal Sketchbook, edited and prefaced by Yoko Ono, Tokyo, 1990

Benzien, Rudi, *John Lennon Report*, Berlin (East) 1989

Buskin, Richard, *John Lennon. His Life and Legend*, London 1991

Coleman, Ray, *John Winston Lennon, Vol. I: 1940–1966*, London 1984
John Ono Lennon, Vol. II: 1967–1980, London 1984

Evans, Mike, *The Art of the Beatles*, New York 1984

Fawcett, Anthony, *John Lennon – One Day at a Time*, revised edition, New York 1981

Goldman, Albert, *The Lives of John Lennon*, New York 1988

Gruen, Bob, *Listen to these Pictures. Photographs of John Lennon*, New York 1985

Haskell, Barbara/John G. Hanhardt, *Yoko Ono – Arias and Objects*, Salt Lake City 1991

Helbig, Jörg, Ein Porträt des Künstlers als Literat, in: *John Lennon. Zwei Jungfrauen oder Wahnsinnig in Dänemark*, edited by Jörg Helbig, Bielefeld 1993, p. 217–234

Herms, Uwe, "O Pflaumenzeit der dungnen Früh". Zu zwei Büchern des Beatle-Häuptlings John Lennon, in: *Die Welt*, 22 September 1966

Hoffmann, Dezo, *John Lennon*, Munich 1986

Lennon, John/Yoko Ono/Bob Gruen, *Sometime in New York City*, New York 1995

Lewisohn, Mark/Piet Schrenders/Adam Smith, *The Beatles London*, Hamburg/London 1994

Logan, Chris, Lennon. Los dibujos secretos de un quinceanero ingenioso y cruel, in: *El Pais Extra*, Madrid, October 1993, p. 55–62

Norman, Philip, *Days in the Life. John Lennon Remembered*, London 1990

Oomen, Ursula, Sprachlicher Unsinn und linguistischer Sinn in Texten von John Lennon, in: *Folia Linguistica I*, 1967, p. 172–193

Posener, Alan, *John Lennon, mit Selbstzeugnissen und Bilddokumenten,* (rowohlts Bildmonographien), Reinbek bei Hamburg 1987

Robertson, John, *The Art and Music of John Lennon,* London 1990

Sauceda, James, *The Literary Lennon: A Comedy of Letters,* Ann Arbor 1983

Schaffner, Nicholas/Pete Shotton, *John Lennon. In My Life,* London 1983

Solt, Andrew/Sam Egan, *Imagine John Lennon,* New York 1988

Stratmann, Gerd, Antiautoritärer Nonsense einst und jetzt: Lewis Carroll und John Lennon, in: *anglistik und englischunterricht 26, 1985,* p. 147–161

Terry, Carol D., *Here, There and Everywhere: The First International Beatles Bibliography, 1962–1982,* Ann Arbor 1985

The Lennon Companion. Twenty-Five Years of Comment, edited by Elizabeth Thomsen and David Gutman, London 1987

White, Michael, *John Lennon* (The World's Greatest Composers), Watford 1992

Wiener, Jon, *Come Together: John Lennon in his Time,* London 1984

Interviews

Lennon Remembers – The Rolling Stone Interviews by Jann Wenner, Harmondsworth 1971

The Lennon Tapes, John Lennon and Yoko Ono in Conversation with Andy Peebles, 6 December 1980, London 1981

The Playboy Interviews with John Lennon & Yoko Ono, interviews by David Sheff, New York

John Lennon. In His Own Words, collected by Miles, designed by Pearce Marchbank, London 1984

Exhibition catalogues

Coventry
"John" by Yoko Ono, "Yoko" by John Lennon, brochure for the National Sculpture Exhibition in the ruins of Coventry Cathedral, 1968

Daytona Beach
John Lennon – Bag One, Museum of Arts and Sciences, September/November 1981

Liverpool
The Art of the Beatles, edited by Mike Evans, Walker Art Gallery 1984

New York
Yoko Ono – Objects, Films, Whitney Museum of American Art 1989

Rome
Let's have a dream. Ommaggio a John Lennon. La Grafica, la Musica, la Poesia, Palazzo delle Esposizioni, 1990

Syracuse, N.Y.
This Is Not Here – by Yoko Ono. John Lennon – Guest Artist, Everson Museum of Art, October 1971

Thomas Grötz, born in 1965, is studying art history, philosophy and ethnology at the University of Trier and working on his doctoral thesis about optical-acoustical interdependencies in popular German culture of the seventies and eighties.

Dr. Dorothee Hansen, born in 1963, studied art history, history and classical archaeology in Munich, received her doctorate in 1992. She first worked for two years at the Hamburger Kunsthalle and since February 1995 has been employed by the Kunsthalle Bremen as curator for Old Masters paintings at the Kunsthalle Bremen.

Dr. habil. Jörg Helbig studied English, French, philosophy and pedagogics at the Free University in Berlin. After completing his habilitation in 1994, he has had visiting lectureships for English literature at the Universities of Trier and Halle-Wittenberg. Editor of the German edition of John Lennon's posthumously published book *Skywriting by Word of Mouth.*

Dr. Wulf Herzogenrath, born in 1944, studied art history, classical archaeology and folklore in Bonn. Received his doctorate in 1970; appointed director of the Kölnischer Kunstverein in 1973, principal curator of the National Gallery Berlin in 1989, and director of the Kunsthalle Bremen in September 1994.

Matthias Höllings, born in 1951, has been a Beatles fan and collector since 1962. Since 1970 specialist for the solo careers of the Beatles; writes works about the Beatles for books, radio and television; works as an editor for the illustrated city magazine *Prinz.*

Astrid Kirchherr, born in 1938, attended the Master School for Fashion, Textiles, Graphics and Advertising in Hamburg from 1957 to 1959. Met the Beatles in 1960, photographed them at Heiligengeistfeld, Hamburg; became engaged to Stuart Sutcliffe. Freelance photographer since 1964, photos published internationally in books and magazines. Exhibitions in London, New York, Washington, Tokyo etc. Lives near Hamburg.

Yoko Ono lives and works in New York City.

Jann S. Wenner, born in 1947, is editor-in-chief and chairman of the board of Wenner Media Incorporated. Its "flagship" is the magazine *Rolling Stone,* which he founded in 1967.

The Art of John Lennon
Drawings, Performances, Films
Exhibition in the Kunsthalle Bremen
from 21 May to 13 August 1995
in cooperation with Radio Bremen

Exhibition organised by
Wulf Herzogenrath, Dorothee Hansen

Catalogue editor
Dorothee Hansen

Catalogue design
Hartmut Brückner
Heiko Aping (assistance)

Photographic work
Lars Lohrisch, Jürgen Nogai

Public relations, organisation
Willy Athenstädt

English copy editor
Stephen Locke

English translations
Ishbel Flett, James Rumball

Production
Dr. Cantz'sche Druckerei, Ostfildern

Published by
Cantz Verlag
Senefelderstr. 9
73760 Ostfildern
Tel. 07 11 - 44 99 30
Fax 07 11 - 441 45 79

US distribution:
D.A.P. (Distributed Art Publishers)
RM 1200
Broadway 636
New York, N.Y. 10012, USA
Tel. 212 - 437 51 19
Fax 212 - 673 28 87

UK and British Commonwealth distribution:
Thames & Hudson
30 – 34 Bloomsbury Street
London WC1B 3QP
Tel. 0171 - 63 65 488
Fax 0171 - 63 64 799

English language edition (Cantz Verlag)
ISBN 3-89 322-734-2
English language edition (Thames & Hudson)
ISBN 0-500-97434-9
British cataloguing-in-Publication data
A catalogue record for this book is available
from the British Library

German language edition (Cantz Verlag)
ISBN 3-89 322-733-4

Front cover: *Bag One*, coverpage,
lithograph, 1970
Frontispiece: *Karuizawa '77*, Sumi ink, 1977
Back cover: John Lennon, photo by Nishi,
courtesy of Lenono Photo Archive, New York
© for the drawings:
The Estate of John Lennon,
licensed by Bag One Arts, New York

Printed in Germany